PE

PENGUIN PORTRAIT

Steve Hare shares a cramped cottage in Wiltshire with his wife, three daughters and 8,000 Penguins. A Penguin addict since his schooldays, he is a member of the Penguin Collectors' Society and editor of *The Penguin Collector*, a bi-annual journal celebrating the design, typography, history and personalities involved in writing, editing and illustrating Penguin Books from 1935 onwards.

Born in 1950, he studied languages at school, drama at Hull University and then, after a number of jobs (including spells as builder, antiques dealer and a manager at Hammersmith Odeon), he became a freelance writer and video producer. He specializes in using the medium of video to bridge the gap between property professionals and the local population and has filmed major construction projects around the country, including recording the construction of the new British Library.

His obsession and his profession happily coalesced while researching a television documentary on Sir Allen Lane and, of course, writing this book.

After the Conference: the Penguin Editors, a painting by Rodrigo Moynihan, R.A. (1955). From left to right: Dr E. V. Rieu, Sir Allen Lane, J. E. Morpurgo, R. B. Fishenden, Sir William Emrys Williams, Richard Lane, Noel Carrington, Miss E. E. Frost, A. W. Haslett, A. S. B. Glover, Professor C. A. Mace, Michael Abercrombie, Sir Nikolaus Pevsner, Dr Gordon Jacob, Sir Alfred Ayer, Miss M. L. Johnson, Miss Eleanor Graham, Sir Max Mallowan, John Lehmann.

PENGUIN PORTRAIT:

ALLEN LANE

AND THE

PENGUIN EDITORS

1935–1970

Edited by

STEVE HARE

PENGUIN BOOKS

PENGUIN BOOKS

Published by the Penguin Group
Penguin Books Ltd, 27 Wrights Lane, London W8 5TZ, England
Penguin Books USA Inc., 375 Hudson Street, New York, New York 10014, USA
Penguin Books Australia Ltd, Ringwood, Victoria, Australia
Penguin Books Canada Ltd, 10 Alcorn Avenue, Toronto, Ontario, Canada M4V 3B2
Penguin Books (NZ) Ltd, 182–190 Wairau Road, Auckland 10, New Zealand

Penguin Books Ltd, Registered Offices: Harmondsworth, Middlesex, England

First published 1995
1 3 5 7 9 10 8 6 4 2

Printed in England by Clays Ltd, St Ives plc

To

Alison, Emily, Joanna, Olivia

Contents

Illustrations

FIRST INSET

Allen, John and Richard Lane at Aust Ferry
Allen and Nora on tour of the Middle and Far East
Allen and Lettice Lane with guard of honour, 28th June, 1941
The Lane brothers at Silverbeck, Stanwell Moor
Richard Lane, R.N.V.R.
John Lane at Harmondsworth
A. S. B. Glover, Allen Lane, W. E Williams and Eunice Frost, c. 1950
Post-war editorial conference
Allen Lane and Eunice Frost
Allen Lane
Early days: the Crypt
Packers at Harmondsworth
The original Harmondsworth frontage
Calm before the storm (*Penguins Progress*)
About to hatch (*The Penguins are Coming*)

SECOND INSET

Post-war Penguin Christmas party
A. S. B. Glover
Nikolaus Pevsner
E. V. Rieu
Betty Radice
Tony Godwin
Tony Richardson
Noel Carrington
Eleanor Graham
Kaye Webb
Advertisement in *The Bookseller*, 14 May 1966
Corned Beef and English Trifle (Len Deighton's *Action Cook Book*)
Cover design for *Guilty Land*, by Patrick van Rensburg
Bill Rapley heading the queue to buy *Lady Chatterley's Lover*
Lady Chatterley's Lover burned outside an Edinburgh bookshop

Introduction

On the main staircase at Penguin's Harmondsworth head office hangs an enormous painting by Rodrigo Moynihan, commissioned in 1955. Entitled *After the Conference*, it shows, in emblematic form, all the editors of the time standing or sitting uncomfortably in a starkly furnished room, frozen in a carefully constructed tableau. J. E. Morpurgo, one of those editors, confirms that the room did exist, had no connection with Penguin or those portrayed, and was the Senior Common Room at the Royal College of Art. Morpurgo continues, in his biography of Penguin's founder Sir Allen Lane: 'Though *After the Conference* is in the eyes of any purist a lie, it uncovers a profound truth about Allen . . . he was genuinely concerned to leave a reminder of Penguin as a venture in which many men and women had played their considerable part.'

This is very much the aim of *Penguin Portrait*. In the course of sixty years, Penguin Books have built up an enormous archive, with files on each and every book. Some contain just one letter, others bulge with several hundred documents. The early files – from 1935, throughout the period of Allen Lane's control, up to his death in 1970 and the purchase of Penguin Books by Pearson – have all now been housed at the University of Bristol Library. Reading this material – the correspondence between Allen Lane, his brothers and the Penguin editors, and authors, publishers and agents – what emerges is not simply a record of the early years of one paperback imprint, but a record that provides valuable insight into Britain's cultural, social and political development between 1935 and 1970.

In those turbulent times Allen Lane and his editors redefined the very concept of books – a revolution that in the course of sixty years has come to be taken so much for granted that the name Allen Lane is now largely unknown outside publishing circles; and whilst a few of his editors are justly celebrated, there are many more who made an incalculable contribution to Penguin whose names are remembered by their friends and colleagues, authors and fellow publishers, but otherwise are in danger of being forgotten.

Bill Williams, very much the dominant figure in the Moynihan portrait, in his 1973 brief personal portrait of Lane, states: 'This book is not a biography of Allen Lane, nor is it a history of Penguin Books.' And now I, in my turn writing about Allen Lane and Penguin, could use these same words to preface my book. I would not presume to compete with Williams's intimate knowledge and deceptively easy style, or with Morpurgo's first-hand knowledge, family ties, painstaking research and elegant accomplishment. I became involved in this story just like anyone else – through Penguin books themselves. They shaped my development and litter my life.

Penguin is not merely a paperback publisher. It is a hugely influential and complex company so tied up with the events of two-thirds of this century that it is impossible at times to tell whether those events are shaping Penguin, or vice versa. Were this book to deal solely with the publisher of reprints of recent fiction it would concentrate inevitably on largely incidental matters: blurb and authors' biographies, misprints, cover illustrations, royalties – and little else. But Penguin had been in existence for barely a year before new series were planned – to reprint classics of literature, and, more significantly, to publish original works. Even the trivia demonstrate, time after time, the original and creative instincts of Penguin's editorial staff.

The early 1930s, though remote and alien now to all but a few, offer nevertheless some striking similarities to our own times. Apart from the obvious – a recent stock market crash, mass unemployment and recession – information and entertainment were being offered in new and unbelievably vivid and exciting ways – Penguin Books came into being at a time when the cinema was reaching the peak of its popularity and BBC radio had become a mass medium, rather than a curiosity for the privileged few. Anyone else might have thought twice about introducing a new series of books in direct competition for scarce funds, against almost universal antipathy from his fellow publishers. Working purely on instinct, Lane's gamble paid off magnificently. Penguin, quite simply, made books a mass medium. Within two years they were pushing the boundaries still further with a series of political Specials that were closer, in terms of speed of production, to journalism than publishing, and closer to the needs and aspirations of their readers and authors than ever before.

The early development of Penguin is a complex and bewildering story which the passage of time has only further obscured. Both Williams and Morpurgo concluded that it is impossible to look in any way at the history of Penguin without examining the life of Sir Allen Lane. The two were inextricably intertwined.

So whilst I shall look a little at both these facets, rather than attempting to emulate either Williams or Morpurgo, I have set my sights rather closer to the portrait of Rodrigo Moynihan. Through their correspondence I have met each of the principal players in Penguin's editorial development, and roughly sketched them. Having finished my task, and placed them in their respective positions I find that some have gravitated their way to the front of the canvas, while others peep around corners – just as they do in the Harmondsworth portrait. Some hardly appear at all.

Unlike Moynihan, my positioning of each editor is neither based on instructions from above, nor on any symbolic suggestion of relative importance. Looking at the development of the company over thirty-five years, rather than a frozen moment in time, everyone could not be fitted in. And whilst I never set out to provide a definitive statement or a perfectly balanced portrait, I find to my surprise and shame that Penguin's enormous output of scientific works has been largely ignored. Similarly there is little indication of the studies of comparative religion; nor is Penguin's significant contribution to education treated adequately. And so it goes on. Much of the selection reflects my own background and interests: having set out to draw my own metaphorical group painting, I find it has only partly covered a rudimentary self-portrait.

Most of all, the selection of material in this book is not intended as a comment on certain personalities' contribution to the Penguin story. The Penguin archive is enormous, but it is not comprehensive. Those who are not represented fairly in the book are simply not represented adequately in the archive. More than anyone else, this apology extends to Hans Schmoller – who as much as any editor was passionate about and committed to the quality of every published book, and the general Penguin cause. A close second is J. E. Morpurgo who made significant contributions to Penguin as the author of several titles, the editor or inspiration behind a number of series, and who was largely responsible for organizing the Penguin archive in the course of researching the monumental Lane biography.

With his example before me, I was aware as I compiled this celebratory book to be published for Penguin's 60th anniversary that the study of Penguin history is a study not only of inspiration and substantial genius, but also one of human frailty. Like any good story, this one is littered with hurt feelings and broken hearts and lives. It lies on my conscience too that to rake over this story might be to open old wounds. Using letters to compile a book is an intrusion on many private lives. There is no fascination for the general reader in the dry matter of simple business exchanges. It is only when personality intrudes that they come alive. And these letters live. They are the records of a dedicated and committed band, pioneering a cause in which they passionately believed. Allen Lane and his two brothers and the first editors were not just doing a job – they were living it and often taking enormous chances. Working under such pressure, it was inevitable, if regrettable, that people's finer feelings would occasionally suffer.

The story, in as much as this book deals with the development of Penguin under Sir Allen Lane up to his death in 1970, cannot avoid an unhappy ending: the death of its founder and the inevitable completion of the long process of gradually releasing, and finally losing family control of the company altogether. Yet that small, personal tragedy is overshadowed by his creation, which had already achieved so much in his lifetime, and continued beyond, thanks initially to the editorial integrity and continuity provided by Dieter Pevsner, Charles Clark, Oliver Caldecott and others; the immaculate attention to every detail of design and typography that is directly traceable to the influence of Hans Schmoller; and the relative financial security that was largely attributable to the considerable management skills of Chris Dolley.

On the death of Sir Allen Lane, one is tempted to rifle through his Thanksgiving Service for some appropriate summary of the man and his life and his creation from the words of those who saluted him. To pick through the tributes and the obituaries which vied at the time with endless speculation about Penguin's fate. To go once more to Morpurgo and Williams and see how their final chapters ended. It is all quite unnecessary – particularly when writing these inadequate words in a room lined with virtually the entire output of Penguin's first thirty-five years. Chris Dolley, who took over the running of Penguin when Allen Lane became too ill to continue, was in no doubt: 'On Allen's death he and Penguin deserved and still do enormous admiration and gratitude – but apotheosis? Never!'

The content and structure of this book is shaped by many people: the editors and authors themselves of course, but also countless unseen hands, who filed and refiled documents over the years, borrowed entire files, occasionally lost or destroyed them, sometimes misplaced them where they have lain undisturbed for many years on a dusty shelf in an ageing building little better than a shed at Harmondsworth. Of the many freelance editors who ran their own autonomous empires, some diligently kept all their papers and, like Noel Carrington, returned every single document to Penguin. In other cases the editorial files have fetched up in American universities. In one particularly unfortunate case, the files relating to the King Penguin series cannot be traced at all.

Allen Lane himself made the biggest contribution to the Bristol archive. From early on he made a point of acquiring a signed copy of every book Penguin produced. The fact that the author was long deceased, or even, in very rare cases, refused point blank to provide a signature, was only ever a minor setback for such a determined and ingenious personality. He would simply approach the author's original publishers and ask them to examine their files for some unimportant letter from the author that might be attached to his book. Thus, on opening a file at random in the archive, a sheet of paper might fall out: a 1920 typed note signed by F. Scott Fitzgerald, acknowledging the receipt of $1,700 'which is an advance on the amount due from the Metro Picture contract or other sales'. Or, now and then, a letter from the author with the signature cut out to be pasted in Lane's library copy. This entire library, virtually all signed by the author bar the Penguin Shakespeare, and Penguin Classics (whose translators at least did sign them), now resides at Bristol.

Taken singly, each file in the archive – when it has not been rendered meaningless by the ravages of time, countless moves from office to office, ill-advised clear-outs and all the other tiny incidents over the years – has a story of its own. The drama of an author struggling to meet a deadline in the face of a huge variety of obstacles; years of work destroyed in an air-raid; a manuscript burnt as a precaution against spreading scarlet fever; the death of the author before the manuscript is finished, or published. Disputes over cover designs, delays in publication. Readers' reports. Lost causes. Misprints. And hugely successful books, reprinted year after year, often developing in size as well as reputation; controversial books, stirring the nation to action; manifestos and polemical pamphlets.

Taken as a whole, the Penguin canon grew to cover every aspect of human endeavour. From frankly amateur beginnings, policies gradually emerged to ensure that no subject worthy of consideration was ignored, and that every subject was treated with erudition and authority. Few writers of distinction were not courted by Penguin, if not published by them. For many years, they were paid what are now considered derisory sums for what came to be seen by most of them as a privilege and the ultimate stamp of authority.

Since 1935 generations of writers around the world have grown up inspired and influenced by Penguin's commitment to making books available to everyone, in huge numbers and at minimal cost. And we all, in turn, have benefited.

At the exact moment when books might have started to become marginal to our existence, Allen Lane made them central – essential. They were at the heart of the nation's growing realization of the horrors and dangers of Nazism. They were carried in every soldier's, nurse's, factory worker's and child's pocket throughout the war; a major influence among voters in 1945; pivotal in the gradual redefinition of obscenity; a force for social change and development in the 1960s. And Penguin was always advocating and leading by example in promoting an international outlook.

While not ignoring the shortcomings, mistakes, squabbles and fights, small acts of cruelty and even stupidity in the course of its development, there can be no doubt that Penguin's sixty years are well worth celebrating, or that Penguin's pioneers deserve recognition and our thanks for their vast achievement: Eunice Frost, Alan Glover, Nikolaus Pevsner, E. V. Rieu, Noel Carrington, Eleanor Graham, John Lehmann, Tony Godwin . . . These people are as near as I get to having heroes. The things they believed in and strove for appear to me to be well worth believing in and striving for: concepts like the quality of the written word and the published book, commitment to a cause, an idealistic belief that the work they were doing was of value and meant something, and would change people's lives.

Published in Penguin. I feel I am in the greatest company.

Steve Hare
November 1994

BEGINNINGS

1935–1939

Myths of Creation: The Founding of Penguin Books

I would be the first to admit that there is no fortune in this series for anyone concerned, but if my premisses are correct and these Penguins are the means of converting book-borrowers into book-buyers, I shall feel that I have perhaps added some small quota to the sum of those who during the last few years have worked for the popularization of the book-shop and the increased sale of books.

Allen Lane, 'All About the Penguin Books', *The Bookseller*, 22 May 1935

I have no aptitude for prophecy, and I do not fancy myself as a reader of omens and auguries, but I fully agree with Desmond Flower that the paperback has many potentialities still to be developed. My own hope – and hunch – is that the present pattern of original publishing, as distinct from reprint operations, is capable of great expansion, and will increasingly make knowledge more accessible.

Allen Lane, Introduction to *The Paperback, Its Past, Present and Future*, Desmond Flower, 1959

If the idea behind Penguin Books was so basic and simple, why had no one ever thought of it before? The simple answer is that they had. The idea of a paperback book in itself was nothing new. Both on the Continent and in Britain many publishers, including the Bodley Head, had toyed with the idea, reprinting moribund or out-of-copyright fiction from their backlists at cheap prices. Ernest Benn even predated the Pelican idea with an extensive sixpenny library of diminutive non-fiction works in drab brown covers. Benn incidentally has a further place in the ample mythology surrounding Penguin's creation. In 1952 Allen Lane wrote to E. Glanvill Benn: 'Incidentally I note that at the foot of your letter you are the publishers of Stead's Books for the Bairns. Could you let me have a list of titles available. I am particularly interested in these as I was more or less brought up on them and I have always considered that they really gave me the first idea of Penguins.'

Claiming to be the ultimate inspiration for Penguin has grown into something of an industry, as Lambert and Ratcliffe remark in their history of the Bodley Head: 'It has often been noted, and it is true, that almost everybody at the time even remotely connected with Allen Lane or the Bodley Head has put in a claim to have inspired him with the Penguin idea. It hardly matters, since only he, in the prevailing conditions, could have shaped the notion, and with an inspiration at once haphazard and calculating, have carried it out, to the great advantage of Western civilization.'

Some of that inspiration – which according to one legend originated on a railway station on the way back from a weekend visit to Agatha Christie and Max Mallowan, her husband, who was to edit the Pelican archaeology series – was later recalled by Ben Travers, a lifetime friend and erstwhile colleague, in an interview recorded in 1970:

I had settled in Somerset by this time. Allen used to visit us there sometimes and my wife and I used occasionally to call on his parents in the Badminton district, where we also became acquainted with Dick and John. Then came one particularly memorable meeting between myself and Allen. I was in London for the day and he came to see me to tell me all about the great idea. He had conceived the project of issuing sixpenny paperbacks of the highest quality. I do not claim for a moment that he sought my advice about it but he was keen to have my opinion. He showed me the list of books on which he had secured an option. His partners at the Bodley Head showed little enthusiasm and Allen felt an irresistible impulse to cut loose, to recruit Dick and John and to go ahead on his own. I told him that I was the last person to consult about the financial prospects of the thing but perhaps more than most people I was entitled to encourage. For, having worked for three years with his uncle, I could recognize the Lane flair when I saw it. And here it was . . . I know very little about the inner workings of the great organization; I know only and cherish always the memory of Allen that morning, full of that exhilarated eagerness of his and with the quick words coming tumbling out of his mouth in the way they did.

The new sixpenny book should be something pretty smart, a product as clean and bright as a new pin, modern enough not to offend the sophisticated buyer, and yet straightforward and unpretentious. And in making what amounted to the first serious attempt to introduce 'branded goods' to the book trade, Allen Lane had the wit to realize the cumulative publicity value of, first, a consistent and easily recognizable cover design, and, secondly, a good trademark that would be easy to treat pictorially, easy to *say* and easy to remember.

I remember well the final conference on this, the most difficult point of all. It was held in a dark little office in Vigo Street, and there were about five of us sitting round a table, with Allen's secretary typing away in her cubby-hole on the other side of the partition. We all fired off suggestions. We had before our minds the successful example of the great Continental series of paperbacks, the Albatross Books, and it was agreed that we too must find a bird or an animal for our mascot. We spent nearly two hours searching the bird and animal kingdoms, until we had narrowed the possibilities down to a short list of about half a dozen. Yet somehow none of these seemed right. We were in despair. Then suddenly the secretary's voice piped up from behind the partition (her name, it should be recorded for posterity, was Joan Coles). She said, 'What about Penguins?'

It was the obvious answer, a stroke of genius. The meeting broke up immediately. I went straight off to the Zoo to spend the rest of the day drawing Penguins in every pose from the dignified to the ridiculous, and the following morning produced, at first shot, the absurdly simple cover design which was soon to become such a familiar sight on the bookstalls.

Edward Young, 'The Early Days of Penguins', *The Book Collector*, Winter 1952

Securing an option of ten books with which to launch the series had been one of the more formidable hurdles to overcome. Most of Lane's fellow publishers were unhelpful, none more so than Gollancz, who failed to reply to all requests. One letter, the only one in the archive, from Harold Raymond of Chatto & Windus tells what must have been a familiar and depressing story.

Your suggestion of the sixpenny series has led to long discussions among us here, but I am sorry to tell you that we have decided not to co-operate. To give you in full our various reasons for this decision would call for a long and boring thesis, but in general we feel that the scheme would create a bit of a rumpus in the trade if you tried to confine the series to Woolworth's. If on the other hand you offered it to the book trade as well, and if they took it up, the sale of the other editions of the titles in the series would suffer very severely. Also there is the other point I mentioned when you were here. The steady cheapening of books is in my opinion a great danger in the trade at present, and I sometimes think that the booksellers have to be saved from themselves in this respect. It is they who have so constantly clamoured for us publishers to 'meet depression with depression prices'. Yet it is this lowering of prices which is one of the chief reasons why our trade is finding it so hard to recover from the slump. And the bookseller thinks that the secret lies in his low rate of discount!

Possibly these arguments might have been over-ruled in our minds if our hopes of the possible profit accruing from the series were greater. But unless we are considerably under-estimating the sales, I can't see that the amount available for us could be even reasonably substantial once we had paid the author his fair ratio and you yours for the inauguration and handling of the scheme.

I am so sorry to be saying no, but I can assure you that we have given the idea a very full consideration and we shall remain very grateful to you for giving us this chance of considering it.

Harold Raymond to Allen Lane, 1 November 1934

The breakthrough was recalled by Allen Lane on his retirement: a story no doubt told many times in his long career.

At any one time, as you know, there are one or two publishers who are the publishers of the moment. At one time it was Gollancz. At that particular moment it was Jonathan Cape. He had the list of the nineteen-twenties: Hemingway, Sinclair Lewis, Beverley Nichols, Mary Webb. I went to Jonathan, and said, 'I want ten to start and ten to follow, and I want ten of them from yours.' I told him which. I was offering twenty-five pounds advance on account of a royalty of a farthing a copy, payable on publication. He wrote back after a while saying, 'You can have them for an advance of forty pounds, all payable on signature, on account of a royalty of three eighths of a penny.' So I got them.

Years later, when the trade was not very good, I was talking to Jonathan and he said, 'You're the b. . . that has ruined the trade with your ruddy Penguins.' I replied, 'Well, I wouldn't have got off to such a good start if you hadn't helped me.' He said, 'I knew damn well you wouldn't, but like everybody else in the trade I thought you were bound to go bust, and I thought I'd take four hundred quid off you before you did.'

Quoted in Michael S. Howard, *Jonathan Cape, Publisher*, 1971

There remain two further tales of legendary significance, which cannot be ignored altogether. Richard, John and Allen Lane set to work to try and raise orders for the series. John, by far the most practical of the brothers, simply wrote to all the contacts he had made on a long world tour nominally on behalf of the Bodley Head announcing that he was sending them a certain number of Penguins as he knew they could sell them. Richard visited London and suburban booksellers, Allen took the provinces. Their total orders fell far short of the minimum number required to break even.

Allen Lane then went to Woolworth's. Woolworth's, like the booksellers, had their doubts, although for different reasons. From the bookshop angle the titles on the Penguin list were all right; it was the format and the price that were wrong. For Woolworth's the price was perfect, the format entirely satisfactory, but the titles were something to think carefully about. Did people go to Woolworth's to buy a book about Shelley by an author like André Maurois? Mr Clifford Prescott, buyer for Woolworth's, listened to Allen Lane with sympathy and attention, but explained that these books were of a kind that had hitherto been outside the Woolworth range. At that point of the conversation, so the story goes, Mrs Prescott called to see her husband. She was asked to consider herself, for the moment, the corporate British public, with sixpence to spend. Would the corporate British public take a look at these books and say what it thought of them? The books were looked at, the opinion quickly arrived at, and warmly given, the sixpences were as good as already in the till. Mr Prescott gave an order. By comparison with the orders then on the new Penguin ledgers it was magnificent, but it was nothing like the repeat order that came from Woolworth's a day or two later. The corporate British public had been most accurately represented by Mrs Prescott.

From *Ten Years of Penguins, 1935–1945*

Lane's initial entry into publishing contained a similar element of pure chance. His 'uncle' John Lane, in fact a fairly remote relation, had moved to the West Country when Zeppelin raids commenced during the First World War. Lane had looked up his relations there, the Williams family, and had taken to young Allen Lane Williams, then at school. John Lane had married in middle age and had no heir. A bargain was struck: on condition that the entire family changed its name to Lane, Allen would join the firm. After a further two years at Bristol Grammar School Allen Lane went up to learn the publishing trade, at the Bodley Head's Vigo Street offices, starting on St George's Day, 23 April 1919.

The financial state of the company was never particularly sound in all his time there, and by 1932 his accountants Smedley Rule informed him that 'Candidly, the situation is desperate and demands that you take most drastic steps to deal with the position, otherwise on the present volume of sales it is only a matter of time before the business will have to cease trading.'

By February 1936 his solicitors Bulcraig & Davis finally admitted: 'There is no doubt that the Company is hopelessly insolvent.' But by this time Penguin Books had already been operating for more than six months, in a complex accommodation with the other principals of the Bodley Head who wanted no part of a venture that was doomed to failure. This venture was already succeeding beyond the wildest dreams of the three Lane brothers.

Several options faced Allen Lane at that point, most of which were considered, including the disposal of Penguin Books. Despite the success of Penguin, the one option that did not remain open was continuing with the Bodley Head. This company went into voluntary liquidation early in 1936. Before the year was out, Lane was trying to buy it back. These complex machinations are neatly disentangled in a letter from H. L. Mason to E. R. Bennett and copied to Allen Lane on 3 December 1936:

The Bodley Head (John Lane) has been in difficulties for some time and when Mr Allen Lane took charge he was very shortly afterwards recommended by the auditors Layton Bennett to put in a receiver. He had the idea for a series of cheap publications which he put before his partners, but they did not care to venture the capital from a concern already in a parlous condition.

Resolving to launch the venture out of his private means and wishing to utilize the Bodley Head machine for the purpose, he loaned the Bodley Head funds to carry on, and launched the Penguin Books as a private venture by arrangement with his partners. In the first year the business reached a sale of several million copies, and he made a net profit of £4,500 in the first nine months plus £1,000 which he drew for himself. Out of his profits he had to find further finance for the Bodley Head which he could not let go at that stage for fear of damaging the credit of the new venture.

Later results have been even better, and he has now felt justified in yielding to the advice of the auditors to put in a receiver to the Bodley Head which is at present the position.

Penguin Books has a capital (nominal) of £100 and has been financed by a bank overdraft at present amounting to somewhat over £7,000 on his personal security and the book stock which is a live asset as he turns his stock over about eight times in the year.

There have been some signs of competition and he carefully considered the question of retiring and leaving others to scramble for the field, but he decided to continue and has taken two very important steps to protect his position. He started the Pelican Books to protect a name which was frequently used by the public under a mistake, and more important he spent money in signing up sufficient suitable works for publication to last him for three years not only securing by this means a first class list of authors and works, but leaving very little of live interest for a competitor to base a business on.

He now requires £20,000 not only to finance the Penguin business on a normal basis, but to acquire the stock, copyrights and goodwill of the Bodley Head which as he points out has a back list of authors and works possessed by few if any other houses and one which when free from other encumbrances will prove a very valuable and workable asset.

He had been thinking of trying for the money on a basis of repayment with a sinking fund, but I pointed out that such a scheme would not be attractive without a sweetener. In any case it shows what faith he has in his own capacity to initiate and bring to fruition his business ideas, and I may say that I was most impressed myself.

If this appeals to your board as a promising project you could not do better than have a talk with him yourself with a view to arriving at an acceptable and mutually profitable arrangement. The figures he has given me, and full details of both the businesses mentioned can be verified of course by Messrs Layton Bennett, and Mr Lane's personal reputation stands very high.

Nothing came of this approach and the Bodley Head passed into other hands. By 1937, premises of a tiny office at 204 Great Portland Street over a car showroom, with the rest of the staff, warehousing and distribution operating from the Crypt of All Souls church in Euston Road, was no longer tenable, and new premises had to be found. For funds, Penguin Books relied as ever on the unconventional preparations of Allen Lane's brother Richard.

Finance was very difficult at this time as apart from an increasing number of titles and consequently larger stocks of books, we also had the financing of the new building. Every couple of weeks I would call on Mr Shankland, the manager of the Cocks Biddulph Branch of Martins Bank, to raise more money. Without the help of Martins we should never have got anywhere. The joint managers shared a large office and after they had dealt with the morning's mail they liked to glance at the *Times* crossword, so on days when I had an appointment at the bank I would spend as much time as possible on the crossword and my opening remark was usually something like 'Have you got one across yet?' This I hoped would give an air of friendliness to our financial discussions.

Richard Lane, unpublished memoir, 1970

From the start the Penguin operation inspired total commitment and dedication. For those in the Crypt, where working conditions were at best primitive, accommodation cramped and the pace of work often frantic, it was essential.

The entrance to the Crypt was by way of a small platform goods lift at the rear of the church. A small notice at the side of the low doors to the lift requested visitors to ring the bell and wait for attention. One of the warehouse staff would then go along to the lift and bring the visitor down. All deliveries from the Crypt had to be taken up on this lift, so it was kept rather busy. London deliveries were by the Penguin van, and daily collections by the railway vans to shipping and delivery agents.

Incoming deliveries from the printers were off-loaded on to a trolley – taken a short way along the side of the church – to a point where one of the grills had been removed to allow access to a chute. This had been built from ground level down to about two feet above floor level in the Crypt – a real fairground slide. The fellows above would throw the parcels – usually consisting of 100 Penguins – down the chute to those below. A lot of the parcels were given a flying start from above and those on the receiving end had to stand well back to effect a perfect catch as it flew off the end of the chute.

Quite frequently deliveries from more than one printer would arrive at almost the same time and, being situated in a rather congested area, it was essential to unload the vehicles as quickly as possible. On these occasions it was necessary to call up reinforcements to assist in the unloading. A phone call would be made to the Great Portland Street office for the additional labour. Whoever was available – AL, RL or JL – would arrive to assist in the operation – usually at the bottom of the chute. It did not go unnoticed that at such times an extra boost was given to some parcels starting the journey down when being received by one of the Lane brothers, but there were never any complaints – only a lot of friendly banter.

Jack Summers, reminiscence, 1984

I remember well that summer of 1937. In July and August we had some very hot days. Of course it was delightfully cool in the Crypt but the things that used to annoy us were the smell and the mice. The smell got into everything and if books were stored there for any appreciable time they got a Crypt smell that lasted for years . . . If John and I worked all night we would knock off at about 6 o'clock and go to Lyons – I think the Corner House in Piccadilly was open early for breakfast, then back to the flat for a shave and a bath and before returning to the Crypt we would spend half an hour rowing around Regent's Park Lake to get a breath of fresh air.

Early in the year we approached the Marylebone Town Hall to try and get permission to install some form of sanitation. An official came down to the Crypt to investigate. He made a thorough inspection and spoke to several members of staff. When he came into the office he told us it was impossible to install sanitation and but for the fact that the staff were happy he would have no hesitation in condemning the premises. He finished by saying that he had never heard of Penguin Books, had never inspected the premises and had never spoken to us, but do please get out as soon as possible. We decided to buy a plot of land and build our own premises. We did not think in our type of publishing that it was essential to be right in London. So I got into our Morris Cowley and drove thousands of miles trying to find a suitable plot of land. This I eventually found at Harmondsworth, about fifteen miles from London, and we arranged to buy three and a half acres for just over £2,000.'

Richard Lane, unpublished memoir, 1970

The foundation stone was laid by the Lane brothers' father Allen Williams on 4 August 1937, just across the Great West Road from what was to become Heathrow Airport. By November the exodus from the Crypt was complete.

Harold Raymond's attitude to Penguin did not exactly mellow during this time; but the best he was able to offer was reluctant acceptance. His feelings were expressed in his lecture on publishing and bookselling, delivered at Stationers' Hall, 21 October 1938:

In my opinion the Penguins are an even greater portent than Twopenny Libraries or Book Clubs, and are already exerting a far more revolutionary effect on the book trade. This may seem odd, for the sixpenny papercovered book is at least three quarters of a century old. But the Penguins and their recent imitators differ from the pre-War sixpennies in four respects: they are far better produced; their average standard of literary quality is higher; they consist of more recent publications, and indeed some of the titles appear in Penguins for the first time; and finally, they are a greater bargain both because a post-War sixpence is of less value than a pre-War one, and because book prices as a whole have advanced since the War.

With such unquestionable attractions to offer it could hardly be disputed that Penguins are finding a new public and training that public to like the best of modern writing. And they are reaching this public through myriads of distribution channels, not merely through the bookshop proper, but through Woolworth's, the village shop, the small tobacconist, and the slot-machine. If the general public are appreciative, no less are the authors. When the sale of an eight-year-old novel has dwindled to a mere five hundred copies a year at 3s.6d per copy, earning for the author about £8 in royalties, it is hardly surprising that he should jump at the chance of receiving several times that amount and extending his public by a Penguin sale of fifty or even a hundred thousand copies.

By now it was considerably too late to try to put a stop to Penguin. Penguin had arrived, and was on its way.

* * *

Allen Lane

In recent years Allen and I often discussed the idea of a definitive history of the Penguin enterprise. He had no doubt that it ought to be written, but he did not want it to be dominated by his own personal part in the saga. He did not want a biography, and he realized that he was not the stuff of which biographies are made. In this I agreed with him. He was not a personality of many facets or, indeed, many interests. This is true of numerous pioneers who have developed great projects – such as Lord Nuffield, Lilian Baylis, Ninette de Valois, Lord Reith, Dr Barnardo. They come to life only in the context of the institutions they create. Allen's characteristics and qualities animated the Penguin story, especially in the earlier years, and that is how he should be revealed in the Penguin history, as a man whose gifts were relevant entirely to the firm he founded.

He pressed me again and again to undertake the job, especially during the long conversations I had with him at Priory Farm in the last year of his life. I suggested other names, such as Asa Briggs, J. H. Plumb, but he used to say that he preferred me because I had been so close to him for thirty-five years and he liked my style of writing. When I realized he was dying I became inhibited about the subject, but over the last bottle of wine we drank together I promised I'd do an outline. And here it is.

W. E. Williams to Hans Schmoller, internal memorandum, October 1970

The proposed 120,000 word book was never quite written. In 1973, however, after several major illnesses, Williams did write a much briefer 'personal portrait'. It was published by the Bodley Head, in size and format replicating an early Penguin biography, except that the author's name occupies the strategic position normally held by the name Penguin Books.

His original synopsis had continued:

The book will be by no means a eulogy. The mistakes which were made will be plainly revealed and the numerous crises analysed in retrospect. There were many individuals who played a part in the development of the firm and their contributions will be carefully assessed. One theme which will be fully considered is the long struggle to subject AL's autocratic tendencies to the needs and demands of good management, and his weakness for 'instant government' will be fully illustrated – but not less so than his flair and intuition. In the early chapters there will be memories of the precarious life the Penguin pioneers lived – the improvisations, the gambles, the shoestring nature of the operations of the first five years, the shocking salaries of the devoted few, the invulnerable devotion of some of the early 'characters' in the firm.

Williams was entirely correct that it is quite impossible to disentangle the facts of Allen Lane's life from the Penguin story. But his suggestion that Lane was 'not a personality of many facets', is a curious observation. As Hans Schmoller was to observe, much later: 'Somehow AL manages to spin his web of ambiguity even nine years after his death.'

Ruthless, impetuous, unpredictable, irrational: each of these characteristics has been attributed to Allen in affectionate appreciations published after his death. And each has its mundane truth. And how delighted he would be! The quick smile, a sparkle in the blue eyes, a slight complexion of guilt. Allen has got away with it again.

Sir Robert Lusty, 'Tribute', 18 August 1970

Sir Allen is a radiant, cleanly scrubbed, fresh looking piece of energy. He is of medium height with a roundish face full of animation. He talks rapidly but clearly. He is widely read and is that remarkable being – a cultured and thinking publisher.

Woodrow Wyatt, 1958

Although Allen became a dedicated publisher, he read very little either for personal or business motives, and he knew virtually nothing about literature.

W. E. Williams, *Allen Lane: A Personal Portrait*, 1973

Williams's book received one particularly telling review:

. . . Because he [Lane] wrought a major contribution to the history of our times his enigmatic personality deserves to be brought out of the shadows of near-anonymity. It is sad, therefore, that W. E. Williams has contented himself with a slight 'personal portrait', for there can be no man living – though there may be some women – who has greater authority to describe Lane's contradictory character than Williams, his friend for over thirty years, and no one with more right to assess his achievements than his enthusiastic, skilful and long-lasting collaborator in the development of Penguins . . . The temptation to follow Williams's example is great, and not to be resisted entirely.

The reviewer was Professor J. E. Morpurgo. Six years later, a good deal of Richard Hoggart's review of Morpurgo's ambitious and much more substantial *Allen Lane: King Penguin* underlined complexities and contradictions barely hinted at by Williams:

I do not remember a biography in which the hum of contrasting epithets is so evident. Here are a few in the order in which they appear: ruthless, engaging, harsh, procrastinating, casual, infuriating, importunate, opportunist, impish, restless, impetuous, ebullient, exciting, infuriating, capricious, awe-struck, bullying, devious, lonely, naughty, idiosyncratic, perverse, malicious, genius, cowardly, prevaricating, bold, precise, vacillating, romantic, dictatorial, mischievous, quirky, spontaneously benevolent, bland, fearful, callous, miserly, implacable, needing support and control from a brother figure, pathetic, inconsistent, bustling, vulnerable, resilient, vital, lovable, pusillanimous, changeable, shifty, solicitous, devoted and enigmatic.

Not all these qualities emerge in his letters. But far from being a man 'of few interests', he was rather a man who found everything of interest. And everything that was of interest to him was of interest to Penguin. So as Lane missed nothing and took in everything, so Penguin came, in time, to give its attention to every subject.

While returning from the south of France by road at the end of August, I got into conversation with a Belgian Professor whom I met while cashing a cheque in a bank at Périgord, and during our conversation he asked if I had been going to the caves. I had read of their discovery a year or so ago, but had quite frankly forgotten that it was in the area. My wife, however, remembered that it was in the Dordogne, and as a result we made a detour and spent several hours there, and in consequence I was so much excited that on my return to London I immediately commenced making enquiries as to the possibility of our being able to produce a King Penguin on the subject.

Allen Lane to Julian Huxley, 8 November 1948

The King Penguin on the Lascaux cave paintings was never published. This letter, however, and countless more bear witness to an intensely interested and committed personality, who in the cause of Penguin never rested and was never off-duty.

Thank you for your letter of the 3rd September pointing out several errors you have discovered whilst reading some of the Pelican books. We shall keep a note of these and in the event of a second printing of any of the titles mentioned, the mistakes can be rectified. About a year ago I was in Portugal and was very interested in the distribution in Lisbon; I was only for about two half days in Oporto, but stayed for about a week some thirty miles out of the city so I did not have an opportunity of seeing the bookstalls and libraries. If you could give me any information or advice regarding possible points of distribution I should be extremely grateful.

Allen Lane to P. Deys, Oporto, 8 September 1937

We are sailing this weekend from Falmouth eastwards. There is a possibility that we may make Torquay by Monday in which case I will call you up on the off-chance of finding you at home. If we don't make it this weekend we certainly will the one after.

Allen Lane to Agatha Christie, 10 August 1938

I have envisaged your work as being an introduction to the subject of Modern Architecture planned to appear as the first book on art in Pelicans (it will not be a Special). I was hoping that you would be able to advise us on further works on architectural subjects with a view to presenting a complete scheme on the subject as a department in our programme.

Allen Lane to J. M. Richards, 16 December 1938

Things are a bit hectic up here, with a constant outgoing stream of evacuees and troops and war material in the opposite direction. However, I rather feel with you, that it is going to be averted.

Allen Lane to Max Mallowan, 28 August 1939

I can assure you that you in America can be no more bored with the war than we are. There is really an astonishing lack of interest in the whole affair, and except for the fact that there are a lot more people about in uniform and there are occasionally slight hitches in getting through supplies, there is very little to denote that there really is a war on. In fact, more and more people are talking of the economic changes which are bound to ensue, than they are of the question of winning or being defeated. As far as publishing is concerned, we are switching very considerably from books on international politics to those discussing the possibility of a new world order when all this mess is over.

Sadlers Wells has been a bit ambitious in putting on a new opera *Dante Sonata*, which I went to see the other evening, and enjoyed thoroughly. Apart from this, the London theatre has gone Crazy Gang-cum-Nudist conscious, with more and more music-hall and revue breaking out weekly. I was told that this was a symptom of the last war, and it is rather depressing.

Incidentally, I have recently read *Charles and I*, and I honestly feel that this might make a good Penguin. May I write to Fabers about it?

In case you haven't seen some of our last efforts I have sent you a parcel today under separate cover.

Allen Lane to Elsa Lanchester* in Los Angeles, 1 February 1940

Your letter (censored) got here the day before the package of new Penguins (uncensored). Since I feel my position as a visitor in this country fairly strongly, I shall not leave the books lying around the house to start up pointless arguments, but I shall read them quietly in bed. When a person pats himself on the back, even with reason, you often want to slap him in the face with a wet fish, so it's naturally better to keep off the subject of war. Many people complain about the lack of news from Europe but I doubt if that means they want to hear the news from Europe. Maybe the combination of California sunlight and actors is accountable for my recent impressions.

* Charles Laughton's wife.

I cannot tell you how pleased I was to hear that you thought *C. L. & I* might make a Penguin. Frank Morley of Fabers once said to me that they thought of bringing out a cheaper edition to get at the film-going public (I suppose he meant the ninepennies as apart from the three and sixpennies) but that was of course before the war . . .

If only I could get a settled feeling here I think I could start off on another book – I've had an idea for a very long time now. But I do think so much about England that I'm partly not here at all. It is really ridiculous to be home-sick for things that do not exist as one imagines them – the sunlight coming through the windows at 34 Gordon Square, the square itself looking so pretty; Stapledown; the pine woods, lazy days, possible days on boats . . . That's of course how I remember it and even now cannot picture brown paper over the windows and the darkness except with an effort. I suppose it's the 'effort' that makes one so stupid.

Elsa Lanchester to Allen Lane, 7 March 1940

I see from the newspaper that you are going to be married. I hasten to offer you my warmest good wishes for your future happiness. I very much hope that when the war is over you will bring your wife to pay your long delayed visit to this house of lost causes and forgotten tunes. I have heard no more from you about the *Desires and Pursuit.* Have you abandoned this project? I shall be grateful if you will send me a list of Penguins in print. My brother is a prisoner in Denmark and I want to send him some books for the Prisoners' Library.

A. J. A. Symons to Allen Lane, 1 April 1941

Our return to work after our holiday was brightened considerably by the discovery of your drawing, which was waiting for us. We think it is delightful and we are having it framed as Clare's first nursery picture. In a letter I had from Geoffrey Smith recently I heard that your new book is to be entitled *Orlando Buys a Farm.* There must be some subtle link between Orlando and myself as the week before I went away I too bought a dairy farm in Berkshire and my time is now fairly equally divided between publishing and study of *The Farmer and Stockbreeder.*

Allen Lane to Kathleen Hale, 10 September 1942

We don't seem to have made ourselves too clear about the Editorial fee for the *Scandinavian Short Stories*. In the normal way we would pay an advance on account of the royalty, out of which you would have to pay any permission fees. Unfortunately, as Allen & Unwin are such sharks they intend to take the whole of the advance royalty but for £5, and as obviously the book won't stand two royalties I suggested to Billy that we should make your fee £25 outright. If you would let me know that this is agreeable to you I will instruct the Accounts Department to post you a cheque accordingly.

Allen Lane to Estrid Bannister, 29 September 1942

For your information our cost of production will amount to almost exactly twice the amount that we will receive from the trade, but so convinced am I of the 'worthwhileness' of the venture, that this causes me no qualms. At the same time, I think it is doubtful that we shall be able to put in hand a reprint so that it would be as well if you let me know how many copies you will require for sale at the Exhibition before we start supplying the general trade.

Allen Lane to Ralph Tubbs, 7 May 1941, on the publication of *Living in Cities*

There are two very exciting machines which I think would capture the imagination of anyone. For instance I have always found a self-binder with its revolving arms a most attractive picture. I think too, perhaps the use of electric fences, which have become very popular recently, might be touched upon and such machines as an automatic cabbage planter, which is equal to Heath Robinson at his best. Apart from these there is a crowd of material on which to draw in such implements as mole-drain diggers, combine harvesters, silage making machines known as cutters and blowers, pocket sized grinding mills as a part of any modern barn equipment, milking machines etc, which linked up with modern methods of transportation are bringing farming once again into its own.

Allen Lane to Margaret and Alexander Potter, 22 November 1943, about the Puffin Picture Book *A History of the Countryside*

This letter comes to you with the best wishes of all at Penguin Books for a good time at Christmas and a New Year which will grow brighter as Victory comes nearer.

In order to help you enjoy the former we are enclosing herewith a postal order which has been contributed to largely by the proceeds of a Dance held in the Co-op Hall, Yiewsley on October 29th.

It was a grand evening with about a hundred and fifty present, ladies in the majority, with Mr Grimes acting as MC. The Committee, consisting of Messrs Olney, Holmes and Hill, Mrs Mixter and Miss Sutton worked extremely hard organizing the selling of tickets, getting the refreshments and gifts for the Raffle and arranging for Brian Dodge and his band to come over from Cowley.

Twelve hundred tickets were sold for the six-prize raffle, including a 'mystery prize' which turned out to be a live rabbit which was won by one of the RAF boys present, who put it up for auction when Mr Grimes, never at a loss for a word, made a most persuasive auctioneer and sold it first to Vera Foster's Uncle Bill for 25/- and on his giving it back put it up again and raised a further 30/-, this time from Mr Ashton Allen who gave it to Reuben Bowerman, and from all accounts it continues to flourish.

There are now twenty-two members of the staff serving in HM Forces, twelve of whom are overseas, including Maynard who is now a Sub-Lieut. RNVR, somewhere in the Middle East: Fry, Summers, Weight, Johnson, Clarke and Kite are all in North Africa or working their way up through Sicily into Italy. Squires is also on foreign service. The Navy has claimed Andrews, Painter, Stevens, Herbert and Blass while the Home Forces include Dyer, Fisher, Lowe, Watts, Webb and White. The ATS and WAAF respectively have claimed Misses Cornell (now a Lance Corporal) and Osborne, who gave us all a pleasant surprise when she turned up at the dance.

You will probably be thinking by now 'Who is there left?' There are eleven of the pre-war staff left, namely Messrs Olney, Ashton Allen, Bill Rapley, Slate, Cracknell, Wheaton, Buckingham, Kendle and Oberndorfer, Miss Frost and Miss Rough. The office staff is now largely composed of boys and girls, while the looking out is mostly done by women.

The firewatching goes on with a rota which takes ten days to run through. We are now running a canteen at West Drayton so that fire-watchers can have plenty of hot water for tea when the de Burgh closes!

My brother Richard is at present 'on-shore' and we hope he'll still be home for Christmas.

This is about all the news for the present; we hope you will soon be back among us when we can fill in the gaps and you can tell us how the war was won.

Allen Lane to Bob Davies, Penguin staff member on active service, 10 December 1943

Talking about *Trees*, I wonder whether seeing a trial plate of the *British Flora* by Richard Chopping might affect your decision about doing a similar book on trees. I will get Cowells to send you one. With regard to your feelings about publishing in Spain, Lane agrees with you entirely on having no truck with Spain at present.

Noel Carrington to S. R. Badmin, 13 November 1946

I was so rushed last week that I did not dictate one single letter between Monday and Friday. At the moment we have a very eminent Swiss typographer, incidentally non-English speaking, staying with us and coming into the office every day, so that there could not really be a worse time for a possible discussion with you on *The Child's Garden* drawings and layout.

Allen Lane to Eve Garnett, 18 November 1946

I have just returned from my American trip (and incidentally I take a rather gloomy view of American publishing prospects for the next year or so), and I am now getting down to the production of our first Group list for publication in early autumn. I think we are all agreed that particularly in view of the Pan announcement, we should make the first list of ten titles, two from each of the five publishers, a really outstanding one, and from your list, if you agree, I would like to nominate *The Ship* and *The Horse's Mouth*.

Allen Lane to Robert Lusty, Michael Joseph Ltd, 9 May 1947

With reference to the birthday gift, we are very short of every type of pre-war locomotive. We are only just getting back into production, with some difficulty. Most of the locomotives, and other goods we make, are ear-marked for overseas. However, if you will refer to page 10 of the enclosed list you will find two of our standard steam locomotives for Gauge O track, and the present-day prices. We also do a better locomotive in steam, the 'Mogul', shown on page 9. If Mr Allen Lane is of a mechanical turn of mind, do you think he would like to build a 'Mogul' for himself? Naturally I will give a discount on our retail price, but I'm afraid in the current circumstances it will be a rather small one.

W. J. Bassett-Lowke to Richard Lane, 29 August 1947

Bassett-Lowke was the author of the Puffin Picture Books on *Trains, Locomotives, Models* and *Waterways.*

Overton has just shown me the blockmaker's pulls of the line drawings for *The Archaeology of Palestine* and from a purely printing point of view I must say I am tremendously impressed with them. The costs have been high, and quite frankly I don't think we shall make a profit on the book. This does not cause me the slightest concern as I feel the publication of this book in our series is a new landmark and I think a number of workers in the field may well think of publishing in our series who previously might have pooh-poohed the idea. However, that was I think our aim when we started.

Allen Lane to Max Mallowan, 11 January 1949

The answers to your first four questions enquiring as to whether I am (a) still alive (b) well (c) rich and (d) happy, are (a) just (b) as can be expected (c) No, and with present levels of taxation never likely to be, and (d) Yes . . .

We have not yet worked out our Royalty Accounts to the end of September, and as you know our normal procedure is to allow for half-yearly accounting. I have, however, asked (pause to watch the Brabazon taking off) for a Royalty Account to be prepared for the last quarter, as soon as the sales figures are in, but if you would like £100 or so on account of these now, just give me a ring.

Allen Lane to Peter Heaton, 12 October 1950

Doyle's signatures are not easy to find. The best chance would be to ask Denis Conan Doyle and all letters to him addressed here are forwarded, for he is in France. I rather doubt whether it would bring any immediate response, for he is separated from the family archives which are locked up in Tangiers. The key is with Adrian Conan Doyle, who is hunting rare fish in the middle of the Indian Ocean.

However, Sir Arthur Conan Doyle's autograph does come up occasionally in booksellers such as Myers of Bond Street.

John Grey Murray to Allen Lane, 13 November 1950 (seeking an autograph for the Penguin *Memoirs of Sherlock Holmes*)

Tuesday July 31st

Mrs Menzies collected us at 8.30 and we started off by calling on the Secretary of the Eastern Provinces, Comm. Johnson, who let me see some of the books and pamphlets the communists are sending here from London. His view is that lack of reading material is so great that they are reading this very largely owing to their inability to find anything else. People have told me of their boys reading out of date postal guides and time tables for this reason. Saw Miss Ogle, chief Women's Education Officer, but didn't get much information from her. Spent the rest of the day at the B.C. writing and in cashing a draft at the bank which took over an hour. Lunched at the Menzies. Mr M. is chief of Police Training. Read the communist literature most of the afternoon. It comes from England and is distributed on the quiet but quite effectively. Dined with Steward and Carpenter, the man I've been chasing. He's the senior Adult Education Officer and is organizing a van in which he proposes to tour the eastern provinces selling books in English and the vernacular.

Allen Lane, extract from his diary of a three-week visit to West Africa, 1951

The Penguin West African series started in October 1953.

The recognition, as of course I realize, is being given for the job of work which has been done by the team here at Harmondsworth over the last few years. On the personal side, it is rather as if I had been prematurely announced as dead in that I can read and hear the sort of things which are usually reserved for obituary occasions – an enchanting experience.

Allen Lane, 19 February 1952, on the announcement of his knighthood

I was very sorry to hear from White that you had been a bit under the weather of late. As a matter of fact the real reason I am going away for two or three weeks is in order to go in for one of those orange juice regimes at Tring in the hope of counteracting the ravages which time, too much food and good drink have reaped on my constitution.

Allen Lane to Hesketh Pearson, 11 January 1954

If you go to Dunedin, you must look up some other relations of mine, Mr & Mrs Will Lane, of 17 Jubilee Street. They run a ginger pop factory there. One of their daughters was in the Olympic Games here, as back-stroke champion swimmer of New Zealand; she is now a doctor's wife in Nelson. Yet another daughter is at the moment in England and is in point of fact spending the weekend with us.

Allen Lane to Eve Garnett in New Zealand, 16 March 1956

Tuesday, July 2nd, Moscow

I'm writing this in the most fabulous room or rather suite I've ever occupied. The drawing room has three large windows on a curve facing the Kremlin, it's about fifteen feet high with a painted ceiling. I've just paced it out and it's 36' × 24', is furnished with a dining table with four chairs, a smaller circular table with a sofa and two chairs, yet another table with two armchairs, an ornate sort of low-boy with a gilt clock and a glass dome, a writing desk with two chairs and a grand piano. The décor is mostly gold brocade with eggshell blue painted wall. Enormous double-double doors lead to the bedroom which is of the same proportions and while lying in bed I can see straight in front of me and not more than a few hundred yards away the red star on the spire of the Kremlin. The dressing table has cut glass and silver fittings, two clothes brushes and is full of ornamental light fittings and ornaments. It has of course a private bathroom.

Allen Lane, extract from his diary of a visit to Prague and Moscow, July 1957

Last Tuesday I was stuck at Orly airport for two hours and I was very much impressed by the fact that the largest jets were starting up outside the main building and the noise inside was so muffled that one did not even have to raise one's voice in conversation. One of our people here, Germano Facetti, was responsible for a part of the architecture at Orly and I asked him what treatment they had given the glazing which occupies the whole of the front of the building, and he said that he thought it was half-inch plate glass mounted on rubber (made by the Société de Glaces Boussois). In view of the noise factor here I feel that it might be worth your while making the trip over to Orly in order to see for yourself. If you would consider this I would be only too glad for the firm to pay the cost of the trip.

Allen Lane to Ralph Tubbs, 12 May 1961

Ralph Tubbs, Penguin author and close friend of Lane, was also an architect. He designed much of the Harmondsworth complex.

The story of Penguin has been a triumph of communication between this one man and a brilliant, if changing orchestra of colleagues which by some strange alchemy of inspiration has kept from the beginning in time and in tune, with only occasional and short-lived discordances.

Allen's friendship, once given, was steadfast through thick and thin. In loyalty he never wavered; if one wanted help it came. Even so, however warm in humanity, however convivial, he often seemed in some strange way a man apart. There was a kind of Allen language it was wise to comprehend. The storm signals might not involve oneself, but it was sometimes kindly to send a message down the line. One might be gossiping with him of this and that and he would be attentive and involved. Some word, some name, some project might strike a certain chord and on the instant Allen would be neither attentive nor involved. Cold little shutters would close upon the light of his eyes. Someone, something, somewhere had had it. The unpredictable was predictably about to happen: and nearly always rightly so.

Sir Robert Lusty, 'Tribute', 18 August 1970

* * *

Richard and John Lane

In summing up, I feel, although I dislike people who call themselves directors, that as this is our job, we should aim to carry it out. I understand even possibly more than you do that when you wander off on a busy day and yourself weigh up books and see how many go to the pound, and what our direct sales postages should be, it is really a form of escapism. I too find a certain amount of relaxation in playing with figures, and this is for the common good, but it is not our main function at the firm.

Richard Lane at Harmondsworth to Allen Lane, probably in USA, 5 August 1947

There has been a tendency to dismiss the contribution played by Allen Lane's two brothers in the birth and development of Penguin. With John this is largely understandable: his contribution was cut short, first by his call-up, and then by his untimely death during the North African landings in 1942. With Richard it is different. The fact that Allen went to considerable lengths to minimize the contribution his surviving brother could make, and further to denigrate that contribution in public, cannot be denied.

Speculation is natural as to what might have become of Penguin had John, 'the brainy level head of the three', survived the war and returned to his position as a Penguin director. Eunice Frost has no doubts: 'The only time I ever knew Allen to be uncalm and unconfident was when his brother John was lost at sea during the war. I am convinced that much would have been different within the firm had he been able to remain Allen's shrewd collaborator.'

Before the war which split countless families and partnerships, the three brothers had been, not exactly inseparable, for all three were seasoned travellers, but remarkably close – in all senses of the word. Again, Eunice Frost: 'Allen's great advantages were the undivided support of his two brothers, Dick and John. Every detail of every day was mulled over by them from breakfast to bedtime – so, of course, much happened for which there can be no accounting.'

Richard contented himself with an early visit to Australia, where he spent more than three years working on a number of farms, before returning and eventually joining Allen at the Bodley Head, after working as an actor and as secretary to A. J. A. Symons. John loved travelling, and, according to Richard, 'always knew how to understand timetables and had an uncanny sense in knowing from which platform trains would go and which end of the train was likely to be least crowded', His wanderlust was put to good use when he embarked on an extended world tour, largely on behalf of the Bodley Head, that lasted nearly two years: an experience which gave him 'an absolutely unrivalled knowledge of the export trade as far as books were concerned'.

When Penguin was first launched, it gained an undeniable boost from John's particular domain. As Richard recalled: 'He built it up into the most efficient export department that any publisher had . . . As he knew the booksellers personally he was able to send them what he thought they could use. I never remember a single occasion in which a complaint was received that too many books had been sent.' A magazine in the Netherlands reported in February 1938 that: 'Many readers will undoubtedly be surprised when I state that the publisher who sells the biggest number of books per year in Holland is an Englishman. And yet it is true. It is 35-year-old Mr Allen Lane, who distributes not less than half a million books among the reading folk of our small country, and then in the English language.'

On a long tour of India and the Middle East undertaken with his sister Nora just prior to the outbreak of war, Allen Lane's fame had preceded him in the form of thousands of exported books. A newspaper in Bangalore introduced him in an article as 'Mr Allen Lane, known to the world at large as the creator of the Poor Man's University'.

J. Hampden Jackson wrote to Lane in June 1939:

> I am just back from looking into the teaching of English in the Baltic States, where it is obvious that the greatest difference in knowledge of English during the last few years has been made by your sixpennies. This applies particularly to Latvia and Estonia. Tartar undergraduates carry a Penguin in their pockets as Americans used to carry a flask. Booksellers strip the outer covers off and paste them on the wall outside their shop as display.

The Lanes' sister Nora was drafted in to contribute to Penguin's affairs from time to time: 'I once did a spell at a Penguin stall at Earls Court . . . Another time I had an SOS to take the family car up to London and drive for a week to help deliver parcels during Christmas week: one of the vans was out of commission.' She also went with John to New York in June 1939 to set up the American company. They returned on the last passenger ship in November: Nora marrying and moving north, John returning to master the additional bureaucracy that exporting in wartime demanded. After Dunkirk both John and Richard were called up within days of each other. From then on the family saw very little of John – apart from Richard, who contrived to accompany him on all but his last posting.

> Although we had lived together for many years, it was the war which really brought John and me together more than ever before. Our business interests had naturally been in common for many years, but whereas John liked yachting I preferred fishing. After we joined up,

and especially during our *Springbank* days, our daily movements, very often literally twenty-four hours a day, were in common.

Richard Lane, unpublished memoir, 1970

Richard Lane's memoir describes in great detail the brothers' childhood, their early careers, the declining years at the Bodley Head and the inevitable tales of the Crypt. But most space is devoted to his and John's adventures as RNVR officers: a good many of them merely amusing scrapes and pranks, usually involving alcohol – some altogether more sober, such as the loss of HMS *Springbank*; though even in these straits something of the Lane spirit prevailed.

We were hit by two torpedoes: one blew off our stern, and the second one, just forward of the engine room, made a large hole in the hold that was filled with empty forty gallon drums. These poured out into the sea making an eerie sound, as naturally our engines had stopped and apart from the sound of the storm, all was quiet . . . There were still about 200 of us on board and to jump into the sea would have been most unpleasant and the chances of being picked up very small. So we just waited. We were naturally in our working gear and John, who had been sunk earlier in the year, pointed out that when we came to claim on all our possessions, it would be assumed we had lost our number ones, our best uniform. So when there was a lull, we went into our cabin and by the light of a torch, changed into our best uniforms – the whole works: suits, ties, shoes and socks.

In the course of their rescue Richard suffered a fractured foot: a minor injury that was to have profound significance. It broke up their partnership, and the two never served together again, and hardly saw each other. Richard was staying with Allen at Silverbeck when he answered a telephone call, to be told that John was missing, presumed killed. The memoir continues, but with none of the earlier verve. Apart from a brief discourse on the books printed privately by the brothers to give away at Christmas, the narrative stops abruptly with the arrival at Penguin of Jan Tschichold the eminent typographer from Switzerland. Whatever his thoughts on his next fifteen years at Penguin, Richard Lane preferred to keep them to himself. In the meantime, it was business as usual.

In looking through our production costs the other day I was horrified to see how much *Alice* is costing us. One of the biggest single items is royalty. I know from a purely commercial point of view, the more we lose on this book, the better you will be pleased, but I am wondering if you would be prepared to reconsider your decision on this, and even though you might decide that 5% is too low, perhaps you might agree to 7½%.

Richard Lane to Rache Lovat Dickson, Macmillan & Co. Ltd, 5 December 1946

I am afraid that we could not possibly consider altering the royalty arrangement for your production of *Alice in Wonderland*. This matter is not altogether in our hands. Definite arrangements which apply to every reproduction of the text and/or the illustrations are clearly laid down. These terms represent the interests of the Estate, and I think are not onerous.

Rache Lovat Dickson to Richard Lane, 9 December 1946

Your letter has conjured up a vision of members of the Estate living in garrets, almshouses and institutions because of our trying to pay less than double the normal royalty usually payable on a shilling edition. I am horrified I ever suggested a reduced royalty and almost feel inclined to offer more.

Richard Lane to Rache Lovat Dickson, 12 December 1946

In response to a complaint about royalty payments, Richard Lane pleaded mitigating circumstances –

Many thanks for your letter of 16th December. I was very glad to learn that in principle you are agreeing to let us have the two shilling and under rights on *Howards End*, but I was horrified to read the rest of your letter. Personally, I was not aware that the royalties on this book were so behind, and as soon as I received your letter I checked up on this point and sent you a cheque by return of post.

I really don't know how to apologize for this, but were you to come down here and see the conditions under which we work, I think you might appreciate how easy it is for a mistake like this to occur. The M. A. P. requisitioned this building during the war, and although we moved back two years ago, we are still terribly badly off for space. The main reason for this is that this building is going to be requisitioned by the Ministry of Civil Aviation for an extension to London Airport, and although we have made plans to move, they will not give us a permit to start building, neither will they give us permission to extend our existing premises or even to connect up a hangar we use for bulk storage with the main building. Our Accounts Department work in a separate building to the main office, which is in fact a Secco Hut, and there is no constant liaison between the two branches owing to the fact that it means a walk of about a hundred yards in the open. This is especially bad in winter. While I realize that this state of affairs doesn't excuse our being so backward in sending out statements, I feel it may help you to appreciate our difficulties. All I can say is that in the future I will see that this doesn't occur and that statements and accounts are sent in on the correct days.

I hope this letter will enable you to feel happier about our accounting system and that you will be agreeable to letting us have the two shilling and under rights on *Howards End*.

Richard Lane to B. W. Fagan, Edward Arnold and Co., 1 January 1948

He had returned to an uncomfortable routine. When his call-up had come, Penguin was already an undoubted success, but it was a young and carefree company, staffed, as Allen Lane freely admitted, by amateurs and run on inspiration rather than deliberation. The postwar world was an altogether more serious place, and everything had changed. Allen Lane had spent five years in sole charge, and the company had prospered and grown under his sole direction. He was now a married man. There was also an indefinable barrier that had built up between them since, and largely due to, the death of John. Through no one's fault Richard's status and position had changed.

He was sent out to the United States when the relationship with the American company started to deteriorate. In his autobiography Victor Weybright the editorial director of Penguin Books Inc. casually dismisses whatever influence, and even abilities, that Allen's envoy might have possessed. It is hardly surprising that Richard's memories of the difficult negotiations that took place should be different, and that if he had achieved nothing else, Penguin Books were at least lucky to emerge with the right to continue using their name in the United States.

In 1948 Allen sent him out to Australia – though this time there was no crisis. Richard had had his reservations about setting up an Australian office from the outset, and had been reluctant to sanction payments. By the time he left, though, Australia had already begun to provide income, rather than act as a drain on it. Nevertheless, the outcome of his mission was something that neither brother could have foreseen. Bob Maynard, the Penguin presence in Australia, recalls:

We had no car but Harmondsworth shipped out an old 1939 Vauxhall that had been rejuvenated for our use. This arrived just prior to Dick Lane coming out in 1948. He had met Betty Snow on the ship coming out and they became engaged. Betty was the daughter of Sir Sydney Snow who owned a chain of department stores here. I was Dick's best man at their wedding in Sydney and I remember the day before the wedding he said to me, 'I do think I'd better visit a chemist's, don't you?' I said, 'Well, if I'm thinking what you're thinking, it might be a good idea.' And he did and I thought he'd supplied himself very liberally. But a week or so later I got a telegram – he'd gone up the coast of New South Wales for his honeymoon – it was rather cryptic. It read:

RE PREVIOUS CONSIGNMENT PLEASE REPEAT AS NOT YET 231 AND RATHER FEAR INCREASE OF A174.

The A174 was the clue – I thought that's obviously a Pelican. So getting out the Penguin list I deciphered his telegram, which then read: As not yet 231, which was 'All Passion Spent' and rather fear increase in A174 which read increase in 'Population of Britain'.

So then, of course, I had to search through the catalogue to find a reply, and I came up with this one – I sent a reply which merely read:

'S55'

And all that said was 'Good God'.

Richard Lane and his new wife returned to England, and the brothers reached a mutually convenient accommodation. Remaining as a director, Richard spent much of his time managing Priory Farm. His influence in editorial matters was confined largely to comments about books concerned with agriculture. His overall influence in the company during this period cannot be gauged. In 1955 he returned to Australia, to take over the running of what had grown into a large and successful business. He remained a director until Penguin's impending stock market flotation precipitated his early and doubtless ill-advised resignation and sale of all his shares.

* * *

Eunice Frost

Penguin history is littered with the significant meetings of people with a mission and the one person who could make their vision reality. This happened so many times it begins to seem as if the whole Penguin organization was beginning to fulfil a grand design. In the early days at least there was no such plan. It all just happened, more or less by accident. Eunice Frost came from a background that was both literary and artistic, but she was not specifically seeking a publishing career when she signed up with an employment agency and was invited to attend an interview at Penguin's Great Portland Street office. There was certainly a vacancy. But Allen Lane, acting as ever on personnel principles of his own invention, tended to create a job to fit the person to whom he took a shine, rather than seeking the person best suited to fill the position offered.

How did I become a literary midwife? Because there was no one else to hold the baby at the time. Somehow I was expected to take on all kinds of reading, negotiating with authors, agents and publishers in addition to general office administration. I remember that in my very first week, instead of being told what to do, I was expected to do the extraordinary. Allen said 'do you like reading?' and pushed a whole pile of books across his desk. And that's how I learned you had to carry the baby home with you every night.

Eunice Frost, reminiscence, *The Penguin Collector*, 41, Penguin Collectors' Society, 1993

I wish it had been possible for me to write this letter earlier to thank you for a very good party but I am sure you will appreciate that with Allen going off to the USA so suddenly I inherited a lot of the things he had left undone which he ought to have done.

Eunice Frost to Mary Field, 6 August 1941

If she was initially employed as a secretary, this was soon forgotten. In addition to dealing with manuscripts, she was soon dealing with publishers, agents, printers, bankers, editors and authors. With the onset of war and the steady exodus of staff, those duties and responsibilities inexorably increased. The publishing world at the time was exclusive and clubbish. Penguin Books were just barely accepted: women were a different matter altogether.

Many thanks for your letter dated June 5th. I am so glad to hear that you can get up to town and have lunch with me on Tuesday. Perhaps you would care to come along to my Club, the Junior United Services Club, Charles II Street. This street connects Haymarket and Lower Regent Street, and the club is at the corner of the western end on the north side of the street. Naturally (!) ladies are not allowed in the main part of the Club, so there is a small private entrance marked 'Ladies Entrance', a few yards up a small alley-way at the eastern end of the Club. If you go to the entrance and ask for me, I shall be there at 12.45 p.m. I hope these instructions are clear and that you will have no difficulty in finding it.

I look forward to seeing you very much, and to discussing the possibilities of 'Story'.

Alan Steele to Eunice Frost, 11 June 1947

She was most at home with artists, and could deal with them on both an equal and sympathetic level. When picture covers were specified for Puffin Story Books, she was delegated to commission the artists, and see their work through. A great many writers and artists were on active service and for a time it appeared that whole barracks were whiling away the intervals between duties with various Penguin commissions.

I have your rough for *Gayneck*. Candidly (and I am afraid I must be) I do not really think it is going to attract the child's eye. I can see what you mean about the brighter colour not suiting the subject. Can't we have a picture of the pigeon itself without any of the war background? It gives me the impression that the contents might turn out to be devotional poems, not at all, I am afraid, a story exciting to children about a pigeon. It is a delicate and difficult business indicating what one wants, but I am afraid this particular pigeon just does not come home.

Eunice Frost to L. A. C. Badmin, 1711928, RAF Medmenham, 7 March 1944

Fortunately Badmin, who did produce illustrative work of the highest order for Penguin, was able in this particular case to pass the job over to one of his companions, whose rough was immediately accepted. Sgt Arthur Hall, 338724 c/o the Sergeants' Mess, subsequently went on to provide several Puffin covers.

About the cover for *Starlight* which I am sending back to you herewith, I rather feel myself that it would be very much more attractive without the mass of bones and entrails on the back page. I hope you will not mind dropping this, otherwise I think it is excellent.

Eunice Frost to Sergeant Arthur Hall, 28 September 1944

During the war, one of the many ambitious schemes hatched by Allen Lane was one more in which Eunice Frost soon became fully involved: the Penguin Modern Painters. Lane first explained the concept to Sir Kenneth Clark in June 1942:

I think you may know that for some time I have been interested in the idea of trying to do the same sort of work for the modern British artist as we have been doing for their opposite numbers, the authors, in introducing their work in a far wider field than has been attempted hitherto. The scheme I have in mind is a series of short monographs, each devoted to a particular artist and containing reproductions characteristic of his work.

Clark was impressed both by the idea, and the quality of colour reproduction that Penguin were achieving with the King Penguins under the technical editorship of R. B. Fishenden. He suggested himself as series editor, and was soon working closely with Eunice Frost.

After all I believe that Betjeman will be the best person to write on Piper. I could help him over the part dealing with Piper's abstract work, which he probably doesn't like. At this rate your authors are going to be almost as distinguished as your artists.

Kenneth Clark to Eunice Frost, 20 July 1942

I have been down to my house in the country and have put aside a fair number of pictures for colour reproduction. As I have had a first choice from the work of three or four of the artists we are including, I dare say they will be representative examples, and in any case it will be a great saving of trouble if I bring the whole lot up to the Gallery. But my name must not appear as the owner in the books, or else the Royal Academy will say I am only editing the books to puff my own collection and then sell it.

Kenneth Clark to Eunice Frost, 10 August 1942

Each book in the series consisted of 'thirty-two full-page reproductions, sixteen in four colour half-tone and sixteen in monochrome, and an introductory essay by a contemporary man of letters and selected for his sympathy with the artist's work'.

About the selection of illustrations in tone. I am afraid my opinion has hardened. Please will you excuse me if I make a selection of drawings and paintings instead. I want it to look more to the future than the past.

Edward Bawden to Eunice Frost, 30 September 1944

Thank you for sending me the coloured plate of Pamela Fry. I am surprised it has come out so well as it has – the general tone is very good, but I heartily agree with you that it wants to be cooler, as you say bluer.

Duncan Grant to Eunice Frost, 9 November 1943

By 1946 plans for the series extended to including artists from the United States, France, Norway, Uruguay, Germany, Australia and Cuba. Of these only the two Americans Ben Shahn and Edward Hopper were published, the books edited jointly on both sides of the Atlantic by frequent letters and cables. Eventually Kenneth Clark found it necessary to give up the editorship because of other commitments. 'I enjoyed being in at the birth of this series and I believe it has done a great service to modern painting.'

After a lull, the series was revived early in 1953, when Eunice Frost again wrote to Clark:

Do you support the idea of adding Braque to the Penguin Modern Painters? . . . and some pressure is being put on us to consider Francis Bacon. The greatest problem in his case is the size of his canvas and the pictures might become disastrous in reduction. Then, too, we have decided to reprint – but in a completely revised form – Graham Sutherland's book. Edward Sackville-West, though, finds it impossible to revise the text since he does not feel entirely sympathetic to Graham's later work and he says, too, that he never considered himself an art critic and that particular piece he did he describes as 'a kind of poem', saying that after all one cannot add to a poem ten years later.

I would much rather my name were not printed as Editor of your new series because I have done nothing to deserve it. You have done all the work during the last ten years, and it is high time your name appeared and you got the credit for it.

Kenneth Clark to Eunice Frost, 8 February 1954

It was Penguin's policy that the names of internal editors never appeared on the series for which they were responsible. The bulk of Eunice Frost's work was taken up with maintaining Penguin's fiction list – this, in between long stints in America, editing Penguin Modern Painters, a number of Pelicans, Penguin Science News and a host of incidental tasks, and occasional minor subterfuge, to secure her namesake Robert Frost for the Penguin Poets.

Thank you for your note of December 22nd and for the copy of Ruth Stark's letter of December 19th about Robert Frost. The point is, as I well know, that Cape controls Robert Frost over here but as he is notoriously uncooperative towards us – and as we don't want to be blocked off from doing a Frost selection in our Penguin Poets series – I was hoping that the willing support of both Frost and his American publisher might help to strengthen my hand.

For instance, I cannot believe that Cape publishes all that Frost has published and in any case our selection would be a matter of, say 120–130 poems at the most.

Luckily I saw Jonathan last night and as he is off to the States on Saturday I plan to drop him a line while he is in America so that perhaps he will be able to consult with Henry Holt while he is there.

But what I want, even more, is that, if and when we bring this off, Robert Frost will himself do his own selection.

Thank you for putting me on to the right person to deal with at Holt's. It may be a help if I get a rejection from Jonathan Cape.

Eunice Frost to Morris L. Ernst, Greenbaum, Woolf & Ernst, New York, 31 December 1952

Had a train not intervened last night, I was going to ask you about a project that we would like to work on and that is a representation of Robert Frost in our series of Penguin Poets, which includes, as you may know, such people as Day Lewis and Edith Sitwell for the moderns, and such others as Donne, Pope, Wordsworth and many more.

What I had hoped would be – as we have done in the case of the other poets – to get Mr Frost himself to make the selection if you, he and Henry Holt are all agreeable.

I do envy you the thought of New York in its winter snow and sunshine. Please take an extra Martini – on me – to celebrate the beginning of 1953.

Eunice Frost to Jonathan Cape, 31 December 1952

I have now heard from America that Robert Frost agrees that there should be a Penguin Frost. Who will you get to make the selection, how long will it be, and what financial terms do you offer?

Jonathan Cape to Eunice Frost, 29 July 1953

Thank you so much for your letter of July 29th. It is delightful news that Robert Frost agrees to becoming a Penguin Poet. What I had hoped – and what I had suggested to you originally – was that Robert Frost himself might do his own selection, which is what was done by Edith Sitwell and Day Lewis when we published their collections.

As regards length, I think we could go to a maximum of 320 pages, though if a lot of copyright fees were involved we might have to cut this down to, say 288 pages.

I think you know our standard rate of royalty and against this we would be prepared to pay an advance of £200.

Eunice Frost to Jonathan Cape, 7 August 1953

Thank you for your letter. I would like you to make the first suggestion as to terms for the publication of the Robert Frost selection in Penguin Poets. I will then put it forward. The trouble with Robert Frost, although I know him personally very well, is that the arrangements go through Laurence Pollinger, who is acting for Henry Holt, who in turn are acting for Robert Frost. Your offer, therefore, should be one that is likely to be satisfactory to everyone in the chain, beginning with Jonathan Cape.

Jonathan Cape to Eunice Frost, 16 November 1953

I am sorry but I am afraid we really can't agree to the suggestion your secretary outlined in her letter of December 15th – that we should pay a royalty of 10% on the published price of a Robert Frost selection, since we do not really mind paying an advance of £200; in fact, we would rather pay an even higher advance, but against 7½% royalty.

And if both you and Mr Frost feel that the extent should be even lower than 256 pages, to this, too, we would agree.

Eunice Frost to Jonathan Cape, 22 December 1953

Thank you for your letter of December 22nd. I will agree to your paying a seven and a half per cent royalty on your Robert Frost selection with an advance of Two Hundred Pounds. Perhaps you will send me a form of agreement.

Jonathan Cape to Eunice Frost, 24 December 1953

I suppose that by this time the first edition (of 35,000) of the *Colossus* has been sold out. I'm wondering if you intend to reprint it, keep it in circulation. I do hope so! No book of mine has brought such welcome letters, such good friends. I hear about the sale of the Penguin edition from remote parts of the globe. (One fellow in Mombasa, Africa, wrote that it was 'selling like hot cakes' there – which sounds incredible.) Peter Owen, England is bringing out a new book of mine in a few weeks – *The Books in my Life*. I rather think it will have a wide appeal. I hope you can spare the time to look at it when it comes out. A friend of mine in Monterey (Roland Bartell) has all the Penguin books and does a thriving business with them. It is a pity the distribution in America is restricted. Your books make friends everywhere.

Henry Miller to Eunice Frost, 10 December 1951

I was most interested in your news that you have a friend in Monterey who has all our Penguin Books. I am wondering, though, whether he or you, on account of your comments about distribution in America being so restricted, know that we have our distribution organization operating in Baltimore. It is run by Mr H. F. Paroissien and the address is Penguin Books Inc., 3300 Clipper Mill Road, Baltimore. I know he will be happy to do anything he could to help.

At the moment *The Colossus of Marousi* is still in stock although the end of the edition is coming in sight. It is not yet time for us to make our decision about a reprint, but you can be assured that we will bear its sales record in mind when the moment comes. I am most happy to know that it has brought so many letters of appreciation. One of the most exciting things about our operation is the fact that one finds

Penguins in any corner of the world and in the most unlikely places, and often they have arrived there by being passed along from hand to hand. During the war we used to be much comforted by the quite extraordinary number of letters which came to us from people serving all over the world who had discovered – through our books – some particular author or subject and in a quite accidental way.

I shall certainly look out for the publication of your new book by Peter Owen.

Eunice Frost to Henry Miller, 23 January 1952

I have enjoyed myself with *The Lift and the Drop* and certainly we shall take it. In ways it is more mature, isn't it, than *Murder on Leave* though I liked the whole setting of the other slightly better than this new one, which here and there (and please excuse the criticism) verged a bit too much on the melodramatic. And I still think, too, that you rely on dramatic feats of improbability or good luck to get you across an awkward spot. But what is such a pleasure about your books is that they are written by an adult for adults.

I am getting in touch with Miss O'Hea. I should warn you, though, that there is no chance of getting it into production for publication before mid-1950. I hope you won't mind this.

Eunice Frost to Geoffrey Galwey, 14 March 1949

I'm very glad indeed to hear that you like *The Lift and the Drop*. I think it's a good deal better than *Murder on Leave* in spite of its melodrama and unreality. It is a vexed question how far a detective story ought to have any of the good graces of ordinary fiction. Dorothy Sayers had begun to lever detection out of its adolescence as fiction with the later books in the Wimsey-Vane love saga. But a detective story must not take itself too seriously – because the crime is nearly always murder, and murder is most often in reality a scrubby squalid business in the Cleft Chin, Brides of the Bath, Acid Bath and Power of Attorney field. A powerful odour of mental corruption hangs over it. As a writer one finds oneself in the grip of a character one has imagined and who have begun to run the story of their own accord when suddenly one comes up against a lump of carrion. Presumably the reader does too. Mind you there are probably many refined and delicately performed murders of convenience which are never even suspected as murders. But unless murder does 'out' there is no story, except an entirely inward psychological one, which Penguins would hardly put in a green jacket.

Sorry! I mustn't go on and be a bore . . . Mid 1950 will be all right with me as a publication date; in fact it is only courtesy of Bodley Head that you can have it by then. Luckily they agree with me that the thing is to get my books out and about and to go on writing. They would rather publish a new than reprint an old, at present.

Geoffrey Galwey to Eunice Frost, 18 March 1949

I do, of course, agree with your analysis of true murder being merely a squalid business, but I don't think a knowledge of this fact need necessarily make a fictional presentation of it affect you to the extent of having to write in a cosy way about it as against a literary and realistic one.

Eunice Frost to Geoffrey Galwey, 28 March 1949

Though the work was demanding, and punctuated by intermittent bouts of illness, the job was not without its compensations – and all the more so given Penguin's international outlook in a period of austerity:

Even more important than *The Quest for Corvo* is the quest for my stockings and I confirm 9½ is my size.

Eunice Frost to Harry Paroissien, Penguin Books, Baltimore, 29 April 1955

Thank you very much indeed for the two copies of the *Manx Fairy Tales*. I didn't mean to ask you for them as a gift, but thank you very much.

I am sending you a small box of Manx kippers, as an Island product. I hope you like them and that they arrive in good condition. I will ask for them to be sent at the beginning of the week, so they won't be in the Post Office over the weekend.

With all good wishes

Dora M. Wild (Dora Broome) to Eunice Frost, 1 September 1955

How more than kind of you to have written to tell me that you are sending me a box of Manx kippers, but I feel quite unjustified in accepting these since the copies of the *Manx Fairy Tales* I sent you will be invoiced to you. This will be done automatically if not immediately, so I shall quite understand if you withdraw the kippers.

Eunice Frost to Dora M. Wild, 7 September 1955

Your letter made me laugh! I am glad the *Fairy Tales* are being invoiced to me, and the kippers will not be withdrawn, but are sent with much good will . . . Please tell me if the kippers don't arrive, as one lot I sent just vanished. I sent two boxes to Sheffield, and one arrived and one didn't. The Island has had a wonderful season. I hear there are 13,000 in this week-end, a record, I should think, for September.

Dora M. Wild to Eunice Frost, 8 September 1955

After all I shall feel justified in accepting those delicious kippers for two more copies of your book have turned up in our Odds Department, and I should certainly like you to have these as a thanks-offering for the kippers which arrived in wonderful condition and were very much appreciated.

Eunice Frost to Dora M. Wild, 21 September 1955

By 1961, twenty-five years dedication to the cause of publishing in general and Penguin Books in particular had brought to Eunice Frost the tangible rewards of an OBE for services to literature, and, soon afterwards, a seat on the board of Penguin, newly listed on the Stock Exchange. At the same time her health, which had never been good, deteriorated to the point that she could no longer work full-time in the role she had created and made her own.

Penguin had offered her a unique opportunity to work with and nurture many of the most creative people, who were constantly drawn to Penguin like a magnet: 'Much of our luck came from the fact that we fitted into a time of very high idealism – and a wish to share a kind of explosive creativity which was so evident in all the writers and editors who themselves had so much to express, and who needed us as a forum.'

In Rodrigo Moynihan's enormous group portrait that looms over the stairs at Harmondsworth stands Eunice Frost in the exact centre, the midwife watching over her charge still.

* * *

Bill Williams

You've often seen in the street of a small town the travelling draper's truck or the travelling grocer's. Why can't you use the same idea to circulate works of art? The answer is: 'We can and, on a small scale, we already do . . .'

If it is true, and I am afraid it is, that standards of taste are poor in England, then one reason, I am certain, is that we get so few chances to see and understand good examples of art. The appetite for art, like other appetites, grows by what it feeds on . . . For thousands of those who see these good pictures it is just a local attraction like the flower show or the crowning of a beauty queen. But there are hundreds who take it more seriously. It sets their ideas about art fermenting. Although they may still be crude and uncertain in their judgment, they are at least not what Plato called 'the man born blind'. We are trying to open people's eyes to the pleasures of art. If we can keep it up on a large enough scale, we shall one day make you tired of those pictures in the room where you are now sitting.

W. E. Williams, 'Art for the People', in *Art in England*, Pelican, 1938

In his scheme for the British Institute of Adult Education, Bill Williams was concerned to expose people, used to a few pictures on their walls of shorthorn cattle which they doubtless no longer ever looked at or thought about, to original works of contemporary art, loaned by their owners for travelling exhibitions. This experience was supplemented by the regular appearance of experts to talk about and discuss the works, and others whose job was simply to coax out of people what they liked or disliked about the works, and so help improve their understanding and critical faculties.

Throughout his life Bill, later Sir William Emrys Williams, was dedicated to the concept of mass education. It led him into a long and unconventional career, and a series of positions where his particular talents could be put to the most effective use. His early experience stood him in good stead during the war, when he launched the ambitious and influential Army Bureau of Current Affairs, in the post-war Bureau of Current Affairs and later running the Arts Council for a dozen years.

The diversity of his interests was matched by the singleness of his aim: that people should be given the facilities to learn, to know, to appreciate, and to enjoy.

Obituary, *The Times*, 1 April 1977

By far the greatest opportunity to put these ideals into practice came from his long association with Penguin Books, virtually from its inception. Together, Williams and Allen Lane made a formidable partnership. In common with their surname and Welsh origins, they shared similar tastes in food and wine; early editorial meetings were more often than not long drawn-out lunches at the Barcelona in Beak Street. And like Lane, William was a complex and elusive character.

For someone who held so many prominent public positions it seems he left hardly a trace. His method of working was very much on a casual and personal basis; yet he was clearly a master at manipulating the most rigid bureaucracy. He made things happen. Which is not to say he necessarily did them himself – individuals could be manipulated as well as establishments. Again, he had much in common with Allen Lane. More often than not he would get his own way.

Baudelaire – Francis Scarfe (Poets Series)

This appears as the poet chosen to represent the Poets series in the list of suggested Jubilee publications in the minutes of the Editorial meeting of 26 January 1959. In March Richard Newnham, as editor of the Poets, wrote to Francis Scarfe telling him that 'we very much hope' that his book would be one of the 25, and asking him to be prompt in the delivery of the manuscript. However, the final selection of Jubilee books was made at meetings without the Junior Editors, and at one of these Baudelaire was replaced by Hardy. Baudelaire then took its normal place in the queue of poets, and is down for publication in July next year.

We were not present at the final selection of Jubilee titles, but presumably Hardy was chosen because WEW wanted it in the 25. I don't see how we can do anything now but apologize and say we are producing the book as quickly as possible, which we are.

David Duguid to Allen Lane, internal memorandum, 20 September 1960

Like Tennyson, Wordsworth and Browning in the Penguin Poets, Hardy was, of course, edited by Williams. His method of working is summed up well in his reply to Moray McLaren, who had been commissioned to write a

Pelican on *The Scots*, and had asked for some general guidance. 'I am only too willing to discuss the contents of the book, so far as we can by writing letters to each other. I will not attempt, in this one, to do more than fling a few bright pieces of cloth which you may care to use for your quilt!' wrote Williams in April 1950. What he actually meant by 'bright pieces of cloth' was best understood in the context of red rags and bulls:

Why are they – if they are – a frugal people? Is it because, in the formative periods of their history, they had such a struggle to live? How far has geography shaped the thriftiness? Or, again, why do the Scots excel in some things – ship-building, engineering, soldiering, exploring – and not in others, such as music? Why are the Scots such remarkable administrators and such paltry poets? Was the Auld Alliance nothing but a mere political axis, for surely the Scots and the French have no cultural sympathies in common?

Moray McLaren took his point:

In the meantime let me say that I can certainly touch on all the points you mention, for they are all subjects which interest me. You made me jump nearly a yard in the air (a considerable feat for a man of my girth) when you said that the Scots were paltry poets, and that we have no cultural sympathies with the French. Really, Mr Williams, how could you? But I suppose you really intended to make me jump.

And in some thirty years of association with Penguin, mostly in a role he usually defined as 'chief editorial adviser', or 'Chief Editor', and ultimately as a Director that is about as much material as can be gleaned from the editorial files of the aims and policies of this crucial figure in Penguin's history and development. Up until 1960 at least, his influence was pervasive: it was, however, casually applied. In all his long association with Penguin he contrived to maintain a quite distinct and separate professional life.

After the war, the question of a closer and full-time involvement was discussed at length, and finally resolved in a revealing letter to Lane from Williams, writing from UNESCO in Paris, 10 September 1948:

About the future. There are two alternatives, round both of which we have skirted from time to time:

1. The full-time idea, which you first raised a long while back, appealed to me very much in many ways. I needn't recite them all, but

the foremost was the certitude at which I have arrived, viz., that Penguins is the most constructive and exciting job I know, or am ever likely to know – it's my permanent love. Although administration is not my favourite occupation, I do it rather well when I have to, and I even enjoy the compulsion of making a machine work effectively. I believe that in time I could have learned to run the office. But two factors to be reckoned with on that point are – (a) the similarity of our temperaments, and, (b) your fervent resolve – which only abates when you are feeling fed-up – to run the show your way. If I were less mercurial than you (and learned the expertise), I would make a Managing Director all right. But my outlook on that side of the show is too like yours, so that I would become a mere duplicate of your method and management. And that would chafe us both, as well as limiting my effectiveness.

2. The part-time idea seems the right one, and there's no doubt that my range of contacts (and even ideas) depends on retaining my present interests and activities. It would please me immensely to continue the relationship. But while we are scrutinizing our cooperation I want to underline one or two relevant points. I don't think you always realize that my 'homework' is as extensive as it has become. The business of reading stuff, for example, takes many hours a week – as it should. Or, again, take blurb-writing (in which I claim to have set new standards lately). In many cases it becomes a fascinating but (very often) difficult exercise. Most of my friends think that I toss off my *bons mots* and fashion my sentences on my head, but the fact is that 300 words often takes me a long night from after dinner to dawn. And then there are other additional tasks (like *Penguins Progress*, or the *News Letter*) which I also cope with (and enjoy) outside the office. I look forward to doing more, not less, of these things, but I have sometimes felt that you don't entirely recognize what all this adds up to, and that you possibly estimate my contribution solely in terms of our weekly meetings or our lunch conferences with authors and the like . . . All this adds up, I suggest, to the fact that a Chief Editor's work is largely extra-mural: that, like the iceberg, there is more to him than looms above the surface of the office . . . Both of us know, thank God, that there'll never be any bargaining between us, and for my part there's no more to be said. I'll be back soon; and then on with the dance.

Professor Boris Ford, who worked with Williams almost from the inception of ABCA and through the Bureau of Current Affairs years, and finally as editor of *Pelican Guide to English Literature*, remembers him as a man of quite extraordinary intelligence, charm and imagination. He was also a person of ideas, with a capacity for putting them into effect. To this end he was perfectly prepared to appoint people he trusted and just let them get on with it.

The genesis of the Pelican Guide demonstrates Williams's attitude and way of working, or at least 'operating'. Returning from an Editorial meeting he informed Ford of Lane's idea to supplement Ifor Evans's brief overview of English Literature with a proper history. Since Williams 'was supposed to know all about Eng. Lit.', it fell to him to return a fortnight later with a plan. Williams was able to think of a number of reasons why he should not, himself, carry out this work, and he certainly had no intention of editing the series. Perhaps it would appeal to Ford? It was then agreed that Ford should be ill for the next two weeks while he worked on a synopsis. Were Penguin looking for one, maybe two volumes? inquired Ford. 'Oh, don't stint yourself, old boy; do as many as you like.'

For reasons best known to Williams, the detailed proposal was then to be presented to fellow editors as his own work, and as soon as discussion turned to the question of series editor, Williams would recommend Ford, and Williams's nomination was sure to be carried. Ford had no choice but to agree reluctantly to this odd subterfuge. The proposal was indeed accepted immediately, and the only flaw in the plan was Lane's insistence that Bonamy Dobrée would make the ideal editor. Williams was then forced to improvise a number of compelling arguments against this idea, before proposing his own choice of editor. The agreement was sealed over lunch with Lane. The question of a contract for Ford was never raised.

Williams and Lane maintained a long and intimate correspondence during their many foreign trips and holidays which would include any or all of: an incisive overview of the commercial scene and its implications for Penguin, a detailed progress report, examinations of every single aspect of Penguin business and personnel – and all inevitably spiced with gossip.

As you know, I feel very much as you do about the risks of spreading our wings too far in a period of such increasing uncertainty. World trade is going to be a heart-breaking gamble for the next few years and, in many respects, would-be British exporters have got the dice heavily loaded against them by the USA. One sign that they intend to keep commercial power in their hands is their behaviour in Japan where any prospect of commercial infiltration by anyone else now seems quite hopeless. To my mind, too, the great reality behind Marshall Plans and the Truman Plans is that strings are going to be attached to the Dollar, and that many countries will be compelled to regard these as zones of commercial expansion for the USA. These are some of the factors which have made me increasingly certain that our line should be (a) consolidation at home, and (b) expansion within the Commonwealth. Our policy therefore, on this basis, should be to withdraw in good order from PBI* and also from regions which, one way or the other, are bound to be overrun by American expansion, i.e. Latin-America and probably Canada. But I should try to dig in in Australia and India. Every conversation I have with intelligent Indians confirms me in the belief that, once they have cast off the political shackles to Great Britain, they will be all the more culturally receptive to us . . . I view with ironic eye the rather hectic activities of some British publishers to horn in on the Continental market . . . I foresee nothing but chaos there, for the franc, the lira, the pengo, the kroner and all the rest of them are in a condition of nervousness from which no security can be expected. These are some of the reasons why I think we are right in our long-term campaigns for building up Penguins at home. Our policy of arranging for several long-term series is, so to speak, a system of vertebrae which will give a firm shape to our enterprise. And meanwhile, we shall fill up the areas within the vertebrae with reprints of many species. We have a prospective list which no one in Great Britain can touch . . .

The magnitude to which Penguins has grown involves, so far as you personally are involved, the exercise of the habit of delegation. I am no lover of Field Marshal Montgomery, as you know, but I am certain he was able to handle his operations because he did not involve himself in the day to day detail but kept his mental energy for viewing his broad objectives. He picked a small group of men on whose advice he put great weight, and once an operation had been argued out in this little council of war he let the event take care of itself. That is the only reality I can see in the much abused word 'leadership'. I have been thinking on these lines, as I have often told you, for some time, and I am convinced they are the right lines. Anyway, until we meet

* Penguin Books Inc., the American branch of Penguin.

again, we can be turning these ideas over so that when we join forces again we shall both have done enough reflecting to settle some important principles for the future.

W. E. Williams to Allen Lane in France, 14 July 1947

Everything is going pleasantly and competently at Harmondsworth and, by and large, the old firm is in sound shape.

My overall hunch is that Penguins will be the last to feel the cold wind of austerity now blowing up again. The general reaction will be to buy cheaper commodities and my bet is that book buyers will be more disposed than ever to buy the cheaper Penguins than the hard cover book. I have always felt that Penguin Books was particularly well rigged, in the nautical sense, to stand up to a slump, and now, for the first time, our belief in that factor will be tested, and, I think, proved. I feel exceedingly confident about our whole enterprise so long as we resist the temptation to go in for any fancy wares.

The heatwave has continued without respite since you left, and the gardeners are crying their eyes out as though that process would water their gardens. I have been leading an industrious and uneventful life, of which the only highlight was a summons last Friday to dine tête-à-tête with Ernie Bevin. What he wanted me for I still haven't a clue, for he was in his most exhibitionistic and sentimental mood, regaling me all the evening with a picture in glorious technicolor of his contributions to the Labour Party, world peace, and what have you. All the same I found the experience entertaining, from a human point of view – and he keeps a pretty selection in alcohol.

W. E. Williams to Allen Lane in Italy, 15 July 1949

I am harbouring one particular notion for the 21st Birthday year, and I would greatly like your opinion of it. What I have in mind is a booklet which would be in the nature of a Penguin Report . . . My idea is to discuss our policies and problems. We should confide in our public, for example, the procedure whereby we select our titles; we should unashamedly disclose the educational purpose that animates all our work; we should describe the ebb and flow of public interest in certain subjects at the expense of others; we should, particularly, stress the creative element, i.e. the extent to which, over the years, we have originated books instead of reprinting them.

Another section which readers would enjoy, I think, would be to trace the influences upon our format and typography, including comparisons between old titles and new ones. We should in this section also describe the processes of production and say why we favour some rather than others. In this journey backstage we might, equally, describe our methods of distribution; describe our efforts – through exhibitions – to widen our public.

Yet another chapter in the story would be our overseas development. In this fairly random selection of contents I ought to have included one final chapter in which we might dare to speculate on the future and the possible impact of television upon reading habits, and in that same chapter we might pin our colours to the mast and declare our intention of sticking to our own particular field instead of wandering after false gods in hard covers!

W. E. Williams to Allen Lane, 13 October 1954

We are both civilized, adult and realistic; we have both spent our best years in creative and exacting activity and, although we have had plenty of fun, we have also worked bloody hard. We have enjoyed no social advantages in our formative years – and for all these reasons we have a kinship together, almost (even) a twinship. We have separate identities, but we belong to the same totem, and I believe both of us have always been conscious of that bond. I can truly say that for you, as for no other man, I have always recognized and cherished a profound and abiding affection. Even when things occasionally went wrong – very rarely in fact – the basic thing was never impaired; and I believe that's as true for you as it is for me . . . I am prouder of nothing in my professional life than the opportunity I had, for nearly thirty years, of being associated with the momentous and exciting enterprise which you created. Sometimes, like an elderly man, I sit and tell my beads! Those years of excitement and innovation, the enlightened boozing in the old Barcelona; the tantrums, the tears, the perspirations. What a compost we created for the harvest which has since been reaped!

W. E. Williams to Allen Lane, 20 April 1965

What we really need and deserve, both of us, is freedom from obligation. We've given the world bloody good value for over half a century apiece. Carried our burdens, coped with our crises, and delivered the goods in a big way. Enough is enough. So far as I am concerned I'd now like to settle for Haddenham and, perhaps, see if I can really write. I'd like to do a kind of outline of Culture in my time, a kaleidoscope of Penguins, the Arts Council, Adult Education, ABCA and so on. It's never been done as a whole, and it makes a significant pattern. Allowing for the fact that I won't be a galley slave any more I would take, say, three years – but years uninterrupted by working on a treadmill. I'm better endowed topside (I believe) than ever before, but I now abominate all routine such as offices, committees, fund-raising, memoranda and such. If I could get that job done, in peace and security, I'd reckon I'd fulfilled my life and would settle for the eventide of a Senior Citizen. If and when the spirit flagged I'd pay a visit to Farmer Lane and swap reminiscences over a beaker of barley-water. The more I think of it, Old Timer, the more I fancy we have something to come . . . I shall now swallow some cold Soave and go for a ride on a steamer.

W. E. Williams in Italy, to Allen Lane, 10 September 1968

* * *

Pelican Books

So far Lane had only printed paperback editions of books that had been published by other companies. 'You should now publish some new and original paperback books,' one of the literary advisers suggested.

The suggestion excited Lane. 'An excellent idea!' he said. 'I'll publish a series of new books and I'll call them Pelicans.' Without delay he appointed some learned men to write books on science, education and several other important subjects.

Extract from an undated pamphlet for schools, c. 1970, published by the Penguin India office.

Penguin stories are never that simple. For one thing there was Lane's delight in the chase, the negotiations, courting and, inevitably, the conflicts that were engendered amongst pretenders. And for another, there was the tendency to surround events and developments in the Penguin history with a deliberate air of mystery.

Like most great leaders Allen was a myth-maker. Many of the myths were about himself; some were almost true, some close to being downright lies and not a few half-truths made apparently entire because he had come to believe them.

J. E. Morpurgo, 'The King And I', *Blackwoods Magazine*, 1979

As with Allen Lane, so with Bill Williams. Which was the master and which the pupil we can no longer tell – but both shared an aptitude for glossing over the facts and leaving a much enhanced story in their wake, which improved in time with the telling. It was a habit which, if nothing else, was highly entertaining.

Bookish Krishna Menon's dark eyes were wide open for new developments in the publishing world, and he took due notice of the Penguins' progress. Also he had an idea, which he hastened to bring to the attention of the enterprising Lanes. The idea was even more enterprising: to move heavily into the non-fiction field, and to publish not only reprints but also original works by big names.

This was all very well, but the publishers needed some assurance that important schools and other organizations would take note of this venture. Krishna Menon had by then lined up an impressive number of contacts, not only in the political but also in the educational world, contacts which the three enterprising Englishmen lacked as yet. So he introduced the Lanes to influential fellow Britishers whom he knew, and who would be of some help. Among these were the Secretary of the British Institute of Adult Education, W. E. Williams, and H. L. Beales, an influential faculty member of Krishna Menon's own alma mater, the London School of Economics. They agreed that the books envisaged by Krishna Menon would be useful in adult education – not the least reason for this being their drastically reduced price – and that therefore they would be ready to lend a hand. This is how the Pelican series of the Penguins came into existence. Krishna Menon became its general editor.

Professor Emil Lengyel, *Krishna Menon*, 1962*

* Letter quoted from André Carvely, Iqbal A. Siddiqui and Ellen Schaengold, *Times Literary Supplement*, 10 July 1973.

This story is corroborated substantially in the booklet *Ten Years of Penguins 1935–1945*, by Edmond Segrave, editor of *The Bookseller*:

In 1936 V. K. Krishna Menon had introduced the Lane brothers to W. E. Williams, then Secretary of the British Institute of Adult Education, and H. L. Beales of the London School of Economics. As a result of this meeting there was planned a new series of books, more serious than the Penguins, and with a definite educational impulse behind them. These were the Pelicans. Krishna Menon was the general editor of the series; Beales and Williams were advisory editors.

By 1973, W. E. Williams, in *Allen Lane: A Personal Portrait*, gave a slightly different bias to the story – sufficiently different to give rise to the above-quoted correspondence in the *TLS*:

I defected to education, I suppose, because in that field I could find scope for my deep social concern and idealistic beliefs. So when I first met Allen I suggested that Penguins might join the current crusade by starting a parallel series of cheap books on a wide range of intellectual interests – philosophy, psychology, history, literature, science. He responded immediately and enthusiastically, and off I went to put the idea on paper. At this stage, a colleague of mine joined in. He was H. L. Beales, then a Reader in history at the London School of Economics, and as deeply involved as I was in adult education.

The books in the new series were to be called Pelicans, and the small editorial board to select them consisted of Krishna Menon, myself, Beales and Sir Peter Chalmers-Mitchell, who had been Secretary of the Zoological Society.

The first Pelican to be published, in May 1937, made Penguin history.

This then had all the ingredients of a good story: one that blossomed and grew over the years with new embellishments in each telling. Allen Lane's own version of the tale has an immediate air of authenticity – but it is the authenticity of a good AL story, rather than the simple ring of truth – a nice, slightly self-deprecating tale that is pure Allen Lane.

One day when I went to a railway book stall at St Pancras to see the manager and try to flog a few books and I had to wait and a woman went up to the book stall and said 'Have you got any Pelican

Books?' I knew there wasn't such a series – she really meant Penguins. But I knew if somebody else started the word Pelican they'd be stealing some of my thunder.

Allen Lane interviewed by Heather Mansell, 1968

At a more prosaic level, the list of Pelican editors inside each book told their own story. In the first two, Shaw's *The Intelligent Woman's Guide to Socialism, Capitalism, Sovietism and Fascism* 'in two volumes with additional chapters specially written for this edition' – making it effectively the first original Penguin publication – the Editor is Menon, and Advisory Editors are given as Beales, Williams and Lancelot Hogben. After just ten issues, Hogben was replaced by Sir Peter Chalmers-Mitchell, a man of substantial talents, not the least of which, according to Morpurgo, was his ability to make the best dry Martini in London.

Number 33 in the series, Sigmund Freud's *Totem and Taboo*, published in October 1938, was the last to carry Menon's name as editor. Not long after this was reduced to two – Beales and Williams, and ultimately only Williams remained – his influence spreading to all Penguin series, and rewarded ultimately with a seat on the Penguin Board.

What, exactly, was a Pelican Book? In a 1938 article in the *Left Review* Allen Lane attempted his own description and explanation:

This series is at present heavily weighted on the side of History, Sociology, Politics and Economics, which together claim sixteen out of the twenty current titles. In addition there are two books on Archaeology, one on Art and one on Poetry. But plans exist for a whole series of books in every field of Art. So that the Pelican books bid fair to become the true everyman's library of the twentieth century, covering a whole range of the Arts and Sciences, and bringing the finest products of modern thought and art to the people.

'Good Books Cheap'. The clue to the success of the Pelicans and Penguins resides in the first word of this slogan. There are many who despair at what they regard as the low level of people's intelligence. We, however, believed in the existence in this country of a vast reading public for intelligent books at a low price, and staked everything upon it. The truth of this we have proved – and in doing so have provided a complete answer to those who despair of the state of England.

So popular did they become from the very start that 'Pelican Clubs are beginning to arise in various places for discussion of the books. These groups may come to play a significant part in the cultural life of this country . . .' According to Donald Kitchen in the same publication, a revolution in publishing was afoot; and only just in time.

The daily newspaper, the cinema, gramophone and broadcasting have all grown so fast that a vast public has learnt to use its ears and eyes in new ways which leave little time for books – or seemingly so. So that intelligent critics, and intelligent authors, were to be found saying: 'Books are finished, the day of the serious work is past. The only thing for it now is to go over to the films or join the BBC.' A gloomy picture indeed. There seemed to be no hope apart from 'crime' and cheap sensational novels. Until two publishers, operating on quite different lines, challenged the situation, realizing that, however great the glut of books at the upper end of the scale, there existed a vast potential public for 'Good Books Cheap'.

One of these publishers was Victor Gollancz with the Left Book Club. The other, of course, the 'standard bearer in the revolution in publishing', was Lane.

The question of defining the nature of the Pelican Book and its audience continued to trouble the series editors, who for a time presided over a number of rather arbitrary decisions as to whether a book would be a Pelican or a Penguin, or, for a while, a Pelican Special. Authors too continued to agonize over the exact nature of the task in hand, and the people for whom they were writing. This much is still clear in 1964, and despite the obvious tensions that had built up in the course of a long and difficult correspondence, this remains as good a definition as could be found for this admired and authoritative series.

You have sent me a number of peremptory letters and I have not answered for I wanted the time to consider points raised in the last discussion I had with you, and to formulate as exactly as possible what it was I wanted.

You ask questions which seem fundamental, but which are almost as unanswerable as 'Who is God?' Of course I can't say exactly who will be buying your book; I can only tell you the sort of person you will be writing for. I agree with you that you ought to assume a modicum of technical knowledge on the part of your reader, and if necessary we can always include a glossary. The BBC series, which in a letter of some months ago, you poured scorn on, seems to me the right level, though sloppily written and rather patronizing. It is clear without being technical, and this is the main thing to aim at. You are not writing for tiny tots, and I never said you were. The same sort of person who reads a book like *Human Physiology* by Walker which was published in 1943 will read your book. You are writing if you like for the Third Programme listeners of the book reading public, that is to say, highbrow in the best sense, intelligent, interested, but also without knowledge. Things therefore have to be explained to them in a way that is clear, stimulating and non-technical. Their first concern is why the subject is important and how it works.

I can't go on for ever trying to define exactly the readership you are aiming at. If you feel that it is impossible to transmit your enthusiasm and experience in your subject to any audience other than one composed of students, then indeed you must be included out. In your last letter which was read to me over the telephone I gather you feel more enthusiastic about the book. I hope this is so because I feel strongly that of all medical topics the nervous system is the most fundamental. It is therefore essential the book should meet the demands of the audience. Without doubt the level of the *Scientific American* is too high: the right approach is much nearer that of the *New Scientist*. The whole basis of this series is the belief that it is possible to write well on medical subjects and bring the readers up to date in medical research without writing a text-book.

I hope you will let me know soon whether you think you meet these requirements. I should not approach Enid Blyton for she lacks your medical experience. By the way, you might get my name right.

Peter Buckman to Dr Peter Nathan, 3 March 1964

I don't remember pouring scorn on the BBC series; I thought the photos and diagrams of the brochure which went with it were excellent; but the level of text was childish . . .

One says things TO someone; one does not talk in vacuo. This is what you don't realize. I have nothing to say to the charwoman about neurology. I have a lot to say to the physiotherapist, a speech therapist, a chemist, a mathematician, a sociologist and so on. I see that you don't know who wants to buy this book. But it is nevertheless fundamental for me at least to be writing to tell someone about the nervous system. I must know what they want to know, what interests them, what they want explained, what they know already.

With regard to the *Scientific American*: this is what one expects. As I said, in nearly all ways America is superior to this moribund museum; and they obviously have a larger number of educated people who can read such stuff, at a higher level than the English.

In about two or three weeks I will have some more stuff for you to read. But you must read it with more concentration.

Final word: if I wrote books as well as I wrote letters, how happy I would be.

Dr Peter Nathan to Peter Buckman, 4 March 1964

* * *

Bernard Shaw

I am against publications in 2 vols. Second vols. don't sell. G. B. S.

The 200th volume to be published in the Penguin series of modern literature, *Back to Methuselah* is the first dramatic work of the world's most famous living dramatist to be published at sixpence. The Penguin edition contains not only the entire text of the play but also the whole of the famous 30,000-word preface. On the occasion of this remarkable publishing event, our Penguin reporter asked Mr Shaw a few questions which we thought might interest *Penguins Progress* readers:

Do you agree with the critics of sixpenny books who say that cheap books are 'ruining the book trade', injuring authors' incomes and generally bringing down the standard of book production, creating thereby in the public mind an idea that all books should be cheaply produced?

Nonsense. Cheap books may be ruining the trade in outrageously dear books which set in after the war; but that sort of thing is always happening. If you invent anything – and a book is economically an invention conferring a monopoly on the inventor – that author or his assignee has to decide whether to put the price at a thousand guineas and sell three copies to millionaires, or sell 150,000 copies at sixpence each to people who are exempt from income tax. Or of course, anything between these extremes. Which end of the scale is the more desirable from the public point of view depends on whether the book is a good one or a mischievous one. But if it has any good in it at all, the cheaper the better both for the public and the author.

What is your attitude with regard to your own books appearing in sixpenny editions?

I should have had all my books priced at sixpence or less if there had been bookshops enough in these islands to make such a price remunerative. Unfortunately, if you except W. H. Smith & Son, who are primarily newsagents and stationers, there are no booksellers in this benighted country, barring half a dozen provincial curiosities and a few London shops. All my attempts at cheap books were commercial failures. Naturally I am receiving the Odhams Press and the great Penguin enterprise with open arms. Thanks to them I am becoming almost a known author now that I am between eighty and ninety.

Extract from *Penguins Progress*, 1939 Summer Holiday Number

By 1939 Bernard Shaw was already well established as a Penguin author himself, and as a self-appointed scout for possible volumes to add to the series.

'Shaw "First Edition" at 6d. a Copy' ran the headline in the *News Chronicle* of 21 May 1937:

One of the inevitable Shaw postcards has resulted in the forthcoming publication of what is virtually a first edition of Shaw – in two volumes at 6d. each . . . and this is how the publishers secured the rights. Mr Allen Lane, the publisher who launched the Penguins, received a postcard from G. B. S. suggesting that he should publish Cherry-Garrard's *The Worst Journey in the World*. Mr Lane thanked Shaw for the idea and added a PS reading 'Of course, the ideal book for the Penguin series would be your *Intelligent Woman's Guide to Socialism and Capitalism*.' To Mr Lane's surprise Shaw replied, 'Right, how much do you want to pay for it?' As Mr Lane puts it, 'the offer rather knocked us', but negotiations were opened, and Shaw agreed to accept royalties which work out in the neighbourhood of a third of a penny a copy on a quarter of a million copies.

There was a Shavian exchange over the signing of the contract which contained the customary clause that the author should guarantee that the work did not contain any libellous, defamatory, obscene or improper material. G. B. S. crossed this clause out, wrote in its place, 'any hidden libels', and added a footnote: 'These clauses are publishers' delusions. A publisher cannot evade his responsibility for every word of the author's. He might as well murder his mother-in-law and produce in defence a contract in which the author agreed to hold him blameless for all murders committed by him.'

I always refuse to sanction school editions, because they make generations of students loathe my name and avoid my books and plays to the end of their lives, and because they have to be provided with schoolmasters' prefaces containing the date of my grandfather's birth and other matters on which the wretched children can be examined and punished. The experienced student reads the preface only.

But I have no objection to your binding ordinary copies in limp calf, or in full morocco if you like, and selling them for ninepence. At the same time I have my doubts as to whether the LCC Education department and the Kentish Director will order many thousands of *IWGS* if they take the trouble to read it first.

I am just finishing the special preface for the Pelican. I have still to pass the paged revises of the two new chapters for press (only a matter of checking the corrections); and the indexer has to index them and to correct the index of the final chapter, as the new chapters are inserted before it. I am sorry all this has taken so long; but I hope to be able soon to signal to Clarks that all is clear for the Pelican.

By the way did I tell you that my professional name is Bernard Shaw and that George is the worst injury that a publisher or manager can offer me.

The photograph I sent with the autobiography was taken by myself and therefore raises no question of copyright. I think the head of the bust, reduced to fit the card, would be far the best heading for it.

Faithfully, [the signature has been cut out from this letter and pasted into one of the Shaws in Allen Lane's collection].

Bernard Shaw to Allen Lane, 11 March 1937

As with G. B. Harrison's series of Shakespeare texts, Allen Lane was proposing that a number of the new Pelican series be bound in limp cloth 'for school use, to retail at 9d. a copy'. The LCC and other authorities at the time 'operated a ban against the use of paperbound books in their evening institutes'. Lane however was 'confident that we shall reach by this means an even larger market than I had at first anticipated'. His letter concluded with the news that Shaw's two volumes of *The Intelligent Woman's Guide to Socialism, Capitalism, Sovietism and Fascism*, with additional chapters written specially for this edition, were subscribing better than any title 'either in Penguin Books or Pelicans so far'. Indeed before too long it was reported in the press that booksellers were arriving at the Penguin stock rooms in taxis, filling them up with Shaws and rushing back to satisfy the insatiable demand for the new Pelicans.

The books continued to sell well for some time, and negotiations were opened, although unsuccessfully, to produce an edition of Shaw's *Prefaces to the Plays*. Shaw made a further brief appearance in Pelican, submitting a foreword, originally published in the *Spectator*, to the work of his fellow octogenarian Beatrice Webb, whose *My Apprenticeship* was similarly published in two volumes. Penguin's practice of publishing longer books in two volumes had its advantages. Unfortunately these were rather outweighed by problems which only emerged later.

In the absence of my brother – Allen – who is at present in India, I am writing with reference to *The Intelligent Woman's Guide*.

When we produced this we printed an equal number of each volume and now we find that we have approximately 10,000 more copies of Vol. II than of Vol. I. It would be impossible for us to sell any copies of Vol. II if Vol. I is not available. Although unfortunately an edition of approximately 10,000 copies is not an economic proposition, William Maxwell of R. & R. Clark has been very helpful and has quoted us a price that will enable us to put this in hand if you are willing to help us.

What I would really like would be the right to print approximately 10,000 copies of Vol. I free of any further royalty, but if you are not agreeable to this what royalty would you suggest, bearing in mind the fact that anything we have to pay will be a loss to us and would only be practicable owing to the fact that if we do not reprint Vol. I, we are faced with the complete loss of the sale of 10,000 copies of Vol. II.

If you can help us in this matter I shall be very grateful indeed.

Richard Lane to Bernard Shaw, 6 April 1939

The result would be sale of the 10,000 new copies, and the 10,000 of volume two still on hand, reproducing the existing situation in six months or so. The effective remedy, as far as I can see without further consideration, is to resort to the shilling public by stopping the separate sale of the two volumes and retailing them henceforth in pairs only at a shilling. On this condition I might forgo a royalty on the new reprint. It is a method of remaindering. But I should like to hear whether the difficulty has not arisen with other works in two volumes.

Bernard Shaw to Richard Lane, 11 April 1939

Rather than waste postcards, for much of the remainder of the correspondence, Shaw merely posted back the original letter, with his handwritten comments added wherever there was space.

In reply to your postcard of 11th April regarding reprinting *The Intelligent Woman's Guide*, I should like to point out that in the event of our levelling up the stock by printing 10,000 copies of Volume I and then selling this number as well as an equal number of Volume II the position would not then be as it is now as we should have sold our complete stock. Our sales on this title have now reached a figure which does not justify an ordinary reprint and it is only by balancing up the stock that we can sell our stock of Volume II. In view of this I should very much like to have your further observations.

Richard Lane to Bernard Shaw, 20 April 1939

– Yes; but the public does not buy equal numbers of Vol. II. As long as the volumes are sold separately your extra 10,000 of Vol. I will be sold without an equal number of Vol. II unless you refuse to sell them separately; and when you have sold the 10,000 you will still be left with a lump of unsold second volumes.

Bernard Shaw, 22 April 1939

I have now worked out our exact stock figures on Vols. I and II of *The Intelligent Woman's Guide* and find them to be:

Vol. I 15,207

Vol. II 4,140

giving a difference of 11,067.

Unless our sales go up it will not be worth while reprinting in our usual quantity of 25,000, but through the courtesy of Mr Maxwell we are enabled to reprint 10,000 of Vol. I. I should then suggest that this figure be increased to 13,000 and then we should end up with – if anything – a slight surplus of Vol. I which we can easily sell.

I should much appreciate your remarks on this proposal with reference to my letter of April 6th dealing with no royalty being payable on the 13,000 copies.

Richard Lane to Bernard Shaw, 9 May 1939

These figures are crazy. Your difficulty was that you had sold so many more of Vol. I than of Vol. II that you needed another ten thousand of Vol. I to pair with the unsold remainder of Vol. II. Now you tell me that you have 11,000 more of Vol. I than Vol. II, which could only occur through people buying Vol. II and not Vol. I. That is midsummer madness.

You go on to say that your remedy for this state of affairs is to print 13,000 more of Vol. I!!!!

Finally you suggest that I should have no royalty on the 13,000. But the suggestion is not in a sane context.

Explain – if an explanation be possible.

Your bewildered Bernard Shaw

Bernard Shaw to Richard Lane, 11 May 1939

Of course, the explanation, as Shaw knew only too well, was a minor error in the earlier letter – the figures were accidentally reversed. Richard Lane wrote in explanation, and asked once more that Shaw forgo the royalty on the additional print run.

I guessed as much; but you have not dealt with the condition I made that if I forgo the royalty on 13,000 new copies of Vol. I they shall not be sold singly. Otherwise they may not affect the sale of a single copy of Vol. II. I should have sent this weeks ago. Forgive the delay.

Bernard Shaw to Richard Lane, 5 June 1939

Thank you for your note of June 5th. I am afraid it would be impossible for us to undertake that our volumes should not be sold separately as a number of our distributors – such as Woolworth's – have a limited price range while with a number of others, such as railway bookstalls, it would be quite impossible to impose any restrictions.

I can only say that in our experience when we have an excess stock of a second volume we do not find it possible to dispose of those other than by reprinting the first volume.

Richard Lane to Bernard Shaw, 12 June 1939

I have now returned from my Indian trip and I find amongst the papers waiting me a note concerning the possibility of a reprint of Volume I of *The Intelligent Woman's Guide* which it will be necessary for us to print in order that the 10,000 copies of the second volume may be made saleable.

I very much hope that you can see your way to give us the necessary permission on the same royalty basis as that now in force for *Back to Methuselah* which I am happy to say is now in its second edition.

Allen Lane to Bernard Shaw, 14 July 1939

– Yes, certainly; but Richard has been demanding 15,000 copies free of royalty. And I still do not see how ten thousand more of Vol. I will sell the remainder of Vol. II if the two volumes continue to be sold separately.

However if, say, 5% of the Vol. I purchasers buy Vol. II, you will only have to print 50,000 more of Vol. I to clear out Vol. II. Further printings can be in that proportion. It is all the same to me in what proportion you print them. But you could put a slip into Vol. I at the end describing the importance of Vol. II with its chapters on Fascism and Communism.

– Have you thought of the *Ingoldsby Legends* as an attractive Penguin? Or Edgar Allan Poe's *Tales of Mystery and Imagination*? Or have you done them already?

Bernard Shaw to Allen Lane, 18 July 1939

Thank you for your letter. I am getting in touch with Mr William Maxwell right away. We will add to the front wrapper of Volume I a note drawing attention to the new material in Volume II.

I am sending you herewith a copy of Poe's *Tales* which I think may interest you in view of your suggestion. We have considered the *Ingoldsby Legends* before but their length put them out-of-court.

Allen Lane to Bernard Shaw, 20 July 1939

Wherever one looks in the archives relating to Shaw, what can only be described as 'Shavian' touches are apparent. His headed note paper for 4 Whitehall Court also carries his 'Telegraphic address: Socialist, Parl. London'. One of the early original contracts still remains – his signature witnessed by 'Minnie Pickering, Whitehall Court Domestic Staff'.

Allen Lane held Shaw in especial regard. Of the publication of the Shaw million in 1946, he declared that 'no venture I have undertaken in thirty years of publishing has given me so much pleasure as that one which we embarked on on July 26th two years ago.' Perhaps for this reason, or simply to protect them, a large number of the famous 'Shaw postcards' were removed from the general files and kept separately with Lane's private papers. Even shorn of their immediate context, they make fascinating reading.

22/2/44 – I think it is perfectly wicked to start an innocent child wasting her time and worrying her neighbouring fellow creatures with the useless practice of autograph collecting (except at the foot of cheques). Why not buy her a Teddy Bear? However, if you will take the moral responsibility, I suppose I must oblige you. G.B.S.

6/1/46 – The experience of fifty years contradicts you violently. In every return of sales during that half century the Unpleasants have been markedly below the Pleasants. The crisis in which my stuff ranked as unpleasant is long past and forgotten: the adjective is now a senseless cry of stinking fish, utterly unintelligible to the Penguin public. However, the venture is yours: do as you please. But you will lose sales on any book you label Unpleasant. As a matter of fact they are *not* unpleasant to the present generation. Old fashioned and sentimental yes; but prudishly pleasant after *Lady Chatterley*. G. Bernard Shaw

10/1/46 – Well have it your own way; but don't ask me to add that you are fifty years out of date, and that nobody nowadays would dream of calling them Unpleasant. *Three Plays for Prudes* would be nearer the mark. G.B.S.

26/8/49 – If you can keep my *Intelligent Woman's Guide* on the market I will not reprint it in my Standard Constable edition. My *Political What's What* is a good seller. If you will take it on I will drop it also. For both I want large circulations at low prices. What do you say to this? G.B.S.

30/7/50 – I am not qualified to write on orchestral strings. What

4, WHITEHALL COURT (130) LONDON, S.W.1.
TELEGRAMS: SOCIALIST, PARL-LONDON.
TELEPHONE: WHITEHALL 3160.

AYOT ST LAWRENCE, WELWYN, HERTS.
STATION: WHEATHAMPSTEAD, L & N.E.R., 2¼ MILES.
TELEGRAMS AND PHONE: CODICOTE 18.

18/1/40.

From Bernard Shaw

O.K. I accept the terms. Make out the contract.

I regret Clark's exorbitance; but I have to pay for the enormous press corrections involved by the addition of the screen version. This gives you an exact copy, like a Bible; so that there will be no corrections except those of Clark's own misprints (if any).

Thanks for the Methuselah advance (receipt in separate letter); but I do not insist on advances unless they are necessary to hurry up production. With income tax and surtax at present rates cheques make me shudder.

G. Bernard Shaw

Bernard Shaw's preferred correspondence medium was the postcard. This is one of a great many to Allen Lane.

you need is not aesthetic twaddle, but good technical stuff by a conductor who began as a violin player. Try Basil Cameron. Failing him Vaughan Williams. I have never had a fiddle in my hands, but I have discussed the strings with Billy Reid and Elgar (both dead) and know what is necessary for the job. G.B.S.

* * *

Penguin Specials

I should be delighted to let you bring out a cheap edition of *Germany Puts the Clock Back*. It is out of print and I do not think there can be any question of John Lane still having rights as the book was sold edition by edition for a fixed sum, to avoid royalty taxes. You know more than I do about this. Don't you think the title is surely clear?

About more material, I wouldn't know exactly what to say. The book is not short as written. Enough has happened since Hitler came in to fill two other books the size of mine. Just what sort of an appendix did you have in mind? Let me know and we can talk it over. Or better, it is possible I shall be in London next week for about 24 hours. Is there any hope of seeing you then?

Edgar A. Mowrer, *Chicago Daily News* Paris bureau, to Allen Lane, 4 March 1937

By God's Grace I could give you a new chapter in about three weeks. Without it, meaning that I found difficulty in getting the new material, it would take six. So say the word and I shall shoot. What did you say you would pay me? You spoke of a halfpenny a copy for Johnny but a common guy like me probably not much more than a farthing. Is sixty pounds for an edition of 50,000 a fair price? Anyway, we probably won't quarrel about it. With best Easter wishes.

Edgar A. Mowrer to Allen Lane, 29 March 1937

Colonel Knox has broken into my work of preparing a new chapter for you with a peremptory order to meet him in Rome this week. I may be gone as much as twenty days, as I may have to take in Geneva on the way back. I am sorry, but this means that I cannot let you have the new chapter with a slightly amended text of the old book before the end of June.

Edgar A. Mowrer to Allen Lane, 10 May 1937

Such was Edgar Mowrer's fame as a writer and thinker that his book *Germany Puts the Clock Back*, which was our first Special, promptly broke all records. This book had originally been published before the Hitler régime, and its prophetic examination of the new Germany was a shock and revelation to all its readers.

Penguins Progress, Winter 1938

S1 followed Pelican's lead – the first book in the new series being the reprint of an established text, updated and with new material written specially for the Penguin edition. And like the Shaw it sold out several editions once it went on sale in November 1937. By this time Mowrer was reading further manuscripts for Allen Lane, suggesting authors for new books planned, working on his next Special, *Mowrer in China*, and reassessing his market value.

Returning from China a couple of days ago I found your letter of May 10 re a possible book. I might do such a book for Penguin but only under certain conditions. I should like

1) to be sure that you can get the book on sale within a minimum time after receipt of the MS as I am writing it primarily as propaganda rather than for literary motives.

2) to remain owner of American and all other but English rights, including reprint, movie, etc.

3) to receive somewhat better financial terms than you gave me for *Germany Puts the Clock Back*: in view of the sales of the latter and the fact that my articles (which would constitute a part of the new book) are being widely syndicated in Great Britain.

I should like to have a halfpenny on a first edition of 50,000 copies and three farthings on all subsequent editions.

Please think this over and let me hear from you at your earliest convenience as I shall have to take a decision within about a week as to whether to do the book at all.

I don't suppose there is any chance of your coming over to Paris in the near future. I am still writing up my China stuff after a whirlwind tour of just under six weeks plus an airplane ride to China and back.

It would be nice to see you. I may go to Geneva in a few days and shall meet Miss Rajchman and hear how her book is going.

PS How are the sales of *Germany Puts the Clock Back*? I am getting in touch with a German in Paris who wants to translate it into the German language but will deal with no translator unless he has a publisher behind him.

May I say that my stuff is rather original? I got cut off with the retreating Chinese army, and later toured the lesser known parts of western China.

Edgar A. Mowrer to Allen Lane, 4 July 1938

Enclosed the signed contract.

I shall do my best to give you the finished MS by Sept. 15 or even a little earlier. But you must not expect me to furnish the maps in the sense of paying for them, as you promised to do this. Nor can I see my way clear to giving you 25% on translations. You see, I consider a farthing a copy very little, as I told you, and am going ahead with Penguin first, because I like you and second, for the propaganda value, but not because I think your terms princely. So I have taken that about the maps out of the contract.

PS Thanks for the new copy of *Germany*. I am afraid we were only too right about Chamberlain.

Edgar A. Mowrer to Allen Lane, 17 August 1938

Mowrer's Specials proceeded at what was almost a walking pace – compared with some of the more frantic productions that characterized the subsequent Specials list, virtually all of which were originals. Geneviève Tabouis's study of European dictators and their methods, *Blackmail or War*, set the trend.

VERY INTERESTED BY YOUR SUGGESTION LETTER FOLLOWS COMPLIMENTS

GENEVIEVE TABOUIS

Telegram, 26 July 1937

POUVEZ VOUS VENIR POUR DEJEUNER OU THE PARIS LUNDI PROCHAIN 24 PLACE MALESHERBES COMPLIMENTS

GENEVIEVE TABOUIS

Telegram, 3 September 1937

With regard to our telephone conversation the other day, I beg to enclose herewith a translation of the outline of Madame Tabouis's book.

Paul Selver to Eunice Frost, 1 November 1937

With reference to our telephone conversation this morning, I find that the transcription of the second chapter is not quite finished, and I am therefore sending you the first one now. The second one will follow, I hope, in the early part of next week.

Paul Selver to Allen Lane, 30 December 1937

On 4 January, Geneviève Tabouis posted the remainder of the manuscript, less the final concluding pages. Chapter five, which was omitted by accident, was sent separately a day or two later. The only sign of stress in the whole production was the translation of the title of the missing chapter. '*Les Liaisons Dangereuses*' became, in the English version, 'Attachments to Beware of'. At the same time arrangements were being made with Joss, the *Star* cartoonist, to provide forty drawings of the various protagonists. *The Bookseller*, 17 February 1938, takes up the story:

In view of the urgency of her material, Penguins have put a special rush on to bring the book out in record time. They only had the typescript from the translator two weeks ago – and then they only had half of it. Then it had to be vetted for libel. With no idea of what the actual length of the whole book was going to be, the production department had to take a risk and make a guess at a suitable type size and page area . . . When galley proofs were ready at the printers, the Penguin production manager went down to Bristol himself and corrected the proofs while the machines were waiting. A few queries sent telegrams flashing backwards and forwards across the Channel. Further telegrams brought last-minute corrections from the author, who had taken a set of galley proofs with her and corrected them on the journey back to Paris . . . The printers have been working overtime and Penguin are expecting copies any minute. They will publish the book on February 25th simultaneously with another important Special, *Mussolini's Roman Empire*, by G. T. Garratt.

By June 1938, sales of the British translation which had been reported to be running at 4,000 copies a day were nearing 150,000 in total, with each subsequent reprint brought up to date by fresh information and necessary revisions. Various translations were in preparation, including Norwegian. The French edition was still to appear.

Every aspect of the growing international crisis was analysed in new Specials. It was an intense two years, during which distinctions between book publishing and journalism blurred and virtually disappeared.

Mussolini's Roman Empire

We return herewith the MS of Chapters 1–14.

We confirm the observations we made on the telephone on the technical definition of 'sedition' as applied to any publication which is calculated to bring the Government by constitution into hatred and contempt, and the ease with which, if they so chose, the Government could put the machinery in motion to stop the book '*pour encourager les autres*' . . .

The book, of course, attacks the Government in the most trenchant manner, but we are of the opinion that a plea of fair comment on a matter of public interest would be an answer to any action by any individual member of the Government, assuming the facts as stated by the author as facts are true, as distinct from any comment made upon those facts.

The book is certainly extremely interesting even if it leaves one with a feeling of utter pessimism as all books of this nature must do. It should prove to be of great interest to students of the Left, and it would probably enjoy a wide circulation among this class. It is impossible, however, to say that one can derive any enjoyment from reading a book of this nature.

Rubinstein, Nash & Co. to Penguin Books, 6 January 1938

I don't know whether you have considered any further the question of the Duchess of Atholl's book on Spain. Possibly I was a little too guarded in what I said about it, but I have been thinking it over and as far as I can tell there is every likelihood of another first-class crisis blowing up about the latter part of April, and it will turn very largely on Spain – when Chamberlain has to put his harvest before the public. It seems therefore very likely that the book would hit a favourable market, as the row will take the form of a Conservative revolt which has been temporarily deferred. The book will have some quite original stuff in it – that is to say information about the immediately pre-war period which has never been published in England. Some of us with Spanish connections have helped her to get it.

G. T. Garratt to Allen Lane, 4 March 1938

With the publication of Garratt's book on Mussolini, in February 1938, and the Duchess of Atholl's on Spain, in June, Garratt was already at work producing a collaborative effort with L. E. O. Charlton and R. Fletcher on *The Air Defence of Britain*. In a letter dated 2 July, Allen Lane enquired: 'Incidentally, is the recent Secrets Act case going to make any difference to *The Air Defence of Britain*?'

I don't think that the stink about the Official Secrets Act need worry authors. It has been there all the time, but no politician worries about such things until it hits one of them. Perhaps Fletcher has put something in which he ought not to have done, but I should think the Government would not want to see another Sandys case.

G. T. Garratt to Allen Lane, July 1938

Edgar Mowrer, Geneviève Tabouis, G. T. Garratt – these three journalists of international repute set the tone for the whole Penguin Specials series, typified, in the eyes of many, by the colour of the covers.

All three were the work of journalists who warned that Europe was drifting towards another war, a drift encouraged by the failure of democratic nations to offer a firm response to Hitler and Mussolini. Edgar Mowrer called for rearmament on a massive scale, Geneviève Tabouis argued that there must be no more surrender to blackmail, and G. T. Garratt demanded British intervention in the Mediterranean. The stupidity of Chamberlain was highlighted, though Garratt detected more sinister forces influencing the British Government, arguing that its 'vacillating, dishonest, and tortuous policy' was the result of a pro-Mussolini attitude prevalent among the Catholics, property-owners, and neo-fascists.

Nicholas Joicey, *A Paperback Guide to Progress, Twentieth Century British History*, 1993

Left propaganda (which by the way is coming perilously close to war propaganda, by the one-time pacifists, of course), is becoming ever more difficult to cope with. Have you noticed the titles of the first three Penguin Specials? *Germany Puts the Clock Back*, *Mussolini's Roman Empire*, (shown in our columns to be violently anti-Catholic) and *Blackmail or War?* by Madame Tabouis, the famous Russophile correspondent of *L'Œvre* who has ways of making herself quoted throughout the world's press. I haven't read the first, but the other two are brand-new books at sixpence apiece, and so rapidly produced that Mr Eden's resignation is mentioned in Mme Tabouis's work. Can there be a profit in this? Certainly only if hundreds of thousands of copies are sold. I don't say that the Penguin owners are responsible, but someone must have been pushing hard to achieve this propagandist coup. I am told that the real reason why these books are Left is that the publishers consider that only Leftish books can sell in sufficient quantity these days to justify the venture.

Catholic Herald, 29 April 1938

It was inevitable that a certain logic would dictate that since Penguin published books that inclined towards the Left, then its editors and owners must be similarly inclined. It did not take too much imagination for such speculation to coalesce into, as Morpurgo put it: 'the canard that Penguin were designed as propaganda for the Soviet Union and Allen himself a paid-up member of the Communist Party'.

There was, for example, the tale that Allen was about to launch a current affairs journal, overtly Communist and edited by a prominent member of the Party. This was founded upon two unrelated possibilities that Allen had been canvassing for some months. His new enthusiasm for periodical publishing had set him to contemplate a Penguin magazine which would deal, briefly and on a regular basis, with the kind of topics handled at greater length, but occasionally, in the Specials; it was said that he intended to appoint James Maxton as the magazine's editor. In truth he was seeking from Maxton a book to go into the Special series and had not for one moment thought of Maxton as editor of his periodical; almost from the outset he had agreed (as he had written to Ethel Mannin) that 'it would be best to have someone with no obvious party affiliations'. But whether as editor or as author, the leader of the Independent Labour Party, like many another British Socialist, was as virulent as any member of the Cliveden Set in his opposition to Soviet Communism.

J. E. Morpurgo, *Allen Lane: King Penguin*

Allen Lane's old friend Ethel Mannin, still reassessing her political stance, was profoundly affected by it all.

Your name is associated with the CP for very obvious reasons – it was John Lehmann who edited *New Writing*, and Krishna Menon who edited (or was anyhow associated with) the series of non-fiction books done by the Bodley Head – the 20th Cent. Library. Both are Communists.

Then again in the Penguins you have published a Communist writer's novel of the Spanish struggle – Ralph Bates's *Lean Men*. In the Pelicans you publish Harold Laski – another Communist.

None of this proves anything, I know, but it accounts for the rumour. If a Communist edits your proposed paper, whether you like it or not you'll be lined up with Gollancz so far as publishing is concerned. Which would be a pity. Better to have someone with no party affiliations, I should say.

I think Maxton is on holiday just now, but I'll find out what can be done. Of course if you could manage to get hold of anything of his to publish it would settle the Communist rumour, which would be what I can only call a Good Thing.

By the way did you do Ramon Sender's *Seven Red Sundays*? Because I feel you should, having done Ralph Bates's extremely unfair book.

If you did something by George Orwell it would again balance the Communist stuff. I wish you could do his *Homage to Catalonia*, but I fear it's too newly out; but there are his novels . . . only I don't suppose Gollancz would release them.

All the best as always.

Ethel Mannin to Allen Lane, 16 August 1938

Lane's reply has not survived.

I am very glad indeed to hear that you published *Seven Red Sundays* and that you are *not* seeking a Communist editor for your paper. I shall certainly firmly contradict *any* party labels attaching to Penguins, and intend to trace down this particular one to its source, and will let you know how it started. There are altogether too many labels handed out these days, and altogether too many rumours current in the literary world – as no one knows better than myself!

Ethel Mannin to Allen Lane, 18 August 1938

The periodical did not appear as a Penguin publication. Lane, as always, had new plans, to which G. T. Garratt's wife could make a contribution.

I am extremely sorry that I haven't written before to thank you for so pleasant a weekend, but on Monday I had my second injection for typhoid and the immediate result was to bowl me over for a couple of days. I enjoyed the weekend immensely and I hope I shall be asked again.

I am leaving at the end of the year and am taking your advice and am extending my tour to include Alexandria, Cairo, Colombo, Calcutta, Benares, Delhi, Agra, Bombay, Baghdad, Mosul, Aleppo, Beirut and Athens. I would very much appreciate any introductions you could give me covering any places in this tour.

On Wednesday the 14th December I am giving a small party – first at the GPO Theatre in Soho Square and afterwards at my flat, 16 Talbot Square – is there any possibility of both or either of you being able to come?

Allen Lane to Mrs G. T. Garratt, 1 December 1938

At a time when Penguin had barely settled into the new Harmondsworth headquarters, and production was running flat out with Specials and Pelicans, as well as the fiction list, the first two King Penguins and a host of further plans ready to take off, Allen Lane was about to disappear, in the company of his sister Nora, on a tour of the Middle East and India that was to last six months.

* * *

Numeracy

Penguin were by no means the first paperback publishers to number their books; but they were certainly the first, and possibly the only, publisher ever to elevate the simple task of assigning a number to an art.

At first all Penguin books simply had numbers, printed at the base of the spine. Within this single series books were colour coded to signify their content. Again, this was not original. From 1932 Albatross Books from their base in Germany had been publishing English language books for sale primarily within Europe, and they had pioneered this approach.

As several generations of readers around the world now know, orange means fiction and crime is green. Penguin chose dark blue for biographies, cerise for travel and adventure, red for plays and yellow for miscellaneous books: anthologies, refugees from an abandoned series of Illustrated Classics, and later, crossword books. After the war, further colours were introduced: sombre grey for world affairs, later put to more lasting use for Modern Classics; and a suitably appropriate purple for essays and belles-lettres. For the sake of completeness there was one further vague category: a sort of lilac which was occupied solely by H. G. Wells's *A Short History of the World.* This guise was soon abandoned altogether for the pale blue covers of the first Pelicans.

In 1937, new series were introduced – initially the Pelicans, with the prefix A followed by a number; then B for the Shakespeare series, C for Illustrated Classics – up to and including Z for Pevsner's awesome History of Art series. By 1970 every letter of the alphabet had been needed, with the understandable exception of O, I and U, and the less obvious omission of M, N, P and W – although these latter were all used in conjunction with additional letters in order to identify what, by 1970, came to number nearly sixty separate series.

Allotting significant numbers rapidly became something of a ritual, and gave rise on at least one occasion to unseemly bickering. Shaw claimed the lion's share. He was the natural, the only choice for the first two Pelicans, and tribute was regularly paid as each round hundred cropped up in the main series: 200, *Back to Methuselah*; 300, *Pygmalion*; 500, *Major Barbara.* 400 was given to Christian Mawson's patriotic *Portrait of England* at the height of the war.

Other series tended to be initiated with volumes by the editor – Penguin Classics with Rieu's translation of *The Odyssey* and Bill Williams's collection of Tennyson and Wordsworth in the Penguin Poets. And every series celebrated numeric centenaries with significant works.

Puffin Story Books produced the large format *Puffin Song Book* as PS 100, published as part of Penguin's twenty-first birthday celebrations in 1956, while two years previously, the one hundredth Puffin Picture Book had been *The Conquest of Everest.*

In 1945 Penguin allowed themselves a rather austere celebration with the publication of an (unnumbered) pamphlet *Ten Years of Penguins 1935–1945*, a simple reprint of articles by Edmond Segrave in *The Bookseller*. This booklet was updated in 1951 as *Penguins – A Retrospect*, with minor changes to the text – and major changes to the design and typography which underline the impact of Jan Tschichold and his successor Hans Schmoller.

Jan Tschichold had been identified, on Lane's enquiring in 1947, as the world's leading typographer. He was tracked down to Switzerland and appointed immediately and at a high salary to overhaul and standardize Penguin design and layout, a mission continued with equal fervour by Hans Schmoller. Schmoller remained rather longer than his predecessor: joining as typographer in 1949, he became head of production in 1956 and a director in 1960 until his retirement in 1976 – not so much a career, more 'a constant pursuit of perfection, as Gerald Cinamon noted in a 1987 tribute.

Penguin's Coming of Age in July 1956 was celebrated with a much more ambitious book, W. E. Williams's *The Penguin Story*, which for 1/- included a full colour cover, numerous illustrations, a Penguin history and a complete catalogue. Published in the Miscellaneous series with the prefix Q, it was possible with a little juggling to assign the number Q21 to this book. Similarly, four years later, the silver jubilee edition *Penguins Progress 1935–1960*, became Q25. They joined a strange assortment, including four wartime hardbacks devoted to aircraft recognition, *The Penguin Atlas of the World*, a book of Saul Steinberg's cartoons, several song books and the de luxe edition of Robert Graves's translation of *The Golden Ass*.

Amongst the Penguin editors and production staff there were people who delighted in any opportunity to make an apposite combination. Thus early on in the war when it was agreed to publish a selection of Fourth Leaders from *The Times*, it made perfect sense to reserve the number 444 for the occasion. Complications ensued when Allen Lane's two brothers and fellow directors John and Richard, who had joined the Naval Reserve in 1938, were inevitably called up and continued to serve together.

You may have noticed a recent announcement of the loss of HMS *Springbank*. Both of Mr Lane's brothers were at sea on the ship and as one of them was particularly interested in the idea of making a selection of your *Times Fourth Leaders* he had the material with him to work on. Unfortunately these went down with the ship. We are sorry not to have let you know of this before, but naturally we could not give you this explanation until the loss became official.

Lieut. Lane had written to us earlier saying that on re-reading the material he did not feel so attracted to the idea of a selection and on going through the further selection which you sent us at the end of September we feel we must endorse this opinion, mainly because of our having to be more than usually selective about what we commission now that we have so much less paper at our disposal.

Eunice Frost to C. S. Kent, 10 November 1941

Thank you for your letter of November 12th. I am glad to say that both of my brothers got away from HMS *Springbank*, although one of them broke a couple of bones in his leg in the process. They are really more concerned over the loss of your cuttings than any item in their belongings.

With reference to the publication of the Leaders, for which we have made a contract on April 30th last, I would very much appreciate it if you would be willing for it to be cancelled. Our decision has been entirely dictated by the worsening of the paper situation.

Allen Lane to C. S. Kent, 18 November 1941

The idea was later revived, and the book was finally published in July 1945, by which time the main series had already reached 500.

555 was allocated to James Laver's biography of Nostradamus: a somewhat recondite reference to the 1555 first edition of *Les Prophéties de Me. Michel Nostradamus*. Rather more obvious was the use of 666 for John Collier's *Defy the Foul Fiend*.

Shaw was once more the centre of an extraordinary publishing coup when, in July 1946, Penguin celebrated his ninetieth birthday with the simultaneous publication of one million books – ten volumes of Shaw plays each in an edition of 100,000. The event became a national celebration in a way that is hard to comprehend today. W. H. Smith in Baker Street was besieged by queues waiting for the shop to open to buy their Shaw ten. The Penguin switchboard was jammed, and the entire million sold out in just six weeks. By the time Shaw died, Penguin were to have sold almost three million copies of his plays, before receiving the dubious compliment of publishing the Shaw Alphabet Edition of *Androcles and the Lion* in accordance with the arcane provisions of his will.

In the wake of the Shaw success, similar celebrations were planned for H. G. Wells's eightieth birthday in September 1946. This, however, turned out to be a somewhat muted affair, following his untimely death during August.

It goes without saying that Penguin 1000 had to be something special. In a typical gesture, however, the book chosen was not the work of a giant of English literature, but that of a little-known war hero Edward Young, entitled *One of Our Submarines*. As Penguin's first production manager, Young had, of course, designed the original cover and drawn the Penguin device.

As from one Old Bird to another, I thought you ought to have an immediate sight of Penguin 1000. These are, of course, very advance ones and your 'regulars' will be coming to you – in order to preserve protocol – through 'your firm'.

I would consider it a fine gesture if you could inscribe some loving words so that you can add me to your fan list.

Don't flash these around, will you, because, of course, they are being hoarded as a surprise for July 30th.

Eunice Frost to Edward Young, 8 June 1954

The very next number, 1001, was immediately assigned to N. J. Dawood's translation of *The One Thousand and One Nights* – much to his and Rieu's chagrin, since the original commission was to make the translation for the more prestigious Penguin Classics, in which it was soon reprinted. Dawood was subsequently commissioned to translate two further Classics, *Aladdin and Other Tales* and *The Koran*.

It was not very long before there was a further opportunity for a little number-juggling with the impending publication of Sir Harold Scott's book on Scotland Yard.

Is there any possibility of reserving Penguin number 1212 for Harold Scott's *Scotland Yard*?

Eunice Frost to A. S. B. Glover, internal memorandum, 29 March 1956

To which there was the handwritten reply from Glover:

Sure: we can and will. But what if the Postmaster General changes their number?

George Orwell's *Nineteen Eighty-Four* should really have been an obvious candidate for this particular game. Unfortunately, the rights to reprint this were granted as early as 1954, and the book was published with the slightly apologetic serial number 972. All was not quite lost, however. Subsequently the company's headed notepaper was seen to carry the new telephone number: SKYport 1984, Richard Lane's suggestion for an unforgettable number.

I'd like to register a mild protest at the arbitrary change of number on PMP10 [Penguin Modern Poets 10] without any discussion with me or indeed with AG [Tony Godwin]. I do of course fully agree that D100 is a number of some significance and that the title which should carry it should be a matter for discussion. On the other hand, there are cogent publicity reasons for using this number on the Liverpool volume and I don't feel it should have been changed without taking full account of these and other possibilities. I am getting a list of all books now in the pipeline which would be eligible for the number and will be discussing it with AG.

Tony Richardson to Hans Schmoller, 7 March 1967

I am sorry this change of number has added to your much more serious worries (I was on the point of dropping you a line). I did not know the number had been specially chosen for this book, nor that editors concern themselves with such mundane details. I am intrigued to know what the cogent publicity reasons might be. Incidentally, I did not change the number. I merely queried whether it had been chosen deliberately. When it was changed, I concluded that this had not been so.

Hans Schmoller to Tony Richardson, 8 March 1967

The next major landmark was number 2000, which had been earmarked some time in advance for the publication in conjunction with Oxford University Press and Cambridge University Press in 1964 of the *New English Bible.*

AL has decided that Pelican A1000 is to be *The Making of the English Working Class* by Edward Thompson, which will be published September 1968.

Dieter Pevsner to Tony Mott, 27 October 1967

1,000th Pelican, 26th September 1968

On Thursday, 26th September, we celebrate a notable event in the social and cultural history of our time – publication of the 1,000th Pelican, *The Making of the English Working Class* by E. P. Thompson.

The idea behind the Pelican series which originated in 1937, was to provide the general reader with inexpensive and authoritative books on a wide range of cultural interests. Over the years the series has developed to cover practically every aspect of modern knowledge. The majority of the books are specially written for Pelican publication and although the general reader has not been lost sight of, schools, colleges and universities all over the world specify Pelicans for required and background reading.

To celebrate this publishing achievement, the *Guardian* will produce a special survey on the 26th September. There will be four pages of lively editorial content, dealing with various aspects of publishing and Penguin Books, supported by advertising from selected interests.

Vernon Brown, Advertisement Manager, to David Smith, W. H. Smith & Son, 29 August 1968

No such steps had been taken to make a similar event out of number 2500 in the main series, which was reserved for the relatively modest *Spanish Short Stories*. It is also assumed that assigning *The World is Not Enough* the number 2001 in 1964 was purely fortuitous. So with the change to ISBN numbering looming, this left number 3000 as Penguin's last opportunity to indulge in this unique pastime. The opportunity was not wasted, the number being reserved for a particularly apt choice of book published to mark Allen Lane's fifty years in publishing.

* * *

PENGUIN AT WAR

1939–1945

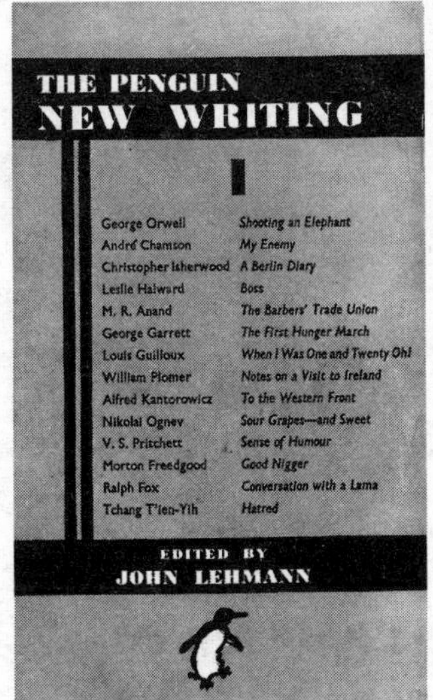

Sixpenny Immortality

As to the Nevinson project, I probably used the word 'Anthology' rather loosely. What I have in mind is a collection of complete essays, and I enclose my provisional list. Some of the books from which the essays are taken you may have by you but I have them all if you need any of them.

Some of Nevinson's books are now quite unobtainable, except by happy accident in Charing Cross Road, and I think it will be a great pity if his work was allowed to die even while he is still alive. A collection, too, would do honour to a great man before it is too late.

George Ridley MP to H. L. Beales, 5 February 1941

The subject of the proposed anthology, Henry Woodd Nevinson, born in 1856, had had a long and distinguished career as a journalist and foreign correspondent. In an Appreciation reprinted in the book, J. L. Hammond wrote that Nevinson remained 'a lover of freedom, and he became the most distinguished representative of his age of the great rebel tradition to which our public life owes so much . . . Nevinson believed in democracy because he believed in the common man, but he never understood by democracy the tyranny of the mass mind. No man attached greater importance to integrity and independence of character, or had a stronger dread of the totalitarian State.'

And in March 1941, Nevinson had a particular reason to despise the totalitarian state. Writing from the King's Arms, in Campden, Gloucestershire to H. L. Beales of Pelican:

I am much obliged for your letter of the 2nd. Considering the risk, I think your terms are generous, but as I have been blasted out of my house, and exile is expensive, I should be ever so glad if, after as little delay as possible, the volume could be finished so that I might receive the £50 advance royalties, for I am now very old and going feeble.

I am indeed delighted to receive your letter of the 11th and to hear that the contract will soon be ready. Also that after the signing of the contract the advance becomes payable.

I have contrived to collect the whole of the Copy now from all the volumes concerned. But if Mr Christian has sent you the volume of *Essays in Rebellion*, perhaps you would kindly forward it to me here, as I have cut my own copy to pieces in order to extract the chosen essays. In some cases I have had the essays typed out from other volumes.

As the whole lot are now collected and arranged as I wish them to appear, I propose sending them all in a registered packet to you tomorrow, including Mr Ridley's Introduction and my own Preface (I implore you not to call it by the German word 'Foreword').

At the very end I hope you will allow a brief Index of the names mentioned in the various chapters.

In these days we must expect delay, but I would remind you that I am now very old, and should be so pleased to see the book published while I am still alive.

Henry Nevinson to Eunice Frost, 17 April 1941

Very many thanks for your letter of April 22nd, returning the contract and so I am able to send you our cheque for £50 and would appreciate it if you would sign and let me have back the enclosed receipt form.

We are very pleased with the selection of Essays and hope to get this in proof as soon as possible.

Eunice Frost to Henry Nevinson, 26 April 1941

My husband has asked me to acknowledge your letter enclosing cheque for £50, as he is not very well today. He wants me particularly to thank you for your gracious words about his Essays, and if I may I will add my thanks to his. In his present depressed state of mind a letter like yours has an immediate cheering effect, and we are both grateful for it.

I also enclose the official receipt and need hardly add that we look forward to receiving the proofs as soon as they are ready.

Evelyn Sharp Nevinson to Eunice Frost, 28 April 1941

I saw Nevinson in London and Campden.

He is now 85, very feeble, and very ill. He thinks he will only live six months or so and it is really the hope of his life that he may see his book in print. If you can do anything to hasten it forward I should be grateful.

George Ridley to Allen Lane, 23 July 1941

Many thanks for your note of July 23rd.

Some time ago we gave particular instructions to our printers that Mr Nevinson's manuscript should take preference over the other material they have in hand, but I am afraid even with this priority there is still considerable delay as now-a-days our printers are held up very badly through lack of staff now that it has been de-reserved as a trade.

We on our part fully appreciate Mr Nevinson's anxiety to see the book published and are certainly doing all we can to hurry the printers, who tell us that proofs should be ready within the next week or ten days.

Eunice Frost to George Ridley, 5 August 1941

I realize that you will have had a great many letters of sympathy, but I wanted you to know how sincerely we regret that it was not possible for us to give Mr Nevinson the satisfaction of seeing his selected writing in print during his lifetime. Every effort was made here to speed up the work, knowing how keenly anxious he was to see it completed, but I am afraid conditions entirely beyond the control of any of us prevented it.

Our aim is that the publication should take place as soon as possible so that the book will serve as a tribute to his memory.

Please don't trouble to answer this letter as I know the many difficulties with which you must now be faced.

Eunice Frost to Evelyn Sharp Nevinson, 14 November 1941

Can you give me any news of Henry Nevinson's Penguin volume, *Words and Deeds*? Your last communication, dated February 13th, intimated that it was waiting only for the permission of the editor of the *Highway* to reprint J. L. Hammond's article as an Introduction. It seems really unfortunate that all this delay should ensue before publication when the book was on the point of coming out before my husband died. I know there are great difficulties just now in the way of publication, but every week new books are appearing that were arranged for later than his could have been, and if I had known there would be this long pause before the appearance of *Words and Deeds* I should have taken steps to secure some other posthumous publication of his while his name was still so prominently before the public. I shall be very much obliged if you will give me some tidings of its publication without further delay.

Of course, I am quite aware of the difficulties, but you will understand how I too am feeling about it. I am my husband's executor, and feel responsible for safeguarding his literary remains. He set great store upon this Penguin volume, which he called his 'Sixpenny Immortality', so I am particularly anxious for it to appear.

Evelyn Sharp Nevinson to Eunice Frost, 11 June 1942

By a very happy coincidence your letter arrived on my desk at the very same time as *Words and Deeds* so I am able to satisfy your questions immediately. We hope to receive the balance of this from our printers shortly and it will then be possible for us to fix its publication to take place early next month.

I am sure it is extremely difficult for you and people outside the publishing trade to understand what seems like fantastic and unnecessary delays, but so many printers are now doing Government work that this always takes precedence and it frequently happens that something on our own production list gets shelved for weeks so that the machines can be used on priority work. This, together with the allocating of our very much reduced paper quota to cover our commitments makes publishing a cross between a nightmare and a maze puzzle.

Eunice Frost to Evelyn Sharp Nevinson, 15 June 1942

I have learnt the reality of Freedom only from the misery of its opposites from the sight of shaggy farmers, rough with mud and storm, clad in leather cut from their starved-out horses; or from the sight of a woman in rags cowering under a ruined wall while sleet hissed upon the charred ground where was her home. Or I see a pale man and girl hurried over the snow between brown-coated soldiers to be shot in a row with others among the sandhills of a Russian town. Or I see a herd of black Africans, men and women, huddled together upon a steamer's deck, like overdriven cattle, gazing blindly towards the two misty islands where they would toil till they died in order that our chocolate creams might be cheap. Or I see a white-robed crew gathering upon a beach where the surf beat heavily under a stormy moon, and from the crowd went up a cry in honour of a prisoner spirited away from his country, untried and uncharged. Or I see an ancient city whispering in terror at the presence of a decrepit and terrified old man who sat in his kiosk like a spider in a web sensitive with treachery. Or I see the state of Europe in this present year of 1941.

I have known them all, and from them too I have learnt the meaning of Freedom as being their opposite. I have learnt that Freedom is a thing like love, which we have to conquer for ourselves afresh every day, and we are always losing Freedom, just as we are always losing love, because after each victory we think we can now settle down to enjoy it without further risk or struggle. But if we would retain love or Freedom we can never settle down. That is why the battle of Freedom is never done and the field is never quiet.

H. W. N.
(in exile from London, 1941)

* * *

'It's This Beastly War . . .'

Regret I have nothing which would be suitable for a Christmas Card unless land girls spreading manure plus winter trees would be suitable.

Extract from a June 1943 letter to Noel Carrington from Stanley Badmin, artist and, temporarily, corporal in the RAF

I always said that in case of war I should have to go to the Ministry of Information to run the Foreign Intelligence Section. So it proves.

One day perhaps you will be able to consider my half-finished Pelican.

I hope the war does not affect your great undertaking.

B. Ifor Evans to Allen Lane, 18 September 1939

I am extremely sorry to hear that you will not be able to complete your MS. It seems to me that it is exactly the type of book which will be in great demand within the next few months as my feeling is that after the first shock of war there will be a great need for books on cultural lines. I wonder if it would be possible for you to reconsider your decision? I am quite often at the Ministry of Information and would be very glad to call in and see you to discuss it some time.

Allen Lane to B. Ifor Evans, 25 September 1939

A Short History of English Literature was, after all, published in July 1940. Lane was absolutely right: it was translated into several languages, was issued in the Forces Book Club, and after countless editions remains in print today.

. . . blood-curdling tales have reached me from Selfridge's Book department and *The Times* Book Club. The former tell me that Puffins don't get reprinted, owing to the paper shortage. The latter told me that they had never received any copies of *Orlando's Evening Out*, in spite of the fact that they had ordered them well in advance. They also said that reprinting was not the order of the day.

Is it not possible to get new editions printed in America? Or at different printers, since they are rationed?

It is rather worrying to think that all the work and lithography that goes into making a Puffin, should die with the first edition.

Kathleen Hale to Eunice Frost, 12 September 1941

. . . [while] in the past we could reprint and reprint each individual title, it is now in many instances an absolute necessity that we should allow it to go out of print so that part of our paper allocation can be put towards the production of another title, which has probably been under contract for a considerable time and which the author – and rightly – is anxious to see on the market. All this means that some form of rationing must be passed on to the bookshops, otherwise the larger concerns would put in fantastic orders which would mean we would be unable to execute orders from smaller shops.

The principle on which we work is that our regular accounts have standing orders whereby we supply them with a regular number of every publication as it comes out and any further copies required must be re-ordered by them in the normal way.

I hope you begin to see that when one considers all the bookshops in England which could, and probably do, stock our titles, remembering that our printers have to be limited because we ourselves are limited for our paper, it is obvious that unfortunately there must be gaps in some places where the stock has been quickly exhausted and further orders have probably come in when the edition has already been exhausted.

I am sorry to go into such detail about this but I feel it only fair to let you know how these things stand and it is for this reason Mr Lane is now in America finding out the possibilities of printing on that side, which to a certain extent would relieve the pressure over here.

Eunice Frost to Kathleen Hale, 17 September 1941

Yesterday I sent you a card to say the Orlandos hadn't yet arrived, this morning a marvellous batch came by post – so many, in fact, that I think he must have had kittens. Thank you very much indeed; I can now send some to relatives and friends abroad.

Kathleen Hale to Eunice Frost, 25 September 1941

I am wondering if you will be sending me a statement of royalties soon, also whether I can take it that I shall receive the money due to me at the end of March, as stated in my contract. And are the American sales included in the same payment? I imagine as the book is sold in America for one shilling, that I get £2 a thousand quoted in the contract?

I will tell you why I am worrying about all this – domestic servants can command a much higher wage than hitherto, and I am in danger of losing mine if I don't give her a rise very soon. I can't do this unless I get my royalties, for my husband's salary is, like everyone else's, halved by the increased income tax and he can't help me. I want to be able to say to my maid that on a certain date I will raise her wages. If I lose her then there'll be no more Orlandos, for I cannot possibly do without her.

I am sorry to trouble you but it's this beastly war.

I should be glad of an early reply.

Kathleen Hale to Eunice Frost, 26 February 1942

As soon as we have straightened out the chaos resulting from our premises having been requisitioned and our Chief Royalty Clerk having been called up, all in one and the same week, we will make up your royalty statement and provide you with a cheque. I do hope though, that you will be tolerant if this doesn't happen for the next few days.

Eunice Frost to Kathleen Hale, 2 March 1942

Thank you very much for the cheque. All was pinched and puny before it arrived and now jubilation reigns. The royalties are to be metamorphosed into twelve hens, two dental plates for my children and a rise for the maid. Could anything be more intoxicating?

Orlando's Home Life is getting on, though repeated bouts of biliousness and 'flu have held up the process till now.

I am, of course, delighted that *Orlando's Evening Out* is being reprinted. I enclose receipt.

PS Will you please let me know what number this second Puffin will be, for I must write it on the plate.

Kathleen Hale to Eunice Frost, undated (March 1942)

Thank you for your letter. The dental plates are in position, the maid is risen, only the hens are vile.

Kathleen Hale to Eunice Frost, 18 March 1942

According to John Lehmann, Allen Lane had a contingency plan in case of invasion to set up office in Canada. As it turned out, Harmondsworth was requisitioned by the RAF and was used for the duration for the repair of fighter aircraft. The Penguin office staff moved mostly to Silverbeck, the home of Allen Lane and his new wife Lettice. The rationed and restricted war years became not a period of retrenchment and consolidation but a period of intense and spectacular growth. 1940 saw the introduction of the Puffin Picture Books, auto-lithographed by the artists, and published in a large format with several pages in full colour, under the editorship of Noel Carrington; and similarly John Lehmann's influential new series Penguin New Writing. In 1941 came Eleanor Graham's Puffin Story Books. Then Penguin Handbooks, Penguin Poets, the short-lived Penguin Hansard, American editions, Reference Books, the single Italian edition, French Penguins, Topolski Prints, Baby Puffins – and, most incredibly of all, two beautifully produced series, Penguin Modern Painters and King Penguins: in all some nineteen new series emerged during the course of the war.

All the same, some compromise was soon necessary.

Now that paper rationing has been introduced, we have found it impossible to publish any work running to more than 256 pages, at the same time we don't like reducing the type size to less than 10pt., as we receive so many complaints from readers when a smaller type is used.

Allen Lane to D. K. Broster, March 1940

The flimsy covers and inferior paper that soon had to be used were equally galling to authors, booksellers and Lane.

Since my return from America I have been very much perturbed by the very shabby condition of our publications on a number of bookstalls. I have not seen Liverpool Street myself but I am told that the display there is very poor from this point of view and from my own observation Piccadilly, both in the stall in the old station and below in the Booking Hall, is appalling. What is to be done about it?

Allen Lane to John Hutchinson, 24 November 1941

This particular letter, the original of which remains in the archive, was probably never sent. Instead the reverse of the original letter sent was used for the file copy of another letter. As paper got shorter, virtually anything would be called on to provide file copies. In most cases, the carbon copy of Penguin's reply would be found on the reverse of the original letter. If this was unsuitable, out of date publicity handouts, old letterheads, the back of sheets from several calendars, and even what appear to be unsolicited manuscripts, torn in half, were called on to save the most precious commodity of all for a publisher. 'Envo-Flaps', adhesive address labels used to seal a folded letter, were much in evidence, in order to 'Save envelopes, save paper, help the war effort'.

I hope I shall be able to see proofs of the Pelican book of *Wild Flowers* before Xmas.

Do you think it would be possible to print it on a dead white paper? If done on the grey paper of recent times, I fear the drawings will not show up well.

You must have many troubles in these days.

J. Hutchinson to H. W. Oberndorfer, 8 December 1944

Thank you for your letter of 8th December. Unfortunately, the paper position does not permit us to think of printing *Common Wild Flowers* on a dead white paper right away, but should the day when the book will go to press coincide with the beginning of a new paper allocation period, we will certainly try and do our best to procure some.

H. W. Oberndorfer to J. Hutchinson, 13 December 1944

During the war Penguin publications contributed to every field of human endeavour and set about, more or less systematically, addressing the various needs of the population – starting with the most basic: food.

I sincerely hope that *Poultry and Rabbits On Scraps* has been a commercial success. I am glad to say that from the Rabbit Section I have had most favourable reports, and luckily, no adverse criticism.

You will appreciate that confined to the Title, the book has been useful mainly to the Novice, and has been used extensively by the Domestic Rabbit Clubs.

Until recently people have just gone crazy on breeding any type of rabbit for meat production; but now practically every beginner has visited a rabbit show, of which there are many every week, and hardly a district without a monthly Show.

The mammoth Club Show is being held at Bradford next week, and there are 11,000 accepted entries, and thousands returned through lack of accommodation.

The Government are in favour of these Shows as it creates interest and brings in fresh breeders, but the effect is, there are hundreds of thousands of rabbit keepers giving up their nondescript table varieties for pure breeds.

I am about to do a much more comprehensive script giving details of all varieties and full information on the Commercial side of the Industry, with a title such as *Rabbit Breeding for Fur, Meat and Profit*.

I am confident that the sale of such a book would be tremendous, and apart from the present demand, would be required for post-war conditions (written partly with that view in mind) and should be a good seller for many years to come.

If you would be interested in publishing such a book, I would be only too pleased to give the matter every detailed consideration.

If the question of paper presents any great difficulty, I might possibly be able to get some concession, as the Government attach great importance to Rabbit Breeding, and are anxious for the development now and for post-war.

C. H. Goodchild to Allen Lane, 28 November 1942

Since the arrival of citrus fruits again in this country I am being inundated with queries about preserving them, so if there should be another edition of *Preserves for All Occasions* being issued this year I suggest perhaps I had better include a section on marmalades.

Alice Crang, Fruit Preservation Instructress, University of Bristol, to Allen Lane, 5 March 1945

The need for shelter was also uppermost in people's minds – whether this meant their usual place of residence, or the strictly literal use of the term.

May I ask you to make a note of my new address? I am sorry to say my house in George Road – a very nice Georgian one in an old garden – was laid in ruins by our discerning enemies last October. My family and I were actually in it at the time, but escaped unhurt by a sheer miracle, although everything came literally tumbling about our heads. Then, in December, while our things were still in the remaining portions of the house, it was hit again and my library was rather badly knocked about, though fortunately nearly all of it is still useable.

All this has rather delayed my start on the Pelican, I am afraid, and only now that we are more or less permanently settled again can I make a real start, though I have thought about it a good deal already and cleared things up in my mind. I think I shall still be able to get it done before the end of the year, for once my notes are in order, I shall be able to carry on fairly quickly.

Eric Blom to Allen Lane, 7 February 1941

Not everyone, of course, was that lucky.

We must get together sometime. I haven't seen you since that chance meeting at Wheeler's Oyster Bar. Incidentally the girl with whom I was lunching that time was killed a few weeks afterwards when the flying bomb hit the Guards' Chapel.

Allen Lane to Vyvyan Holland, 11 August 1945

Since this war started, there has been a remarkable revival in the interest shown in crossword puzzles. Many thousands of people who never did them before now do them regularly, and, of course, there has always been a public, running into many millions, who have always indulged in this pastime.

ACROSS

1. What Adolf will soon be begging for
6. Keep clear of him or you'll get it in the neck
9. It's guaranteed to put the wind up the enemy
10. Take one if you're thirsty
11. Star men at sea?
12. One expects him to have foreign ideas
17. The British army doesn't know the meaning of the word
18. Something to bring back from the battle
19. Eventually Germany will be forced to do so
21. He's only half a man!
24. Is it eaten slowly in France?
27. It might be a six
29. Contents of Yvonne's lipstick
30. Instrumental in the downfall of the enemy!
31. Mope for a change
32. It has more than two feet

DOWN

1. What the Nazis will never do!
2. Descriptive of that smart French girl
3. Pull the vessel
4. It may indicate which service you are in
5. Something for Tommy to speak French with
6. It has explosive possibilities
7. Quarters for the general
8. It's all up when you're at your last one
13. Obviously not a lady's gun
14. Lamed perhaps, but coveted by a soldier
15. This vehicle might follow Annie, we hear
16. The base deceiver—no wonder he gets the cat!
20. Pretty dangerous when Mac and Ian get together
21. " His age " (anag.)
22. The right kind of stools to provide rest for the army?
23. A useful sort of line for oil supplies
25. One jumper your wife will never knit!
26. You wouldn't expect to find it in the Christmas Pudding!
28. Name for a " musketeer "?
29. A piggish sort of place

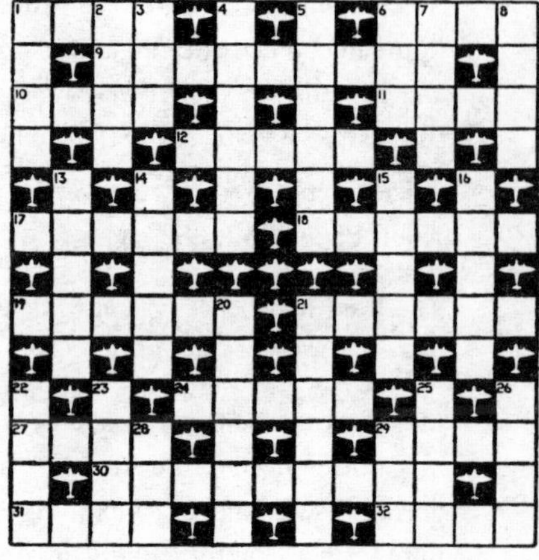

'Our soldiers, sailors and airmen will find a whole section compiled for their special benefit' in Morley Adams's *Second Penguin Crossword Book*, 1941.

It has occurred to me that a book containing 150 puzzles would be a good proposition.

If you are interested we could supply you with this number of puzzles, the same having appeared in the London papers during the last few years.

The book would contain all grades of puzzles, some with the clever cryptic clues such as we do for the *Evening Standard* and *Manchester Evening News*, others would be plain, straightforward squares like those we contribute to the *Star* every day. The book would also contain some of the skeleton crosswords which I invented many years ago and have had a run for the last twenty years in the *Sunday Express*. There would also be a section for children, containing the children's puzzles from the *Evening Standard* which we supply.

We shall be pleased to supply these puzzles on a royalty basis to be decided.

Morley Adams, Morley Adams Ltd, Newspaper Feature Specialists (evacuation address: The Fox Inn, Cane End, near Reading) to Penguin Books, 25 September 1939

Your Penguin Crossword Puzzle book has helped me through many bad hours in an Air Raid Shelter, although the Skeleton Crosswords floor me at present.

From a reader's letter, 18 October 1940

Thank you for your letter. As a matter of fact the second edition of the first Crossword Book is already in hand.

About the week-end – I think the best thing would be for me to come over to the Fox Inn, if this is all right for you. Our address is The Warren, Ipsden, and our telephone number is Chackenden 84, but it is a pretty difficult place to find, even for a crossword expert, in these signpostless days.

Allen Lane to Morley Adams, 11 November 1940

Selections from the *Telegraph*, the *Manchester Guardian* and *The Times* soon followed, the latter being rather nonplussed at finding themselves in such company, and requesting, without success, a more exclusive status in the Penguin canon, or at least a colour coding of their very own.

Of course the most pressing need that Penguin could address was that of amusing and entertaining readers. As George Orwell observed:

The people who were penned up in the Tube shelters for hours together had nothing to do, and there were no ready-made amusements available. They had to amuse themselves, so they improvised amateur concerts, which were sometimes surprisingly good and successful. But what is perhaps more significant than this is the greatly increased interest in literature that has appeared over the last two years. There has been an enormous increase in reading, partly owing to the great numbers of men who are in the army in lonely camps, where they have little or nothing to do in their spare time.

George Orwell, *The War Broadcasts*, ed. W. J. West, Duckworth/BBC

W. D. Denning, Manager of W. H. Smith's in Port Talbot, took up this point in October 1940: 'We are frequently asked for a volume of patriotic speeches, verses etc. – something that could be taken into an air-raid shelter to pass away the time. There is an immense amount of material available and I feel sure that if such a volume were produced it would fill a very real need.' He suggested extracts from Shakespeare, 'the inspiring speeches of Winston Churchill', Kipling's patriotic poems, J. B. Priestley's nine o'clock broadcasts, and other material likely to take people's minds off the destruction of their neighbourhood and the loss of friends and relatives. The suggestion was taken up by the elusive Christian Barman, under his pseudonym Christian Mawson, though *Portrait of England* did not appear until the end of 1942.

Penguin had needs too, only for the duration these tended to be strictly controlled by various authorities set up for the purpose. For Allen Lane this was merely one more challenge:

Few things pleased him more than reading the rules so that the game would be played his way; he seldom enjoyed himself more than when he was using his charm to gull some stony-faced official into believing that it was he who had first dreamed up a gracious concession which would allow to Penguin an advantage that had at first seemed unwarrantable.

J. E. Morpurgo, *Allen Lane: King Penguin*

National Service (Armed Forces) Act, 1939–1941

With reference to your application on form N.S. 300 for the deferment of calling-up for service of your employee BADMIN, Stanley R., I have to inform you that after careful consideration the District Man Power Board has decided that deferment cannot be granted.

The employee will be regarded as available for calling-up for service when required.

District Man Power Officer, Ministry of Labour and National Service, to Allen Lane/Penguin Books, 26 October 1942

You have probably heard the bad news with regard to your deferment. I gather from Geoffrey Smith* when I saw him this week, that you were making good progress with the work. I suppose it is impossible for you to complete it before you are seized.

Allen Lane to Stanley Badmin, 29 October 1942

* A director of Cowells, the Ipswich printing firm.

Badmin's work – writing and illustrating the Puffin Picture Book on trees, that was to become a popular book with children as much as their teachers, and students at agricultural colleges – was published in October 1943. Lane, who had an ambitious series in mind, for which Badmin's services would be indispensable, continued with his attempts for most of the war.

Lane's optimism that mountains could be moved and bureaucratic authorities neatly side-stepped must have been at work when the Countess of Longford was approached in 1943. Amongst the many wartime shortages, there was apparently a lack of good crime fiction – and some years previously she had been commissioned to edit and shorten her fellow Dubliner J. Sheridan Le Fanu's *Uncle Silas*, written in 1864. This work had been completed and the manuscript returned just as war broke out. In 1943 another opportunity arose with John Meade Falkner's *The Nebuly Coat*, which required considerable abridgement as 'thrillers were slower in 1903 than they are today'. So too were the authorities.

I have managed to trace a little of the wanderings of *The Nebuly Coat* proofs.

They were sent from here to our West Drayton office on April 12th and our van took them up to London the next day. They were left at the Press and Censorship Division of the Ministry of Information – because we thought that would save a little time. From there, apparently, they were sent up to Liverpool and then back to London again. Finally they were passed and posted off on May 1st.

Presumably the Censor enjoyed the book so much that he sent it round for all the others to read too – one can only wish they had managed to curb their enthusiasm until it was published. I hope the Irish Censors will not be equally keen and hold on to it for another month.

Joyce Harley to Lady Christine Longford, 6 May 1943

At least the war provided a new and valid excuse for the number of dilatory authors, who would squeeze a few more weeks out of Penguin in much the same way as Allen Lane would win concessions from various authorities.

I am terribly sorry about the appalling delay in finishing off my anthology about the Poets and their damn critics. Beales may have told you that last summer I was pushed into the Ministry of Food, and that my life has become more and more hectic as there was less and less food. For the last few months I have been travelling almost in perpetual motion, while my wife has been struggling with the copyrights. This has been made difficult by the various blitzes, and dislocations in the publishing world.

Hugh Sykes Davies, editor of *The Poets and Their Critics*, to Allen Lane, 1941

William Grimmond, a particularly dedicated artist responsible for several Puffin covers and illustrations, and work for other series, was able to provide a concrete excuse for unavoidable delay in preparing the cover for *South Country Secrets*.

I went last week to Uffington and Blewbury – it was an interesting and useful trip though I was very disappointed to find that the White Horse has disappeared! It has been so completely obliterated, by such skilful camouflage, that I could not discover its exact whereabouts in the short time I had for exploration. But I got a very good idea of the surroundings, and if there is no great hurry for the cover I may be able to go again armed with more exact data. In Blewbury I had a long talk about possible illustrations with Mrs Bower, and made a sketch of the cottage which is referred to in the book. She likes the idea of the White Horse as a cover (the camouflage will of course be removed as soon as the war is over). She is going to find me some more material for illustrations, and was altogether very helpful. I hope to let you see the proposals very soon.

William Grimmond to Eunice Frost, 19 October 1944

Thank you for letting me know the result of your visit to Blewbury. It is rather disappointing about the disappearance of the White Horse, particularly as I would not want the whole book to be held up until such time as they take away the camouflage which might not be for a very long time. Having got the general idea of the lie of the country, would it not be possible for you to do it?

Eunice Frost to William Grimmond, 2 November 1944

Then there were the people in the wrong country altogether: many by choice, though not all.

In reply to your letter of March 19th, we are tentatively scheduling *Jam Tomorrow* for Autumn publication. About the advance, I think our generosity might be a little more evident if you were to approach us in two or three months time.

Elizabeth Creak to H. P. Morison, Thomas Nelson & Sons, 21 March 1946

Many thanks for your letter. I will report to Miss Redlich. My suggestion that the £50 would be acceptable was made because, though you may not know it, Miss Redlich has been under German 'protection' for the last five years.

H. P. Morison to Elizabeth Creak, 25 March 1946

Thank you for your letter of March 25th. I had no idea of Miss Redlich's plight, and I am arranging for the advance of £50 on *Jam Tomorrow* to be paid to you during the next few days.

Elizabeth Creak to H. P. Morison, 8 April 1946

The headed notepaper of the publishers Martin Secker & Warburg Ltd showed a not uncommon progression during the course of the war. By 1942, and probably earlier, it was felt advisable to state, when listing the firm's directors: 'J. H. Lothar (German, of Austrian origin)'. Soon after this his name is inked out, and finally removed altogether. Life was not easy for such people, as one distinguished Pelican author was to discover. In January 1940, Dr Leonhard Adam, author of *Primitive Art*, wrote:

Being a refugee in this country I feel I must avoid publicity personally. This is necessary on account of my relatives who are still in Germany. I would, therefore, very urgently ask you not to publish my photograph, nor a biographical note nor even to say that I am a refugee. If something must be said, however, it should not be more than the following: 'The author's academic studies include ethnology, oriental languages, and primitive law. He made a special study of the tribal organizations and arts of the Northwest American Indians and, on the other hand, the Himalayan peoples and published various articles on all these subjects.'

I would also ask you to omit my Christian name on the title page and jacket of the book. Simply print the initial 'L' instead, please.

By June 1940 letters from Penguin were being addressed to Dr Adam at '32 Shepton Road, Aliens Internment Camp, Huyton, Liverpool', and a year after that, he was to write as 'Dr Leonhard Adam (No. 35000) Internment Camp No III Tatura (Victoria). More happily, by March 1945 he was able to write as the Research Scholar in Anthropology, University of Melbourne, Tutor in Anthropology at Queen's College, Melbourne.

Gradually, with the return to peace, there was a drift back to peace time concerns, and the slow revival of a normality that had almost been forgotten:

The Lanes think that wartime rocket developments should be included, but as the war is over I think we should end on the note of life-saving. Is it known, by the way, whether the rocket was the first development of the firework? Perhaps we had better see how this revised plan works out before asking the artist for more roughs. By the way, he has not yet tackled the rather technical part of how fireworks work. I expect you will agree that these need to be very practical and not at all impressionistic. If fireworks can be bought again, I wish you'd ask your people to send me a ten shilling box for my children's birthday, and send the account to me here.

Noel Carrington to Alan Brock, author of the Puffin Picture Book, *Fireworks and Fêtes*

Thank you for your letter of the 10th October, and please forgive my answering it (a) so late, (b) on such peculiar paper, and (c) in such an odd envelope. I'm living at present among the (late) Herrenvolk, which must serve to explain it all.

Yes, I shall be delighted to do you a cover for *Columbus Sails* – even though I'm rather out of practice nowadays. Will you let me know:

(i) The date you want the finished drawing
(ii) The method of reproduction you wish me to draw for
(iii) The size of cover . . . (presumably the same as *Jehan of the Ready Fists* which you enclosed) and whether you are normally using drawings on front and back, as in the Jehan example
(iv) THE PRICE. (I hope you propose to pay me?)

I think that's all. I can't remember what else one used to discuss in the distant pre-war days when I used to do this for a living. I feel rather like Lazarus trying to order a meal in a restaurant.

C. Walter Hodges, H.Q. School of Infantry, B.A.O.R. Training Centre, 20 October 1945

* * *

and revert to a system of grunts and squeals, like the animals?), but actually, I suspect, because he was a gentleman, a type hated by the modern intelligentsia. He is pretty certain to come back into favour. One of the surest signs of his genius is that women dislike his books.

The article ends:

But on the whole the Penguin Books are keeping up their high level. There are some very good ones in the next batch of ten, and in bulk on my mantelpiece they are as inoffensive to the eye as any sixpenny books could conceivably be.

New English Weekly, 23 July 1936

Just a few years later – with several million Specials and Pelicans and a world war in full swing – Orwell's conversion towards Penguin was complete.

Reading is one of the cheapest and least wasteful recreations in existence. An edition of tens of thousands of copies of a book does not use up as much paper or labour as a single day's issue of one newspaper, and each copy of the book may pass through hundreds of hands before it goes back to the pulping mill. But just because the habit of reading has vastly increased, and people cannot read without educating themselves in the process, the average intellectual level of the books published has markedly risen. Great literature, no doubt, is not being produced, but the average book which the ordinary man reads is a better book than it would have been three years ago. One phenomenon of the war has been the enormous sale of Penguin Books, Pelican Books and other cheap editions, most of which would have been regarded by the general public as impossibly highbrow a few years back.

George Orwell, *The War Broadcasts*, ed. W. J. West, Duckworth/ BBC

Numbered amongst that 'impossibly highbrow' Penguin output was *Down and Out in Paris and London*, issued in 1940 under a contractual agreement whereby Orwell was free to issue a cheap edition two years after publication if Gollancz himself had not.

With reference to your letter dated 5.3.43 I am not absolutely certain without looking up my contracts how I stand about the rights of my books, but I am almost certain that if the publisher has issued no cheap edition two years after publication, the rights revert to me. I can verify this, but in any case neither of my publishers is likely to make trouble about the republication of books which appeared some time ago. The books of mine which might be worth reprinting are (I give date of publication with each):

Burmese Days (1934–1935)
Homage to Catalonia (1938)
Inside the Whale (1940)

I should say *Burmese Days* was much the most hopeful. It was first published by Harper's in the USA, then a year later in a slightly bowdlerized edition by Gollancz. The English edition sold 3,000 to 4,000, the American about 1,000. I think it deserves reprinting, and it has a certain topicality owing to the campaign in Burma. Gollancz's stock of it has come to an end and it is totally out of print, but I possess a copy of the American edition. *Inside the Whale* is also totally out of print, the stocks of it having been blitzed, but I have a proof copy. It didn't sell much but got me a certain notoriety owing to parts of it being reprinted in magazines. *Homage to Catalonia* I think ought to be reprinted some time, but I don't know whether the present is quite the moment. It is about the Spanish civil war, and people probably don't want that dragged up now. On the other hand, if Spain comes into the war I suppose it would be for a while possible to sell anything which seemed informative about Spanish internal affairs, if one could get it through the press in time.

I shall be happy to give you any further information you want.

George Orwell to Penguin Books, 8 March 1943

Orwell's agents, Christy & Moore, were soon able to confirm this to Eunice Frost:

The position in regard to George Orwell's *Burmese Days* is quite all right. Mr Gollancz regrets he cannot do a cheap edition himself but is quite agreeable to your having the book. When you have finished with it, and after the war, Gollancz may indeed do a cheap edition himself, but, as I say, only when you have finished with it.

I am returning herewith the proofs of the Penguin edition of *Burmese Days*. I have corrected them carefully. There were very few misprints, and most of these I think carried forward from the original edition, but I have also made a few minor alterations. I draw attention to these as it is important that they should not be missed. Throughout, whenever it occurs in the text, i.e. not in the dialogue, I have altered 'Chinaman' to 'Chinese'. I have also in most cases substituted 'Burmese' or 'Oriental' for 'native', or have put 'native' in quotes. In the dialogue, of course, I have left these words just as they stand. When the book was written a dozen years ago 'native' and 'Chinaman' were not considered offensive, but nearly all Orientals now object to these terms, and one does not want to hurt anyone's feelings. If the corrections I have made are followed there will not be any trouble. I don't think they cause any overrunning to speak of.

George Orwell to Penguin Books, undated (November 1943)

* * *

For the Forces

G. B. Harrison was the first in a long line of distinguished scholars who became attached to Penguin as advisers or series editors. He edited one of the first volumes in the Pelican series, later transferred to the Penguin Poets, *A Book of English Poetry, Chaucer to Rossetti*, first published in 1937, and constantly in print thereafter to this day. Similarly his 1939 original Pelican, *Introducing Shakespeare*, remains in print. His main contribution, however, was to edit the Penguin Shakespeare – thirty-seven volumes which appeared between 1937 and 1959.

In 1939 however there were more pressing matters to be addressed.

I am enclosing a letter from Mrs Risdon, who is my secretary, asking for certain Penguins to be sent to her husband who is now in France.

It occurs to me that Penguins might perhaps care to undertake this sort of thing on a larger scale. If you were to advertise or let it be known that you would send off direct parcels of, say, not less than six Penguins, it would be a good thing, and I think popular. If one does want to send books to people at the Front it is a bore to order them from Smiths and then subsequently pack them oneself. Doubtless there would be obstacles to get over, but I think the direct service idea is worth considering.

Do I gather that the book of Verse has been reprinted? And have you started to publish in America, and if so, what luck?

G. B. Harrison to Allen Lane, 25 October 1939

I have sent off the books to your secretary's husband. As a matter of fact we are now working on a scheme for a group of books to be posted direct in cartons holding five or ten copies.

Yes, we have reprinted your book of Verse which still continues to sell merrily.

Our American house opened in July and the first three months' trading looks extremely promising.

Allen Lane to G. B. Harrison, 30 October 1939

In the event, after Dunkirk the immediate need to dispatch books to the British Expeditionary Force evaporated. All the same, the prospect of many thousands of potential readers and purchasers of Penguins, with money to spend and time for reading, was not lost on Lane.

Confirmation came from B. Ifor Evans, Professor of English Literature at Queen Mary College, the University of London, who had recently 'compressed into a bare 200 pages the whole story of English Literature from *Beowulf* to *Finnegans Wake*' into an extremely successful Pelican.

I am sorry your dates for a meeting last week were impossible. I sent a copy of my 'brilliant' Pelican to Lord Macmillan, President of the Pilgrim Trust. He replies: 'I discussed the other day with the Secretary Tom Jones, whom you probably know, the idea of providing a few thousands of your book for our sailors, soldiers, and airmen. The men in our services nowadays are drawn from all classes and there must be many among them who would find in your history just the sort of reading they want in their scant leisure. So I hope to carry out this plan.'

Here surely is an idea bigger than anything that affects my book. I think you should consult W. E. Williams who knows Tom Jones.

We ought to meet soon.

B. Ifor Evans to Allen Lane, 10 August 1940

Bill Williams was certainly the ideal person to consult. In his wartime role he

Something in the air? From *Penguins Progress*, 1939 Summer Holiday Number.

held a unique position of influence, as Director of the Army Bureau of Current Affairs, his brainchild.

In the long period between the retreat from Dunkirk and D-Day it had soon dawned on the military authorities that it was absolutely essential to find some means of maintaining the morale of the forces at large and keep their minds active and alert. Large numbers of troops spent long periods manning anti-aircraft batteries or searchlight clusters, often isolated and remote from civilization. It was Bill Williams who developed a number of programmes to inform, motivate and educate troops through the medium of discussion groups. Dealing with current affairs – the progress of the war, and ultimately the details of post-war reconstruction – it became the most extensive adult education programme ever undertaken in Britain. Despite some official opposition, and the initial suspicion and reluctance of participants, the scheme flourished and prospered, and had far-reaching effects.

At times it seemed that the Armed Forces were populated solely by men and women keen to learn – and read. What was required was a plentiful supply of books that addressed that need: well-written factual books, current literature of a high quality, light reading, short stories, quizzes and puzzle books. What was required, in other words, was a plentiful supply of Penguins and Pelicans.

There were immense difficulties with the supply of books to the troops. Added to this was a growing number of service personnel in hospitals, convalescent homes and prisoner of war camps. Throughout the war the task of supplying books for the Forces fell to voluntary organizations, such as the Red Cross, who launched regular appeals for second-hand books with which to stock libraries or parcel up and post. A good many Penguins published during the war carried a notice on the title page:

FOR THE FORCES

Leave this book at a Post Office when you have read it, so that men and women in the Services may enjoy it too.

In the first year of the war the London headquarters of the Red Cross received half a million books, apparently donated by many Londoners in the process of giving up their homes in the face of air raids. In later years, however, the number of books donated fell sharply, as the effects of paper rationing began to feed through, and homes and property were destroyed by enemy action.

Penguins, sold in vast numbers before the war and after its outbreak, were especially popular, being small, light and consequently easier to transport. But with constant reading they inevitably deteriorated. At the London headquarters of the Hospital Library Service, rooms were set aside solely for the repair and rebinding of Penguins.

In these various ways several million second-hand books were in constant circulation amongst troops at home and abroad. This was all very well; but it did not help Penguin. In wartime, all publishers found themselves in the happy position of being able to sell almost anything they published, a complete contrast to long years of recession. Strict paper rationing, about to be tightened still further, meant a severe curtailment in the production and supply of books. But because paper rations were assessed according to sales during the year immediately prior to the outbreak of war – the year which had seen phenomenal growth in sales of Penguin Specials – Penguin were in a far more comfortable position than any other publisher. They could well have exploited this position by using their ration on more expensive books: instead they maintained their pre-war stance, and kept faith as best they could with their mass audience, a good proportion of which was now in uniform.

As Allen Lane had intimated to Harrison, Penguin had from the outset been dispatching books directly to individuals in the Forces by means of the Permit System. Under this scheme individuals or relatives could place orders for books with Penguin which were then delivered through the Services Central Book Depot. Allen Lane argued that if this casual arrangement could be formalized through the existing machinery of the Armed Forces, then there might be an opportunity to bypass paper rationing and increase Penguin's paper allocation. And Bill Williams was probably the one person in Britain at the time with the connections to make this happen.

With reference to our conversation at the War Office on Friday with Brigadier General Morgan, Colonel Jackson and the representative from the Treasury, I am writing this letter as my recollection of the conversation.

As you know, for the past two years we have supplied the bulk of reasonably priced books for the Forces, either through the channels controlled by Colonel Jackson, by books supplied direct to units by us or through the normal bookselling channels both in this country and abroad. In spite of the paper rationing we have been able to maintain a reliable selection although in recent months this has dropped from something like 400 titles to about 100. In order to do this we have had to ration the home trade severely.

The scheme I proposed was that we should produce 10 books a month for the Forces alone: that we should supply these parcels ready for distribution to Colonel Jackson who would affix the labels, stamp them and hand them over to the Post Office. The price I suggested was 5d. a copy or 4/2 per parcel of ten books which would allow Colonel Jackson's organization a margin of 2d. per copy for office expenses after deducting 8d., being the cost of postage to any part of the world.

The only figure about which I was not certain was what the immediate requirements might be and Colonel Jackson seemed to be confident that we might place at least 75,000 of each title or three quarters of a million books each month.

Colonel Jackson also said that there would be no difficulty in getting the necessary paper allocation as his namesake at the Paper Control was quite willing to co-operate provided that all the paper thus released would be used wholly and solely for the Forces. This, of course, I was quite willing to agree to as I would propose that when once we had delivered the agreed number of books to Colonel Jackson for distribution there would be no further reprint and, in fact, that the scheme would work as a sort of 'Forces Book Club' which, when once distribution of each title had been effected, would thenceforth become unavailable under the scheme.

This was the scheme in a nut-shell and as soon as I hear from you that my recollection is correct I will proceed with the production of a first list, which I think we could guarantee to have ready for circulation by March.

PS I am enclosing herewith a 'rough' of a cover which I think might be suitable. I would not propose to use either my own name or that of this firm in connection with this series as I feel that by so doing I might give rise to a certain amount of antagonism among the publishers.

Allen Lane to W. E. Williams, 24 December 1941

The scheme, though admirably simple, still had to negotiate the tortuous red tape of Services bureaucracy. The fact that the scheme, first proposed in November 1941, was officially approved by July 1942 and the first ten Forces Book Club issues were parcelled up and posted by October 1942 was due solely to the fact that, as J. E. Morpurgo wryly observed, 'once the principle was agreed, Allen left the details to his chief adviser, W. E. Williams, who had no difficulty in making a sound working relationship with the General's nominee, the Director of the Army Bureau of Current Affairs, W. E. Williams'.

The main hurdle, in fact, was alluded to briefly by Allen Lane in the throwaway postscript to his letter. 'A certain amount of antagonism among the publishers' was of course a deliberate understatement, the prospect of which no doubt gave Lane considerable delight. And after due consideration over Christmas, he decided to make an eminently sensible and practical suggestion which doubtless enraged them still more:

In all probability it would be better if we used our own imprint in connection with the series as this would obviate any necessity for having to refer back any books which we might have under contract to the original publishers.

We suggest that the title page might bear some such imprint as this:

Published for
H. M. Forces
by
Penguin Books Limited

George Orwell and Penguin

The Penguin books are splendid value for sixpence, so splendid that if the other publishers had any sense they would combine against them and suppress them. It is, of course, a great mistake to imagine that cheap books are good for the book trade. Actually it is just the other way about. If you have, for instance, five shillings to spend and the normal price of a book is half a crown, you are quite likely to spend your whole five shillings on two books. But if books are sixpence each you are not going to buy ten of them, because you don't want as many as ten; your saturation point will have been reached long before that. Probably you will buy three sixpenny books and spend the rest of your five shillings on seats at the 'movies'. Hence the cheaper books become, the less money is spent on books. This is an advantage from the reader's point of view and doesn't hurt trade as a whole, but for the publisher, the compositor, the author and the bookseller it is a disaster . . .

In my capacity as reader I applaud the Penguin Books; in my capacity as writer I pronounce them anathema. Hutchinsons are now bringing out a very similar edition, though only of their own books, and if the other publishers follow suit, the result may be a flood of cheap reprints which will cripple the lending libraries (the novelist's foster mother) and check the output of new novels. This would be a fine thing for literature, but it would be a very bad thing for trade, and when you have to choose between art and money – well, finish it for yourself.

George Orwell, *New English Weekly*, 5 March 1936

Later, his attitude softened, and by July 1936 his criticisms were confined strictly to the quality of the books Penguin had on offer: in this particular batch there was Conrad's *Almayer's Folly*.

At present Conrad is out of fashion, ostensibly because of his florid style and redundant adjectives (for my part I like florid style: if your motto is 'Cut out the adjectives', why not go a bit further

Many of these 'original publishers' had already joined forces as the British Publishers' Guild. They got to hear of the scheme – for Lane wrote to them about it – and Walter Harrap was soon writing to J. Mulligan, the Secretary to the Services Committee for the Welfare of the Forces, from the British Publishers' Association. A copy found its way to Allen Lane, along with annotations in the margin courtesy of Bill Williams:

Many thanks for your interesting letter. The idea of producing cheap paper-bound books entirely for the use of the Forces has already received some consideration, for, among my various activities, I am largely responsible for the existence of the British Publishers' Guild, which, as you may know, issues Guild Books.

We have already discovered the difficulty of obtaining additional paper for volumes of this kind, but I feel that sooner or later the Services will have to do something to make the publication of such books possible, if they really feel that the troops must have light reading in a cheap and handy form.

I am afraid it is quite useless to proceed on the lines that you briefly outlined. [emphasized] Quite obviously you have not studied the manufacturing angle . . .

If the paper can be made available, I have no hesitation in saying that a scheme could be presented that should work easily and without complications. Through such an organization as the British Publishers' Guild the interests of all members of the Publishers' Association are adequately safeguarded. Such a scheme could not be worked through an individual firm because all the books you would require are copyright and the copyright owners might have views of their own when it comes to granting permission for such cheap reprints.

Walter G. Harrap to J. Mulligan, 13 April 1942

This long letter continued by raising the very arguments used against Penguin Books in 1935 when they first started publication. The difference now was the prospect of Penguin operating in tandem with the military authorities, with the means to gaining additional paper over and above their already superior allowance. What the Guild may not have realized was the significance of having Bill Williams on the team as well.

I enclose, for your private information, a copy of Harrap's reply, and the comment upon the reply which I have immediately made for the consideration of the Adjutant-General. I must ask you to keep Harrap's letter to yourself.

I think the end is in sight, and I suggest you go ahead with your preparations.

W. E. Williams to Allen Lane, 18 April 1942

Memorandum to C.A.D.G.W. & E.

1. I have read Harrap's answer which is what I expected.

2. On the penultimate paragraph I would say this:

Harrap's declaration that 'such a scheme could not be worked through an individual firm' will be flatly contradicted by Allen Lane who, as you know, has the paper and can get the copyrights of most of the books he needs. The fundamental difference between publishers as-a-whole and Penguin Books is that the first insist on using their paper ration for expensive books, while Allen Lane produces only cheap books. The project we have in mind is, therefore, a continuation of his present activities.

One factor in the situation is that Allen Lane, in this matter, is mainly a philanthropist, he wants to give the Services priority in book supplies, and he wants to mitigate for them the consequences of the impending book famine. As his profits inevitably go in EPT (Excess Profits Tax) he would prefer to see them utilized instead for the Services.

3. The next step, I suggest, is that Allen Lane should be asked the same question as was put to the Publishers' Association.

W. E. Williams, 18 April 1942

BOOK CLUB APPROVED OFFICIALLY STOP GO AHEAD WITH JACKSON STOP CONSULT CHAPMAN AT WAR OFFICE AND HAVE ANNOUNCEMENT READY FOR ABCA BULLETIN BY TUESDAY STOP WILL BE BACK WEDNESDAY

WILLIAMS

Telegram, W. E. Williams to Allen Lane, 23 July 1942

There can be little doubt that the idea was potentially a brilliant one. Penguin stood to gain immeasurable goodwill – from authors, faced with the prospect of receiving an additional £75 royalties in a patriotic cause; printers, suffering as much as any other trade; and the many eager readers. Added to this was the prospect that the selection 'include some books not likely to be otherwise available in cheap editions for some time to come – e.g. William Shirer's Berlin Diary.'

A number of books were published in the Forces Book Club before publication as a Penguin on general sale, a fact pointed out in the announcement of the Club's closure:

The Club has thus functioned for exactly a year, the first distribution having been made in October 1942. During these twelve months subscribers have received a hundred and twenty books which are believed to have been representative of the best in contemporary literature. In the majority of cases Club members have received their copies before the book has been available in any comparative edition to the general public, and in a number of cases they have in fact been first editions appearing for the first time in the Club edition.

There were two clear reasons for its ultimate failure. The first is that the Club simply did not reach the audience for which it was intended. Richard Lane could testify to this, as Allen pointed out to Williams:

You are, I think, aware that my brother has been serving in a battleship on foreign service and has been stationed at one of the largest of our foreign bases before being transferred to one of the main home establishments. He tells me that with the exception of one Admiralty Fleet Order he has come across no publicity for the scheme and in point of fact, no one with whom he has spoken seemed to be aware of the Club's existence.

We are constantly being asked whether it is possible for units to obtain regular supplies direct from us and obviously the writers have no knowledge of the service which the Club gives or they would have availed themselves of it; on the other hand on more than one occasion I have had letters from private individuals who have wished to donate a subscription to a ship's company (not to an individual) and their application has been turned down by the Services Central Book Depot.

On visiting the Army Educational Corps on Salisbury Plain recently I found a few of the larger units had sets in their libraries but the officers asked me whether it would not be possible for them to have some publicity material enabling them to introduce the scheme to their

ABOVE: The Lane brothers, Allen, John and Richard, caught by their sister Nora contemplating a return to their Welsh roots, at Aust Ferry. (*photo: Nora Bird*)

LEFT: Allen and Nora on their extended tour of the Middle and Far East shortly before the outbreak of the Second World War. (*photo: Nora Bird*)

Allen and Lettice Lane with guard of honour, 28 June 1941.

The Lane brothers at Silverbeck, Stanwell Moor. (*photo: Hulton Picture Library*)

Richard Lane, R.N.V.R.
(*photo: Gilbert Adams*)

John Lane at
Harmondsworth.
(*photo: Tunbridge*)

A.S.B. Glover, Allen Lane, W.E. Williams and Eunice Frost in conference, c. 1950.

ABOVE: Post-war editorial conference: Tatyana Kent (later Schmoller), J.E. Morpurgo, Richard and Allen Lane, W.E. Williams, Eunice Frost, A.S.B. Glover. (*photo: Pictorial Press*)

LEFT: Allen Lane and Eunice Frost discuss the possibility of another volume of Low cartoons for the Penguin Specials. (*photo: Bristol Archive*)

Allen Lane. (*photo: John Gay*)

LEFT: Early days: the Crypt. (*photo: Bristol Archive*)

CENTRE: Packers at Harmondsworth. (*photo: Bristol Archive*)

BELOW: The original Harmondsworth frontage, demolished 1970. (*photo: Topham Picture Library*)

LEFT: Calm before the storm. (*Bristol Archive*)

BELOW: About to hatch. (*Bristol Archive*)

May 25, 1935 THE PUBLISHERS' CIRCULAR AND THE PUBLISHER & BOOKSELLER 707

THE PENGUINS ARE COMING

IF YOU WANT TO KNOW WHAT ALL THIS IS ABOUT, TURN OVER QUICKLY TO THE NEXT PAGE →

outlying stations, the people in fact we were hoping to reach when we first discussed the idea.

We are carrying out a similar scheme for the Prisoners of War, particulars of which are enclosed herewith and it would entail no serious re-organization of our Despatch Department to add the Forces Book Club, and this I propose to do unless the present state of affairs can be remedied.

The other factor was that the Club openly reflected the ideals of ABCA, at the expense of a more general appeal. Lane wrote later to Jackson:

It seemed to me that it was obvious that we are not supplying the type of book which you feel is best suited for the services – you mentioned three categories stressed by you – 'warm' fiction – Westerns and Crime, and as we have never published any books in the first two categories and no more than two titles a month out of a total of ten of the last category, I can readily understand how unsuitable our list as a whole must be.

Penguin's individual subscription scheme was still in force, acting almost as a rival to the Club – and, it appears, it was considerably more successful: 'which is proved by the vast number of orders coming in – £5,000 worth yesterday'. The idea was revived towards the end of the war, with a number of Services Editions which were, for the most part, selections from the current publication list in different covers. For a while too, during 1942–3, Egyptian Editions were produced under licence, when Cairo was the secure base for Allied forces in North Africa.

None the less, between them, Penguin and ABCA helped many thousands not just to while away the war, but to use what free time they had to good effect. Professor Richard Hoggart recalled that:

The rise of Penguins in the mid-1930s and in particular the degree to which the more thoughtful soldiers, sailors and airmen took them as a kind of template of their aspirations, was very important. We had a kind of code that if there was a Penguin or Pelican sticking out of the back trouser pocket of a battledress, you had a word with him because it meant he was one of the different ones. I think I would want to put with that W. E. Williams's Army Bureau of Current Affairs which, after the war was coming to an end and after it ended and we were still in the Army, every week taught us something about what might happen in Britain. I think those were elements in creating a change in climate which finally produced the Labour Government in 1945.

The Penguin Collector 41, Penguin Collectors' Society, 1993

* * *

Prisoners of War

Thank you for the six copies of *Preserves For All Occasions* and for having the four dozen copies sent to me. I am disappointed that no mention could be made in this edition that the royalties were to be paid to the British Red Cross Prisoners of War Fund, but note that you will have this added in the next edition. Perhaps your accounts department will keep me informed of the accounts sent to the above fund.

Alice Crang to Allen Lane, 14 April 1944

The author, after being shot down in an air fight, made five attempts to escape from Turkish captivity in 1918. The first brought him punishment in the criminal jail at Nazareth. To prepare the successful fifth, he feigned lunacy in Constantinople. His later adventures were as exciting as anything in Buchan's *Greenmantle*: he and his Australian companion, Captain Tom White, hid for weeks in a steamer near the Sultan's palace on the Bosphorus; went about the enemy capital in various disguises; crossed the Black Sea as star stowaways in 'a shipload of rogues'; came into contact with the Russian revolution; again voyaged as stowaways; and on reporting at British headquarters in Salonika, with much information, were taken to be 'dagoes'.

From the blurb for *Eastern Flights*, Alan Bott, published 1940

Many thanks for your letter of April 24th, and for sending me a copy of *The Tunnellers of Holzminden*. I read this book when it first came out and I would welcome the opportunity of including it in our series.

In my opinion, there is a certain urgency about this, and with a view to saving time I have taken the liberty of preparing a draft contract which I am enclosing herewith in duplicate. If you find this in order, perhaps you could sign and return a copy to me.

We would very much like to use the illustrations. I wonder if by any chance you have the half-tone blocks? – or failing this the original photographs?

Allen Lane to R. G. L. Kingsford, Cambridge University Press, 26 April 1940

The Tunnellers of Holzminden by H. G. Durnford was indeed published in July 1940 in the cerise covers of the Travel and Adventure books in Penguin's main series, shortly after another 'Classic of Escape', *Within Four Walls*, by Major M. C. C. Harrison and Capt. H. A. Cartwright, a book which includes the touching dedication:

To MY MOTHER whose untiring efforts to get my invisible ink developed and send out all requirements according to instructions never failed.

H. E. Hervey's *Cage-Birds* and *Eastern Flights* were also concerned with escape from enemy prisoner of war camps during the 1914–18 War. History was now on the verge of repeating itself, and Allen Lane soon saw opportunities here that were not to be missed.

Each month, in consultation with the organizations responsible for the distribution of printed matter to Prisoner of War Camps, and if necessary the Censors, the publishers select ten works of Modern Fiction, Crime, Travel, Biography, Humour, Science, etc., which are packed and dispatched direct to individual Prisoners of War through the usual channels. The annual subscription of three guineas payable in advance can be sent through any bookseller and will provide 120 books delivered regularly throughout the year at a cost per book, packed and delivered, of just over sixpence; six-monthly and quarterly subscriptions will be accepted pro rata.

This advice was printed inside each slim wartime volume, specially printed for the Penguin Prisoners of War Book Service. It is now impossible to say exactly how many of these special editions were published. It is fairly certain that the majority of the promised 120 were issued in POW livery, during 1942 and 1943, with, presumably, the remainder made up from ordinary

Penguin publications. Whatever paperwork passed between Penguin and the military authorities and the Red Cross whilst this enterprising sideline was in preparation and operation is nowhere to be found today.

It might easily be assumed that the escape tales brazenly issued in the POW Book Service never actually made it to the camps – but that is not the case; in a postscript to a letter to Allen Lane, A. J. Evans reported: 'As I expect you know, *The Escaping Club* was translated into German and Italian and was compulsory reading for guards in the POW camps.' Furthermore, 'It was used . . . for the education of the RAF and sent round to their libraries.'

Other books in the mainstream Penguin series also failed to find favour with the German military authorities and were rooted out of Red Cross parcels destined for prisoners; Llywellyn Maddock, one of Penguin's early 'travellers', recalled in 1970: 'At one time there were little advertisements at the back, and one of the drawings was of a British soldier sticking a bayonet into the backside of a German soldier, poised in mid-air with a terrified look on his face, and the German soldier was obviously Hitler with a little black moustache. And the Germans would not allow any Penguins with that picture to be sent to troops in the internment camps. They took exception to the fact that this little figure had a little black moustache.'

Elliott Viney of printers Hazell, Watson & Viney, the Librarian of a large POW camp, takes up the story:

> All Penguins were banned from that day and were held up by the Censors, but they continued to be sent from England and eventually filled two rooms in the German Censor's office. When the invasion forces were approaching the Rhine two years later the ban was suddenly lifted and over 25,000 Penguins were released on one memorable day and probably served as fuel to make almost as many cups of tea.
>
> *Penguins Progress 1935–1960*

Of course some of the books that arrived at POW camps were actually read, including the few escape stories that had escaped the camp censor's notice and were, according to Viney, 'carefully rebound with the first and last pages and cover of some other more innocuous title to escape the frequent and censorious security searchers'.

Prisoners' own books were not permissible under any circumstances, and it was some time before secondhand books were permitted into camps, and even these first had to pass through the Educational Books Section, where every book was first carefully examined and each footnote, under-

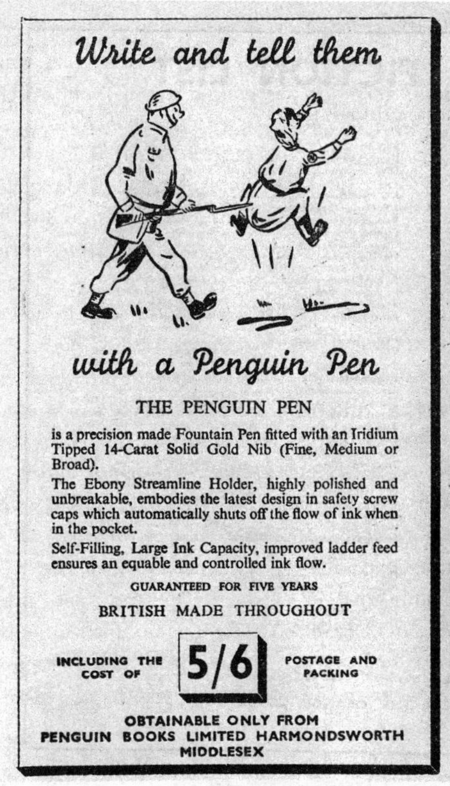

Penmanship by Bob Maynard, Penguin Production Manager.
German POW camp officials were not impressed.

lining and marginal note carefully erased, before being sent abroad, where they were used in the growing number of educational courses that had been organized.

This volume contains the substance of a course of nine lectures on English literature which I delivered to brother-officers prisoners of war in Germany, a first time at Oflag VI B, during the winter and spring of 1941–42, and a second time in Unterlager, Oflag IX A/H during May, June and July 1943. On each occasion I was guided by the following considerations. Most other ranks in captivity in Germany have been put to work. Not so officers. Theirs is a situation of whole-time leisure. And since the latter part of 1941 there have been plenty of books. So for reading, British officers in German hands have an opportunity such as few of them can ever have had before. Indeed, not only have many never before had so much time available for reading; many have found themselves reading for the first time.

So started the Preface to Montgomery Belgion's Pelican, *Reading for Profit*, published shortly after the cessation of hostilities, although Belgion himself had been one of 'the fortunate 2,000 odd prisoners of war repatriated the other day from Germany', in September 1944.

Not all Penguin authors and editors had the same good fortune as Belgion. 'Here are the biographical notes for the *Irish Short Stories*. I think they might have had a more original touch if Alan Steele had been here, for he knows so many of the people personally. But as things are they are as full as can be managed.' So starts a letter to Eunice Frost in August 1942.

The writer was Joan Hancock, Steele's co-editor on the *Irish Short Stories* and a selection of *American Short Stories* – and later his wife. Alan Steele had also edited two volumes of *Selected Modern Short Stories* for Penguin. He had joined Butler and Tanner before the war, printers for both the Bodley Head and Penguin, and had known Lane for some years. The situation referred to in Joan Hancock's letter is the fact that Steele had been reported missing in action. In July 1943 she was finally able to report to Penguin that he was in a Japanese prisoner of war camp, where he was to remain for the duration.

An airmail letter marked post free – 'Liberated Officer P.O.W.' – and addressed, 'Aboard HMS *Implacable* Mid-Pacific':

It seems, and is, many years since I had the pleasure of writing to you. I had the misfortune to be caught in Java. We were hostages to fortune there from the moment we landed and the less said about that disastrous campaign (?) the better! I was moved up to Japan in the autumn of 1942, reaching there after an . . . voyage at the end of November.

We had a swine of a commandant all the time we were in Japan, and he was the direct cause of, literally, hundreds of deaths. We put in a hell of a report on him and his Satellites to the Americans, so hope they will be suitably dealt with. We had a fairly good supply of books to read, but had little opportunity for reading as (a) our huts usually had no windows and we weren't allowed to take a book outside, and (b) we were working all day. There were two big deliveries of American Red Cross books, one in November '43 and the second about the same time last year. The first lot they divided into lots of fifty books and sent them round to the twenty-three camps in our Fukuoka, Kyushu, area. They looked on books as 'books' – so the result was that you might, and did, receive fifty Jewish prayer books, instead of fiction etc. After many protests, I was allowed by the Japs to go to the warehouse in Fukuoka, and sort them myself for the various camps. You will be amazed to hear that Penguins (American) were forbidden, as they said they had been found to 'unsettle' the men!? They were always terrified of detective fiction, as they thought they would give the men 'ideas'! Eventually this ban was lifted.

Their dealings with Red Cross supplies – we had four parcels in three years, books, clothing etc. – was criminal. Still it's all over now, thank God. We were rescued by the Americans on September 8th, having had air-dropped food and supplies about a week earlier. Their dropping of this was so accurate that our camp was completely devastated and burned, and we had to evacuate! Fortunately our only casualties were a couple of broken legs, and a Korean killed. I was lucky enough to be one of the British officers moved to Korea in April this year. Our treatment was better – we had *glass* windows – and we missed the bombing of Japan – or most of it.

From Korea the Yanks took us to Manila. They were more than kind, but it is good to be on a British ship again, and to learn that England *did* do something in this war, for, reading the US papers and listening to them talk, one wouldn't think we'd done much! We didn't like the production of the American Penguins as well as the English editions. Those picture covers are a mistake – we thought, but I suppose they are competing with the Pocket Book editions. Incidentally, Penguins were plentiful in Java and Japan. There's no doubt the potential market for English books in the Far East is colossal. Every race out here tries to learn English. Very many Japs can read English and boast of it – but only a few can speak it with any fluency. I fear the Japs will have no money for some years, so nobody (?) will be able to buy much. I found an Australian edition of the *Irish Short Stories* aboard this ship. I hope they've done well, and that Joan Hancock has received some welcome cheques in my absence! I hope Dick and John have got through the war safely. I heard that Edward Young had done well, and that you had got married – I believe the latter event happened before we went into the bag. We are now en route for Vancouver, so God knows when we shall eventually reach England.

I hope to see you one day before very long.

Alan Steele to Allen Lane, 30 September 1945

Steele, of course, was not to know that John Lane had been killed in action two years previously.

Allen Lane had underlined part of this letter. It was not the comments about Far Eastern markets; it was rather the sentence about the garish illustrated covers which had proved to be necessary for the American market, a theme which was to recur throughout his Penguin years.

By the mid-1950s, war fiction was the vogue. It was a boat that Penguin missed, or rather, it is said, that Allen Lane deliberately avoided. A few titles were secured: *The Cruel Sea*, *The Great Escape*, and Edward Young's submarine adventures. All the same, in January 1956 A. J. Evans was having no luck trying to persuade Penguin to reprint his earlier classic of wartime escape:

We are very conscious that *The Escaping Club* has good claims to being reprinted. The bother is that we now have so many successful books for which reprints are urgently demanded that we cannot possibly do more than a small proportion of them, and the choice, especially when the claims of new books also have to be taken into consideration, is an extremely difficult matter. Moreover printers are so over-worked and we have so many things in hand at a given time that getting a reprint through is by no means a quick business and I don't think there would be any hope of getting *The Escaping Club* into this year's programme at the best. The present 'go-slow' among printers will make the position a good deal worse. When Sir Allen is back, however, I will see that we consider the matter again.

A. S. B. Glover to A. J. Evans, 20 January 1956

* * *

A. S. B. Glover

Many thanks for the proof of The Miracle Boy, *which I herewith return. I am deeply grateful to Mr Glover for suggestions he has made, each of which I have incorporated. I feel he must have read the book with a certain devotion.*

Louis Golding, 5 May 1944

There is a Penguin legend that a certain Penguin reader pointed out in long letters the many errors of fact and misprints that occurred. Time passed, and the lists grew so long that ultimately there was only one solution. He was invited to join Penguin, and was immediately assigned work of this nature. In a letter to Allen Lane in May 1944 the author Norman Douglas notes, '*Fountains* and *Old Calabria* are full of misprints; these would have to be corrected.' In a pencilled note alongside, Lane has simply written 'Glover'.

The first recorded instance of his involvement is in July 1942, two years before he joined Penguin, when Raymond Bush, who wrote a number of Handbooks on fruit-growing, was informed that 'one of our readers' was going through the manuscript for literals.

To hear is to obey, though I haven't a notion what a 'literal' is. I have sent the MS along to Mr Glover and hope he won't find too many, if they are bad, or too few if they are good things to have in a book.

Raymond Bush to Jean Osborne, 22 July 1942

. . . The other had a face scarred by excised tattoo-marks. He wore a suit of massive tweed, a red shirt, a shocking-pink tie and on one hand a grey suede glove. He carried a large gladstone-bag and, before ever the meeting had started, he tipped its contents carelessly on to the polished table. This was Alan Glover, the unacknowledged genius of Penguins and the best informed man I have ever met, as knowledgeable about Russian literature, psychoanalysis and the more obscure religions – to most of which he had been converted at some time in his life – as he was about cricket scores or bus time-tables, and the only man I have ever known who could correct galley-proofs whilst strap-hanging in a rush-hour tube-train.

J. E. Morpurgo, *Master of None*, 1990

When he joined Penguin in 1944 Alan Samuel Boots Glover was nearly fifty years old, with a long and varied career behind him that included several published scholarly works, a stint at *Readers' Digest* and a life devoted to the accumulation of both practical and esoteric information. It was this encyclopaedic knowledge, coupled with an eye for detail, consistency and accuracy that characterized his editorial career at Penguin.

On page 168 of the Collins edition you say of your hero at the beginning of the second paragraph, 'He reached Wembley Park to find a steam train about to start for town', but this is surely impossible. Under the act passed at the end of last century which provided for the extension of the Manchester, Sheffield and Lincolnshire Railway to London along the lines of the Metropolitan, it was expressly provided that no Great Central trains should stop between Harrow and London and therefore they never stopped at Wembley Park. The direct journey from Wembley Park to Marylebone has in fact never been practicable, and no steam trains have used Wembley Park station for stopping purposes since the Metropolitan Line was electrified. This is a point of very minor importance, but I thought you might like to know how careful an eye your publishers keep on the transit facilities of the United Kingdom.

A. S. B. Glover to Freeman Wills Croft, 12 November 1952

With regard to the proofs of this book, you will note that there are a number of references to a convent 'Mars Elias'. Should this not be 'Mar Elias'? 'Mar' is the Syriac honorific appellative equivalent to 'Saint' in English, and we take it that this is what is meant here.

A. S. B. Glover to Joan Haslip, author of *Lady Hester Stanhope*, 22 January 1945

Forgive me if I have found a mare's nest, but in preparing for press the Penguin edition of your Edmund Campion (I quote from the second edition, 1947) you say on page 78 near the bottom, 'A Salesian Father' did so and so. This refers to 1580, but at this date St Francis Sales was only thirteen years old and the order known by his name, the Salesians founded by Don Bosco, did not come into existence until the nineteenth century. Has something gone wrong here, or have I fallen into some stupid misunderstanding?

A. S. B. Glover to Evelyn Waugh, 3 February 1953

Thank you for your letter of yesterday. I consulted the MS to see what I wrote nearly twenty years ago. It was, of course, 'Silesian'. It doesn't surprise me that I let the slip pass – I am the worst proof reader in the world but it is extraordinary that the book can have been read aloud in refectories, commended to students and so on for years and no one should have spotted it. I am most grateful to you . . .

Evelyn Waugh to A. S. B. Glover, 4 February 1953

One small point has struck me going through your proofs of Donne. On page 50 you give a footnote explaining the title of the poem, but it struck me on reading it that this may slightly confuse the reader who happens to know that St Lucy's Day is not December 22nd but December 13th. The point, of course, being that in Donne's calendar before the Gregorian revision had been adopted in this country, December 13th and not December 22nd was the shortest day and I wondered whether you might think it worth while to indicate this in your note. On the other hand you might quite well feel that the reader ought to have the common-sense to work this out for himself.

A. S. B. Glover to John Hayward, 20 April 1950

He was not quite infallible.

A reprint of the Penguin edition of your *Public Faces* is going through the press, and our reader has noticed that in one place something appears to have gone slightly wrong with the text, and on checking back with the first edition, we find that it also appears there.

The passage in question is in the middle of page 209 of the original 1932 edition, of which you probably have a copy. Here you say 'the familiar smell of the boat-house creaked open as he swung the door'. It looks as if at some points in this sentence some words have been omitted. If you will let me know if you would like any corrections made, I will see that it is done.

A. S. B. Glover to Harold Nicolson, 18 October 1945

Many thanks for your letter of yesterday. I am afraid the phrase which you question was deliberately written in the form it stands. I was rather pleased with it myself, feeling it was an interesting experiment in post-impressionism. I should hate to see it altered in any edition.

Harold Nicolson to A. S. B. Glover, 19 October 1945

Thanks for your note of October 19th. The phrase shall, of course, not be altered.

You have made me feel thoroughly miserable, and my tail is

noticeably between my legs. To say that I am not usually so dull would look too much like making excuses.

A. S. B. Glover to Harold Nicolson, 22 October 1945

Whatever else Penguin provided for Glover – as with many others there was no such thing as a hard and fast job-title or clear definition of duties – it provided the opportunity to cultivate friendships with like minds – such as William King, at the British Museum, the friend and literary executor of Norman Douglas, author of an early, and long popular Penguin, *South Wind*, about to be reprinted in 1953.

Thank you for the first part of *South Wind*. We can manage the new paragraph on page 83 all right, but I am afraid the omission on page 133 is a practical impossibility. If we cut it out it will leave a line and a bit at the top which will look simply horrible and there is no way in the preceding pages of adding a line by re-arranging the type since all the paragraphs break off short. I hope that Mr Douglas looking down from Olympus or up from, I won't say where, but whichever it may be, will forgive us for not making this deletion. I have tried hard to think of some reason for myself, but all I know about Beelzebub is that he was the God of Flies and this doesn't really seem to throw much light on the matter. The other omission on page 150 we can manage.

A. S. B. Glover to William King, 16 June 1953

Thank you so much for your letter. I quite understand about the difficulty of the omission on p. 133. And I am sure that N. D. would have understood too. I certainly shall not mention it to Secker or the Authors' Society. Here is the final instalment. By the way a third omission of N. D.'s was at the very end, from the last line of p. 314 'Too surprised . . . fairy-tale' on p. 315. But that I should hate you to leave out. N. D. knew that I loved that passage, and I know when I see him again he will forgive me. Perhaps I ought to say 'if I see him again'. In any case I am quite certain that if we do meet we shall be down below, looking up at you.

William King to A. S. B. Glover, 17 June 1953

Thank you for the final proofs of *South Wind*. I hope that our new edition will when it comes out be relatively free of blemishes. I take it in rather bad part your suggestion that I am to be committed to the celestial regions and separated without deserving it not only from all my existing friends, but from the opportunity of making nice new ones including N. D. and Mr King. But probably God will maintain his reputation for pawky humour by sending you both to Heaven too. I believe harping is quite interesting after the first few thousand years.

A. S. B. Glover to William King, 18 June 1953

Thank you so much for the copy of *South Wind*. I opened it at p. 148 and saw to my horror a ghastly misprint, 'frabric' for 'fabric'. I apologize most humbly. The blurbs seem all right, except that Norman Douglas's only post abroad was St Petersburg. I am pretty sure of this, but will confirm, if you want to make an alteration later.

William King to A. S. B. Glover, 12 September 1953

Life is like that. We have to have one misprint in order to avert nemesis and prevent hubris. We shall make a note to see that this one is removed in the next edition. No doubt some other one will creep in to take its place.

A. S. B. Glover to William King, 14 September 1953

Four English Tragedies

The editor of this book is making herself unpleasant about proofs. While not taking her too seriously, can you see if possible that she gets them before Christmas so that publication is not delayed more than a year from the fixed date?

A. S. B. Glover to John Overton, internal memorandum, 2 January 1953

I wonder if the editor of *Four English Tragedies* is aware that the book will not be published before August 1953, and that therefore she could not possibly expect the proofs to arrive much before the end of June. However, to give her a little breathing space and not to hurry her overmuch we have specially arranged that we shall have at least two days for the reading of the proofs some time towards the end of March or during April.

John Overton to A. S. B. Glover, internal memorandum, 7 January 1953

On behalf of the editor of *Four English Tragedies* thank you for your memorandum of January 7th. It would be a generous gesture if the two days at the end of March or during April to which you refer could be April 4th and 5th as this would enable me to have a clear Easter week-end with your secretary at Brighton while the editor in question was confined to her desk.

A. B. S. Glover to John Overton, internal memorandum, 9 January 1953

Janet Morrell, the editor in question, was better known to all at Penguin as Mrs Alan Glover.

J. M. Cohen, a man of many talents, amply illustrated by his at least fifteen appearances in Penguin, as author of *A History of Western Literature*, translator of Cervantes, Rabelais, Rousseau and more, and editor of several verse anthologies as well as the *Penguin Dictionary of Quotations* with his son Mark, found himself in regular correspondence with Glover. It soon became obvious that they shared, amongst much else, a taste in humour and a similar outlook on life and by the time Cohen was appointed as an advisory editor, their correspondence had developed into something not far short of a double act.

In January 1951, Cohen's anthology *Comic and Curious Verse* was well under way, his Cervantes translation had been published, and he was on the verge of a new work: 'About the Classic: I have translated a few pages of the Rousseau and intend to do another extract from another part of the book. This I have discussed with Rieu. I certainly want to do *The Confessions*. I almost come to like the old scamp. I shall forgive him everything in the end.'

It is not entirely clear if 'the old scamp' is a reference to Rousseau, or the venerable Dr E. V. Rieu, translator of *The Odyssey* and *The Iliad*, and editor of the Penguin Classics, then aged sixty-four.

Glover replies: 'I am glad Rousseau is interesting you and I hope something will come of it. I don't remember whether the idea was mine or not, but as I once translated some parts of *The Confessions* myself, I hail you as a brother.'

Cohen's next letter concludes: 'I await the contract. Rousseau, Rieu tells me, is now at Harmondsworth for your final decision. Look after the morals of your secretaries, he's a dangerous fellow to have loose in a Middlesex village.'

I am hurrying up the contract as much as possible. Our Contracts Department is at the moment struggling with auditing, but I don't think you will have to wait long.

I haven't had Rousseau yet, but no doubt it is on the way to me.

Thank you very much for the warning about Dr Rieu. I had often had my suspicions, but am sorry to have them confirmed. I have warned all my secretaries to be very careful when he is about, but if they take measures not to excite him I have no doubt that prudence will combine with cunning to moderate his approaches. If we get three years for slander we'd better do half each!

A. S. B. Glover to J. M. Cohen, 1 March 1951

With very great regret I say that although I have no personal objection to your biographical note, I hope you won't mind if we extract the bare facts and use those. There is a feeling that the attempt to introduce an element of humour or facetiousness into these rather otiose biographical notes is to be deplored, for Penguin readers are very serious-minded and learned young men and women in quest of truth and the elusive light of pure intellectual satisfaction. You must remember that the new generation is not like our own. It doesn't drink, it doesn't smoke and it is existentialist. God be praised it will all be destroyed by an atomic bomb in a very short time.

A. S. B. Glover to J. M. Cohen, 26 July 1951

I'm sorry that the average Penguin reader is such an earnest fellow. Clearly he will not appreciate the 'Selected Letters of A. S. B. Glover', which, with your permission, I was thinking of preparing for publication.

If we are going to be seriously biographical, I was a scholar of St Paul's School, and Exhibitioner of Queens' College, Cambridge, though who would care to know that I can't guess. My greatest single achievement, of which I am still proud, was to teach myself to read Russian in the train between Maidenhead and Paddington. As you may guess, I travelled the route on more than one occasion.

J. M. Cohen to A. S. B. Glover, 27 July 1951

Thanks for the royalty schedule. I don't propose to pay these fees now but to wait until the book goes into production as is the usual course. I don't think we can do much about the doubtfuls and we can only wait until they sue us though by then we shall probably all be in quad for publishing your Rabelais, an event which I understand is more probable than ever with our new Home Secretary. As a matter of fact I think he will be a bit down on Penguin Books because I once rejected a manuscript of his for the School Magazine and he has probably retained a grudge. Still we hope for the best.

Your St Teresa should be reaching you within the next few weeks if our contracts staff, which seems to do nothing but prepare contracts for you, has time to do it.

A. S. B. Glover to J. M. Cohen, 19 October 1954

The new Home Secretary was Gwilym Lloyd-George, the son of David, and a Conservative who had started in the same year as Glover at the City of London School – a fortunate choice for Glover, an LCC scholarship boy who had previously run away from Christ's Hospital. It was an extraordinarily advanced school for its time: the first in the world to install practical science laboratories, it had Sanskrit on the curriculum and was an early advocate of the teaching of English Language.

Much of Alan Glover's life remains a mystery. He was born Allan McDougall in 1895. In 1916 he translated the collection of Old Breviary hymns *Pange Lingua* and was married, shortly before, one assumes, he was conscripted. At the time he may well have been a Quaker; he was certainly a pacifist, and took this stance rigidly. He became one of the 985 'absolutists', who chose prison rather than any form of occupation which might contribute in any way to the war effort.

Typically, details of his eventful life emerge almost accidentally in the course of his ceaseless correspondence. In 1954 he wrote reminding an author that his manuscript for Pelican on *Crime and Criminals* was overdue. The book, incidentally, was never completed.

I hope you have been able to time one of your prison visits while a riot was on so that you had a front stalls view. Unfortunately when I was doing time we lived a very quiet life indeed and there was hardly any excitement.

A. S. B. Glover to T. C. N. Gibbens, 28 June 1954

Did you say it was Wormwood Scrubs which you knew so intimately? If one could choose, the best place would be a snug little local prison such as Durham, with its magnificent view of the Cathedral, or perhaps Bedford or Canterbury.

T. C. N. Gibbens to A. S. B. Glover, 2 October 1954

Speaking somewhat as an authority on the subject though not a very recent one, I wouldn't agree with you about snug little prisons.

Exeter, in which I spent some little time is a dull place; the library was rotten and the bread was bad. All things considered my own choice was Winchester though I took a lot of dislike to it in my last days there when they took to forcibly feeding me. The trouble about Wormwood Scrubs is that it is too large to be really friendly; and whatever you do keep out of Pentonville.

A. S. B. Glover to T. C. N. Gibbens, 6 October 1954

His time in various penal establishments provided him with the opportunity to continue his own education. Possessing a near photographic memory, he is said to have read the entire *Encyclopaedia Britannica* during this period. Equally important was the influential and distinguished company he found himself in, not the least of whom was Francis Meynell, publisher of the Nonesuch Press for whom Glover would later compile several works – including revisions of Rousseau's *Confessions*, *Madame Bovary*, *Candide* and *Old Goriot* – and, in 1951, the Nonesuch *Shelley* which he edited.

His job developed in the Penguin way: from reading proofs he soon became a vital part of the Penguin editorial team – sharing responsibilities and duties with Eunice Frost across the Penguin list.

His lifelong study of comparative religion had for a period in his life been undertaken on a practical basis, as a Franciscan tertiary and an initiate in a number of obscure oriental sects, one of which may well have demanded the legendary tattoos. By the time he came to Penguin he was a confirmed Buddhist, who maintained a fascination for the Catholic faith in particular, and took whatever opportunities arose to continue odd quests.

The total stock of the book that we have left of the 40,000 we had printed is now only 1,500 and these will be absorbed probably within a month. We shall reprint as soon as we can . . . Frankly, I don't think we have done at all badly with a book which several of my colleagues anticipated would be a complete failure and only let it get past as a sop to my personal crankiness.

A. S. B. Glover to Christmas Humphreys, author of *Buddhism*, Pelican, 23 July 1951

There's often a touch of sly humour in the patrons the Roman congregation appoints for particular professions – as with Bernardine of Siena for advertising men, presumably because he used to go about with a kind of sign saying IHS; or Clare for television because she's alleged to have telepathed a message to Benedict. But Sebastian for street cleaners has me beat. Is it because they poke down drains with arrow-shaped sticks to clean them?

A. S. B. Glover to Dieter Pevsner, reporting on the MS for the *Dictionary of Saints*, 19 February 1964

If he had looked it up, the word 'worship', or its Latin equivalents, have always been used to cover any kind of honour paid by believers, not only to God, but to other religious persons or objectives. The technical distinction is that there are three kinds of worship. (1) Latria, which can only be offered to God Himself (I say 'Himself' without expressing any opinion as to whether there are actually one or three of Him); (2) Hyperdulia, which is a particular and superior kind of (3) which may be paid only to the Blessed Virgin Mary; (3) Dulia, which is the kind of adoration or honour paid to any person remarkable for singular holiness. The third kind is as much a variety of worship as the first. I strongly suspect that the variety of Catholic faith which your correspondent represents, is that peculiar combination of superstition and bad history known as the Anglican heresy.

PS You can even worship a Mayor. The distinction here, I think is that you pay latria to the Mayor, hyperdulia to the Mayoress, and dulia to the Chairman of the Urban District Council.

A. S. B. Glover to Nikolaus Pevsner on a theological point raised in a Buildings of England proof, 19 October 1950

His other principal interest was the study of psychology – in which, once more, his interest had been practical as well as theoretical. From an early involvement in English Freudianism, he was to become a formidable Jung scholar – and tireless worker. Norman Franklin of Routledge recalls: 'he worked by day for Penguin, in the evenings for us and throughout the night for Bollingen.'* For many years, continuing after his retirement, he was involved in the monumental task of checking the scholarship, making translations and compiling the general index to the Bollingen/Routledge *Collected Jung*.

Under the editorship of Professor Mace of Birkbeck College, a substantial Pelican sub-series on Psychology was introduced – which Glover naturally oversaw, in common with a vast number of general and detailed scientific topics, not always entirely seriously.

In Maynard Smith's manuscript, when talking about genetics, he uses

* The Bollingen Foundation.

the forms 'D/d', 'd/d', and so on to denote homozygotes and heterozygotes. Don't we usually refer to red-haired white rabbits with dumpy wings, a short stalk and puce eyes, or whatever it is, as just Dd, or dd, like that?

A. S. B. Glover to Michael Abercrombie, Department of Anatomy, University College, London, 13 September 1957

Glover was not treated well at Penguin. Those who knew him well, the people who worked most closely with him, and whom he trained and in whom he instilled his exacting standards, admired and respected him unreservedly. At other levels he was very much taken for granted. He bore this stoically for many years, but in 1958, on an occasion when whatever authority he had been led to believe he possessed was totally undermined, he tendered his resignation in a long letter which revealed the humiliation he felt.

We've always all of us given lip service to the idea that our future is considerably bound up in the serious side of our list, in spite of the fact that it is less spectacular, sells more slowly, and is from the editorial and production points of view considerably more costly. Perhaps it's also partly due to the fact that the Classics, for example, and parts of the Pelican list that are organized in sub-series, aren't heard of much at editorial meetings, but go on their quiet way in the background. It is by no means so quiet really, of course: I mean that, when once we've organized, say, a medical series, and found an outside editor, the books in due course come along and take their place in the list without any particular intervention by the editorial board as such; but they keep me and my boys and girls busy enough. What I want to get across is the point that when we've agreed to have a series of Pelicans on, say, medicine, and have found our outside editor, it doesn't mean that we have now finished with that one and can get on with something else in its place: we've started a job, not finished one, and thereafter it goes on all the time while the series lasts.

Dieter Pevsner, the son of Nikolaus Pevsner, who in 1958 started working with Glover on the Pelican series, remains convinced that the meticulous care that went into each and every Pelican, ensuring its factual accuracy, stylistic consistency and authentic scholarship, was directly responsible for the universal conviction that simply because a book was a Pelican, it was the authoritative statement on its subject. The series that was founded on the erudition of Lance Beales, the commitment of Krishna Menon and the energy of Bill Williams was always regarded as timely, radical and reputable. Under the inspiration of Glover, it came to be regarded as definitive.

After his retirement in 1960 his involvement with Penguin continued – notably with his contributions to *The Penguin Encyclopaedia* on religion and mythology.

I have looked at Glover's list for Religion. It is a relief to have one in which the contributor has been at pains to eliminate the hackneyed or superfluous and I find it a very good list.

Sir John Summerscale to Dieter Pevsner, 15 May 1961

First of all I should explain that my interest in it is no longer an official one, for I retired from Penguins last year, and now content myself, so far as my old firm is concerned, with incarnating the Jungian archetypal figure of the Wise Old Man, any deficiency in wisdom being supplied by an excess of oldness. But this doesn't in the least lessen my interest in your book, and I shall be only too happy if at any time I can be of any help in regard to it.

A. S. B. Glover to Dr F. C. Happold, author of *Mysticism*, Pelican, 3 March 1961

The Times, 8 January 1966

Sir Allen Lane writes:

Mr A. S. B. Glover, who died on January 5 at the age of 70, had a long and distinguished career as an editor. My own acquaintance with him goes back to 1944 when I invited him to join Penguin Books so that he could apply his exceptional gifts as a scholarly reader to manuscripts rather than published books on which, as a member of our public, he used to send in detailed lists of factual errors and misprints, usually saying these had not spoiled his enjoyment of the books as such.

Soon the scope for his work widened, and as resident editor of Pelicans and the Penguin Classics he made a remarkable contribution to our post-war development when paper-rationing was abolished and the range of our publishing activities began to grow. One of his outstanding qualities was a retentive and encyclopaedic memory: authors and translators were forever being amazed by his detailed knowledge of their particular field of study. Since his retirement from my firm in 1960 he remained as active as ever, particularly as editorial adviser to the Bollinger Foundation.

The last line contained what might just have been a Freudian slip on the part of Sir Allen Lane. If so, Glover would have enjoyed it: he would never have allowed it into print.

At his funeral, J. M. Cohen read from Juan Mascaró's translation of the *Bhagavad Gita* for the Penguin Classics: 'The Spirit that is in all beings is immortal in them all: for the death of what cannot die, cease thou to sorrow.'

* * *

Noel Carrington

When, please, is Misha Learns English *actually coming out? This does seem a wonderfully opportune moment for it, doesn't it? And I hope with all my heart that besides amusing the children it may help to cement good relations between the Russkies and the Angliskies.*

Extract from letter to Allen Lane from Pearl Binder, 23 June 1942

In the thirties my own young family was growing up, its members demanding to know the how, why and wherefore of what they observed; not only about animals and insects but equally of how locomotives pulled trains, how motor cars and tractors worked and how aeroplanes flew overhead. There were of course books and children's encyclopaedias which would provide all the answers, but increasingly I felt the need for simply written and well illustrated books in which children could find for themselves what they wanted to know; to have them in their nursery at bedtime; and the books so cheap that they could easily be replaced. I was confident that there must be many thousands of other parents who would not grudge their children the expenditure of a few pennies.

For fifteen years I had myself been engaged in the business of book publishing. At that time I was employed by the *Country Life* group to edit and produce their books, which, naturally enough, reflected the chief interest of those who read the magazines, that is to say the architecture and furnishing of country houses, field sports, gardening and also natural history. However I was also editing some stories for children. It was a short step therefore to set myself to planning a series which, if printed in large editions, could be priced at a few pennies each.

In the thirties, when the series was still in the stage of dreams, I was greatly encouraged by the example of just such a series for the education of children. It had been produced in Russia and it had been brought to my notice by the artist Pearl Binder, a devoted admirer of the Soviets. The books were lithographed in bright colours and were very cheap. I had also examined the Père Castor books, lithographed in France.

Noel Carrington, reminiscence

By 1938 Noel Carrington had assembled a stable of artists eager to experiment in auto-lithography, and had found in Geoffrey Smith of Cowells a printer sympathetic to the idea. When *Country Life* turned his scheme down, he naturally turned to the publisher who was preaching the philosophy of popular education through books.

Meeting Allen Lane to discuss a book on design, he set out his scheme. 'He thought it over for perhaps a minute. "I already have children's books in mind," he said, "and if you can show me that you can produce such books in colour and which can be sold at sixpence, it's on." Too good to be true, was my thought.'

It was – Lane immediately disappeared with his sister Nora on their lengthy tour of India and the Middle East, and by the time he returned war was threatening. Carrington assumed the new series would be shelved indefinitely, but, on the contrary, to Lane's mind the new circumstances gave it added impetus.

To my amazement he phoned me to arrange a meeting. 'The worst has happened,' he owned, 'but evacuated children are going to need books more than ever, especially your kind on farming and natural history. Let us plan to get out half a dozen as soon as we can.' It was agreed rather reluctantly that some of the first batch must be geared to the all-pervading war efforts, so that one of the early titles was *The Battle of Britain*, written by David Garnett and illustrated by James Gardner, perhaps the most versatile of my artists.

As evidence of this versatility, Gardner recalled:

During the war, when I was in camouflage at Farnham Castle, I was informed that a civilian wished to see me. It was Allen Lane. So I gave him lunch in the mess. After lunch he told me he wished, after the war was over, to buy a farm in the country and be a gentleman farmer part-time, but knew nothing about farming, so could I join him. This was a real joke as though I wrote the book *On the Farm*, it was based on a local farm in Hertfordshire, near my home, which I visited and on which I based the illustrations and story – written in the first person. I remember ending the story with a suggestion that the reader visit me one day at my farm. In fact I knew no more about farming than he did.

This was soon to change. Farming, as he delighted in pointing out, was in Lane's blood; and Carrington's too for that matter. And it was not long before the boot, as it were, was on the other foot.

I think your new layout for *On the Farm* will do very well indeed. There are one or two points I'd like to make:

The picture of the farmer on page 3 has been criticized a good deal as being a bit of a caricature and not quite the modern farmer. Maybe you'd consider redrawing it while you are about it.

Then on page 29 you don't mention which breeds of cattle you propose to put in. Remember that Allen Lane has Ayrshires on his farm, and you might also remember that I have Guernseys on mine. I'm wondering if you couldn't give page 29 to six cattle breeds, and just put a caption under each. After that I should say the sooner we can get on with it the better, as the new style of production seems to take a hell of a time anyway.

Noel Carrington to James Gardner, 10 April 1946

Shortly after, he wrote once more to Gardner: Allen Lane wanted a hay-loader put in, and found the milking machine 'rather confused'. Richard Lane also chipped in with a long report detailing a number of criticisms: 'The plough is of an old-fashioned type without tripping gear . . .' Eventually the strain began to tell.

Gardner has at least turned in the corrected copy of *On the Farm*, and we have his revised drawings complete (unless the amateur farmers around the place think up some more improvements, which is all too likely). What I suggest is that you prepare an estimate for a revised edition with the substitutions of the new drawings and complete resetting of the text, so that Penguins can see the greatest possible advantage in using existing plates as far as possible. I hope you catch my meaning.

Noel Carrington to Geoffrey Smith, R. S. Cowell, 26 September 1946

Carrington's job as editor of the series was a delicate balancing act. Except in these special instances, it was Lane's policy to give his editors a completely free hand, but nevertheless, more often than not, Carrington would find himself having to mediate in disputes between Penguin and printer, printer and illustrator, illustrator and author. Cowells were by no means the only printers involved, and many of the artists commissioned had no experience in the specialized techniques required. It fell to Carrington to coax them through to a satisfactory result.

Thank you for your letter about the reproduction. I do not think you have got the idea of the process quite right and I will try to explain it as follows:

You draw in ink or chalk on a grained paper and these are reproduced photographically on the plate. For the black and white plates that is all you need to do. For the colour plates, you get three zinc plates with offsets of your black and white drawings and on each of the plates, you will draw in black lithographic ink or chalk for those portions you want tinted, having to separate in your own mind from your coloured originals what parts you want to go in each colour. These plates you then return to the printer who proofs in colour. I have asked Cowells, the printers, to send you a piece of grained paper so that you can try an experimental colour plate.

Noel Carrington to Jacques Groag, 21 November 1944

In a 1949 booklet, Noel Carrington would add:

We owe much to the artists. Usually they have dedicated far more time and pains to the making of their books than seemed to be justified by the immediate reward. Some of the subjects meant months of preliminary field study or research.

Of the 119 books eventually published in the series, it is freely admitted that a good many were no more than satisfactory – and a few not even that. Many more, particularly the natural history books, proved to be happy combinations of text and illustration, such as those by S. R. Badmin, Richard Chopping, R. B. Talbot Kelly and Bernard Venables. Some, like Phyllis Ladyman's *About a Motor Car*, were translated into more than twenty different languages, and found a ready market all around the world. Badmin's *Trees in Britain* became a set text at agricultural colleges, and for a while a number of the books were issued in board covers in response to demands for their use in schools. One or two books stood out as Carrington's personal favourites.

I had a really stunning scheme for a book: *Wild Flowers* by Paxton Chadwick, the whole job superbly finished in water-colours. When Allen and I looked through it he exclaimed: 'But this is absolutely tops! Who is this chap? Of course we must do it.' I said: 'But he makes conditions. It's to be in colour on every page.' (Puffins were usually black and white on every other opening.) Here I brought out one of Chadwick's lithographic plates which he had done as a sample. It was really a masterpiece. Allen compared it with the water colour and handed it round the table. Somebody said: 'Almost too good for a children's book.' 'Nonsense,' said Allen, 'nothing is too good for Penguins. We will double the print and bring the cost down. Bring this chap along to our next meeting. I want to see him.'

Reminiscence of Noel Carrington, *Penguin Collectors' Society Newsletter*, 1979

Similarly, persuading artists of the calibre of Edward Bawden and C. F. Tunnicliffe to contribute to the series helped enhance its reputation.

Thank you for your letter. I am so sorry that up to now I have not been able to get at the little book *Birds of the Estuary*. I have been so desperately hard-worked these last twelve months, and have been so messed about by my publishers and authors, that I am sadly behind with the fulfilment of my promises.

However, before I really get down to Estuary Birds I should be glad if you would give me some information. On looking at some of the Picture Puffin Books I see that the colours are harsh and, in some cases, crude. Have you made any advance since, say, *Butterflies in Britain*? I hope you won't mind my asking this, but I am tired of seeing bad reproductions of my work, and being blamed by the experts for wrong colours. Looking at the Picture Books on Butterflies, Trees, Insects and Village and Town, there appears in each case some limitation to the number of colours one can use. Is this so? Judging from these books there seems little chance of expressing the difference between the grey of the back of a Common Gull and that on the back of a Black-Headed Gull.

Are you able to reproduce pencil drawings or must those be a hard ink outline?

Is the format to be the same as in previous picture books – one double spread of colour alternating with a double spread of black and white?

C. F. Tunnicliffe to Noel Carrington, 2 November 1948

Many thanks for your letter. I think I can answer your questions satisfactorily.

The early Puffin Picture Books were nearly all printed from plates drawn directly by the artist, partly from economy, as the original books were sold at 6d., and partly because of the difficulties during the war of getting photographic reproductions done. We are now reproducing most artists' work by photolithography, which would give you a complete range of colours, and also enable you to use pencil as much as you like on the black and white pages.

Regarding the quality of the reproduction, we would put it with the best printers we can find for the job. I am enclosing a copy of *Fish and Fishing*, where the colour plates were done by photolitho, I think in about six printings. The format would be the same as in similar books – that is to say, colour alternating with black and white. We have occasionally gone to all colour, but its costs make production a good deal more expensive.

What I should like to do is to try and fix a time when you could complete the book so that it could be fixed in our production schedule.

Noel Carrington to C. F. Tunnicliffe, 6 November 1948

Many thanks for your letter and for the *Fish and Fishing* book, a very nice book, and one that gives me confidence to begin *Birds of the Estuary* as soon as I am able. Would it be satisfactory to you if I promised to have all the material in your hands some time during 1949? I cannot give you a more precise date as my programme is rather full, but I think I can complete the book with reasonable certainty during the next year. I have no doubt that some author or publisher will wreck my plan of campaign for 1949 as they did for 1948 so your book may be done sooner rather than later.

C. F. Tunnicliffe to Noel Carrington, 7 November 1948

The early 1960s, with the retirement of Noel Carrington and a virtually complete change of editorial personnel at Harmondsworth, heralded the gradual decline of the series. One of the last books he supervised personally was *The Human Body*, 'perhaps the most difficult subject to offer either parents or squeamish booksellers'. It was nevertheless a bestseller, and survived into the 1980s.

Along the way several variations had been tried – Baby Puffins, exquisite books for infants based on the same principle, but half the size of the Puffin Picture Books: an ingenious means of making the paper ration go further; and a number of Cut Out Books, including two sets of three large format books, *A Half-Timbered Village* and *A Cotswold Village*, with text by L. A. Dovey, and notes and beautiful drawings by Margaret and Alexander Potter, who had contributed two further volumes to the series. The Cut Out Books were ultimately defeated by bureaucracy: classified as toys by the Board of Trade, rather than designed for educational purposes, they were subject to Purchase Tax and did not sell well at a higher price.

Arthur Mould, a long serving member of the sales team, summarized the series' decline:

I believe you know my views about PP's in general – after some sixteen years of trying to get them well shown (and therefore automatically well sold – in the West Country). It is hard work – and it gets harder still as the price goes up. Usually the PP stock ends up in an obscure, soon to be dog-eared pile on some remote shelf in the Juvenile section. But they sell like hot cakes in the few shops where they are appreciated, understood and properly displayed. Most Penguins, and even Puffin Storybooks will, at a push, sell briskly with only the spines showing – but the PP has no spine to show.

* * *

Eleanor Graham

... We were right only in one point: as soon as the two parties saw each other they began to fight. Many were killed on both sides, but the whites won. Next morning we saw that some of the browns were hanged on trees. The rest, blacks and browns alike, carried the loads and the whites goaded them with whips, and everywhere in this country there were whole camps of the blacks burned by the whites and whole piles of white corpses ...

Cranes Flying South, N. Karazin, 1936; Puffin edition, 1948

I have for some years past been in the habit of snapping up every Puffin Story book I could find, having been impressed with the quality of the first of them and having found that my children like them.

My confidence was badly shaken today when by chance I picked up *Cranes Flying South.*

My first disappointment was on finding that the cranes are endowed with the psychology of human beings. More serious, they seem also like good Russian cranes to have absorbed the ideology of *Pravda.* Is it reasonable to represent human life in Africa in terms such as are used on pp. 122–3 and again pp. 139 and ffg. What historical reality is indicated? Is it the Italo-Abyssinian War? Or the era of slave trading by the European nations? Or is it just meant to be typical of European imperialism?

I am sorry to find that in future I cannot take for granted that a Puffin Story book will be a good book and I write to let you know of the disappointment of one of your customers who has in the past recommended the series to other parents.

John M. Graham to Eleanor Graham, 14 January 1949

Thank you for your letter about *Cranes Flying South*, and for making the criticism of it to me. I think I understand your feeling.

I, myself, brooded for some time on the African passage and took it to refer to the horror of the Abyssinian War. I first read the book in 1936. Re-reading it much later for Puffins, I weighed it up as a whole, feeling its value lay chiefly in the most stimulating account of bird migration, of which very little has been written for children though it is a subject that fascinates most people and starts many a pregnant question.

I should have preferred a treatment which did not involve the personification of the birds, but I felt (and still feel) that even so, there is so much of value to children that it was worth bringing to them. Also, while respecting your objections, I feel it is perhaps good to recognize the dreadful pages which have spoilt the records of white men's treatment of other nations. To my mind, the point was not laboured here, and I believed that the young reader would most probably be too absorbed in the strange history of the birds to take the passages in question as more than features in a strange landscape.

I should be sorry to think they could be harmed by them, or absorb even the rudiments of any foreign ideology; but my opinion for what it was worth was (and is) that they won't.

All the books in the series I edit have been well known to me over a period of years, many of them since before their first publication and it has always been my habit to keep reasonable track of any I was interested in from the Public Libraries, schools and some homes, in order that I should check my own reactions. None of us is infallible, but you can be sure that I am very earnest in my desire that only books which come up to certain high standards of writing and integrity and which are, in my judgment, Good Books for Children, should be in the series.

The use of propaganda, I abhor, in any literature for the young, and neither I nor the Penguin organization would allow it for a moment, of that you can, at least, rest assured.

I hope you will go on reading Puffin Story books and that you will find many to please you.

Eleanor Graham to John M. Graham, undated (January 1949)

In all her letters Eleanor Graham was quite unable to conceal her passion for the job she was doing and the books she was publishing. This absolute certainty about the direction in which she was heading, and the qualities and value of the books in her series could easily give rise to a feeling that she was unbending and dogmatic – with the implied suspicion that a book must germinate and grow in her opinion for so long that it would be out of date by the time it finally found its way on to the list. This impression would be contested with equal passion by the new authors she helped – including a number whose first works were published as original Puffins – and equally the people who worked with her at Penguin.

Being still young in publishing experience, I found Eleanor at first somewhat intimidating – sometimes almost dogmatic in her opinions, unyielding in her judgments. No doubt I showed this in my reactions, but she was very shrewd in the way she dealt with my often ill-considered enthusiasms for certain books – being tolerant and sympathetic to my views, but sticking firmly to her verdict, and leaving it for me to find out for myself how her sound judgment of books was based on a lifetime of reading, assessing and reviewing.

Margaret Clark, *Signal*, 1972

This dogmatic attitude also is used as evidence by a number of critics who found the early Puffin list too predictable, stodgy – conservative. This is hard to reconcile with her initial fervour and inspiration for the publishing of children's books:

It is worth mentioning perhaps that some wonderfully good work was being done then – after the Revolution – in Russia, for they had to raise a *literate* people – *quickly*. Excellent stories were written for them, well illustrated, and they were printed in huge numbers, so that every child in the land could have one – and they were not *sold*. Great piles of them were set at street corners, to be taken freely as children went by . . . Two Russian books from that period which I liked specially were *Mourzouk*, the story of a lynx, by Vitali Bianchi, and *Cranes Flying South* by N. Karazin. Later, I put them both in Puffins.

Eleanor Graham, 'The Bumpus Years', *Signal*, 1972

All the same, that ardour was tempered by a certain ingrained attitude, which could never really be overcome. It was not concerned with the quality of book published by Penguin – 'nothing but the best is good enough when publishing for children' – but rather with the quality of the audience she was publishing for, specifically when a certain degree of 'intelligent appreciation' was called for.

None of these three volumes (*Enjoying Paintings*, *Going to a Concert*, *Going to the Ballet*) are likely to appeal to the general run of Secondary Modern children – who, I suppose, make up the greater part of the up to 15 age group. There has to be some consciousness: some extra upward yearning before they will bother with them, but this quality certainly lies in the make-up of the rather better educated – say Grammar School and High School level – from even 13 up. Moreover I fancy there is a good adult market for them as well. So many of the parents who never managed to find the right introduction to the arts, long to get hold of some means of pulling themselves up on to the fence from which the sights may be seen. I think they would find what they need in these which have that genuine breath of enthusiasm in them which calls the ignorant on and never makes them feel ashamed of ignorance.

Eleanor Graham to Eunice Frost, 14 January 1952

While giving books away in vast quantities was never seriously considered a possibility, publishing at the cheapest prices and for a mass audience was undoubtedly in her mind throughout the 1920s and 30s, during which time Eleanor Graham accumulated experience in various aspects of publishing: as an author, her first children's book being published in 1925, as a librarian, bookseller, and, most of all, a reviewer of children's books. They became, quite simply, her life.

Once Penguin had started publishing books – albeit closer in conception and inspiration to Stead's Books for the Bairns than the Russian ideal – a familiar story unfolded: a meeting with Allen Lane, already an acquaintance of long standing; discussion of the possibility of adding a children's list to Penguin; a long silence and the assumption that the war had put paid to the notion. Then the sudden phone call, and a rush of urgency and excitement that impelled another new editor towards the creation of another new series.

I had prepared a very long list of books I wanted for Puffins – many of them ones I had known well in my days at Bumpus's. Allen and I had already agreed in general terms the shape Puffins were to take: definitely not a series of out-of-copyright classics. What we wanted was the best of *new* classics of the new generation, so that Puffins could be a worthy partner to the now established Penguins. I realized that Allen might have difficulty in getting rights. I knew also from other publishers that there was very little paper to spare – or printing capacity either, for that matter. It was a curious, courageous, and very tough moment to start.

Eleanor Graham, 'The Puffin Years', *Signal*, 1973

In short, the launch of Puffin Story Books was in many ways comparable to the launch of Penguin itself: bringing quality contemporary juvenile fiction at the lowest prices, after extracting the rights from the reluctant first publishers. In appearance and style the first Puffins followed their adult equivalents with plain, typographical covers and, as the series developed, a mixture of fiction, biography, verse, puzzles and humour, and no shortage of mystery and crime titles to add spice to the list. Before too long, many of the best known children's classics were added, and further old tales brought up to date.

As well as translating *Two Satyr Plays* for the Penguin Classics, Roger Lancelyn Green was to become one of the staple Puffin authors, contributing *Tales of the Greek Heroes*, *The Tale of Troy*, *The Saga of Asgard*, *The Adventures of Robin Hood* and his best known work, *King Arthur and his Knights* – the majority of which remain in print in Puffin today.

I had a letter from Roger Lancelyn Green at the weekend in which he said he had sent Arthur Ransome a copy of *King Arthur* and had quite lyrical praise back of it. I wondered if we might use it, but Roger says he'd rather not. He feels it would show him in a bad light, so we must leave it. I wish some of the reviews would hurry up and recognize what a good thing it is. Perhaps the *TLS* will. They will have two others, I think, to review, and should do all together, so that anyone with discrimination should be able to point out Puffin's excellence effectively.

Eleanor Graham to Eunice Frost, 16 November 1953

What commenced as a purely business relationship, or even a speculative submission of a manuscript, for many became a long-standing friendship. One such arose between Eleanor Graham and Marjorie Lloyd, who wrote and illustrated a series of stories set in the Lake District, of which *Fell Farm Holiday* was the first original manuscript to be published in Puffin.

I simply posted the MS to Penguin Books, Harmondsworth. Shortly afterwards, to my surprise and delight, I had a letter from Eleanor Graham, accepting it for Puffin Story Books. I don't think she asked for any alterations. The contract was signed in May 1947. So soon after the war years paper was still rationed and the book was not published until March 1951.

As far as the writing of books was concerned I think she taught me all I ever knew. She was easy and amusing to talk to, ready with praise for anything she thought well of, but severely critical of anything she thought less than good. In later years, even after her retirement she read many of my MSS before I offered them to publishers. I remember her returning one to me with the terse comment: 'This will not do.' I immediately burnt it.

Marjorie Lloyd, reminiscence

William Grimmond was commissioned, for a tiny fee, to prepare the cover illustration for *Fell Farm Holiday*. Grimmond was a perfectionist. Not content with merely reading the manuscript, he took it with him to the Lake District, and using clues in the text, located the actual farm that had been used as the basis for the story.

There was a similar dedication from the series editor herself, as she explained to Alison Uttley, who had complained about the rearrangement and presentation of her stories in her book *Magic in my Pocket*.

I gave so much thought to the arrangement of stories, and it was put to the test, as the printers were given the Faber list of permissions instead of my setting list, by accident. When I saw what had been done, I was quite shocked. The sense and continuity had gone – and you know there is a sort of rhythm and continuity of feeling somehow in them as they stand. For one thing, think how many a Christmas ends with riddles round the fire? To my mind there is an almost poetic satisfaction in the present ending, and that delights me. Won't you see it a little my way? Do try. It would give me so much pleasure to feel you were happy about it again, and you know you could be, for nothing but loving care has gone into it – none of the critical feeling I am afraid you have imputed to me.

Eleanor Graham to Alison Uttley, 20 May 1957

Undoubtedly the Puffin in which she took the most pride was one of her own contributions, *The Story of Jesus*. It was a book that had a curious history, at which she only hinted in a letter written some ten years after her retirement:

I'm not sure that there was ever a contract. AL had asked me to do it and when I'd finished I sent it direct to him. He read and approved it, though I think against the views of his readers. He had wanted it for his children, but warned me at the start that if he did not like it he would not publish it. I wrote it, sent him the MS. He rang me up in a very short time to say that he'd read it, he liked it and would publish it. However Penguins were generally against it – but it sold out its first edition, though it was not reprinted.

Eleanor Graham to Doreen Scott, 22 March 1971

After her retirement, Eleanor Graham, in a letter to her successor Kaye Webb, expanded on this initial antipathy. One member of the editorial staff in particular, Alan Glover, was particularly antagonistic to the project. A man of encyclopaedic knowledge, he was particularly well versed in comparative religion, and had little doubt that once the manuscript was delivered, he would be forced to reject it. In the event, his report on the book told a very different story.

I have searched out what Glover wrote about it – not for my eyes, be sure: but perhaps he was a 'just beast'. I enclose that and only two of the excellent reviews it received.

Glover wrote: Although I would personally disagree very widely with EG's interpretation of the NT story – I say this only to show that my prejudices would, if anything, be against her – she seems to me to have done a marvellous job very judiciously, and with great feeling for her theme, and with reverent yet lively treatment. However individuals may differ from her reading of the story, nobody could reasonably fail to admire the deep sympathy and appreciation with which she has told it. It is practically impossible to find a hole to pick.

Eleanor Graham to Kaye Webb, 29 March 1969

On the strength of his folio and obvious passion for the subject, the task of illustrating the book was entrusted to a young unknown artist, Brian Wildsmith – a controversial choice, but the start of a long association with Penguin, producing cover designs, point of sale and press advertisements.

You propose to devote the next three months to this work and to give us up to fifty pages of illustration, divided into half pages, full pages, head-pieces or tail-pieces as you wish, or as Miss Graham may suggest . . . You have also agreed to provide us with a cover design, but this we should like done last of all. The work will, as you know, have to be done in close cooperation with the author, and we suggest therefore that you send the drawings to her in batches whenever you have dealt with two or three chapters for her approval.

Margaret Clark to Brian Wildsmith, 10 October 1958

Brian brought me more drawings on Friday, most of them very promising. We spoke together about the drawings I kept back from those you and I went over. The Judas he feels he intended just as it was, not because he thinks Judas was anything like that, but because it expresses the treachery and the meanness. He feels strongly about it, so I agreed to keep it . . . He is getting dreadfully tired, and rapidly reaching the point at which he can't bear to do any more, but he has now covered everything, about fifty-six drawings, and at least one for every chapter. I asked him for something small for the title page, and I forgot about the map, but have dropped him a line. He may feel now that he simply could not do it. I don't know. He is so tired. And he has done so much.

Eleanor Graham to Margaret Clark, 4 January 1959

The book, one of the last Puffins produced before her retirement, was perfectly summed up in a letter to her from Allen Lane, for whom this had always been much more a personal than business matter.

I'm delighted you like the book. I think that on the production side Hans Schmoller has excelled himself. I was a little worried that some of the drawings might become thickened up in the printing but I think now that they have improved in the reproduction. To my mind it is one of those books which have 'come off' in that there has been a perfect fusion of the author and artist and that their work has been blended with just the right feel of paper, print and binding. As you say, it is a lovely book to handle: that indefinable quality which few people outside those whose work has been concerned with the making of books will understand. I'm delighted with it in its every aspect.

Allen Lane to Eleanor Graham, 14 October 1959

After its disappearance during the entire 1960s, the book was eventually reprinted, edited entirely with Eleanor Graham's approval by David Thomson. It has remained in print since then, and still sells today.

* * *

Penguins Arrive in America

At last we've taken the plunge and a brass plate on 41 East 28th Street, New York, announces that Penguin Books Inc. have arrived. For four years we have been planning to commence distributing in America, the only country barring Germany and Italy in which Penguins were not readily accessible, but in spite of almost running a ferry service across the Atlantic by the brothers Lane, countless difficulties, the two main ones being that of finding the right man for the job and squaring copyright complications, delayed the matter until by a happy chance H. L. (Pelican) Beales introduced Ian Ballantine, one of his students at the London School of Economics. From that day the matter was as good as settled, and at the end of June, after allowing himself only twenty-four hours in which to get married and obtain new passports, he and Betty sailed on the Nieuw Amsterdam. The first home of Penguin Books in America is reminiscent of our early days, when the editorial department consisted of three rooms over a motor car showroom, and the stockroom was the crypt of a church, only in this case the entire firm is housed in one room half way up a sky-scraper.

Penguins Progress, 1939

Looking so far ahead may seem wildly optimistic, yet, I think, I have come back from England with a combination that will finally make the quarter book a permanent feature of American publishing . . . As the agency is to justify itself by sales we are starting an office with the barest minimum necessary – a secretary (my English wife), and a stock boy. We all find ourselves having to do a great variety of things at which none of us are experts. There are books to be kept, publicity to be obtained, creditworthiness looked into, small advertising to be written, copyrights to be obtained, Customs Officers to be handled, plus almost anything else you might think of. I have, since I import, all the advantages of low costs without any of the disadvantages of large stocks which must be immediately merchandised, as well as a list of first-rate titles which I have been working hard to release from the clutches of American copyrights owned by regular publishers.

Penguins migrate west, August 1940.

If one can build up sales in America on the basis of importations and so organize a distributing system which can handle 25,000 of a single title, the point will have been reached at which Penguin Books Inc. starts publishing in America. With a consistent editorial policy in London, with a single price and with the support such an effort deserves from people interested in widespread distribution of worthwhile books, that may not be a completely wild dream.

Ian Ballantine to Professor Louis Hacker, 5 August 1939

There were, however, a number of minor problems to overcome in the meantime. Some of the titles imported were ‘a bit too British for American merchants. On a visit to Sears & Roebuck, Ian tried to convince a buyer that Americans really were interested in British agrarian practices – which caused the Sears buyer literally to fall from his seat laughing.’ (Philip Patrick, unpublished article, 1994)

There was also a certain resistance from booksellers, which could only be overcome by selling books on an exchange basis. Hardback publishers too hardly welcomed the competition. Nevertheless, in less than a year, under the missionary zeal of the Ballantines, Penguin Books Inc. had become well established, and had scored several notable successes:

We have gotten better publicity than any other low-cost publisher has ever obtained. We have sold more books in educational markets than thought possible by trade publishers, who all attempt to secure school sales by travellers who devote their whole time to seeing professors – a very expensive procedure. Though we have established a reputation for quality in all fields, our costs of distribution have been lower than any other publisher. We have secured reprint rights at a lower figure than anyone else.

Ian Ballantine to Professor Louis Hacker, 5 August 1939

Setting up a distribution network in America had initially seemed to be impossible: according to American law any book carrying a US copyright could not be imported into the States. Effectively this meant that virtually every Penguin reprint could be seized. In London Ian Ballantine had researched the problem for Lane and had discovered an obscure US Customs decision that provided a loophole: if copyrights were first resigned by their authors, then Penguin copies could be imported legally. It was this discovery that had first led to his appointment. Before too long, however, the cost advantages of importing were far outweighed by the many problems facing their British supplier.

War conditions necessitating the use of smaller type and poor paper have resulted in a rising volume of complaints. Pocket Books, who, I have discovered, go out of their way to harm us, constantly emphasize to booksellers that their print is superior to ours. The regular bookstore is not impressed a great deal by this propaganda. However, centres of mass distribution, i.e., department stores, have dropped our books in several cases, due to what they call their decline in quality. Of course in some cases this has reacted in our favour as the bookstores realize the seriousness of the problems facing England.

The scope of our distribution is limited almost completely to the normal book-trade outlets. Until we use a laminated cover, similar to Pocket Books, it will not be possible to get news stand distribution. News stands in the States are far more exposed than in England. In addition they have been taught bad habits by the magazine distributors. The indestructible Pocket Book has the advantage in chain stores as well, where the personnel knows very little about selling books. Here the laminated cover is needed to make exchange possible. This is the only device which can make up for the store manager's lack of knowledge in selecting books.

Ian Ballantine to Allen Lane, 23 November 1940

Ballantine's problems were mostly a matter of uncertainty: 'Shipping lines between the United States and Britain were harried by German submarines. Whenever a merchant marine vessel was torpedoed there was the possibility that 50,000 Penguin titles went to the bottom.' It was quite obvious that the only solution in the special conditions that ruled was to publish in America.

All this was confirmed when Allen Lane managed to visit New York in 1941. Paper rationing had now been introduced in the States, on a similar basis to that in force in Britain. Unfortunately pre-war paper consumption by the British firm counted for nothing in America. Added to this, new finance could not be introduced from Britain. In the face of possible closure, Kurt Enoch, who had fled first Germany and then Paris before settling in the States, intervened. He agreed with Lane to raise the necessary capital to underwrite Penguin's American production and publishing operation, and joined Ian Ballantine for the duration.

Following the example of the Forces Book Club in Britain, Penguin Books Inc. produced a series of Fighting Forces Specials to help the war effort, acting in close co-operation with the officially sponsored *Infantry Journal* who supplied additional paper for the purpose. The first of these, again profiting by British experience, was *What's That Plane?*, which was put together by the Ballantines and Walter Pitkin, their first editor, and Pitkin's wife Suzenna, around a dining room table in the apartment the two couples shared. The book was a collection of aeroplane silhouettes accompanied by a text written by Betty and Walter, based on R. A. Savile-Sneath's Penguin Specials, *Aircraft Recognition. What's That Plane?* was published in March 1942, nearly four months after Pearl Harbor, and was followed by ten printings which put more than 360,000 copies of the book into circulation.

This and further successes led the army to make it quite clear that if Ballantine were called up, he would be sent straight back to his office in uniform. In many cases Penguins, such as the *New Soldier Handbook*, were central to army training. At the same time their popularity and semi-official status helped break down whatever prejudice lingered against Penguin, along with the virtual monopoly that Pocket Books had enjoyed. Both fiction and non-fiction titles were successfully published and bought in large numbers by an eager public – the books initially reprints from Harmondsworth series, but soon developing into a genuine American list. This process was completed by the replacement of staid typographical covers with prominent illustrations.

The partnership came to an end soon after VE day, when the Ballantines sold their 49 per cent interest in the company back to Allen Lane – for one dollar. Quite apart from the question of attention-grabbing covers, American practices, particularly the emphasis on popular fiction and the obligation to take back all unsold copies, remained alien to Lane's vision. Ian and Betty Ballantine left to start Bantam. Kurt Enoch stayed, as President and Director, while Lane went in search of a replacement.

Eunice Frost was drafted in to provide editorial continuity, and to seek local replacements to guarantee long term stability. She recruited two young American editors and enlisted a number of prominent editorial advisers. As proof of the new Penguin Books Inc.'s revived adherence to the British model, American Pelicans started to appear.

Meanwhile, Allen Lane's searches bore fruit, to the considerable surprise of Kurt Enoch:

Sometime in 1945 Victor Weybright called on me at my office, without prior notice, and a stranger to me. He explained that Allen and he had become personal friends after having had frequent official and personal contacts during Victor's activities as Representative of the Office of War Information attached to the US Embassy in London. With the end of the war his job in London had come to an end and Allen had proposed that he join his American company in an executive position. The purpose of his visit was to discuss that proposition.

Kurt Enoch, reminiscence, 17 June 1971

Despite this impromptu introduction, an agreement was reached whereby Weybright would be Editor in Chief and Chairman of the Board, while Enoch was to be President, Chief Executive Officer and Treasurer. In October 1946 Morris L. Ernst, Lane's American legal representative and friend, wrote: 'I have seen something of your American boys and recently Harriet and I had lunch with Victor and Kurt. I am quite sure that the marriage is working out between these two individuals.'

Victor Weybright was well connected and familiar with the American literary scene. More important still, as Bill Williams observed, was that he appeared to be a kindred spirit, possessed, like Lane, of the necessary mercenary and missionary qualities.

However, whilst the 'marriage' of Enoch and Weybright developed, that between Lane and Weybright soon began to break up, and the American company once again disintegrated, this time with considerable ill-will from which only their respective lawyers gained any tangible benefit.

The underlying reasons for the rift between Lane and Weybright were never completely revealed. It came as the culmination of a number of differences, summarized by Enoch:

> He [Lane] had apparently expected that our editorial programme could include more books which were published by him in England. He did not sufficiently recognize or concede the peculiarities of the American market and the preferences of the American readers. He disliked picture covers which were a vital instrument of selling books merely by display in magazine outlets. Last but not least, he was disturbed by the fact that sales had to be made subject to the right of return since our books were distributed in quantities determined by the publisher and his national distributor to about 100,000 magazine dealers and not on orders from professional booksellers.

Morris Ernst could only suggest to Eunice Frost: 'It is hard to picture One World when people differ so widely in glands and attitudes as do Allen, Victor and Kurt. Not everybody can be in tune with everybody else.'

The American market remained an unsolved problem. Even in 1956, so far as Bill Williams was concerned, it was characterized by 'a commodity with garish and sensational eye-appeal . . . geared to a rapid turnover; the wares it handles are designed to last a week or so on the news-stands and then to be replaced by fresh attractions from the endless conveyor belt.'

It was into this marketplace that Allen Lane's latest ambassador, Harry Paroissien, was sent, towards the end of 1949.

> This is to report progress. I had hoped that I would be able to write and say that I had fixed on a location. Since Monday I have been searching in and around Baltimore so far without success. One likely place was an old Mill – shades of West Drayton. But it was 6,000 sq. ft. and $2,500 a year. Another snag was that it was not near any public transport and it was thought I should have difficulty with female staff as the neighbourhood was not considered very good and girls would have to walk three quarters of a mile to the bus stop in the

winter. Other places would be good from some points of view but lacking in an entrance, or the cases would have to be carried through a front door and then put on a goods lift. I got footsore but not discouraged as I feel sure that with perseverance I shall get what we want.

I moved to this place yesterday, it is 25 dollars a week against 42 for a room at an hotel. I have a bed which disappears into a cupboard and a small kitchen where I can cook some breakfast. Furnished apartments for the family, two bedrooms and a dining-living room cost from $125 a month! I have been offered a small house at 200 dollars a month. However the important thing is to get started so that the dollars roll in.

Harry Paroissien to Allen Lane, 18 November 1949

You may remember that it was about twelve months ago I called to see you in company with my sales manager, Mr Paroissien, who had just returned from making a survey of the cheap book-publishing field in the United States. As a result of his trip we commenced operations in Baltimore at the beginning of this year, and I have just got back myself from a visit to our new branch which, aided by the recent devaluation of the pound, has got off to a good start.

Allen Lane to Bernard Shaw, 19 June 1950

In 1953, news that Victor Weybright had approached two Pelican authors while in Britain to offer them 'some massive inducement' to edit a volume on the major philosophers for his New American Library, revealed a continuing animosity:

Better than anyone you know that Mentor Books are a sop to respectability, and that Mickey Spillane and Erskine Caldwell are the authors which Weybright really cares about. Of course, they can pay a larger advance than a British publisher for the initial printing is much bigger. Hampshire could also get a bigger salary by working at an American University, (especially if, like royalties, it was paid in the UK). Would Weybright have paid a large advance for Spinoza? Would he have published it at all? Would he have dreamt of approaching Berlin or Hampshire if we had not started the series of philosophers? All this you know and summarize when you say it is a difference of attitude in mind and economics, but it can and should be refuted.

Harry Paroissien to Eunice Frost, 6 November 1953

His vitriolic and largely groundless dismissal of Weybright was as much a reflection of his unquestioning loyalty and allegiance to Allen Lane, as an indication of the commercial threat that his predecessor represented. Nevertheless, surely and steadily under Harry Paroissien's direction, Penguin comfortably achieved what Allen Lane had sought for the last ten years and more: presence, stability and growth. What is more it achieved this through close connections with the educational market, rather than relying on the somewhat ephemeral success of popular fiction. The new American company's first venture into publishing was the highly regarded Pelican Shakespeare, launched in 1956.

In return for ten years' service in Baltimore Harry Paroissien was elevated to the board and brought back to Harmondsworth. In due course Chris Dolley took over in Baltimore, moving into new premises at the earliest opportunity and extending the successful exploitation of the schools and college market. And in his turn, Chris Dolley returned to a seat on the board and, for a brief period, was joint managing director with Paroissien, before assuming full control of Penguin shortly before Lane's death in 1970.

Foreplay

'Do you call that a hat?' said Miss Morland. 'I don't call it a hat at all. Good Heavens, I wouldn't be seen dead in a ditch in a thing like that.' But she was! The next morning she lay by the side of the drive with Francesca's absurd hat perched grotesquely on her severed head.

From the blurb for *Heads You Lose*, Christianna Brand

I have yours of 4 Sept.

This is the first I have heard of your Penguin of Chinese Room.

I have no interest in biographies nor photographs of any author or of myself.

What do you think I am? An author, or a model?

For Christ's sake, man, get on with the bloody story, if you want to publish it, and leave Wardour Street to supply personal pars for buggered-out old bitches in Bournemouth, in the Pitchers column.

Aren't you ever going to grow up in that dreary country?

Vivian Connell to David Herbert, 12 October 1950

From the very start Penguin provided a short biographical piece about the author and a 'blurb' outlining the book. Unfortunately, for the first few years this information was to be found only on the flaps of the dust wrapper. Once, as usually happened, this disintegrated, the blurb and biographical details were lost. In 1939 Penguin gradually became aware of this fact, and the blurb was duplicated on the half title (that is, the first leaf of the book). Separate dust wrappers were an early casualty of the war with the introduction of paper rationing – although for a brief time in 1940 a sort of compromise was achieved with flaps incorporated into the covers themselves which were of inferior quality altogether.

A typical biography would read something like:

A son of A. H. Evans, Founder and Headmaster of the famous private school, Horris Hill, he was educated at his father's school, Winchester and Oxford, where he gained many athletic successes. He and his father both captained Oxford at cricket, a unique record. After a short time as master at Eton, he went into business with Edward Lloyd Ltd, the paper makers. A. J. Evans volunteered immediately war was declared and served until 1918. Awarded an MC at the battle of Loos, he was captured at the Somme battle, but escaped after nine months' captivity. He spent the last months of the war in a Turkish prison and received a bar to his MC for his attempts to escape. He is married and has four children. He is also a well known cricketer, having played for Hampshire, Kent and England.

Along with each biography was a photograph. Originally not much bigger than a postage stamp on the dust wrapper flap, this was eventually enlarged to fill the remainder of the page above the 250 or so words allowed.

Requests for blurb and photographs litter every file – along with the most common reply: 'details may be gleaned from my entry in *Who's Who*'. Photographs presented more of a problem. The authors of the day were notoriously camera shy, and would usually claim to have no portrait at all in their possession – and direct the enquirer to the original publishers who had a block used for the first edition, often some twenty or thirty years previously.

Thank you for your letter of Nov. 27, which reached me today. I return herewith one contract with my signature. I will see if I have a photograph. Possibly my wife, who is away, may know if one exists.

R. H. Tawney to Allen Lane, 30 November 1937

Indeed it was evidently so difficult to acquire a photograph at all, let alone one still bearing any resemblance to the author that Penguin came to an arrangement with the West End photographer Howard Coster to photograph authors free of charge.

For those writing under an alias the matter of the biography was usually side-stepped. Not so for D. B. Wyndham Lewis, writing as Timothy Shy.

About that biographical note: I don't quite see how there can be one, since as I explained to Mr Lane, I want to keep the pseudonymity of T. Shy. If you like I could write a brief note to take its place – which would make a change, also – explaining that for Government reasons the identity must on no account be revealed. A photograph of Thackeray or somebody might make this quite a tiny joke, if you think so.

D. B. Wyndham Lewis to Eunice Frost, 25 January 1941

We agree that it is a good idea to go completely haywire with your biographical note and portrait in *Beyond The Headlines*. I should be grateful if you could let me have this material at your convenience.

R. W. Maynard to D. B. Wyndham Lewis, 11 March 1941

You will remember that it was suggested that we should use a portrait of W. M. Thackeray (alias Timothy Shy) in *Beyond The Headlines*? We have written to Macmillans regarding this, and as they have not one available, they suggested that we should get in touch with the National Portrait Gallery. We feel however, that they would hardly approve of the use to which we would put this, and are wondering whether you have any other suggestions as to whose photograph we might use in place of this. What about Lear, Beau Brummell etc., etc.?

R. W. Maynard to D. B. Wyndham Lewis, 8 September 1941

I have borrowed from the *News Chronicle* photo library (they want it back please) the enclosed Victorian child, which I think would do admirably for the photograph facing the title page. Walter Leaf was, I believe, a banker who died some years ago; anyhow I don't suppose there'd be any difficulty over a photo like that.

I will send on the biographical note next week.

D. B. Wyndham Lewis to Jean Osborne, 28 September 1941

Many thanks for the biographical note. This is one of the few I have

THE AUTHOR

Young, bronzed, fit, cleanly, ribald, fearless, masterful, frank, rich, yet possessing a lofty character and a warm, warm heart, Timothy Shy of the *News Chronicle* is personally perhaps, the most fascinating columnist in Fleet Street, which is saying something; an outstanding example of Dr. Julian Huxley's newest discovery, the Group (or Croup) Mind.

Over the pen-name of "Disgusted" Mr. Shy's work is familiar to readers of the correspondence-columns of every leading organ of opinion in the country. As "Henry Bessemer" he is well known to science and industry as the inventor of the Blast Furnace. As "Dulcie Merrythought" he has long edited the "Stop-Me-If-You've-Heard-It" Fun page of *The Economist*. Long one of the best-dressed men about town, as the photograph shows, Mr. Shy has from time to time been entertained in pre-war days by rich women, but not very much. To-day, in uniform, he is Simpson's favourite model. On being nodded to by Professor Joad in the Lavatory of the Athenaeum (3.28 p.m., 18/7/32, Washbasin No. 5), in mistake, as it turned out later, Mr. Shy at once abandoned Literature, resigned from the P.E.N. Club Wolfcub Patrol, and took up thinking in a big way. The present Penguin is the principal result to date, barring a few minor contusions which are neither here nor there, as the actress said at the séance when the spirit of the Elder Pitt struck her with an imaginary bicycle-pump.

The reader will perceive, on getting down to it honestly, that relatively little of World War II has been allowed to creep into these fascinating pages. This important step, taken after long conference with Penguin Books Ltd. (if that *was* Penguin Books Ltd.—a very attractive face, not strictly handsome, perhaps, but manly and *good*) is deliberate.

The illustrations are by Landseer.

Timothy Shy successfully conceals his true identity despite detailed biographical notes in *Beyond The Headlines*.

really enjoyed reading and typing out to send down to our printers. The Production Department was pleased to receive it as a means of breaking the usual Monday morning ice.

Jean Osborne to D. B. Wyndham Lewis, 7 October 1941

Some authors fumed, albeit belatedly:

I happened to pick up a copy of *All Passion Spent* at a friend's house – and read the biographical note describing me as 'the wife of a diplomat'. I do most strongly object to this expression, which evokes a dreadful type of person, only too familiar to me: the social, bridge-playing woman, who writes a little in her spare time and turns her foreign experiences to good account in the pursuit of publicity and pocket money! I hope to goodness you are not repeating this in your edition of *Passenger to Teheran*. If it is possible, I would be awfully grateful if I might see whatever you do intend to put; I am not unreasonable, I think, but I must confess to certain prejudices – and, as a professional writer, I dislike having my private life and circumstances exploited.
Please forgive me.

Vita Sackville-West to Eunice Frost, 14 December 1942

We hope to put *Orlando* in hand very shortly and are wondering whether you would care to revise Virginia Woolf's biographical note which was used in conjunction with her photograph in *The Common Reader*.

Eunice Frost to Leonard Woolf, 23 January 1942

Both Leonard and Virginia Woolf had been published amongst the first Pelicans to be issued. Virginia, who had died in 1941, was described thus, in the 1938 Pelican *The Common Reader*:

Virginia Woolf is the daughter of the late Sir Leslie Stephen, KCB. She ranks high among literary critics and essayists. Is the wife of Leonard Woolf (author of *After The Deluge*, also in the Pelican series) whom she married in 1912. Her hobby is printing, and her interest in typography led her and her husband to found the well-known Hogarth Press in 1917. Two of the best known of her many books are *Orlando* (an outstanding example of the 'stream of consciousness' technique) and *The Waves*.

With reference to your EEF/VD of 23 January, I have revised the biographical note as enclosed. I don't think I have read the note in *The Common Reader* before; it is rather absurdly inaccurate for *Orlando* is notable among my wife's books for having absolutely no 'stream of consciousness technique' in it at all!

Leonard Woolf to Eunice Frost, 2 January 1942

On one memorable occasion, the matter of biography came close to losing Penguin one of their most successful authors.

Thank you for your letter. Here are a few notes about Graham Greene:

Graham Greene is descended from Whyte Melville and Robert Louis Stevenson so that writing is in his blood. He went to Oxford and very soon after made his name with *The Man Within*; since then with each of his unusual books, particularly *Brighton Rock*, he has added to his reputation.

In 1938 he went alone to Mexico and travelled there for three or four months; and this was the exotic background he used for his last novel *The Power and the Glory*, a book which, according to the late Sir Hugh Walpole, 'proves that he is the finest English novelist of his generation'. It has just been awarded the Hawthornden Prize for 1940.

Several of his books have been made into successful films: *Stamboul Train* which was called '*Balkan Express*', and *A Gun for Sale*, renamed '*A Gun for Hire*'.

He himself has always lived a quiet life and shunned literary circles. He lived with his wife and children in a Georgian brick house on Clapham Common, beautifully furnished in period, and now alas bombed. At the beginning of the war he worked for a time on the Ministry of Information, and he is now on active service in the Middle East.

He is now at work on a new book which he calls 'An Entertainment'. It is called *Ministry of Fear*.

I hope this will help you.

Grace Cranston, William Heinemann Ltd, to Jean Osborne, 19 January 1942

This information was faithfully passed on to readers in the Penguin edition of *England Made Me*.

We are shortly reprinting our edition of *Brighton Rock*, and I wonder if it is still your desire that our usual practice of printing a short biographical note and photograph of the author in our books should not be followed in your case. We did not do so in the previous edition, as we understood it was your wish, and if you can be induced to change your mind, we would be very glad.

A. S. B. Glover to Graham Greene, 3 May 1945

My objection to the biographical note and the photograph in Penguins was that the biographical note was horribly chatty and personal and the photograph was quite wildly out of date. I have no rigid objection to your putting a note in if you will confine it to the details given in *Who's Who*, and obtain the photograph from my agents, Pearn, Pollinger & Higham, who have the only authorized prints.

Graham Greene to A. S. B. Glover, 10 May 1945

Mr Robert Chris, of Cecil Court, mentioned to me a day or two ago that you had been annoyed to find that a biographical note is still appearing in the Penguin edition of *England Made Me*.

I am very sorry that there should have been any annoyance to you over this: but I hope, when I explain the circumstances, that you will absolve us of intentional neglect of your wishes.

In 1943, when we were first printing *Brighton Rock*, your agents wrote to us saying that you did not wish any biographical note or photograph to appear. In accordance with your wish we did not insert one, and none has ever appeared in our edition of that book. In looking through our files concerning it, when the question of a reprint arose, I found this letter, and it was in consequence of this that I wrote to you last May asking if your wishes in this matter were still unchanged. You will perhaps remember replying that you had no rigid objection to a biographical note provided it did not go outside the details given in *Who's Who*, or to a photograph provided that it was taken from one of the authorized prints in the hands of your agents.

We then obtained an authorized photo for future use, and I made a record of the fact that in any future reprint of any of your books the biographical note, if one appeared at all, was to conform with the wish that you had expressed; and I am taking care that the new printing of *Brighton Rock*, when it appears, shall conform with your wishes.

Meanwhile, however, the new printing of *England Made Me* had been published. The biographical details there given were supplied originally by Heinemann's when the book was first printed, and when the reprint was arranged for at the end of last year, they were automatically included in the 'copy' sent to the printers, as in the case of that title no question had been raised about them. Had I then known your views, I should of course have referred to you before allowing them to be reproduced; but it was not until some months afterwards, when the question of reprinting *Brighton Rock* arose, that I was aware that you had ever raised the point.

We shall, of course, ensure that not only in the case of the forthcoming reprint of *Brighton Rock*, but in all future printings of any of your books, no portrait or biographical matter appears that has not your own approval.

While writing, may I revert to Miss Frost's letter to you of October 12th last about the possibility of your consenting to a Penguin edition of *The Power and the Glory* or *The Ministry of Fear*? I cannot trace a reply from you to this letter, and Miss Frost is in America. We should like very much indeed to do one or both of these, if we might.

A. S. B. Glover to Graham Greene, 30 July 1945

Your letter of July 30 crossed mine of the same date to Miss Frost, and I feel rather shattered and appeased.

Actually it was because of the blurb in *England Made Me* that I insisted on no photograph or blurb appearing in *Brighton Rock*. Anyway, let us say no more about the matter as I have your promise that no future reprints will contain this material.

I am afraid there is no possibility whatever of a Penguin edition of *The Power and the Glory*, as I feel it would damage the sale of the 5/- edition. I cannot say anything about *The Ministry of Fear* at present as I am trying to arrange a reprint at the original price, and until this has been done I am unwilling to give it to Penguin.

I believe that at the moment you are considering *The Lawless Roads*, which was the travel book on which *The Power and the Glory* was based.

Graham Greene to A. S. B. Glover, 31 July 1945

I return the two books with insulting comments on your awful publicity matter on the back of *England Made Me*!

With tardy best wishes for the New Year,

Graham Greene to Allen Lane, 18 January 1946

Very many thanks for signing and returning the two books so promptly.

I am sorry that the biographical material which appears on *England Made Me* has pained you so deeply. I have taken the matter up with my Editorial Department who have shown me the correspondence which they had with you last summer. They have also shown a letter from Heinemann of January 1942 on which the 'blurb' was based. I am sending you a copy of this letter herewith so that you can see that the blame was not entirely ours for some of the alleged mis-statements.

I am also enclosing a proof of a wrapper which I have just received from New York. Is there anything in this which you would like me to try to get altered?

The ideal thing would be for you to dictate a note to your secretary of what you would like to appear both on this side of the Atlantic and in New York.

Allen Lane to Graham Greene, 28 January 1946

GRAHAM GREENE

He is a bit upset – and I dare say you will be more upset – to see that on the spine of your edition of *The Lawless Roads* his name is misspelt.

Anything that I can tell him?

David Higham to Richard Lane, 3 July 1947

* * *

RECONSTRUCTION AND CONSOLIDATION 1946–1960

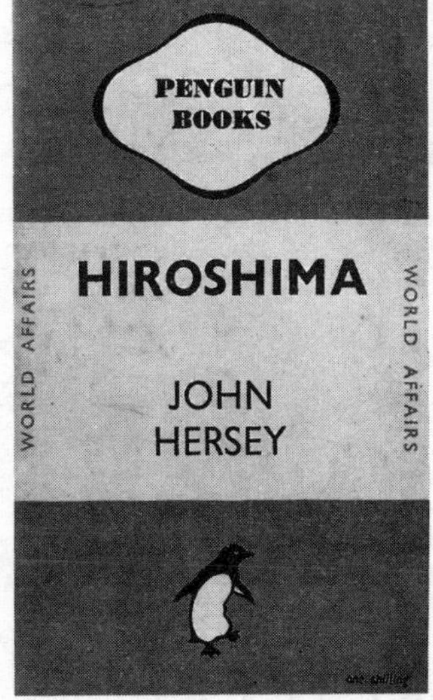

Mass-Observation

Mass-Observation, a movement started early in 1937 by two young men and now embracing some two thousand voluntary observers all over the country, exists to study everyday behaviour in Britain – the Science of Ourselves.

Cover blurb to *Britain by Mass-Observation*, Penguin Special, 1939

During December 1946, 'unknown to anyone but the managing director', a Mass-Observation investigator was employed to work at Penguin, supposedly as a trainee. 'Her object in doing so was to study the reactions of staff to their working conditions and to attempt to assess the degree of satisfaction or dissatisfaction which they felt in their work.' In the course of this work she was able to observe the editorial staff in their daily work, and at an editorial 'conference'.

The driving force of the house comes from the managing director, Allen Lane, who, having established an efficient working organization with a policy which can be quickly absorbed by newcomers, contrives not so much to impose new directives upon it as to canalize and direct the forces now at work. At editorial meetings, 'partisanship' is sometimes evident. Here, suggestions for future titles are brought forward by various members, and discussion runs high, particularly if the subject or author concerned brings in an element of personal feeling. Thus, contemporary literary works will generate more heat than classics; questions of contemporary interpretations of trends (e.g. aspects of architecture or education methods) will be more hotly debated than those more remote from the immediate experience or opinions of the staff concerned (say, archaeology, history, etc.). It appears to follow that special knowledge of a subject or interest in aspects of it involves an element of partisanship which becomes exaggerated beyond cool judgment when confronted with opposition. Hence the need, appreciated by the editorial staff, of delaying final decisions.

To this scene, Eunice Frost provides the dynamic of the partisan. Because of her participation in the younger contemporary intellectual circles, she is able to bring to editorial meetings suggestions for subjects and authors which, when adopted, assist in the publicizing of contemporary attitudes, and, also, in bringing the authors concerned into the level of established rather than controversial opinion. This participation has the effect of keeping the house policy abreast with contemporary thought. On the other hand, it did sometimes seem that this same participation, implicating emotional forces, could distort balanced judgment and leads to the excessive pressing of a point in the face of sound objections. To balance this tendency, however, other members of the editorial staff, notably 'Pelican' Williams, are able to maintain their objections and their own judgments with the result that on the whole the final decision represents the preponderance of advantages over disadvantages. Mention should be made, too, of A. S. B. Glover, in charge of general editorial, whose erudition, judgment and pungent irony provide a stabilizing element to the editorial side of the house.

Editorial meetings are conducted with a certain amount of hilarity, and they commence on a conversational basis as the members assemble, drop into chairs and get down to the day's business. Eunice Frost reports the relevant correspondence:

Frost: 'The man from UNRRA wants to do a book on Czechoslovakia.'
A. Lane: 'I can think of 10,000 reasons why we should not . . .'

Williams: 'There are books which people can't read and think they are marvellous.'
A. Lane: '*Mathematics by the Million.*' [no such title: probably *Microbes by the Million*]
Frost: '*Interglossa.*'
Williams: 'That should be a main exhibit for Penguin's Follies. In a glass case.'
Frost: 'This question of their doing us a book on coal. They say they don't think it will overlap with "*x*".'
A. Lane (on intercom with Cash Sales): 'Hill, what orders do you get for "*x*"? You are almost out, aren't you? Yes. And how would that compare with, say, *Lives of the Great Composers*? He thinks there's a steady demand for it.'
Frost: 'There's a new bookshop being opened devoted completely to the subject.'

A. Lane: 'I think this needs a reprint.'
Frost: 'If we want to do a new one at all . . .'
A. Lane: 'We do want to do one. We are interested in the raw materials aspect. Would you like to take it further with . . .'
R. Lane: 'Marvellous salmon. Have you ever caught a salmon?'
Williams: 'I can't exactly say I have ever caught a salmon. It was represented to me that I had. When I get to Newfoundland . . .'
Frost: 'What are you going there for?'
Williams: 'To recuperate from all your unkindness.'

Frost: 'This letter from . . .'
A. Lane: 'TK* is going to Paris next week. Tell her to go and see him. I should write in advance and be careful not to hold out hopes, explain that we are not really enthusiastic. He wanted me to go over by plane, wine and dine me and get me to sign on the dotted line.'

Williams: 'I would like a large Scotch.'
A. Lane: 'Not for me.'
Frost: 'What's come over you?'
A. Lane: 'I'm off spirits. It was suggested by someone up here that there might be time for a snifter, but it was turned down.'

And so on.

* * *

Hiroshima

The following note appeared in the *New Yorker* of 31 August 1946 as an introduction to John Hersey's article.

The *New Yorker* this week devotes its entire editorial space to an article on the almost complete obliteration of a city by one atomic bomb, and what happened to the people of that city. It does so in the conviction that few of us have yet comprehended the all but incredible

* TK is Tatyana Kent. Allen Lane's personal assistant for many years, she set up a South American Penguin offshoot, before returning to England, eventually marrying Hans Schmoller.

destructive power of this weapon, and that everyone might well take time to consider the terrible implications of its use.

I am sending you herewith the most impressive piece of journalism in all of my experience and acquaintance with periodicals in America – a total issue of the *New Yorker*, just out, devoted to 'Hiroshima' by John Hersey.

Immediately upon seeing it and reading it, I got in touch with Lesser of Knopf, not only on your behalf but on behalf of PBL. Obviously, I could not speak for you or commit you, but I knew I was on safe ground in assuming that you might be interested in this as an immediate Penguin Special for England.

Gollancz did Hersey's last book – but I don't think Gollancz has a firm claim on this. Lesser is going to take up with Alfred Knopf tomorrow the question of whether an arrangement might be possible with PBL, skipping a trade edition altogether, or perhaps a trade edition and a PBL edition simultaneously.

All this, of course, is contingent upon your being interested and making a bid for it.

I would appreciate it if you could write or cable me your views as soon as you have studied this extraordinary issue of the *New Yorker*.

Victor Weybright, Penguin Books Inc., New York, to Allen Lane, 29 August 1946

FROSTIE AND I NOT ENTHUSIASTIC HERSEY. NEW YORKER ARTICLE FOR THIS SIDE STOP ALLEN IN SWITZERLAND WILL CABLE ON HIS RETURN IF HE IS MORE IMPRESSED

DICK

Telegram from Richard Lane to Victor Weybright, 4 September 1946

BELIEVE HIROSHIMA RIGHTS MIGHT BE AVAILABLE IF FIRM OFFER WERE MADE TO KNOPF WHO ARE RUSHING OUT BOOK FOR NOVEMBER FIRST PUBLICATION THIS COUNTRY BEFORE ACTUAL HERSEY CONTRACT IS FINALLY SIGNED STOP APPARENTLY GOLLANCZ IS PRIORITY BRITISH PUBLICATION BUT NO FORMAL CONTRACT YET EXISTS

VICTOR WEYBRIGHT

Cable from Victor Weybright to Allen Lane, 6 September 1946

I was disappointed to hear that you and Frostie are not enthusiastic about the Hiroshima article by John Hersey, which occupied the entire editorial content of last week's *New Yorker*.

I read it on the Wednesday evening when my subscription copy arrived, and the first thing Thursday morning attempted to get it for PBL. The whole issue of the *New Yorker* was sold out by nine o'clock and the *New Yorker* office was flooded with requests to reprint it. Knopf was equally beset by book propositions, and it looks as if it will be a Book of the Month Club selection here.

Meanwhile, hundreds of newspapers throughout the country are reprinting it in serial form, including the *Herald Tribune* in New York.

If there is any hesitation at PBL, I imagine the best thing to do would be to let it go to Gollancz. If Allen is more impressed than you or Frostie, please let me know – although everything is moving so rapidly that I don't imagine Knopf can wait longer for evidence of interest.

Victor Weybright to Richard Lane, 6 September 1946

JUST RETURNED FROM CONTINENT ARE RIGHTS HIROSHIMA ARTICLE STILL FREE CABLE REPLY

ALLEN LANE

Telegram from Allen Lane to Victor Weybright, 9 September 1946

INTENSELY ANXIOUS SECURE NEWYORKER HIROSHIMA ARTICLE SINCERELY HOPE YOU CAN YET ARRANGE FOR US PUBLISH HERE

ALLEN

Telegram to Victor Weybright, 9 September 1946

I very much hope that we have not missed the John Hersey Hiroshima book. I was in Switzerland on business all last week, the results of which I hope to be able to give you in the very near future as I think they may conceivably interest you, and while there saw a note in the *New York Herald Tribune* (Paris edition), of the *New Yorker* number devoted to this article, which incidentally the *Herald Tribune* are running serially commencing yesterday.

On my return I was about to cable you for information when Dick told me that he had already more or less turned it down. I read it in bed last night, and this morning Glover also read it. We are both intensely enthusiastic, and think that it should be published by us without delay. I am keeping my fingers crossed that someone has not already snapped it up. In any case I am grateful to you for the promptitude with which you acted.

Allen Lane to Victor Weybright, 9 September 1946

NEW YORKER URGING HERSEY WHO IS ABSENT FROM CITY TO RECOMMEND PENGUIN FOR HIROSHIMA IN ENGLAND STOP MEANWHILE BELIEVE AN OFFER FROM YOU WOULD INTEREST KNOPF WHO ASSUME THEIR CONTRACT WILL INCLUDE RIGHT TO PLACE BOOK IN ENGLAND

VICTOR WEYBRIGHT

Cable from Victor Weybright to Allen Lane, 10 September 1946

HAVE JUST SPOKEN TO GOLLANCZ WHO HAS WIRED NEWYORK EXPRESSING INTEREST IN HIROSHIMA STOP WILL YOU CONTACT KNOPF AND MAKE FIRM OFFER OUR BEHALF OF ONE THOUSAND DOLLARS STOP IF HIGHER ADVANCE REQUIRED PLEASE CABLE OR TELEPHONE REVERSED CHARGES PERSONAL

ALLEN

Telegram from Allen Lane to Victor Weybright, 10 September 1946

SORRY TO MISS YOU PERSONALLY BUT HAVE CONFIRMED HIROSHIMA WITH KNOPF FOR YOU TO HAVE FIRST BOOK PUBLICATION IN ENGLAND 250,000 PUBLICATION DATE FIRST WEEK IN NOVEMBER STOP I AM DELIGHTED

VICTOR WEYBRIGHT

Cable from Victor Weybright to Allen Lane, 11 September 1946

It was a joy to hear your rippling English voice and to note, if I am not mistaken, that Allen had infected you with my own enthusiasm for *Hiroshima*. I only regret I missed a direct connection with him because it has been so long since we have been in touch. You will never regret doing *Hiroshima*, which is certainly destined to become a classic of its kind.

There were wheels within wheels in the effort to secure it for PBL and money wasn't the prime mover – but the auspices of the Penguin imprint and the Penguin audience were. Both Harold Ross and Truax recommended the Penguin deal to Hersey and Hersey in turn was responsible for upping the guarantee to a guarantee of a quarter of a million copies – even though the $2,000 which he will have to split with Knopf is peanuts compared with the guarantee he might have expected on a trade edition.

It is necessary, of course, to permit Gollancz to bring out an expensive edition after your publication – making him wait quite a decent interval, I hope.

I will keep sending Allen promotion material of possible use in dramatizing your edition. I would be most interested in a report on all your editorial reactions to it, including Billy's. I had a curious hunch that Allen would see it as I did, with his flair for the timely that transcends mere journalism.

Victor Weybright to 'Frostie', Eunice Frost, 11 September 1946

I am frantically excited about the Hiroshima book, and am enclosing herewith our contract which I would be glad if you would let Knopf have, and if, as I hope, it is in order, I shall be glad if you will get one copy from him for return to us.

I would like you also to take the opportunity of thanking the Knopfs personally for letting us have the book. It seems after all that perhaps your lunch at Claridges was not in vain.

What thrills me even more is this instance of co-operation from your side. It will I hope prove to be the forerunner of many such plans, and it demonstrates how usefully we can run in double harness.

Dick has just gone off to Denmark for a long weekend. I am afraid he does not share all my enthusiasm for the Hersey book, nor in fact does Frostie, as you will by now have gathered, but although I can see reasons why it might not be liked here, I am sure that we have made a right judgment.

We are now announcing our first three post-war Specials, namely *Hiroshima*, *The Nuremberg Trials*, and *The Anatomy of Peace*.

Allen Lane to Victor Weybright, 12 September 1946

I am writing this personal note of appreciation of your helpfulness in steering the John Hersey Hiroshima book in our direction.

At the time when we first had news of this exciting project I was in Switzerland on a short business trip, which accounted for the slight delay there was in our making up our minds, but the speed at which the final decision was arrived at impressed me considerably, and we are now fully engaged in meeting the contractual publication date of November 1st. As you know, our first printing is a quarter of a million copies. Final page proofs were passed today, and despite the current threat of a printers' strike we hope to get the first copies in the house within the next two weeks.

After the public acclaim with which the account has been received it would be superfluous of me to write in its praise, but I would like you to know that I feel its publication here may do a great deal towards a future peace.

Allen Lane to Blanche Knopf, 24 September 1946

I have just gone over the *Hiroshima* contracts with Messrs Lesser and Koshland and initialled several changes.

Two of them are important: (1) the published price is held to a shilling at two pounds per thousand royalty; (2) the advance guarantee, payable on publication, of the first edition of 250,000 copies is $2,000. That was the understanding that Knopf had on the day we struck the bargain after my telephone call to England. If, for any reason, the payment on publication seems too steep, let me know, and I can have PBI assist in part.

It is actually of considerable value to us, as well as to PBL, to have been involved so intimately with everyone concerned in this Hersey tour de force.

Victor Weybright to Allen Lane, 26 September 1946

I feel I ought to write to you regarding my first reactions to the Hiroshima book. As you know, my main job in the firm is not editorial and I only coped with this during Allen's absence. My job, however, apart from finance, is to see that when we have paid advances on books, that these are not shelved, and at the present time, while we are still rationed for paper, to see as far as possible that a book, having once been signed up, flows to its final publication without too many hindrances. Naturally, one of the biggest hindrances is the production of rush and special books, which upsets the routine.

As we still ration booksellers, the question of whether a book is a potential best seller or not hardly comes into the picture.

We have quite a number of books signed up and advances paid well over ten years ago. We also have the case of a book on which we have publication rights for five years only from January 1st, 1945, which has not yet been set. Every time we do a Special, it naturally hinders the production of these books.

I read *Hiroshima* right through during my critical hours commencing 5 a.m. I thought it an able piece of work and I thought it would sell, but more important to me was the fact that it would hinder the publication of books already in hand. As you know, there is a terrific bottle neck in binding at the moment, and an extra 250,000 copies do make a difference.

I can quite see Allen's point of view. It is something new and exciting; it involved cables and transatlantic phone calls, which he loves, and also there is the question that if we got the book, a certain other publisher would not.

I thought I would like to explain this to you so that you would not think my lack of enthusiasm was entirely due to the book itself.

Richard Lane to Victor Weybright, 26 September 1946

Once again a thousand thanks for the way in which you have handled and are handling this most significant publication.

The contract as sent with your letter of October 1st is ok with me. I have had it stamped and put in the archives.

Although we could publish in a limited way by say November 5th, the two printers who are working on it cannot give us better delivery than 5,000 to 6,000 copies a day, and we are therefore holding up the publication until we can make a really good distribution. The date we have fixed as being for a number of reasons the most apt, is November 10th. This you will note is a Sunday, so that the books will only be on sale on the Monday, but it is a day fixed as a commemoration of all those who were killed or died during both Great War 1 and Great War 2. The King is unveiling a new inscription on the Cenotaph on that morning, and the two minutes' silence which has hitherto been observed on the 11th is being transferred one day earlier.

I am not anticipating any trouble with the Exchange Control, but if we do run into snags I will certainly call on you for help.

The BBC a fortnight ago started what they call the Third Programme, i.e. an addition to the normal Home and Light Programmes, a feature which has been an outstanding success, and they are serializing *Hiroshima* in I think three instalments in this programme next week.

I am glad that Blanche Knopf is pleased with us, and I hope that this may lead to further co-operation in the future.

Allen Lane to Victor Weybright, 11 October 1946

The *New Yorker*'s original intention was to make the story a serial. But in an inspired moment, the paper's editors saw that it must be published as a single whole and decided to devote a whole issue to Hersey's masterpiece of reconstruction. For ten days Hersey feverishly rewrote and polished his story, handing it out by instalments to the printers, and no hint of what was in the air escaped from the *New Yorker*'s office. On August 31st, in the paper's usual format, the historic issue appeared. It created a first-order sensation in American journalistic history; a few hours after publication the issue was sold out. Applications poured in for permission to serialize the story in other American journals, among them the *New York Herald Tribune*, *Washington Post*, *Chicago Sun*, and *Boston Globe*. A condensed version – the cuts personally approved by Hersey – was broadcast in four instalments by the American Broadcasting Company. Some fifty newspapers in the US eventually obtained permission to use the story in serial form, the copyright fees, after tax deduction, at Hersey's direction going to the American Red Cross. Albert Einstein ordered a thousand copies of the *New Yorker* containing the story. Even stage rights were sought from the author, though he refused to give permission for dramatization. British newspapers and press syndicates immediately cabled for reproduction rights; but the *New Yorker*'s executives insisted that no cutting could be permitted, and with British paper rationing, full newspaper publication seemed to be impracticable. The book production rights for the United States were secured by Alfred A. Knopf, Inc., and the American Book of the Month Club chose it for publication as an 'Extra'; and the BBC obtained permission to broadcast the article in four episodes as part of their new Third Programme.

Penguin Books, feeling that Hersey's story should receive the widest possible circulation in Great Britain, immediately cabled to

Alfred A. Knopf for, and were accorded, permission to issue it complete in book form. It here appears – save for following English spelling conventions – in an edition of 250,000 copies, exactly as it appeared in the pages of the *New Yorker*.

Many accounts have been published telling – so far as security considerations allow – how the atom bomb works. But here, for the first time, is not a description of scientific triumphs, of intricate machines, new elements, and mathematical formulas, but an account of what the bomb does – seen through the eyes of some of those to whom it did it: of those who endured one of the world's most catastrophic experiences, and lived.

Extract from Publisher's Note introducing Penguin edition

* * *

Penguin Periodicals

Having moved book publishing into the realms of pure journalism with the Specials, and finding that a good many of their customers would buy every book that came out, or at least every book of a certain type, led Penguin to experiment with further innovations. Coinciding with the launch of the first Penguin Special was the first tentative step in this direction, *Penguin Parade*, edited by Denys Kilham Roberts. This miscellany of new stories, essays, poems and woodcuts by contemporary writers and artists was planned as a quarterly publication, with the possibility of monthly editions mooted in the first issue. Readers' contributions were welcomed, and were printed, along with contributions by the likes of H. E. Bates, Sean O'Faolain and Sherwood Anderson.

During the war this idea was taken a stage further, with the launch of a magazine, the periodical *Transatlantic*, published in London, with 'the collaboration of the Writers' War Board, New York', which came with a full colour cover, a good deal of advertising, articles on American current affairs and a lofty ambition: 'to assist the British and American peoples to walk together in majesty and peace'.

On the home front, the return to peace prompted the launch of a number of periodicals: the *Penguin Film Review*, *Penguin Music Magazine*, and *Russian Review*, along with two successful and long-lived scientific journals, *Science News* and *New Biology* both of which lasted until 1960.

Penguin *Russian Review:* 'that uncomfortable porcupine'.

The *Russian Review* lasted for four issues, a victim not so much of the Cold War, as its own ambitions:

The general reader in this country, in spite of an intense interest in Russia, has been impeded in his desire to understand her by the lack of suitable and adequate information . . . To supply this want, to contribute to nothing less than the initiation into the spirit of the Russian people which is embodied in its history and literature, its arts and sciences, its philosophy and religion and in its economic life, the *Russian Review*, under the imprint of Penguin Books, intends to publish periodically numbers containing a selection of articles on these various aspects of Russian life. In another section, Russia will speak for herself through her imaginative writers and poets. The *Review* is intended throughout for the general reader, whom it hopes to attract by the variety of subjects, and by their popular yet comprehensive treatment.

From the start it was not a success, and only survived as long as it did thanks to the efforts of Edward Crankshaw, who replaced Count Benckendorff as editor. It was a rare, though not unique, example of Allen Lane giving an editor complete trust and editorial freedom – and then regretting it.

I have just seen a report on the material submitted for *Russian Review* 3, and owing to the criticism I have heard of the volume already published and of the material already in hand for the second issue, I have been looking into the balance sheet side of the publication, and I must admit that I am very much concerned over the results of the investigation.

As I think you know, we went into this on a somewhat idealistic basis without thoughts of making enormous profits, but even bearing this in mind, the results are pretty catastrophic. As a matter of interest, our cost of production on the first issue came to something in excess of the price received from the booksellers, not taking into account our overhead expenses here, and in addition we are having a hitherto unknown experience in that copies are being returned in fairly considerable quantities from the trade as being unsaleable. To date out of our first printing of 25,000 copies, we have received back over 4,000.

Page proofs of number 2 came in today, and are by now on their way to you, and under the circumstances I feel that the best thing would be to await the public's reception to number 2 before deciding whether in fact we can proceed further with the publication of this venture. For the moment, I am not proposing to have any further work carried out on *Russian Review* 3.

Allen Lane to Count Benckendorff, 24 January 1946

The first issue had come out with no editorial explanation of policy. This appeared belatedly in issue 2, which, apparently, was liked a little more by readers, apart from a long article on Polish prison camps, which 'seems to involve a great amount of gruesome details which will certainly please readers of the lurid Sunday papers, but which hardly seems quite in place in a serious periodical, and isn't altogether calculated to appeal to the best instincts in man'. Lane, who had recently visited the Nuremberg Trials, opined: 'My own feeling is that everybody has had enough of this "death camp" business, and that the sooner we all block it out of our minds, the better for everybody.'

Lt. Col. Edward Crankshaw was initially recommended by Bill Williams as co-editor of 'that uncomfortable porcupine' *Russian Review*. In October 1946 it was agreed that he would take over the editorship from the fourth issue, with an undertaking to edit at least two more after that. But with Lane's admission that 'at the moment our balance sheet on this publication is a sorry affair', its days were numbered.

'We have come a good deal closer to the division of the world into two opposed camps. People are finding it harder than they expected to make head or tail of the Russians, so hard that many have decided it is useless to go on trying. We have to go on trying, all the same.' In these words Edward Crankshaw introduced the fourth issue of *Russian Review* to its readers. By the time this appeared in print he had already written to Lane: 'Naturally I am sad about *Russian Review*, of which I once had great hopes; but that is really part of a greater sadness! I have no doubt, however, that what has been done had to be. And I'm very glad the final scuttling was conducted in amity.' Crankshaw's next contribution to Penguin was the 1963 Special *The New Cold War: Moscow v. Pekin*.

The film and music magazines fared better, and shrank rather than disappeared, first with a reduction in size to the standard Penguin format, and then assimilated into the Pelican series as annuals which lasted until 1952. *Penguin Parade* was revived after the war under the editorship of J. E. Morpurgo: an international collection of 'critical and informative writing without prejudice of school or subject, with, so far as it is possible in the circumstances of postwar publishing, an accent on topicality, and with a belief in the continuity of the arts and of social development', embellished with colour and photogravure illustrations. Its aim was to be 'a microcosm of all the fields covered by Penguin publications', an ideal pursued more explicitly by the free booklet *Penguins Progress*, again the direct responsibility of Morpurgo, then in charge of Penguin's public relations. Mailed directly to Penguin readers, it was as close as Penguin then came to general advertising. There were fourteen postwar issues of *Penguins Progress*: *Parade* lasted three, with two further completed issues never making it to the presses.

One reason for the decline from 'periodical' through 'occasional' to demise was explained to Henry Williamson, when, in February 1949, he wrote asking if Lane might take over *The Adelphi*. Alan Glover replied that: 'We have, as you know, made some incursions into the field of publishing what we call "occasionals", but times are extremely bad for them, and we are closing down one or two of those for which we are responsible. Our distribution is geared up to publications in very large numbers, and to take over a review with a circulation figure in the two or three thousand region would be against what has been our whole policy.' Moreover, the pressures that such topical publications imposed on the Production department were difficult to sustain without the mainstream publications suffering delays. It was becoming increasingly clear to editorial staff that periodical publishing was a diversion that Penguin could ill afford.

One Penguin periodical, at least, was an outstanding success throughout the war years, from both a critical and, for much of its life, financial point of view. John Lehmann's *New Writing* had originated in 1936, and was one more of Allen Lane's parting gifts to the Bodley Head. In 1940 Lehmann contributed an original survey of current trends in English and European literature for the Pelican series, *New Writing in Europe*, and before this was published, he agreed to a suggestion of a Penguin reprint of selections from his prewar *New Writing*. Having persuaded Lane that two volumes might be gleaned from the existing material, he set to work compiling them. But by the time Lehmann's first *Penguin New Writing* appeared in December 1940, radical developments had occurred.

The second selection never appeared as planned. Things began to move very fast during the summer. I pressed on with the work with a sense of urgency, inspired partly by the idea at the back of everyone's mind that an invasion was imminent, and partly by the fear that I myself might be called up at any moment. During our discussion Lane had tentatively mentioned that Penguins might start a monthly literary magazine. The more I thought about this, the clearer it seemed to me that in Penguin's selections from *New Writing* he already had a magazine in embryo. Why shouldn't the selections appear each month, but with half of every number consisting of *new* contributions, stories, poems and articles?

Penguin New Writing 1940–1950, edited by John Lehmann and Roy Fuller, 1985

As Lehmann wrote in his autobiography, *I Am My Brother*, 'The details were settled with what – considering the difficulties that were cropping up on all sides from the intensification of the attack on Britain – seems to me now incredible speed, and a contract for six numbers of a monthly *Penguin New Writing* was signed by the end of October.'

During 1941 eleven issues of *Penguin New Writing* were published, and by the end of the year enough paper was scraped together to produce editions of 75,000. It was a time of feverish activity, which in itself helped a good many get through these dark days.

My recollection of those early months of *Penguin New Writing* is of continual train-journeys accompanied by a suitcase full of manuscripts and proofs which I worked through; of frequent halts on the line during an alert . . . Sometimes dusk fell over the darkened train and reading had to be abandoned, and passengers in silent gloom reflected that their plans to arrive – or leave – before the evening blitz were going to be in vain; guns started to bark and the faraway thump of bombs changed, disagreeably, to the swish-swish of a stick of them swooping down close by. Also I remember blissfully peaceful nights at Cambridge, where my secretary, Michael Nelson, would often join me, typewriter in hand; and of trips to the works where the Penguin was being printed, sometimes to find there had been a raid the night before and a tarpaulin was being hurriedly stretched over jagged holes in the roof under which the machining of the next number miraculously proceeded. And all the time the letters and manuscripts poured in . . . More and more were coming in from young authors who had been drafted into the Army, or the Navy, or the Air Force, and some of them so interesting that before long I began to see that it would be possible gradually to reduce the proportion of contributions reprinted from the old *New Writing*, and make the Penguin a completely contemporary magazine.

John Lehmann, *I Am My Brother*, Longmans, 1960

In 1942 the worsening paper situation forced the change to quarterly publication, along with editorial changes, introducing articles on contemporary arts, supplemented by a photogravure insert. Issue 13 also saw the first of the regular contributions of Jack Marlowe, who 'has had more than a nodding acquaintance with the world of writers, journalists and publishers ever since he can remember'. Among a number of writers operating under pseudonyms, Jack Marlowe was Lehmann's own creation. It was not only paper that was in short supply.

As the war goes on, it is not only the increasing difficulties of the paper supply and labour in the printing and binding trades that a literary periodical has to contend with. As formidable, if not more formidable, is the steady drain of authors of every sort into the war-machine . . . Some have been directed, wisely if belatedly, into positions where there is scope for their particular gifts; others, far too many, are being squandered in routine office jobs which could equally be filled by those incapable of making the artist's special contribution to a community at war; and some are quite simply submerged in spit-and-polish and foot-slogging. One can only record – and I know that I do it on behalf of thousands of people both in uniform and in mufti whose belief that the war has to be fought is above question – one's enormous regret at the loss of so much that might have been precious to us; one cannot hope to change it.

John Lehmann, Foreword to *Penguin New Writing 12*

Writers and artists who had abandoned their magnum opus still found time for less ambitious works, to the great advantage of *Penguin New Writing* which provided the perfect outlet for their work, along with a ready audience. Their contribution celebrates and epitomizes the whole decade.

There are no editorial files on *Penguin New Writing* in the archives at Bristol; and all Lehmann's papers now reside at the University of Texas at Austin. Letters remain in the Contracts file at Harmondsworth, which chart the slow decline of the periodical towards its demise. From a peak of 100,000 copies printed of the first postwar issue, by 1949 this was reduced to 40,000, in a smaller and more modest format.

I am glad you have settled in principle that *Penguin New Writing* must go on. I am sure it would have been a mistake, after building something up that has had such a success and is already an institution that people (particularly in the Forces) look to for intellectual food of a kind they can't get elsewhere, to let the war destroy it. If we can keep it going while the fighting is on, it will be much easier to develop its many possibilities in the visionary days to come when paper and labour are no longer a problem.

I quite understand your difficulties about production and publication and would like to co-operate with you in finding a reasonable solution. I think myself, having announced that it was to become a quarterly, we should at least complete a year of it on those lines, i.e. try and get out number 16, as well as a number 15, roughly to time. After that I don't see why we shouldn't allow ourselves more manoeuvring room, always provided that we can bring it out sufficiently often to make people feel it really is a periodical, and to keep the features to some extent topical.

I suggest that we agree, by exchange of letters, to something like this. We will bring out number 16 in the same way, and we will continue it thereafter to its majority, i.e. number 21 (assuming that we will discuss the matter again on the outbreak of peace or the call-up of either of us or a sudden worsening of the paper situation here) but not fix anything more definite about time than that these six numbers – 16 to 21 – should be ready for publication, if not published in the course of two years, that is by December 31st, 1944.

I would like to think out a way of bringing in more unknown writers in the future – a sort of beginners' section. It may need some planning, but I believe it would be an advantage.

John Lehmann to Allen Lane, 26 October 1942

I have been giving a great deal of thought to the future of *New Writing* during these days since our talk . . .

I promised to give you a decision one way or the other by January 1st, and I am keeping to my promise. At the same time I regret that the decision will have to be a negative one, so that the present arrangement will have to come to an end with *Penguin New Writing* No. 30.

As you can imagine, it is a sad decision to make. I liked a great deal of what was in *New Writing*, and I have to a certain extent basked in reflected glory. Hard facts, however, must have their place in this unholy business of publishing, and with the many difficulties which I see ahead, I think it is fairer to all concerned to clear our minds of delusions and face these facts now.

Allen Lane to John Lehmann, 31 December 1946

I should confirm to you, I think, the agreement that we have arrived at, and that is that, because of the sales trend, we shall bring out *New Writing* only three times a year instead of four. This will not, of course, affect our financial arrangements in any way, but the change shall take effect as from No. 33 (already published). 34 is in production at the moment, which will leave 35 for publication at the end of the year.

Eunice Frost to John Lehmann, 5 April 1948

In future it has been agreed that *New Writing* should be reduced from 160 pages to 128 and that as a consequence the editorial payment of £300 shall be reduced by £35 per issue. Overton has, at present, the manuscript for No. 37 and as soon as I am satisfied about the cast off for this I shall ask you to send him his cheque for this reduced amount for No. 37, plus the normal amount for No. 36 on publication, which is now due.

Eunice Frost to Jack Summers, internal memorandum, undated

Following our most enjoyable meeting, Eunice Frost and I have had several talks about the future of *New Writing*, and we brought the matter up for discussion at a full meeting of the Editorial Committee last week.

The points under discussion are simple: you on your side don't feel that you can continue to edit *Penguin New Writing* unless it comes out more frequently than twice a year, as you stand to lose money thereby. We on our side have lost money on every issue for some considerable time, and we don't feel in the more realistic publishing conditions of today that we can afford to increase this rate of loss.

Quite frankly, however it was 'improved' or broadened in its scope, in the very tough field of magazines published today I don't see that we could, without considerable optimism, think of largely increased sales.

In view of this I don't feel that there is any alternative but to close down, and as there is little point in prolonging the agony, I suggest that we should make the next issue, No. 40, the last.

It is with the very greatest regret that we have arrived at this decision: we have at all times been proud to be associated with *Penguin New Writing*, and it is indeed something to be able to look back on ten years of uninterrupted publication.

Allen Lane to John Lehmann, 26 April 1950

This cannot be the place to recall the hopes and enthusiasms of the early days and the excitement of *Penguin New Writing*'s rapid growth during the war: nor to recapitulate the opportunities that wartime development gave us, the enormous variety of readers it brought us, the young authors from all over the world we were privileged to encourage in their early beginnings, and the young artists whose pictures we were proud to reproduce – even at one time in colour. It would take more than two pages, and it would be a pity to spoil a good story; for it is a story, we believe we can say without vainglory, that forms part of the history of our time.

John Lehmann, Foreword to the final issue of *Penguin New Writing*, 1950

* * *

Rieu and the Classics

I tried to telephone you today, but in vain, and am therefore writing in case you are unable to ring me up this evening.

You will, I think, be pleased to hear that I have made an arrangement with my firm which allows me to accept your offer and become General Editor of your new Translation Series from the Greek, Latin and other classics, though they will continue for two years to require my services here for four days a week. This will, I think, give me ample time to undertake your work, and I am delighted to be able to do so. The great point about the arrangement is that I can start for you on November 1st (if you agree) and have not got to delay active work on your behalf until the war ends and Wait comes back, either of which events seem at the moment to me to be pretty remote.

I have prepared with great care a list of some forty Greek and Roman authors who should, I think, be eventually included in the scheme, and I have tentatively selected batches from each series for priority treatment, with your approval. I should very much like, therefore, to meet you and settle all these details, including questions raised by Carrington in a recent talk I had with him and a letter which followed it.

I am also considering a French list and consulting some friends, and I am quite ready to set one or two Scandinavian translations afoot, in particular Ibsen's plays, if you wish it. So we shall have plenty to discuss. Perhaps you could kindly ring me up just to confirm the main arrangements, and to make a date (preferably for lunch with me at the Athenaeum) when we could get ahead with the scheme.

E. V. Rieu to Allen Lane, 19 October 1944

So started the Penguin Classics. In common with many of the Penguin offshoots, it was a risky business that seemed doomed to failure. Translations of *The Odyssey* already abounded, and their total sales figures in the recent, albeit rationed, past amounted to little more than dismal. Rieu's translation, it need hardly now be said, was an instant success, another case of Allen Lane's hunches paying off.

Why should this venture in particular have succeeded so well? Bill Williams, in *The Penguin Story*, suggested that 'Dr Rieu's object was to break away from that academic idiom in which so many of the world's classics have been put before the general reader, and to present them in contemporary English without any transgressions of scholarship or textual accuracy.' Or, as Rieu put it: 'Write English'.

As he translated, he was in the habit of reading aloud each section to his wife, in order to gauge its effect. And Nelly Rieu was herself no stranger to the art of translation: she could claim the substantial distinction of having introduced Babar to an English-speaking audience.

'On every spare evening for over a year, I sat and translated Greek and Latin books to that patient lady, in the best English I could muster as I went along,' wrote Rieu in an article in an early postwar volume of *Penguins Progress*.

I began on *The Odyssey* three years before the second World War started, and completed the first draft as France fell. Home Guard service intervened, and I could not finish the job till 1944. Even so, its revision was undertaken to the sound of V1 and V2 explosions and the crash of shattered glass – an accompaniment which should have chimed in better with the more warlike *Iliad*, and which, I hope, is not reflected in my style. Actually I went back to Homer, the supreme realist, who puts his magic finger every time on the essential qualities of things, by way of escape from the unrealities that surrounded us then – and still surround us in a world of fantastically distorted values.

The 'essential qualities' of both Homer and his translator were widely appreciated.

Would you mind handing the enclosed order for the despatch of three copies (on my brother's behalf) to the right person? You will be amused to hear that the King has accepted the copy I sent him. His secretary writes: 'The King is already familiar with your admirable translation of *The Odyssey* and looks forward to reading *The Iliad*.' What a pity that one must regard this as top secret. I also have a charming note from Churchill. Nothing from Attlee! I must have failed to send him a copy.

E. V. Rieu to A. S. B. Glover, 16 April 1950

I have laid down your translation of *The Odyssey*, read in a great books course. Never before in my life, dogged by unhappy bouts with Latin, did I suspect that anything 'classical' could give me real pleasure. There were moments in Virgil when I knew there were beauties, but the forced labour (and eternal failures) poisoned it for me.

Now I have read 'your' *Odyssey* and have had a real experience. Thank you for opening my eyes to what must have been the essential quality of the minds of those ancient people. It has not only abbreviated the distance between them and me, but, strangely enough, has given me the feeling that I can find my own place in the life sequence thus. Those men and women had a strength to endure, and thank goodness, the gift of enjoying life too. There is something in the tale that includes you, bears you on in its enchantment and yet leaves you with a certainty on which to rest when it has passed on.

I realize that the vividness and the naturalness in the story is your own contribution. Why else did I always reject the standard translations before? Please accept my sincerest appreciation for your marvellous gift to my enlightenment and happiness. I look forward impatiently to your translations of Virgil's *Eclogues* and the *Iliad*.

Harriet D. Adams, Director, Junior Art Gallery Inc., Louisville Public Library, to E. V. Rieu, 8 April 1950

This was exactly the 'principle of equivalent effect' that Rieu strove to achieve in his translations, and those he commissioned: a certain quality in the translation capable of creating the same impression on modern-day readers as the original had on its contemporaries. It is a fine line, for nothing dates a translation and jars so much as yesterday's expressions. Eventually 'some tactical revision', as his eventual successor Betty Radice tactfully put it, was required almost everywhere in the series.

For eighteen years the Penguin Classics grew steadily. Translations from Greek and Latin were joined by virtually every European language, as well as a number of Middle and Far Eastern works. By the time of his retirement there were nearly 150 translations published or in preparation, and Rieu had accumulated a substantial number of academic and literary honours.

Rieu's latter days as editor were marred by an increasing friction with the abrasive personality of Tony Godwin. In Betty Radice's capacity as his assistant it became a principal concern of hers to 'keep the peace between the Edwardian old fogey and the half educated young upstart as they termed each other'. There was more than a difference in age and outlook at stake. Rieu's series had been inaugurated with the specific aim of making the Classics accessible to the widest possible audience, primarily for their enjoyment; and with few exceptions this aim had been met by any standards. In the United States however, it was their educative value that was quickly appreciated. Penguin's principal American market was the colleges, where the privilege of set-book status would automatically guarantee sales in their thousands.

This was not in the mind of the founder of the series, who thought of something enjoyable for the 'general reader' and met with a certain amount of criticism from the academic world; the idea of a 'crib' was somewhat disreputable. Now we know that the Classics are widely used in teaching, and they must be 'useful' as well as enjoyable.

Betty Radice, internal memorandum, undated

She was, therefore, well aware that 'Classical teaching was changing and I saw that there was a great opportunity for the classics to meet new demands if new titles were provided with line references, notes, indexes, bibliographies and fuller introductions, designed for use in teaching courses.' ('A Classic Education', Betty Radice, *Times Higher Education Supplement*, 19 October 1984)

Rieu was equally aware that 'every generation should re-examine its interpretation of the Classics'. But he was long used to having a totally free hand, and working at his own pace and to his own agenda. Tony Godwin was a man in a hurry, and Rieu was beginning to be regarded as an obstacle. Indeed it was not long before change was imposed on the series – the introduction of Germano Facetti's new design: the black spine and colour cover illustration. In April 1963 Godwin's plans to update the series were regarded by Rieu with fury. He immediately wrote to Allen Lane:

I find it hard to believe that you would allow a newcomer to the firm, without discussion with me, its editor, to mutilate a series that you and I had created in 1944 and have since made world famous. However I will not at the moment detail my many reasons for thinking that Godwin's plan (even if it were feasible, which it isn't) would not only lower the standard of the Classics but grievously affect the reputation of Penguin Books . . . About a year ago you told me that you saw yourself and me staying in harness for five years more. That is just what I should like. I cherish the Penguin Classics and want to continue to edit them for you in their present shape: the question of salary is of comparatively little importance.

No doubt these differences played their part in hastening Rieu's decision to step down, which he did in January 1964, though one month short of his seventy-seventh birthday it could hardly be said that he had been forced into premature retirement. Robert Baldick and Betty Radice, authorities on modern and classical languages and literature respectively, were appointed as his successors. Since both had published translations for Rieu, and Betty Radice had worked for some time as his assistant, he could be confident that they would cherish his series as he had. Splendid celebrations attended his retirement, in the company of many of the surviving translators who had contributed to the series – overseen and coaxed gently into being by its creator and mentor.

In 1964, when E. V. Rieu retired from the editorship of the Penguin Classics, we gave a party for him at the Arts Council. Harry Paroissien asked me to get hold of a bust of Homer which, crowned by a laurel wreath, was to be surrounded by a complete set of specially bound Classics we were presenting to Rieu. After a long search I managed to borrow a plaster cast from the British Museum. A few weeks earlier Goya's painting of the Duke of Wellington had been stolen from the National Gallery. As I was staggering along the corridors of the B. M. with the light but huge plaster cast in my arms, doors were helpfully opened by uniformed attendants everywhere, but in the forecourt, where I had my car, somebody shouted: 'Now, now – where's the Goya?' The order for the laurel wreath at Moyse Stevens' read: 'One classical wreath made to measurements of customer's bust.' It finished up on Mrs Rieu's hat.

Hans Schmoller, 9 April 1976

* * *

Robert Graves and *The Golden Ass*

I return the proofs; they seem to be without errors, from a few specimen galleys I have read. Please let me have a revise of the Latin verses I have inserted at the end of the Author's note in volume I, returning original copy. If necessary, to allow for the lengthening of the Author's note, put the quotation from Tacitus after it, instead of before. The verses are not to appear in volume II. I have made out a list of my other books to go just after the title page in both volumes on the page giving the numbers of editions *I, Claudius* went through. Penguins are far more useful to an author as advertisement for his other works than as royalty earners, and I suggest that a select bibliography ought always to figure in them.

Meanwhile, here is a short biographical note to take the place of the one you kindly sent me.

Robert Graves to Penguin Books, 21 January 1941

I have just received a letter from Mr Robert Graves which explains itself. He writes:–

'Will you please ask Penguin whose address I don't know, to send back the prelims to *I, Claudius*, from which they printed without sending me a revise, and so made several shocking misprints, especially in the Latin verses. I should have thought that somebody at the Penguin Pool would have been able to proofread Latin, if they were in too much of a hurry to return the proofs to me.'

May I hear from you in this matter, at your earliest convenience?

A. S. Watt, A. P. Watt & Son to Allen Lane, 4 June 1941

By 1944 Penguin did have a member of staff who could proofread Latin, who had doubtless already pointed out the errors in the early edition of *I, Claudius*. For many years, Alan Glover was to be one of Graves's two main contacts at Penguin. The other was E. V. Rieu who just weeks after accepting Lane's offer to edit the Penguin Classics series, wrote to Graves, fired with obvious enthusiasm.

I am delighted that you are interested.

I have read your admirable translation of Seneca's horrible effort and have tried to judge from that where your tastes would lie. Here are some notes and my suggestions:

1. Caesar's *Conquest of Gaul* is your own. It would make one volume, and I have it pretty high on my list.

2. Mattingley of the British Museum is doing Tacitus *On Britain and Germany*, and will want to follow it up with *The Histories*. But I

don't think he would mind me placing *The Annals* (2 vols.) elsewhere. Do you fancy Tacitus?

3. Horace's *Odes* will I think be rendered into verse by Day Lewis. But his *Satires and Epistles* should make an attractive prose volume.

4. There are Juvenal and Persius too to be considered.

5. Herodotus (2 vols.) is not yet booked up. A very delightful task for anyone who tackles him *con amore*.

6. I am thinking of doing Arrian's *Alexander*, on account not of the greatness of the author but of the theme.

7. Rex Warner is doing Xenophon's *Anabasis*, and Thucydides. That leaves Plutarch, and I don't want him just yet.

I admit that Marsh is excellent, but quite apart from copyright questions, I have advised Lane to go in every case for new translations prepared for the Penguin market.

I am sorry we cannot meet and have a talk, but I have picked out the possibilities I think most likely to appeal to you, and I look forward with great interest to your reply. Time is not of the first importance, though I don't want my own *Odyssey*, which is the first volume of the series and due in 1945, to remain solo for too long.

E. V. Rieu to Robert Graves, 6 December 1944

Graves, however, had an idea of his own, which did not figure on Rieu's list. It was, at the time, a rather controversial choice.

I don't want Caesar for myself, thank you all the same. He was offered only as an example of an author who was not so dry as he seemed.

Will you secure *The Golden Ass* for me? Or is that too barbarous for your public? I am also very fond of Apuleius' *Apology*.

No: Tacitus is so affected that I need him only for information, not for pleasure. But Apuleius was an honest man, and I think that Adlington's superb translation is a bit too Elizabethan for modern reading. But what is the Penguin policy about Classical obscenity?

Robert Graves to E. V. Rieu, 7 December 1944

I am glad to have your choice, though sorry it was not one of those which stand early on my list and which I think it will be easiest to get across to the modern public. I had put Apuleius' *Golden Ass* down for late consideration only, when we had established the series.

However, in view of what you say, I have been looking again both at the original and at Adlington's translation. I agree that the latter will no longer serve, excellent as it was. What I cannot quite imagine is how it is going to shape in modern prose. Will you at your leisure have a shot at it, and when you have satisfied yourself and chosen your style, send me something to look at?

As for obscenities in Apuleius, we are not writing for schools, and I should put my trust in your confidence and skill. The 'Pasiphae' passage in Book X is a bit of a pill. I think you might have to bowdlerize a bit more than our Elizabethan friend.

By the way, I have an excellent version of Ovid's *Metamorphoses* coming along nicely. I think that on the whole this is more likely to find new readers more readily than *The Golden Ass*.

E. V. Rieu to Robert Graves, 15 December 1944

I'll have a go at the first page of *The Golden Ass* some day and send it to you. You need not worry about readers for the Ass!! (You'll sell 200,000 copies.) What you call the Pasiphaë bit is most interesting to me as anti-Christian mockery: apparently Jesus was secretly worshipped as an ass-god by some of his near-Eastern devotees, and the graffiti which are generally regarded as libels are nothing of the sort. They even found an ass-crucifix at Rome. It all develops from the text in Isaiah XXXII 20 which is Messianic. Most translators leave out the Matron's Christian leanings – I write from memory. By the way, why not publish a skeleton Classical Dictionary without which your series won't be complete, using Smith as a basis. It would have a huge sale. (Not for me!)

Robert Graves to E. V. Rieu, undated

I was glad to have news of you.

Very well. I look forward to your tackling Apuleius in November. It is true that I was in no great hurry for the completion of the work, but I was eager to reach the stage when it could be regarded as settled. Actually I am allowing myself to do so now! So don't run off and get yourself done in in a new civil war in Spain.

A slight defect in your handwriting (of which, otherwise, I speak with the greatest respect) leaves me uncertain whether you refer to your new book on Jesus as disgusting or disquieting. In either case I am intrigued and want to know more about it. Don't forget that I shall not forgive a visit from you to London that does not include a lunch with me at the Athenaeum. We have some very good Marsala.

E. V. Rieu to Robert Graves, 7 April 1945

In the meantime, Rieu had already completed his translation of *The Odyssey*.

Translation is admirable and brings out all the charming frivolity of the original.

I read somewhere that Butler's theory of the 'authoress' has Classical support of which he was unaware: Alexandrian said that 'Homer' borrowed most of *The Odyssey* from an Egypto-Greek poetess called Phantasia. There is certainly something in the book which suggests the hand of a predecessor of Aphra Behn, Anita Loos, Amanda Ros and who was it wrote *Gone With the Wind*?

I have recently been thinking about Proteus: he seems to have been an oracular god, ex-demon-of-the-year, living on a sacred island, in a cave tended by orgiastic priestesses – a type common all the way from Leuce off the Danube to Torey Island off the West coast of Ireland; probably at Pharos since pre-gnostic times, brought from Byblos.

Robert Graves to E. V. Rieu, 8 September 1945

Thanks for returning my proofs and for your very kind comment upon my version of that strange little Odyssey, the *Menelaid*.

Translating a man teaches one more about him than ten years' study of text and commentaries at school and at Oxford. And frankly I have never yet succeeded in detecting a woman's hand in Homer – nor, come to think of it, a man's either. He seems to me to have the bisexual prerogative of supreme genius, which is one reason, I think, why I put him higher than the writers of the classical period.

Proteus fascinates me too. Why don't you work up a little study of him. If he is proto-Egyptian, he is another example of the way the Greeks humanized everything they touched. I have been studying what I can of Egyptian literature, with a view to a possible Penguin, but I find it is practically all founded in magic. The Western mind had not begun to work.

E. V. Rieu to Robert Graves, 10 September 1945

I will ask Watt to stop 'pestering' you and when I come round to translating the Ass, I shall not send you a specimen because that is not my way. If you cannot commission a translation on the strength of my other translations, then you will have no more than first refusal of the completed work, which will be saleable elsewhere without difficulty. Possibly Watt has professional pride in not allowing his authors to sell work to a popular-books firm before it has gone to a library edition public. Not supercilious: just Scotch and very shrewd. He has been a very good friend indeed to me since 1921, and I find it best to give him his head.

This is a very hot day indeed but I hope this afternoon to bathe in very clear water in the bay; one can see one's shadow on the rocks below, 5 fathoms deep as one swims.

I was delighted to find that Calypso's island was groved with alder and frequented by sea-crows; this makes an important mythological link with Early British folk-lore. Heigh-ho the heat and the flies.

Robert Graves to E. V. Rieu, 27 July 1946

Many thanks for your letter of July 27.

You did undertake to let me see a specimen of your proposed translation of *The Golden Ass*. However, in view of what you say, we are not going to bother you, and I am asking Penguin Books to negotiate an agreement with Watt, on the understanding that the book will come to about 280 pages in the style of my *Odyssey*, including an Introduction of adequate length.

Don't hurry yourself over the job, much as I look forward to seeing it. As for style you have pointed out to me – not that it was necessary – that you can translate. I will only remind you, if I may, that my series is not designed for scholars, or even for highbrows only, but for the general public, so that both classes of readers have to be satisfied, if possible. It isn't too easy, as I know to my cost, for I am nearing the completion of the *Eclogues* and would often have torn my hair out, if I had any.

Well, the best of luck with a fascinating job. And I envy you your sunshine. We have had the bloodiest summer on record. But I did manage to get away to Ireland for a month.

E. V. Rieu to Robert Graves, 22 August 1946

I have done about one third of *The Golden Ass* (though the *Transformations of Lucius* is the real title) and have been surprised etc. to find how incorrect Adlington's translation was, and how much of the inner sense of the story I missed in my casual readings of it. It really is a wonderful book. I agree with what you say about the need of being contemporary though not topical. I am appalled to find how difficult it is to be modern without falling into US slang (especially when doing the bandits' hide-out part of the story), but it can be done.

There is another moral point which crops up. Apuleius sometimes gets his sentences in the wrong order, unless one can blame the copyists, and spoils his own points. And the logic of Latin prose is not the logic of English. However, I am taking less liberties than Adlington. The obscenity is not impossible by 1946 standards, I find. It is clean obscenity, at least . . . My translation is beginning to read as smoothly as a modern novel, but I have yet to polish it a lot more.

PS We have had four months of sun and are very short of water and green vegetables.

Robert Graves to E. V. Rieu, 1 October 1946

The following is a copy of those parts of Mr Graves' letter which I read to you on the telephone this morning:

'Rieu asked me to help him with the Penguin Classics. I myself suggested translating *The Golden Ass*, a book I have always been interested in: he told me there was no hurry. The job has taken me much longer than I expected and has not been an economical proposition because of the unforeseen expense of living here unless I can also sell it, and get a decent advance, in a hard-cover edition. I had hoped that it could be published simultaneously with a Penguin edition, or within a reasonably short time; but if the Penguin people want to be able to say that it was translated especially for them, this is true and I daresay Methuen would not mind my inserting a note to that effect. One thing is certain, that the so-called obscene passages cannot appear in Penguin because the books sell indiscriminately, but could go in an 8/6 or 10/- volume out of reach of the pockets of minors. And I want the uncensored edition to appear first. You will have the copy in three weeks.'

A. S. Watt to Eunice Frost, 5 September 1947

I have just returned from a magnificent holiday in the South of France, which incidentally looks like being our last excursion abroad for the time being. If conditions permitted it, we should dearly like to come to visit Majorca, although we hear fearsome accounts of the high cost of living there.

Among the matters awaiting my attention on my return was the problem of your translation of *The Golden Ass*. I gather that you are a little perturbed about the possibility of a charge of obscenity being brought against the publication of an edition destined for the widest possible public. I am personally not at all apprehensive on this score, and would be prepared to consider the deletion of the usual libel and obscenity clause from the contract in this instance. My view is that we are publishing for a sophisticated audience, and I would be perfectly willing to justify this policy were it to be brought into the Courts.

In the past certain portions have been printed in the original Latin, which seems to get over the Censor's conscience, and this might be a way out in this instance. I would, however, rather like to see your translation before committing myself on this point. I may say I have had a word with Mr Rieu who feels as I do in this matter.

We are in negotiations with A. P. Watt & Son regarding the contract, and I hope to get this settled within the next few days.

Allen Lane to Robert Graves, 10 September 1947

I'd have answered your letter before, but we have had rather a time. I got a viper bite in the foot, William (our eldest boy) got run over by a car and broke most of the bones in his foot, Beryl had to have a minor but very painful operation. We are really out of the wood now, though Beryl is still abed and Wm. cannot yet walk.

Anyhow, I'm very glad to hear from Watt that *The Golden Ass* pleases you, and that you have come to an agreement with him about it.

As for the bowdlerized edition – if you really think it isn't too thick for the Penguin public (and you ought to know), then naturally I should prefer to have the same translation in both editions. It is not pornographic in the nasty way that Lucian is, or the *oeuvre badin* of many a French *abbé*, but I should welcome a *nihil obstat* from Max.

So glad you got your holiday in before the austerity curtain rang down. Yes, the cost of living has risen 60 per cent since we arrived here, and it was high enough then. At the moment we have no potatoes, bread, flour or any of the staples, and even the black market is not so easily [illegible word] as it was. Best wishes to you both, and to Max [Mallowan] and Agatha [Christie] if you write to them.

Robert Graves to Allen Lane, 1 October 1947

I have read your *Golden Ass* with the greatest delight – an admirable piece of work, which I wish I could have done myself! I understand that Lane, after a talk with me over the phone, has put in for the complete rights. I have no doubt that you heard from Watt. So I need not go into that side of it. But let me hear from you on questions of production. I expect you want the full title on the title page, but will be content with *The Golden Ass* on the cover. Anything else?

Are you fed up with translation or will you consider something fresh – at your complete leisure of course – I am in no violent hurry, for production has lagged far behind my deliveries. I doubt whether you would find Thucydides exciting. But what of Herodotus, whom I have not yet fixed up? And then there is *Daphnis and Chloe*. Or do you think that is too pretty? Do let me hear from you.

I have delivered the *Eclogues* after much sweat and am nearly half way through the *Iliad*, which is incredibly magnificent but by no means easy.

With renewed thanks and congratulations.

E. V. Rieu to Robert Graves, 10 October 1947

On the question of the publication of the Penguin edition unexpurgated, we have spoken to Max Mallowan, and although he is quite willing to adjudicate, he is really terribly busy in getting going in his new job, and says he can't possibly look at it for a couple of weeks or so. At the same time W. E. Williams, our Chief Editorial Adviser, who as you know is prominent in educational circles – he is on the Arts Council, and a founder of the Army Bureau of Current Affairs – has read it twice, and says without hesitation that it would be a crime if we were to cut a word from the edition as it now stands.

Would you in the circumstances still want me to wait for Max Mallowan, or are you willing to accept our feelings?

Allen Lane to Robert Graves, 24 October 1947

Pencilled reply on original letter: 'My dear Allen, All right. Have it your own way. W. E. Williams ought to know. Best wishes. Robert Graves.'

I am really delighted to hear that you approve of *The Golden Ass*; you can appreciate all my problems and sympathize with me.

Yes, the rights are all fixed up now and I am very glad that Lane feels no bowdlerization is necessary.

Yes, I suppose it had better be *The Golden Ass*, but only on the cover. I leave production to you.

Sorry, I have no more time for translations. I am writing a Utopian novel, a collaboration in a 16th Century historical novel about the She Admiral Isabella de Barreto, and collecting my essays on poetry. Your *Odyssey* has been very much enjoyed by my wife as well as by me. Looking forward to the *Eclogues*; I hope you have a good translation of Theocritus, by the way.

Is there a decent translation of Plutarch's religious essays available? It is my greatest need at the moment. Is there an original text in print anywhere?

Robert Graves to E. V. Rieu, 7 November 1947

Many thanks to you and Lettice for your Thackeray Christmas Card – poor Victorians, by 45 they had one foot in the grave – something to do with the way they dressed perhaps? Or was it too much food and church-going? Anyhow –

W. P. Watt – Tweedledee to A. S. Watt, noble Tweedledum (who has had an operation on his eyes and is more or less retired) – writes to me that he can't get any reply to two or three letters he's sent you about *The Golden Ass* contract and thinks that 'an author of my standing' shouldn't be treated so. I'll write to dissuade him from taking any violent action in the matter, but if you could stir up someone in the Contract Department to provide him with what he wants, I should be grateful, because, between you and me, he writes as though you'd spoilt his nice new rattle. Please! And soon!

An agent of such standing . . . a publisher of such standing . . . an author of such standing . . . An Ass of such standing . . . a rattle of such standing – Heigh-ho! tonight the three Kings come and fill the children's shoes, Father Christmas having already filled their shoes to overflowing . . . Children of such standing . . .

Robert Graves to Allen Lane, 5 January 1948

The Golden Ass was published in the Penguin Classics in April 1950. The following year, Penguin issued their own hardback version – a limited de luxe edition of which the entire 2,000 numbered copies were first sent out to Majorca to be signed by Graves. The book was seized by Australian Customs and prohibited in Ireland, on the grounds that it was 'indecent or obscene'. This decision could, under the Irish Censorship of Publications Act, 1946, be appealed. This was never considered a worthwhile proposition; banning was a fairly regular occurrence with Penguin publications, so much so that it had long ceased to have the slightest publicity value. Nor did it have any noticeable effect on sales, which continued uninterrupted in Britain and elsewhere.

I haven't got the de luxe *Golden Ass*, but the ordinary ungilded one is fine.

Translating the Four Gospels eh? I've been doing nothing else for the last nine months, but it's a recension rather than a translation, in about 500 pages. I daresay you know that according to Menaeus the way they wrote the Gospels was to take the [illegible word] and shuffle the texts about in order to prove special doctrinal or political points. I have stumbled on the clues for restoring the correct sequence, and what a much better story it makes.

By the way: doesn't the Fourth Gospel sometimes make your stomach turn over? It's even more dishonestly written than the whitewashing of King David in I Kings. As for 'Epimanondas', the stupid editor of Matthew who misreads glosses, and Telescope Timon the literary wizard of Luke who makes a mad nonsensical sequence of five or six separate parables found under the same subject heading!

Matthew, Mark, Luke and John –
What a show you sure put on.

Robert Graves to E. V. Rieu, undated (April 1952)

Thank you for sending me Graves' letter. I share your own uncertainty as to what exactly it means, but one morning when the weather is not quite so hot I will put a wet towel round my head and think it out and then I will have a word with Williams and Frosty about it. At any rate we will write to him as soon as we can.

A. S. B. Glover to E. V. Rieu, 30 April 1952

* * *

Dorothy L. Sayers and Dante

By one of those happy coincidences that occasionally delight the world of letters, Miss Sayers's enthusiasm for Dante reached its climax just at the time when the Penguin Classics were launched. She had written *The Mind of the Maker* and *The Man Born to be King*, and had translated *The Romance of Tristan*. To bring Dante home to English-speaking people in all his moods, from the homely and humorous to the terrible and the sublime, was perhaps an even greater task. It called for a poet, and it has found one.

From the blurb to *The Divine Comedy*, Penguin Classics, 1949

So it was that in March 1945, some time before *The Odyssey* was published, Dorothy L. Sayers set out to visit its translator E. V. Rieu, with an early draft of her Dante translation.

'Dorothy Sayers had arrived in Highgate for lunch with her script of Dante, stayed to tea and then to dinner, still talking, and just when we were about to offer her bed and breakfast said she must go.' (E. V. Rieu, quoted in *The Passionate Intellect*, Barbara Reynolds, 1989)

Rieu, having read the thirteen cantos of translation, had no hesitation in accepting it for the series; 'It is full of fire, swift movement, poetry and vigour, and above all, for my purpose, it is clear.' (ibid.)

With pleasure! – though I shall have still more pleasure in autographing *The Divine Comedy* when the time comes. I think it is very courageous of you to venture in it, and only hope it will not unplume all the Penguins and destroy the nest! The reviewers of *The Odyssey* don't seem, so far as I have read them, to be paying much attention to the idea of the series *as* a series, which is tiresome of them, because it really is an exciting venture, and particularly well-timed, just when we are being exhorted to get together with other nations.

Dorothy L. Sayers to Allen Lane, 22 February 1946

Dorothy L. Sayers: Agreement

Thanks for your note of March 1st. It goes a little against the grain to drop the approval clause in any of my agreements, but as I think we are agreed that Miss Sayers's Dante will do well and must be swallowed whole, so to speak, I feel I must climb down in her case.

E. V. Rieu to Allen Lane, 2 March 1946

Dorothy L. Sayers's Dante translation was to dominate her life for more than a dozen years until her untimely death in 1957, the translation still incomplete. It was a long and arduous task – a true labour of love, of 'intellectual ardour'. The first part of *The Divine Comedy* was delivered to Rieu almost exactly two years after their first meeting. What immediately followed was not a well-earned rest, but renewed intellectual exercise of a quite different kind: taking on the Penguin staff in general, and Hans Oberndorfer in particular, in a prolonged series of sorties and attacks, gradually shaping the printed text into as close an approximation of her ideal as was possible.

In March 1946 she had written to Rieu 'setting forth very lucidly her ideas on the style and layout for her Dante', which Rieu passed on in due course to Glover: 'A few specimen pages would enable her to complete the annotation of the Cantos to the required length and also to write an introduction which would not cause the book to exceed a total length of 256pp., which is, I suppose, your maximum for profitable production.' The paper situation, a prime consideration in 1946, had eased somewhat by the time the book was published. Her translation ran now to 348 pages, spiced with extensive notes and commentaries which might confirm Julian Symons's observation that 'An originally admirable desire for accuracy in details became pedantic . . . as was often the case, she mistook accuracy for art.' (*Sunday Times*, 14 March 1993) This might well be true, but few pedants surely ever took such an obvious delight in their quest for perfection, or attacked the task with quite such passion.

I know all about the bottle-necks in the printing trade, and all about Bernard Shaw's 90th birthday, and all about the sudden death of H. G. Wells and the necessity for celebrating his funeral with ham and sherry and memorial volumes. I do not want to argue that Dante is a greater man than Wells and Shaw rolled into one – I want only a specimen page, or else a simple postcard saying "500 words to the page", or whatever it is. And I want the typescript. NOW. Dear Mr Rieu, will you please convey my modest requirements to Mr Oberndorfer in "winged words", such as may penetrate his apparent stupor and bring about action . . . You might remind Mr O. that there is a Vestibule to Hell, in which persons unable to bring themselves to any decision run perpetually, stung by wasps and hornets.

Dorothy L. Sayers to E. V. Rieu, 18 September 1946

'Would it not be nicer if we used single quotes?'* enquired Hans Oberndorfer in all innocence on 30 May 1947.

And now I tune my brazen throat
To sing in harsh, emphatic strain
With what abhorrence, rage and pain
I contemplate the Single Quote.

I hate it. For one thing the eye slips over it too easily (especially when it is combined with the beastly modern habit of insufficiently indenting the beginning of a paragraph) and may easily miss it altogether. Dante is difficult enough already, without our conspiring to prevent people from seeing where dialogue ends and narrative begins. Since indentation is impossible in verse, clarity on this point is the more essential. Never mind your house-rule, or the look of the page – we want to be intelligible; and anyhow, we can't be frightfully aesthetic with all the lines numbered and economy margins.

Moreover, I think the Single Quote is ugly in itself. It looks an ass if it comes up against a final apostrophe – so much so, that one sometimes harks back, wondering whether it is a misprint.

And it looks a thundering ass when it comes to quotes within quotes. A mimsy pale Single Quote trying to enclose and contain a fat black Double Quote reminds me of a negro baby whose woollies have shrunk in the wash.

I can truthfully say that I never read a book where the Single Quote is the rule without consciously or subconsciously noticing it and resenting it, like something scratchy next the skin. It is an offence to me. I cannot away with it. I see you have allowed Mr Rieu Double Quotes all through *The Odyssey*, and I claim as much for Dante. I will not have him put upon!

Dorothy L. Sayers to Hans Oberndorfer, 2 June 1947

Thank you for the proof. Yes, this looks better; we are getting on.

No, no! You must NOT "delete the headline on page 1"! What would become of the valuable information "Maundy Thursday, night"

* It was at this time becoming Penguin's house style to use single quotation marks, and then double quotation marks for quotes within quotes.

which now appears there? That night is over by the time we get to page 2. Do pray recollect: –

> These are not "headlines", added to conform
> To some time-honoured, quaint, aesthetic norm,
> But "running heads", compendiously designed
> To aid the reader and improve his mind.

If you really think that by the time the reader gets to this page he will have forgotten what book he is reading, you can either add: INFERNO *under* the running head and above CANTO I; or you can cut a dash with the paper, and stick INFERNO all by itself on the recto of the preceding page.

I quite agree that "INF. I" looks awful. (If Mr Rieu would have allowed me to call the book "HELL", which is the proper English title, we should have been spared that the choice between the truncated "INF." and the over-long "INFERNO" – however!) My own preference would be to remove it altogether, and simply display, at the beginning of each left-hand page, "CANTO I", followed not by a dash, but by a colon, introducing the contents of the page in a different type, thus:

CANTO I: *The Dark Wood – Good Friday evening*, etc.

All the *reader* needs to know is what canto he has got to and which bit of Hell. But I suppose, if I ask for this, a howl will go up that the printers will then not know which book they are setting, and that the binders will cheerfully mix the sheets up with those of *The Iliad*, or *Rosmersholm*, or whatever else happens to be lying about. Yet I see books all about me in which the printers and binders are left without the assistance of any heading at all to remind them of what they are supposed to be doing, so it must be possible for them to get over this handicap. After all, a remembrancer could be set up over each desk to assist them:

> The title of the book you have to set (bind)
> Is The INFERNO – please do not forget; (please bear this in mind);
> The English word is HELL, so you will know
> In case of doubt, exactly where to go.

You are going to send me paged galleys, aren't you? There will, I fear, be a number of corrections to allow for. I keep on thinking of improvements to make in the text, for greater elegance and/or clarity. I have just thought of two in this canto!

Dorothy L. Sayers to Hans Oberndorfer, 14 July 1947

Around this time, Hans Oberndorfer the Penguin production manager was eventually pressed to take desperate action – a 'translation' of his own:

I don't know whether I should be proud of so successfully concealing my previous identity or not, but I am afraid that for better or worse I am the same . . .

John Overton to Dorothy L. Sayers, 22 October 1947

I am very glad to know you are still yourself; that was my first impression, but I was shaken by the disappearance of two praenomina, and a control over the form of your handwriting which should qualify you for a distinguished career in forgery if the printing profession should ever grow wearisome to you . . .

Dorothy L. Sayers to John Overton, 23 October 1947

It is as you know increasingly the accepted practice to use single quotation marks as far as possible where they are necessary in printed texts and to use double quotation marks for quotations within quotations or where for other reasons it is necessary to make distinction and this is the rule we now generally follow in all our publications. At the time we printed *The Inferno* we were not so consistent and in this as you know double quotations were normally used. Unless you have any strong feelings in the matter we would propose in *Purgatorio* to use single quotations and to make the change in *The Inferno* to single quotations when the book is next re-set. I will take it, unless I hear from you to the contrary within a few days, that you have no objections to this course.

A. S. B. Glover to Dorothy L. Sayers, 27 January 1954

URGENTLY IMPLORE DEMAND INSIST DOUBLE QUOTES PURGATORY INFERNO AS BEFORE STOP DEEPEST PASSIONS ROUSED WRITING
SAYERS

Telegram, Dorothy L. Sayers to Penguin Books, 28 January 1954

It may perhaps be partly the temperature which at the moment is about 28 degrees below zero Centigrade, but I feel that I am in a very low position in the Inferno after receiving your telegram. I was not aware of your interesting correspondence with Mr Oberndorfer (now Mr Overton) on the typographical details of *The Inferno* or I would never have raised the point in my letter. Of course you shall have your double quotes, though you will allow us here to maintain our opinion that you are all wrong and dreadfully outmoded. None the less like Voltaire although we hate everything you think, we are quite willing to die for your right to think it; all the more willing to die since you presumably still have some vacancies to spare in Paradise, but have now safely filled up Hell and Purgatory and our post-vital adventures can therefore be counted on to be pleasant. I am unearthing your correspondence about Hell and we will give it careful study before *Purgatorio* goes to the printers. No doubt some points will arise that will call for deep and bitter protests on both sides, but the first round is yours.

A. S. B. Glover to Dorothy L. Sayers, 28 January 1954

Many thanks for your swift and sympathetic reaction to my impassioned telegram. If you were to look up your files, you would find, I think, an equally impassioned letter on the same subject, in connection with the *Inferno*, which was printed as it now stands at my earnest solicitation.

Only over my dead body shall such ditches and hurdles be placed in the way of readers toiling through a work which already presents intrinsic difficulties enough. Punctuation marks and other diacritical signs are surely intended to make things easier for the reader, and not to bitch, bugger and bewilder him. When I die, you will find the blessed, unambiguous, but rapidly disappearing double quote written on my heart. And I know many other persons, engaged in reading or writing works of scholarship and criticism who would emphatically endorse what I say.

I am deeply grateful to you for so kindly respecting my wishes. If my representations could persuade you to turn this "accepted" into a "rejected" practice, I should feel that I had struck a blow for English letters!

Dorothy L. Sayers to A. S. B. Glover, 29 January 1954

It was the start of an all-too-brief friendship between like minds.

Thank you for your letter. Strictly between ourselves and provided you will not use this confession in evidence against me, I have a good deal of sympathy for your remarks about double and single quotes. My own feeling has always been that it might be a very good thing if we could introduce the Continental practice of square quotes instead of the common English ones whether double or single, thus avoiding any possibility of confusion with apostrophes, but we have never yet felt at Penguins that we dare to be so revolutionary.

One day I hope that you and I will have an opportunity of going over the Recording Angel's big book jointly and making a few suggestions for the improvement of the celestial record keeping.

At any rate, if you do find any single quotes left by error in the proofs of *Purgatorio* you will now know that accident and not design put them there.

A. S. B. Glover to Dorothy L. Sayers, 2 February 1954

Throughout 1954 the proofs were corrected, and the text polished and perfected. Odd points were regularly raised and answered, which then led off at a tangent:

– Mr Collins (was it?) said that you (was it?) had objected to the phrase "older version" of *Deus summae clementiae*, saying that it was not a "version". I am not quite clear what the objection is, but please alter it if you feel strongly about it. [Sayers]

– As for the Latin hymn I have forgotten myself what the point was that I raised about it, but on looking at the proofs as they now stand it seems all right to me. I always get so infuriated with those abominable Jesuits who spoilt all the best hymns in the seventeenth century that any remote allusion to anything they did tends to infuriate me. [Glover]

– The trouble with the Jesuits is that they are post-Renaissance – it was the Humanists who killed the living Latin. However, let us remember that comforting remark of somebody's: "We are commanded to love our neighbour, but not, thank God! to like him". [Sayers]

As part of the preparations for the publication of *Purgatory*, John Curtis from Penguin Production wrote, once more in all innocence of previous correspondence, to enquire of Miss Sayers how she was progressing with writing her blurb.

Dr Rieu is a wicked old man, who has basely deluded you. He knows perfectly well that I have never written my own blurbs and never will, because it is a corrupt and degrading practice, and I could not do it without my tongue in my cheek.

I am, however, willing to indicate the lines on which somebody else might write the blurb for the *Purgatory*.

In the first short paragraph you will flatter the reader into buying the book by indicating that this, the tenderest and most beautiful of the three parts of the Comedy is the one that most endears itself to really intelligent Dante-lovers, and that by buying it, and subsequently boasting of having read it, he will immediately distinguish himself from the common herd who only know the *Inferno*. (You can pinch some phrases for this from the first page of the Introduction, where I have put it all nice and handy.)

In the next paragraph you will say that all the scholastic philosophy and stuff has been explained, for the modern reader, with that lucidity of which I am a master – but that anybody who knows it already or can't be bothered with it can easily skip the footnotes and things, owing to the admirable way in which the volume is arranged.

In the third paragraph, you can say how awfully well I do this kind of thing, and that good as my translation of the *Inferno* was, this is even better.

To this effect, sir, after what flourish your nature will.

Dorothy L. Sayers to John Curtis, 5 May 1954

Dorothy Sayers died suddenly, shortly before Christmas 1957 – and so it happened that Barbara Reynolds found herself following her friend's footsteps – both literally and metaphorically:

My visit to Dr Rieu in his house in Highgate is still vivid in my memory. It was the first time I had met the originator of the Penguin Classics. We spoke of the tragic interruption that had occurred. 'We want you to finish *Paradise*,' he said, coming straight to the point. I was horrified. Being still in a state of shock and grief, all I could do was to expostulate at some length. He let me have my say. Then, looking at me over his glasses in a shrewd but kindly way, he spoke one word: 'Try.'

Barbara Reynolds, *The Passionate Intellect*, Kent State University Press, 1989

I knew Dorothy Sayers so well, especially in connection with her Dante work, about which she talked to me and wrote to me a great deal. And to all of this I listened, a most interested and delighted but quite passive receiver. Then, so suddenly and unexpectedly, I had to take over and convert my participation from passive to active. The task of completing the translation came at a time when I was very heavily committed and the only hope of accomplishing it lay in tackling it immediately, while conversations with her were still fresh in my mind and the imprint of her personality still vivid. This I did, mostly by forgoing sleep, and if the book presents anything approaching a satisfactory blend of two minds and styles, it is because of the very unusual circumstances in which it was produced.

Barbara Reynolds to David Duguid, Editorial 2,* Penguin, 21 February 1961

* * *

Pevsner and The Buildings of England

'To the Inventor of the ICED LOLLY'

Dedication by Pevsner in *Bedfordshire, Huntingdon and Peterborough*, Buildings of England BE34, 1968

I think I will start with the prehistory of the King Penguin books which is how I got into the Penguin outfit and it's a very characteristic Allen story. What happened was that the King Penguins were started just before the war and they were edited by a very brilliant young woman, Elizabeth Senior. They brought out Redouté's *Roses* and they were very good; and I signed the contract to do something on illuminated manuscripts. Well, then some more books came out and the colour work was atrocious, so I wrote a polite letter to Elizabeth Senior and said I wanted to contract out of this because the books were not good enough.

* The commissioning editorial department at Penguin was (and is) known as Editorial 1: the copy-editorial department as Editorial 2.

Well, Elizabeth Senior was killed by a bomb and the correspondence must have gone back to Penguin Books. Allen must have seen it and in a very typical Allen fashion he wrote to me and said, 'I see you find that the King Penguins aren't good enough: can you do better?' So I wrote back to him and said, 'No, not in that way because the basic mistake is that the series ought to have a technical editor as well as a library editor,' and this was done. Fishenden's services were obtained and all went well after that; so I was literary editor for a number of years, getting a little fee for each volume. At that time Penguins were still so small, relatively speaking, that we had actual meetings on King Penguins once a month, with Billy Williams, and Eunice Frost, of course.

I must say there was a difference between meetings in the morning and meetings after lunch, because after lunch everybody was rather gayer, but rather less responsible. I had intended to do a King Penguin on certain excavations in the Far East by a French archaeologist called Shafer in a place called Agarit. When I brought this up it was Billy after lunch who said 'Agarit, oh bugger it', and that was the end of it and I could never get this through. On the whole though the decisions were right. In fact my own King Penguin on *The Leaves of Southwell* was a spectacularly bad seller.

The war came to an end and optimism amongst publishers was enormous, because paper was again there and everyone was starved for books. The Lanes asked Lola and myself to come for a weekend at their house, Silverbeck. We were sitting in the garden and Allen said, 'You have done the King Penguins now and we are going on with, them, but if you had your way, what else would you do?'

I had my answer ready – and the answer was very formidable, because I outlined both The Pelican History of Art and The Buildings of England on the spot: each about 40 to 50 volumes. Allen Lane said, 'Yes, we can do them both,' and that was the end of the meeting.

Sir Nikolaus Pevsner, from a taped interview

Is there any chance of getting the use of the Austin 10 again for a very short time, partly because I find that on the guide books for the boroughs of south London, travelling by buses etc. takes far too long, the boroughs being so very much bigger than north of the river, and partly because I have reached a stage in my driving lessons when I feel that sitting next to Lola and asking her hundreds of questions would help me a great deal. I want, of course, to get through my test in time for the next county which will be some time during late summer. We could pick up the car at Harmondsworth and deliver it back there.

Nikolaus Pevsner to Allen Lane, internal memorandum, 11 June 1946

Here is the cheque for the 5,000 frs. and also coupons for 21 gallons of petrol, the balance of what I was granted and did not use. What is going to happen next Spring? Do you think there is any chance of getting the petrol permit for Cornwall? It cannot be done with less than 60 gallons plus the journey, which is long. I suppose we shall have to start applying about Christmas, and I hope you will help. It is a case of all or nothing; for a county just cannot be done with less petrol or without a car.

Regarding the car, she has been like a lamb since the repair I had done. But here are still the following things which need attention, according to the mechanics who have seen it:

The direction indicator does not work

The spare wheel has a puncture

The solenoid (is there such a thing?) is broken and needs replacement.

I should be grateful if Mr Smith could examine it thoroughly. I shall of course if I get petrol start in time reminding you of the date at which I intend to go on tour. It's probably going to be March 28.

Nikolaus Pevsner to Allen Lane, 5 October 1947

Many thanks for your letter of the 5th and for your cheque for the francs and the petrol coupons. I certainly think that in the New Year we should start to work on the authorities for sufficient petrol to enable you to proceed with the Cornish Guide. I think it will be a good thing if we can get the Middlesex volume into such shape that we can show it as evidence of the type of book we are doing, and a useful point might be that such a series would prove of considerable interest to the tourist trade, which the government is obviously very interested in encouraging.

We intend to have the car thoroughly overhauled this winter. At the moment my Rover is in the hands of the best garage I know. The engine is being taken down completely and rebuilt, and the body work repaired and repainted, and I intend to do the same thing with the Wolseley, which is, I consider, an extremely good job for your purpose.

Allen Lane to Nikolaus Pevsner, 9 October 1947

Just a line to commemorate the fact that on my guidebook tour of Notts I passed through West Drayton today and duly noted in three lines what little there is to be said. Nothing like our West Drayton.

The tour goes well, although I am this time all alone with the big machine. She is very nice and obliging to use and only occasionally makes protesting noises.

The tempo is again a little frightening – I mean of work, not of driving – but my slaves have done their jobs well, and there is little library checking I have to do at this stage. It's all checking with my own eyes. One church in ten deserves enthusiasm, and they are by no means always the famous ones. The big houses like Welbeck and Thoresby I have not reached yet. Villages range from full (?) character, almost Dutch, to prim suburban colliery estates.

I'll be back in less than three weeks, ready to start on the office jobs for the Notts volume: notably the masses of checking letters to vicars, 'occupiers', My Lord Dukes, Venerable Archdeacons, public librarians etc.

Remember me to Lettice and the children, and of course to Eunice, JO, JT, Mr Glover an' all.

Nikolaus Pevsner to Allen Lane, 8 September 1948

WEST DRAYTON

St Paul. Nave and chancel in one; Norman masonry apparent. The S doorway with a scalloped label-moulding and zigzag on front and soffit above the one order is in a very decayed state.

The Buildings of England, *Nottinghamshire*, 1951

I forgot yesterday to give you the left-over petrol coupons from Nottinghamshire. I hope you can make good use of them.

In the meantime you will have heard Mr Smith's tale of woe, and in a way we are quite glad that he has seen for himself what remains the one serious snag about the CMJ 615. As soon as she goes she goes so well that even I without any previous experience have not once had trouble during the month in Nottinghamshire and as soon as she is in use every day she starts all right too. But when she has been out of use for some time there is just no starting her. When we were in Cornwall in the Spring we had to pay garages every morning for the first four days and when I arrived in Nottinghamshire exactly the same thing happened. Now this time I have had her at a good garage for a while because I succeeded in making several scratches and dents, and then she had to come back and stand in front of our house for a week. The result, unfortunately, Mr Smith has seen.

My suggestion would be now that when the Rover is back, an Austin specialist should get her for the one purpose of discovering this starting trouble. Don't you think this should be possible? As I hope to use her again next Spring it would mean a lot to me if there were not those initial difficulties and I would be willing to go fifty fifty on the investigation. Would that suit you?

Nikolaus Pevsner to Allen Lane, 9 November 1948

My two volumes are emphatically not drafts but intended for setting. However, they could not, at this stage, go to the printers because we are still waiting for sample pages. Glover's amendments refer chiefly to such matters as cross-referencing, which, in such an elaborate job, would probably have to be gone over in the galley proofs anyway. I am seeing him tomorrow to discuss with him that he should go over the Cornwall one from that same point of view as well. It is true that he has pointed out one mistake but then where would Glover not be able to find one mistake? The rest of his suggestions are very valuable but mostly technical things. Incidentally, he says that he is surprised there is no mention of London Airport. My reason was, of course, the complete absence of permanent building. However, do you think some reference to size and length of runways, etc. should be made? I should be glad to have your views.

PS Glover is absolutely wonderful. Here is one of his points. 'Hanwell, London County Mental Hospital. The name of this is, and has been for some years, St Bernard's Hospital.'

Nikolaus Pevsner to Allen Lane, 7 November 1949

The logistical problems of getting to and around each county – begging a petrol ration, then a car, organizing an itinerary, visiting each town and village by day, and writing up notes into a first draft each evening and night – was an exhaustive and exhausting process in itself: 'I should now fill the rest of this page with nice human bits, but it's no good. The journeys just are not human. To bed 11.00, 11.30, too tired even to read the paper. Up this morning at 6 to scribble, scribble, scribble. If only one could be proud of the result.' But even this paled in comparison both to the earlier preparatory work involved, and the task of finalizing and setting each book.

The preparatory work is described by Pevsner in the final volume in the series, *Staffordshire* published in 1974, four years after Lane's death, and some eleven years after the death of his wife, Lola – both of whom 'helped as long as they lived'.

I have often been asked how the volumes of The Buildings of England came about. Their genesis is the same every time. An assistant first spends a year or eighteen months full time on reading and extracting the literature on one county. The first assistants were German refugee art historians, Mrs Schilling, Miss Schapire, Miss Bondi. I could not think of others competent to do the job. Then the Courtauld Institute of Art began to produce the right type, and ever since nearly all the assistants have come from that source. Nearly all are mentioned in their respective volumes. Armed with files of extracts written by one assistant, her or his county is then travelled by me, and what I see is described. The early volumes are slimmer than the later and were moreover printed in larger type. The reason for this is plain enough. I knew less, and the assistants knew less. The most valuable sources were not tapped, because we were in ignorance of them.

For nearly thirty years during which the series was in preparation, Pevsner was both witness to, and the victim of, the fundamental changes that inexorably took place in post-war England. At one time he could travel around an area throughout the day, then seek out a modest hotel for the night, with no need to book in advance. 'Is it that there are more tourists around? Undoubtedly, but it seems in fact rather the commercial travellers, the reps, who have multiplied. Can social investigators explain?' And, even more pertinently, no longer were churches left open and unattended all day. 'The reason is growing vandalism, and nothing else.' At the same time of course he was eloquent witness to physical, concrete, change:

It is not only the appearance of buildings which has changed in the course of my Buildings of England years, it is also the appearance of the town and the countryside – the towns by high blocks of flats, often unneeded and nearly always unwanted by those who have to move into them, and by speculative centre renewal, i.e. usually shopping precincts without interference by car traffic. Some of these precincts are architecturally good, some of them are bad, most of them are indifferent. In the country the principal changes are the murder of the local train routes and the abandonment of tracks and the appearance of the motorways. One got used to them quickly, and it seems odd already now that only twelve years ago I sacrificed one of my hundred illustrations to so rich a county as Northamptonshire for the purpose of showing the M1.

As ever, the foreword ends with an appeal for readers to point out errors and omissions. 'I know by now to the full how many mistakes I have made and an unsuspecting publisher has published. The next round will be revised second editions. The publisher is ready for them, an excellent reviser is busy. The more of these improved volumes I shall see the happier I shall be. Don't be deceived, gentle reader, the first editions are only *ballons d'essai*; it is the second editions which count.'

For the very first editions, the substantial onus fell mainly on Alan Glover. It was hardly surprising in the early days, while the overall style and approach of the series was still in a state of flux, that occasionally tempers would fray. Glover's encyclopaedic knowledge, in every subject from church dedications to London Transport, was to prove invaluable: 'Osterley Park station was so called under the form of Osterley Park and Springrove until about 1913, when the name was changed to Osterley.' Gradually, over the course of several years, a mutual understanding and appreciation was to develop between the two.

I am looking at the specimen pages that have been set up for the guides and will let you have any comments together with the others here.

Don't you think that the National Grid references will look rather ugly set under the place names in the text? Would it not be a better idea to give them in the index in brackets after the name of the place concerned? Surely by the time anybody has got to the reading of the text itself, he will no longer be interested in the National Grid references. It is when he is looking for the place that it will be of use to him. I take it, incidentally, that you will be adding these National Grid references to the copy at your end.

A. S. B. Glover to Nikolaus Pevsner, 24 March 1950

Middlesex, page 90, Harefield

You will remember that you quoted a Greek inscription on a tomb in the church at Harefield. I was suspicious of this and queried it on the galleys. You crossed out my query and left it as it was. I was still suspicious of it on the page proofs and queried it again, but the query was again crossed out. Even so my suspicions were not laid to rest so I had the bad taste to ask Mr Collings to go to Harefield and look up the inscription. As I suspected it was wrong, two letters having been left out which made all the difference between meaning and meaninglessness.

A. S. B. Glover to Nikolaus Pevsner, 4 June 1951

Here are the eight boroughs back with very little comment. As a fellow resident of Hampstead I did my best to catch you out here, but as you will see I have had to give you best. Your contemptuous dismissal of West Hampstead is the hardest blow I have had to endure for a long, long time. I will return to Marylebone as quickly as I can. It has just come to me.

A. S. B. Glover to Nikolaus Pevsner, 27 November 1950

In 1951 the first volumes in the series began to appear, and continued regularly, despite Pevsner's other trifling ways of passing the time as stated in this early biographical note: 'He is Slade Professor of Fine Art at Cambridge, Lecturer in Art at Birkbeck College (University of London); Editor of the Pelican History of Art and the King Penguin Books; an Editor of the *Architectural Review*, and one of the most learned and stimulating writers on art in England.'

Apart from writing thirty-two of the forty-six volumes in the Buildings of England series, and co-writing the rest, he also wrote *An Outline of European Architecture* and adapted his *Pioneers of Modern Design* for the Pelican series; in Peregrine *The Englishness of English Art*; he helped compile *the Penguin Dictionary of Architecture*; and of course wrote *The Leaves of Southwell* for his King Penguin series.

The Buildings of England series was never profitable. Nor, in truth, was that Allen Lane's first consideration; as Pevsner observed:

> Somehow it seemed to a literary editor like myself that he really accepted the book because he believed in the book and he fervently believed in the educational possibilities of books of my kind and accepted them, and somehow or other, the money was there . . . I can only repeat that I have never seen him put finance first and the quality of a man or a book second.

Regular losses were borne for as long as possible, but by the end of 1954, after eleven volumes had appeared, there was a pause for serious thought and a search for sponsorship.

> The publisher has lost on these books heavily ever since we started them. His loss is, in fact, on an average as high as £3,000 a volume. This actually stands to reason for with the length and illustrations which these volumes have, profit would only become possible if 20,000 were sold immediately. Instead, Penguin Books sell six to eight thousand quickly and then continue very slowly. In addition, there is the research organization which although very small comprises one full time and two half time assistants, a secretary and the occasional work of a geologist, a prehistorian, and a photographer.

At two volumes a year he estimated that another sixteen years was required to complete the task.

In 1957 the interrupted flow started once more. As Pevsner explained in the foreword to *Northumberland*:

> After striving to find some way out of this impasse the immediate problem has been solved by a generous grant from the Leverhulme Trust which will provide for the cost of research; Birkbeck College of the University of London at the same time accepted the responsibility for administering the grant. In addition Messrs Arthur Guinness, Son & Company Ltd have placed at the publisher's and my disposal a substantial sum with which to cover part of the production costs and establishment expenses particular to the series.

But this was only part of the story. What followed was referred to by the Hon. C. M. Woodhouse, briefly Penguin's chief editor, as a 'generous decision'.

> Somebody in your department has been ingenious enough to dig out the original contract for The Buildings of England. According to this I would receive a royalty from the middle of this year onwards.

However the contract also stated that by that time I would have finished the whole country. As I have only just reached the half-way mark I have arranged with Sir Allen that the whole contract is cancelled. The result of this will be that I have not broken a contract and that you don't owe me royalties.

Nikolaus Pevsner to Jack Summers, 30 May 1960

In a possible rehearsal for his own eventual retirement, Lane discussed with Pevsner the possibility of setting up a Buildings of England Trust. It never happened, and Pevsner continued until the Buildings of England were complete, and a start made on the Buildings of Scotland as well as Ireland. Just occasionally it was with wavering enthusiasm: 'The two volumes I shall tackle next year, however, will be unrelieved hell: Lancashire.'

* * *

Misprints

I can assure you, as the result of long experience, that things can drop out anywhere; I am not at all sure that sometimes, after a book has been finally printed, letters don't drop off the page.

A. S. B. Glover to Glyn Daniel, 7 September 1959

Germinal, page 46, line 3. For 'bit-bottom', read 'pit-bottom'.

Instruction to copy editors on first reprint.

I see that in the publicity matter of some of your November books, I appear as Glyn Jones. It's the difference of one sound (like ermine and vermin), but if this can be altered in the future I'd be glad.

Gwyn Jones, 1940: author of *A Prospect of Wales*, King Penguin; editor, *Welsh Short Stories*

George Bernard Shaw had once told his printers, the Edinburgh firm R. & R. Clark, that a single misprint upset him more than the death of his father and sister, 'with whom I am on good terms'. He was not alone in this sentiment – but then it did, very much, depend on the misprint in question.

I recently received copies of the Abyssinian book (*Guerrilla War in Abyssinia*) which I thought very well produced. There were a certain number of misprints, the worst of which was a reference to Colonel Wingate in 'a shapeless wet toupee' instead of topee! This certainly ought to be corrected in the reprint. I have not got a copy of the book with me now but it comes in the last ten pages – in the account of the Italian surrender at Ajibar.

PS We are in the midst of a coup d'état here at the moment.

Captain W. E. D. Allen, Press Attaché, British Legation, Beirut, to Eunice Frost, 22 November 1943

Your letter of November 22nd has just reached me. I admit the error about Colonel Wingate is rather horrifying, but it can be put right when we reprint, which I think very possible as the book has gone extremely well.

Eunice Frost to Captain W. E. D. Allen, 13 December 1943

In dealing with an organization capable of changing 'some pretty standardized blocks of flats' to 'some good-looking standardized blocks of flats' and of changing '2/9 of £900 = £200' to '2s. 9d. of £900 = £200', arguments about the meanings of words are perhaps a waste of time. Presumably, however, you can grasp the principle involved: it is not just that it is generally understood that no changes shall be made in a book unless the author is going to have a chance to inspect them; after changes had been made at an earlier stage, I received your personal assurance (see your letter of May 31) that I need fear nothing of the kind that has in fact been pulled on me.

Stanley Alderson, author of the Penguin Special *Housing*, to Dieter Pevsner, 28 November 1962

Mistakes were not confined solely to the printed text – and the Puffin Picture Books, along with every other series, could boast its faithful band of more fastidious readers. In this case the original letter of complaint, from a young boy, does not survive; Kathleen Hale's reply does:

What a nasty little boy Christopher must be – nearly as horrid as my own sons, though not quite, since they pointed out more than one discrepancy.

Anyhow, those circus tickets weren't made of cat, they were of the usual cardboard variety and got blown by the wind to Orlando's other side. (What excuse did you give?)

If any other precocious monster should ask why the men and women on page 6 are basking on their balconies when it is obviously winter, tell them that they are having an affair, and feeling rather hot.

Kathleen Hale to Eunice Frost, 28 December 1941

* * *

An Auden Selection

The poems in this volume are arranged more or less in the chronological order of their writing: the first dates from 1927, the last from 1954.

I am sceptical of all attempts to draw the line between what is poetical and what is not, whether in theme or in treatment. However such frontiers may differ, they all place some poetry outside the pale which I like too well to surrender. I can understand, for example, the arguments which have led some critics to disapprove of *Lycidas*, but if they tell me they *dislike* the poem, I find it difficult to believe them.

On the other hand, the sensibility and experience of every poet set bounds upon his own writing which he cannot transgress without making a fool of himself. I admire and envy those poets who have such an instinctive sense of what they can and cannot do that they never write anything for which, subsequently, they will have to blush. Though I hope the years have taught me some caution, I fear I shall never be among them.

I have been taken to task, and rightly, for employing such rhymes as *law* and *door*. The trouble is that in the speech of many middle-class Englishmen born south of the Border and educated at a public school and Oxford or Cambridge, they do rhyme. Thanks to my residence in the United States, my ear has learned to wince, and I promise not to do it again.

W. H. A.

I am delighted that you have been able to send me your MS so very quickly. There are several things that I would like to be able to discuss with you, though, and I am wondering whether you are likely to be in England before too long or whether you would prefer me to write to you about them.

In particular perhaps I should say that I had hoped for a longer Introduction. And in view of your textual alterations would you feel it reasonable to refer to the changes you have made since, without any such comment, I fear we are only too likely to be attacked by purists pointing out how and where our edition differs from the Faber versions. Then, too, oughtn't we to mention the original books from which all the poems have been taken?

A meeting would make it very much simpler and easier for us to discuss these points but if you will not be in this country for some while then I can send you a letter in fuller detail.

Eunice Frost to W. H. Auden, 12 February 1957

I ought to have answered your letter of Feb 12th (EEF/JB) long ago, but I have been very occupied.

I shall not be in England until the middle of next month, when I hope we can have a meeting and discuss the points you raise.

In the meantime, may I say:

(1) As regards the Introduction, I feel it is unseemly for a writer to jabber on about his own work. I know the French do it, but I find it embarrassing. Besides, if there is any room to spare, I would much rather add a few more poems.

(2) Textual alterations. If any reader happens to notice a difference between the Penguin text and the original, I imagine he will attribute the change to me, not to Penguin Books. If, however, you think it worth while adding a sentence in my preface to the effect that some of the poems have been revised, I have no objection.

(3) Since the poems are in chronological order, it hardly seems to matter in which book they originally appeared. Again, I will do whatever you prefer in the matter.

W. H. Auden, in Italy, to Eunice Frost, 13 March 1957

When the book was published in August 1958, there was no Introduction: just the briefest of notes, almost hidden at the foot of the list of Contents:

NOTE

The poems in this volume are arranged more or less in the chronological order of their writing: the first dates from 1927, the last from 1954. Some of them I have revised in the interests of euphony or sense or both.

W. H. A. 1957

* * *

Triffids

Before I tell you the real purpose of this letter I do want to let you know what an absolutely fascinating experience it was for me to discover you as a writer. I found it impossible – as the cliché goes – to stop reading *The Day of the Triffids* and even more so *The Kraken Wakes*. Both I and my colleagues are immensely enthusiastic about the fact that we are going to be able to put them into Penguins. You may know, perhaps, that we are planning to publish *The Day of the Triffids* in January.

What we want to do, on the cover of the book, is to have some little pictorial illustration since I believe that something visual – in conjunction with the title – could be very helpful.

Of course, on the half title page of the Michael Joseph edition there was a little thumbnail drawing taken – I rather imagine – from the American edition. Or am I wrong? It seems to me that perhaps we might do a little better than this, and although you do give a quite detailed description of what one of your triffids looked like, I thought I would like to ask you whether you have ever sketched one out or would like to do such a thing – even in the roughest form – from which we might do a finished drawing? It may be, of course, that you thought the Michael Joseph one entirely satisfactory, but it does seem – in some details – that it contradicts your description.

Just to show you how differently everybody imagines these triffids I enclose some of the very roughest of rough sketches by some members of our staff here who couldn't resist the desire to nail down the Triffid.

Eunice Frost to John Wyndham, 21 October 1953

Thank you for your letter of the 21st and the pleasure of hearing that you are intending publication of *Triffids* for January – Mr Lusty had told me on the telephone that he and Mr Lane had spoken of the matter, but he also added in a somewhat vasty manner 'probably in 1954'; so the imminence comes as a pleasant surprise.

It was most kind of you to write so enthusiastically about both the books; and from the source of so many books. It is always such a pleasure to be told one has entertained – particularly with these imaginative excursions where he always has the haunting misgiving that he may have got just on the wrong side of acceptability in places. Besides, it encourages one who is thinking: 'What the devil am I going to do this time? – can't destroy the world for a third time in four years.'

For my part I can only say that my honour of being recognized by Michael Joseph's mermaid could only be exceeded by my presentation to your penguin.

Regarding the aspect of a Triffid – and I do think it is an excellent idea to have a small illustration of one – I am in some difficulty. Any rough ideas I may have had some time ago have since been overlayed by other people's, and become composite.

In the description I gave them leaves to rustle because I wanted some audible sound of approach. That turns out to have been a mistake pictorially; if they are given many leaves, they invariably start to look domesticated, which isn't what's wanted.

The Joseph version was the original English type. I don't think it is at all bad, except that it could well have a sting and a little more action and venom about it. I'm not sure that the one from your office marked 'A' wouldn't do very well, given a little more flexibility it could be more decorative than the others. However you may well feel that something more aggressive is required, so I enclose a selection of types with the suggestion that from this array you should select what seem to you the most telling features, and get a craftsman to put them together. (Of course what is really wanted is something capable of

Hybrid triffid developed by Penguin production staff from John Wyndham's sketches.

being simplified effectively in a kind of colophon way – which is just what we don't seem to have here.

I am sorry to feel that I have not been as helpful as I ought to have been after your very kind letter, but I do hope that a draughtsman may be able to solidify some satisfactory kind of creature out of these.

John Beynon Harris (John Wyndham) to Eunice Frost, 24 October 1953

All your Triffids caused a lot of talk and pleasure here. Our Production Department has developed – from them – the one which we would rather like to settle with the slight variation from the design which I am enclosing that the head will be more bell-shaped. I do hope you approve, and that you will be kind enough to send it back to me right away, since I should like to be able to rely on having it by me to work with on Monday.

Somehow most of your own drawings made the Triffids look too cosy and even endearing. In any case, it's difficult to make any drawing of a Triffid seem as inimical as your own description.

Eunice Frost to John Wyndham, 13 November 1953

I must apologize for the delay in returning the enclosed drawing of a Triffid – it had to be forwarded to me here in Derbyshire, and the word 'Urgent' seems not to have registered. I do hope this has not caused you inconvenience.

The compromise that your Production Department has made is just the sort of thing I hoped they would be able to evolve. My only criticism would be yours – that the head should be more bell-shaped. It is rather like a cut-off hose as it stands.

John Wyndham to Eunice Frost, 20 November 1953

Very many thanks for returning the Triffid drawing. I must tell you that I had begun to get rather anxious since we are working to a difficult schedule, and I am only sorry that I had to chase you into the heart of Derbyshire with the problem.

I am so glad you think we have brought it off. After all, though, it is a very composite Triffid, and what you did to help was invaluable.

Eunice Frost to John Wyndham, 25 November 1953

Thank you very much indeed for the advance copy of *The Day of the Triffids*. It was very kind of you to think of it.

The little drawing has come up well. I imagine it should be well up to its function, which I take to be a pause, a figurative scratch of the head, followed by a 'What the . . .?' So let us hope a lot of them look inside to find out.

I am enclosing the second copy, signed for Sir Allen Lane.

John Wyndham to Eunice Frost, 15 January 1954

* * *

Bosoms and Bottoms

The most familiar feature of the Penguin look is, of course, the avoidance of pictorial covers. In America the lurid cover is considered essential for securing mass sales of paper backed books; and in this country also, most of the cheap reprints are presented in picture covers. It has often been urged that Penguins might do better business if it conformed to this general practice; but whatever truth there may be in that supposition, the decision has been made, as a matter of taste, to reject the American kind of cover.

W. E. Williams, *The Penguin Story*, July 1956

By the time Bill Williams's celebratory review of Penguin was published (with its photographic covers in full colour), the first regular use was being made of an altered cover grid in the fiction series to allow room for a small black and white illustration, suggestive of the contents of the book to the browsing customer. What is more, Penguin were already planning the issue of certain fiction titles with pictorial covers.

It has long been regarded almost as an article of faith that Allen Lane despised lurid covers – by which he meant colour illustrations of any kind – and referred to them dismissively as 'bosoms and bottoms'. Yet it would appear that in the long debates on the subject he held with Williams, the impetus to use such covers was actually Lane's. Pictorial covers were still assumed by both to be inextricably tied up with fiction of a type which Penguin had tended to leave to their rivals. Nevertheless, the discussions allowed Williams to introduce his own, rather unexpected agenda:

I give you notice that I am going to make a further determined effort to talk you into an entirely new series called Penguin Westerns. The appetite for Westerns in this country is already strong and I believe it could be increased if we went all out to popularize Westerns on a new basis . . . Also, I would concede you, at last, the picture covers you are secretly pining for. I would get Schmoller to do us a grand new cover in a new colour and I would go all out on the title Penguin Westerns. I could promise you, too, a really high standard of literary product. I am, I suppose, the only Western addict in the firm, and I guarantee that there are far more first-class Westerns to be found than there are first-class Detective stories. Why not have a go? None of our competitors has tried this line yet, and here is a chance to steal a march on them.

W. E. Williams to Allen Lane in Iraq, 20 April 1953

These private talks developed into the prospect of exploiting this very market which they had studiously avoided, and a Penguin offshoot referred to contemptuously by Williams as Parrot Books – a phrase often used by Lane when disparaging his rivals – was proposed. It was not adopted immediately, and Williams could honestly state in *The Penguin Story*:

The dominant motive in the firm's endeavour is to provide good reading for people who have acquired a sound taste for books. For those who lack an habitual appetite for reading, Penguins have nothing to offer; they do not deal in those products which aim to excite and contaminate the mind with sensation and which could be more aptly listed in a register of poisons than in a library catalogue.

In a long memorandum to Williams, Lane compared Penguin with Lilian Baylis's Old Vic Theatre, and, more to the particular point under discussion, the BBC. 'As Sir Ian Jacob had no difficulty in reconciling the Light Programme and the Third Programme within his organization, so we should not consider it impossible to embrace series as wide apart as the Pelicans on one side and light fiction in glossy covers of the Pan/Corgi variety on the other.'

The memo continued:

When Lilian Baylis devised the [Old Vic], she, I think, must have had an attitude similar to our own in our early days in that she set out to provide the plays that she considered that the public should have at a price they could afford, and that in order to do this, her overheads were cut to a minimum, and no one, including the stars, drew anything but the most modest of salaries. The whole thing in fact was run on a shoestring in the same way as Penguins was in its early years at the Crypt and Great Portland Street, and later here at Harmondsworth, which was at that time a sort of glorified warehouse.

The Old Vic when it went across the river changed all this . . . In the same way we ourselves have changed from our policy of the early days as publishers of reprints which we felt were up to our standard, into publishers of original work setting standards as high as any reached by any publisher, including the University Presses, of our generation.

When Lilian Baylis was struggling in her early days, I am sure that the box office, when the company was faced with a difficult financial time, must have put forward suggestions, that if, without lowering standards too far, they could bring in a little more sex and perhaps show a leg from time to time, they would do much better, in the same way as our travellers and some of the critics suggest that a little more breast and bottom, if possible in colour, would do a great deal to relieve our financial tension when it exists. Some time ago I suggested that there was a lot of money to be made if we lowered our sights and produced a series outside our existing Penguin/Pelican range, into which we could put such titles as we knew we could sell but which we didn't want to have associated with our existing imprint . . .

At the present time, our standards from an editorial or from a production view are higher than they have ever been, and I think that it would be a considerable mistake to do anything which would alter this position, and I continue to defend our policy, when faced with such criticisms as we have been receiving lately on having missed the bus over the war books. At the same time, if it is now felt that we should, in addition to our Third Programme, as exemplified by Pelicans, the Scores and Buildings of England, or our Home Programme, as represented by Penguins and Puffins, add a Light Programme on the lines of Bantam, Avons, Dells, Pans or Corgis, and that this could be encompassed without injuring our Penguin/Pelican relationship, I am not opposed to the suggestion, although I think it should be borne in mind that this policy has led to the chaotic conditions among paperbacks in America, and which I fear may well come in this country as a result of the rapid increase in competition in books of the cheaper literary content.

Allen Lane to W. E. Williams, 21 February 1955

In his similarly detailed reply, Williams added:

There is one imponderable which troubles me a great deal. If we set out on Parrot Books we should do it with every intention of keeping the bird from contaminating the other birds in our aviary. But despite that intention, might there not be a pressure of various kinds – e.g. of production and handling which might militate against the enlargement and improvement of our present series? You remember Gresham's Law which lays down the theorem that bad things tend to drive out good. As you see, my present disposition is to doubt the wisdom of Parrots. You and I never feel any sense of shame about changing our minds, and so I find no difficulty in recording these doubts. It is only by coming back again and again to these ideas that we will find the right answers in the end.

There still remains the other possibility: viz. an experiment in colour covers with Penguins only. I cannot see for the life of me any objection to our coming out with a few coloured covers – just to see what would happen in the trade. Is it worth considering, for example, whether our Penguin Westerns, now agreed upon, should not be used for an experiment of this kind?

There is an obvious logic in choosing them. I think, indeed, it would be regarded by the publishing trade as a further example of Penguin initiative and Penguin willingness to try everything once. There is no need to look further at present; but if we found that Penguin Westerns with coloured covers were a thumping success, we might decide to put all our green-backs into colours.

W. E. Williams to Allen Lane, 2 March 1955

The influential artist and graphic designer Abram Games was recruited as consultant art director in 1956 and the experiment took place. Whether or not they looked to America for inspiration, these covers undoubtedly had a stylistic resemblance to the Signet and Mentor editions published by Victor Weybright in the States, which were in turn a development of the US Penguins of the war years. A few Westerns and other titles, thirty-three in all, duly appeared in full colour livery, unannounced and unsupported by virtually any publicity. Games himself provided a number of highly regarded covers: 'probably the first fully pictorial paperback covers in England with any kind of artistic integrity and a sense of adventure'. (*Typographica*, June 1962) It was a relatively short-lived experiment however, and was abandoned as much for reasons of cost as the fact that it tended to have the opposite effect to that intended:

As far as I can see the unanimous opinion within the firm is that we should desist from coloured covers as soon as possible. There is now evidence from many quarters that those of our titles which wear this kind of Joseph's Coat are not being treated as proper Penguins by most booksellers and are finding their way into the miscellaneous racks of lurid covers. We can all comfort ourselves anyway by the fact that we have given this conception a fair trial, but I do not think it would be in our interests to persevere with it.

W. E. Williams to Allen Lane, 23 July 1957

The subject was still not dropped altogether. Under the supervision of John Curtis Pelicans, Handbooks and Specials and the new Modern Classics all began to announce their presence on the shelves in a much more enterprising fashion and both photographic and full-page cover illustration were much in evidence by 1961. 'Parrot Books' were revived late in 1958, in a compromise based on the repackaging of existing popular titles under the guidance of an advertising agency. Amidst considerable agonizing over 'cheesecake', 'financing the good by mass selling of the inferior' and 'loss of prestige', the idea was abandoned with the books in production. Tony Godwin would ultimately complete the move from purely typographical covers, appointing Germano Facetti to oversee the exacting task of attuning all Penguin series to the rapidly changing marketplace of the 1960s.

It is our policy to produce books that are not only good but also good-looking, and in the last year or two we have emphasized this principle by many innovations in the appearance of our series. It is a fallacy to suppose that good design costs more than bad, but what it certainly does call for is a progressive Art Department which can produce, for example, book covers in the best contemporary idioms of graphic design.

Allen Lane, Chairman's Statement, 18 April 1962

* * *

Obscene Libel

. . . Mere pornographic literature, the filthy, bawdy muck that is just filth for filth's sake. Probably you ladies have never seen such a work, except, perhaps, by accident. Some of the men, in their younger days, may furtively have glanced at the literary output of Port Said and felt rather ashamed of themselves afterwards . . .

Mr Justice Stable, from the summing up in the prosecution of Secker & Warburg and *The Philanderer* for obscene libel, July 1954

By the time Penguin started publishing, the law relating to obscene libel was already out of date and in growing disrepute. In anticipation of the 'wives and servants' argument of the *Lady Chatterley* trial, a rule of thumb operated that while it was generally acceptable for a slightly risqué book to appear in hard covers at a correspondingly high price, its mass sale in a cheap edition rendered it liable to prosecution. In the particularly repressive climate of the mid-1950s, however, even price was no guarantee of immunity. Virtually any work, whatever its supposed literary quality, could, on the basis of just a few words in the text, become prey to the 'common informer', seizure and prosecution. Unfortunately at this particular time a whole rash of 'difficult' Classics, including L. W. Tancock's translation of Zola's *Germinal*, were in preparation. Despite the seriousness of the situation, Michael Rubinstein was unable to avoid a small, rather Freudian, joke.

Germinal, by Emile Zola

It should be axiomatic that a book recognized throughout the literary world as a Classic will not be suppressed on the grounds of any alleged obscene libel even under the impetus of the present campaign. However, immunity on the grounds that a novel by Zola is such a Classic cannot be taken for granted, and one is reminded that Zola's first English Publisher was imprisoned as well as ruined in the late Victorian Era, to the tastes of which the authorities seem to be reverting. For this reason I think we must take seriously the possibility that passages in this translation of *Germinal* might give rise to a prosecution.

You will be aware that the definition by which a book is judged is that of Cockburn C. J. in 1868, 'the test of obscenity is this, whether the tendency of the matter charged as obscenity is to deprave and corrupt those whose minds are open to such immoral influences and into whose hands a publication of this sort may fall'.

Having read *Germinal* with this definition in mind, I must advise that passages on the following pages would certainly not pass the test: 42/43, 95, 108, 115/123, 142, 145, 326, 339/340, 357/359 and 374. I have little doubt but that the translator has been reasonably faithful to the original text, and it could hardly be alleged that the motives of either the author or translator were other than creditable, yet the fact remains that in law all, or any of these passages could be held to be obscene, and might lead to prosecution. I am loathe to advise any emasculation, but the danger must under existing conditions be regarded as a practical one, and you will no doubt wish to consider with the translator some modification of the passages to which I have called attention.

On a number of pages vulgar words are printed on the principle referred to in the Introduction. I don't think the publication of these words would in itself lead to any trouble.

Michael B. Rubinstein to Elizabeth Knight, 11 May 1954

A meeting was held with Tancock to discuss the problem, with the upshot that Penguin resolved to take the risk by not interfering with the translation, or, as Tancock put it: 'Sir Allen offering to stand by my side in the dock.' Glover's reply was typical: 'When we are walking around the exercise yard at Wormwood Scrubs we will be able to tell each other what nice people we are. I will of course pass on your message to Sir Allen who is always ready for a fight if a fight is pressed on him.'

Germinal appeared, but the police did not. After a few weeks Tancock wrote tentatively: 'So far I have heard no mutterings about obscenity, but admittedly I have not had my ear to the ground. Judging by the accounts of the recent *Decameron* case, the line taken by the prosecution is that if a book is sold in a respectable bookshop it is classical literature, but if it is sold in a shop that also deals in surgical goods it is pornography. If that is to be the case we are all right, I think.'

Rabelais

In view of possible Swindon cases, Doctor Rieu has asked me to point out any particularly earthy passages, but this I can't do. The book is full of smutty and realistic language: bollocks, roger, screw, tool, john-thomas, etc., etc., and there are plenty of passages both sexual and lavatorial. I haven't toned it down, though I have avoided one or two very ugly words, such as that stand-by of the Public Bar, f**k. I think we agree we can't translate Rabelais in any other way: Urquhart certainly didn't. But if you want to give the book to your solicitors to read, they'll have to read it all.

J. M. Cohen to A. S. B. Glover, internal memorandum, 20 September 1954

As they did. Michael Rubinstein would have been failing in his duty had he not pointed out the numerous passages likely to cause problems. In the particular circumstances of the times, the publisher was faced with a real dilemma, for the law offered no certainty, only risk. With regard to a quite different book under consideration at the same time, Desmond Flower, of Cassells, in an internal memo copied to Penguin, summarized the problem as succinctly as was possible: 'In my opinion there is nothing obscene in this book, and Penguin's Solicitor is merely covering himself because no one knows what the hell is going on in these prosecutions.' About Rabelais Rubinstein was, of necessity, more circumspect:

The crucial question is whether such risk attaches to a new translation of this work, which is known to every schoolboy as one of the masterpieces of French literature. You will recall a recent reversal on appeal against an Order for destruction of *The Decameron*. The copy seized in that case was an expensive one (£3.3.0. if I remember rightly) and so deemed out of reach of the purses of young persons whose minds might have been 'corrupted and depraved'. On the other hand it had been on sale in a shop mainly retailing cheap novels, many of which were ordered to be destroyed as obscene, having been seized at the same time. Undoubtedly the Penguin series of Classics has established itself as fulfilling a need amongst serious students of literature, but at a price which would make it readily available to an adolescent seeker after pornography – clearly a class of persons whom it is an object of the present campaign to 'protect'.

While in these circumstances it would be impossible for a mere lawyer to go so far as to advise for or against publication of this book, at least one may hazard the opinion that the prestige of your series of Classics should save you from any charge of intending to publish obscene literature as such. On the other hand if the book were to be seized from a shop where it was on sale alongside pornographic publications which were not classics, the Director of Public Prosecutions might feel obliged to include your Company, and at least one of its directors among the parties to a prosecution.

Michael Rubinstein to A. S. B. Glover, 12 October 1954

The Classics were not alone in causing dilemmas for the Penguin editorial staff. Ironically enough, the earliest opportunity to print the word 'fuck' had arisen in 1947 in Morris L. Ernst's *The Best is Yet*, which Penguin were reprinting. Ernst had successfully defended *Ulysses* and other censorship cases in the States: the word was simply used in the context of these cases in his memoir. In Britain, the legal advice was perfectly clear: if prosecuted they would be convicted; but whether they would actually be prosecuted was entirely a matter of conjecture. The Penguin edition compromised with 'f---'.

'What cowards you people are. See your page 116,' wrote Ernst, to which Glover could only reply: 'And as for our page 116 – we know we are cowards, horrible cowards: we only wish we weren't . . . But our lawyers assure us that if we do, any policeman or Wesleyan Methodist who happens to read the book, will immediately become a common informer and tell the Home Secretary, who will then proceed to prosecute us, collect very heavy damages, and not use his profits to reduce our Income Tax, so I think we must leave it as it is.'

I checked up with W. H. Smith on their action in regard to *Woman of Rome*. It would appear that all that has happened is that copies of the book have been removed from their open shelves, and are held for those customers who definitely ask for a copy on loan. I asked them precisely why this action had been taken and got the answer that it was because the police were supposed to have made some gesture of a menacing character towards Harmondsworth. At the time of writing it all looks like a storm in a teacup.

Fred Warburg, Secker & Warburg, to Eunice Frost, 11 May 1954

Towards the end of 1957, Penguin published the first paperback edition of *The Philanderer*, by Stanley Kaufmann. Added to the end of the text was Mr Justice Stable's summing up in the 1954 trial.

I do not suppose there is a decent man or woman in this court who does not wholeheartedly believe that pornography, filthy books, ought to be stamped out and suppressed. They are not literature . . .

But in our desire for a healthy society, if we drive the criminal law too far, further than it ought to go, is there not a risk that there will be a revolt, a demand for a change in the law, so that the pendulum will swing too far the other way and allow to creep in things that under the law as it exists today we can exclude and keep out?

Members of the jury, that is all I have to say to you. Remember what I said when I began. You are dealing with a criminal charge. This is not a question of what you think is a desirable book to read. It is a criminal charge of publishing a work with a tendency to corrupt and deprave those into whose hands it may fall. Before you can return a verdict of 'Guilty' on that charge you have to be satisfied, and each one of you has to be satisfied, that that charge has been proved. If it is anything short of that, the accused companies and individual are entitled to a verdict at your hands of 'Not Guilty'. Members of the jury, will you consider your verdict?

The jury returned verdicts of NOT GUILTY in respect of all the accused.

In the uncertain climate leading up to the 1959 Act Penguin, despite their claim in court and elsewhere that only complete works were published, occasionally forestalled possible problems by cutting texts. Gide's *If It Die* was published with two short omissions, indicated 'by a space and the word [omission]'. And it was only in 1968 that Paul Turner's translation of *Daphnis and Chloe*, published in 1956, was issued complete. In *Penguin News* there was a brief announcement: 'Former Penguin editions of this third-century Greek novel, the prototype of all Arcadian love-stories, were, we regret to say, bowdlerized. Paul Turner has added the missing passages for this new edition, in which the text is unexpurgated.'

1954, 'a true annus mirabilis for the Home Office: there were five prosecutions against reputable publishers, a new drive against homosexuals, a notable crop of hangings, and the Secretary of State's torch of Liberty was handed on from Lord Kilmuir to Lord Tenby' (Roy Jenkins, *Encounter*, October 1959), ended on a more positive note with the formation of a Committee composed of frustrated authors, publishers, critics and lawyers under the Chairmanship of Sir Alan Herbert. With the formation of a Select Committee, the publication of a report and the necessary preparation of a draft statute, after several false starts progress towards a change in legislation came eventually to apparent deadlock. The decisive moment came with the somewhat bizarre intervention of Sir Alan Herbert, announcing his candidature for the East Harrow by-election on an Obscene Publications Bill ticket, which set the wheels in motion once more. Eventually Roy Jenkins's Obscene Publications Bill became law in 1959, with the crucial provision of allowing expert evidence in future prosecutions to prove literary merit intact.

* * *

Lady Chatterley's Lover

A Landmark in Evil

There has been brought to our notice within the last few weeks a book which we have no hesitation in describing as the most evil outpouring that has ever besmirched the literature of our country. The sewers of French pornography would be dragged in vain to find a parallel in beastliness. The creations of muddy-minded perverts, peddled in the back-street bookstalls of Paris are prudish by comparison. The book is by one of the best known of modern English novelists, Mr D. H. Lawrence. It is entitled Lady Chatterley's Lover.

John Bull, 28 October 1928

From its first appearance in 1928, Lawrence and his best-known work suffered such vilification, and more – the book was pirated, bowdlerized, banned and seized. Though a certain notoriety was inevitable, through an accident of history the book was thrust into the glare of publicity as the harbinger of an age to which it had no direct relevance – and for which, according to many outside, and one or two within Penguin, it lacked the necessary credentials. The book was forever dislocated from its own time, becoming permanently associated in the popular imagination with Penguin Books. Even Penguin shares, offered to the public soon after the book's appearance, were known in the City as 'Chatterleys'.

In the Penguin archives at Bristol University, under Penguin number 1484 there is a small, bland file containing nothing of any particular significance. The large and comprehensive files, taking up two full drawers of a filing cabinet, are still kept locked away at Harmondsworth.

Few prospects are more daunting than describing yet again events so well

The Book of the Trial of the Book: Rolph's erudite exploitation.

known as to have achieved mythic status. And not just Allen Lane or Penguin myths – those many stories told to friends and journalists so often that over the years they have grown and developed and finally acquired a life and meaning of their own. The trial was, of course, reported extensively at the time and is still referred to today. It has been recreated on television. It has been the subject of books – not least by Penguin who capitalized on the trial itself with a full and detailed account, edited by C. H. Rolph, and issued with the customary speed of a Penguin Special on 2 February 1961 (and with the less than customary green cover). The same book, in hard covers, designed by Hans Schmoller was published in a limited edition of 2,000 as Allen Lane's Christmas book of 1961. Each copy was signed by Lane and numbered, with the message:

Some of my friends were concerned because they did not receive a card from me last Christmas, and wondered if they had been forgotten. As a matter of fact, I have taken one of the few vows of abstention in my life, and have resolved that I will no longer burden the December mails with expressions of wit and sentiment. Instead of a card, I propose, as the spirit moves me and the occasion warrants, to send a book or keepsake, the current offering being a limited edition, printed for private circulation only, of *The Trial of Lady Chatterley* which includes as an appendix a report of the House of Lords debate on the motion to ban certain works of D. H. Lawrence.

It was a subject on which there appears to be very little left to say. Yet it remains a pivotal event in the history of Penguin Books, and is of undoubted significance when examining social and cultural change in the 1960s.

By a combination of perspicacity and good sense, all the papers relating to the trial were retained by Michael B. Rubinstein, of Rubinstein, Nash & Co., Penguin Books' solicitors at the time. Originally founded in 1825, in October 1994 the partnership, then Rubinstein, Callingham, Polden and Gale, was finally dissolved on the impending retirement of its principals. In an act of altruism and generosity, Michael Rubinstein donated all the records to the Penguin archive at Bristol University. Together with the Penguin files these papers help recreate something of the sense of urgency and moment that the book's progress towards publication held for all concerned.

It is hardly necessary to sift the printed and available evidence of the many witnesses who appeared for the defence, nor to speculate yet again on the approach of the prosecution which appears to be so much like incompetence – but, conducted by persons of such conspicuous competence, it seems that their approach could only have been inspired by deep reluctance, or some agenda that will remain hidden. C. H. Rolph pointed out in the Introduction to the *Trial*: 'The decision to prosecute was a great surprise to many in the world of publishing – and of the law. There were many books, some of them much in the news, that had seemed more likely targets.' It was more likely that the reasons for the choice of *Lady Chatterley's Lover* as the test case were mostly negative: 'there was nothing and no one in the legal machine able or willing to stop it'.

PARLIAMENTARY QUESTION FOR WRITTEN ANSWER

FRIDAY 5TH FEBRUARY 1960

QUESTION – Dr Alan Thompson: To ask Mr Attorney General, whether he will give an assurance to the board of directors of Penguin Books Limited, that their forthcoming publication of *Lady Chatterley's*

Lover, by D. H. Lawrence, will not be the subject of criminal proceedings.
Member's Constituency: Dunfermline (La.)
ANSWER – The Attorney General: No.

I passed on the gist of our conversation of yesterday to Allen Lane and Bill Williams (of the Arts Council as well as Penguins) this morning. We all agreed in being grateful for your initiative, and wishing you well in organizing a deputation to ministers on behalf of *Lady Chatterley's Lover* if you decide to do so. Naturally any or all of us would be willing to be associated with such a deputation if that would help to reinforce the case, but equally willing to stand aside if that would be preferable.

Lest we appear to be lukewarm in supporting your initiative, I would just like to make our personal feelings clear. Allen Lane is not anxious to add unnecessarily to the publicity the impending publication of the book has already had: in other words, we are not seeking a *succès de scandale*, and we would like to see it come out in exactly the same way as any other book in the series. Bill Williams, with a long experience of deputations to Ministers, is doubtful whether a deputation would make the slightest difference. I was personally impressed by the arguments you put to me yesterday, particularly about the latent official hostility which you suspect. In sum, we would not urge you into action on our own account, but we would give you every support if you think it the best course.

C. M. Woodhouse to Dr Alan Thompson, 29 April 1960

The first edition, of 200,000 copies, had originally been contracted to the printers Hazell, Watson & Viney. In view of shopfloor protests and the risk of prosecution, Elliott Viney was obliged, reluctantly, to inform Penguin that his company could not undertake the order. Penguin had to change their plans rapidly, and the first printing was transferred to the Bristol firm, Western Printing Services Ltd.

Perhaps it would be for your future possible convenience and mine were you to be informed thus early that a subsidiary printing company of the Group of which I am Chairman will be helping the well-known and highly esteemed Penguin firm in the printing of *Lady Chatterley's Lover* for the coming anniversary of the death of Lawrence.

Sir Allen Lane of Penguin has been put in a very difficult situation by the decision of Hazell, Watson & Viney to discontinue the printing. It was put to me as a matter of principle that – particularly with a firm of the standing of Penguin – it is not for the printer to act as censor, making impossible of achievement (or even more difficult) the decisions of publishers to publish, who after all take the prime responsibility.

As a publisher also myself I take precisely that line. As it happens, the firm in question – Western Printing Services – are very full of work, and it is therefore clearly as a matter of principle that the action is proposed by the Directors of that Company, and that I have not discouraged them notwithstanding whatever public position I may occupy.

I am writing not to ask you any questions, but rather to place on record at the time my reasons and the facts – should it be that later, questions are asked in the House.

I. J. Pitman to R. A. Butler, CH, MP, 21 April 1960

Once a new publication date had been set for 25 August and announced in the press, speculation began to mount, culminating with a visit by Sir Allen Lane to Scotland Yard, at their invitation, on 4 August, before leaving for holiday in Spain.

A period of frantic activity ensued, co-ordinated for the most part by Hans Schmoller, the most junior Penguin director, and Rubinstein. An immediate meeting was arranged to discuss the choice of junior and leading counsel. Lists were drawn up of people to contact, and 'paperbacks available on bookstalls with lurid covers and blurbs'; review copies were recalled and advance orders cancelled. Directors and staff members shared the task of placating both the press and major retailers.

Traditionally, in such cases, a book was published, and a copy seized from a bookshop, ideally in Charing Cross Road, which, according to Rolph, had an 'undeserved fame as the spring-board of all the big dirty-book prosecutions'. By co-operating fully with Scotland Yard, and forestalling publication Lane and Rubinstein were able to persuade them not to involve an unfortunate bookseller in the prosecution, by making copies available for them to collect – in itself a technical 'act of publication'. There was, however, another crucial point at stake, which Rubinstein pointed out:

Our Clients appreciate that it is open to you, as an alternative to the procedure referred to above under Section 3 of the Act, to proceed by way of Summons under Section 2 of the Act upon receipt of the

Post-war Penguin Christmas party. (*photo: Bristol Archive*)

RIGHT: A.S.B. Glover.
(*photo: Bristol Archive*)

BELOW: Nikolaus Pevsner and one of his monumental series.
(*photo: Frank Hermann*)

E.V. Rieu. (*photo: Sam Lambert*)

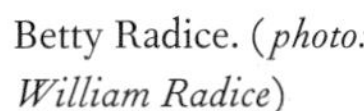

Betty Radice. (*photo: William Radice*)

LEFT: Tony Godwin.
(*photo: Fay Godwin*)

BELOW: Tony Richardson.

LEFT: Noel Carrington.
(*photo: Bristol Archive*)

BELOW: Eleanor Graham.
(*photo: Sam Lambert*)

RIGHT: Kaye Webb.
(*photo: Tom Hanley*)

BELOW: Advertisement in *The Bookseller*, 14 May 1966.
(*photo:* The Bookseller)

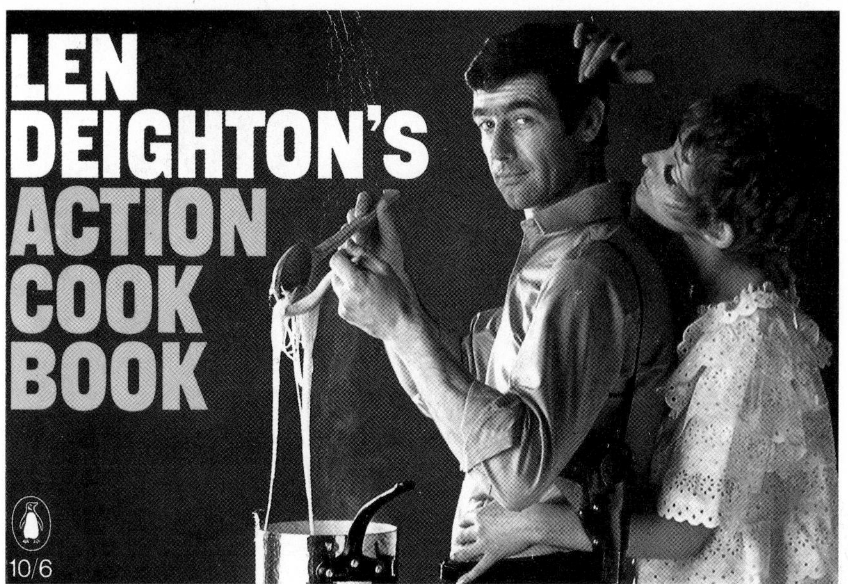

ABOVE: Corned Beef and English Trifle. (*cover design: Raymond Hawkey*)

LEFT: 'I must make it clear at once that Penguins' use of the poster for this book involved no deceit. You knew that we wanted a photograph or photographs of South Africa for a book but we were never asked the subject of the book.' Raleigh Trevelyan, Penguin editorial, to the South African Tourist Corporation, 16 January 1962. (*cover design: Frederick Price*)

ABOVE: Bill Rapley, a member of Penguin staff, assisting Mrs Freedman at the Leicester Square bookshop. Queues extended for hundreds of yards around the square. (*photo: Topham Picture Library*)

RIGHT: Having bought her copy in an Edinburgh bookshop, and carried it outside held in a pair of tongs, this lady then proceeded to burn it for the benefit of the press – and ultimately, Penguin Books. (*photo: Bristol Archive*)

books from them, which would give our Clients the right to elect trial by jury.

Michael B. Rubinstein to Scotland Yard, 15 August 1960

The symbolic gesture of publication was not made by Lane, who was still abroad, but by Schmoller – although this turns out to be a simplified version of the event:

On 16 August 1960, at 11.15 a.m., I met Sir William Emrys Williams at the London Office of Penguin Books, 303 High Holborn, WC2. At 11.30 a.m., as arranged through Rubinstein and Nash, Detective Inspector C. Monahan, accompanied by Detective S. Sayers, arrived and was shown in to us. He identified himself by showing us his warrant, and we gave him our personal details which Detective Sayers recorded. He asked whether we knew the purpose of his visit, to which we replied 'Yes'. I do not remember the word 'caution', which appeared in the Law Report, to have been used. Sir William then produced twelve copies of *Lady Chatterley's Lover* saying that he did so on behalf of the Board of directors of Penguin Books, and handed them to Inspector Monahan . . . Shortly after the departure of the two Scotland Yard officers Sir William began to have misgivings about his having been the person who was recorded to have handed the book to Inspector Monahan. He said this might cause trouble at the Arts Council, whose Secretary General he is. He telephoned Inspector Monahan in my presence and asked him to substitute my name for his (Sir William's) in the official record. Inspector Monahan accepted his request.

Deposition by Hans Schmoller

LEGAL ACTION IMMINENT STOP ADVISE YOUR IMMEDIATE RETURN
BILL AND HANS

Telegram to Allen Lane, 16 August 1960

The following day Monahan phoned Rubinstein to inform him that the summons would be issued and served immediately – under Section 2, allowing the defendants to elect trial by jury. Now that prosecution was inevitable, the publication date was cancelled, all copies recalled from wholesalers, and the defence prepared. No effort was spared to seek opinion and involvement from the most illustrious representatives of any profession that could be construed as relevant. And it remained, right up to the moment the jury returned their verdict, a very real possibility that Penguin would lose the case. Filed as 'Unhelpful or rejected', 'Likely', 'Doubtful', 'Hostile', 'Helpful', 'Witnesses not being called but with helpful views' – writers, publishers, churchmen, students, teachers, doctors and journalists – all were approached. Potential witnesses were subsequently categorized:

A: Probably excellent, or necessary
B: Probably necessary
C: Proof not yet prepared or not yet completed or approved
D: Not in top category

Bill Williams, on his own initiative, had written to a number of leading authors, inviting their support and the submission of brief essays of some 200 words on D. H. Lawrence and the desirability of the book's publication.

Lady Chatterley's Lover is a literary work of importance, written by a leading 20th century novelist. It is surprising that such a work should be prosecuted here, and if it is condemned, our country will certainly make itself look ridiculous in America and elsewhere.

I do not think that it could be held obscene, but am in a difficulty here, for the reason that I have never been able to follow the legal definition of obscenity. The Law tells me that obscenity may deprave and corrupt, but as far as I know it offers no definition of depravity or corruption.

I am certain that it is neither erotic nor pornographic, nor, from what I knew of the author, would there have been any erotic or pornographic intention in his mind.

E. M. Forster

In reply to your request, you may use the following if and when it is needed:

Lady Chatterley's Lover is without any obscene element or intention. It represents an experiment by a novelist of genius, and though I do not think the experiment succeeds, it would be the height of absurdity to regard it as a pornographic work.

J. B. Priestley to W. E. Williams, 16 August 1960

Williams's personal appeal bore several such fruit, and the idea was taken up by Rubinstein in order to gain opinions from a much wider field. Pre-publication copies of the novel were either sent to or withheld from potential witnesses on the strength of their original replies.

I first read *LCL* when I was in Germany just after the end of the War. I recently re-read it in the proposed Penguin edition. I strongly support the publication of the unexpurgated edition of *Lady Chatterley's Lover* as being for the public good. Opinion that there is artistic merit in all Lawrence's work is accepted and I consider that his work has even more significant merit as the vehicle for his ideas. It seems to me therefore of the utmost importance that the entirety of his writings, including, that is to say, the full text of the work under discussion, should be freely available to any member of the public.

It is incontestable in my view, that Lawrence was one of the most influential thinkers of his time. His importance as a thinker on class relationships is not relevant to this trial. On personal relationships – in which I am both personally and professionally interested – he had particularly important ideas to impart, important to society as well as for individuals, beset as we all are at one time or another with problems involving relations with members of the other sex. He advocates in his books and in this particularly greater seriousness, reverence and frankness in matters involving sex and a human concern for the deepest needs of men and women. His intention was not to incite readers to promiscuity or cynicism – quite the contrary, these are the debasing influences affecting attitudes to sex in our modern society. I am married and have two sons (12 and 11) and a daughter (6). When my children are old enough (by which I mean when they want to read it) I would have no objection to their reading the book freely.

Kingsley Amis, 22 September 1960

Of less help, and consequently filed as 'Unhelpful', was the following.

I cannot IMAGINE why Penguin Books Ltd have put my name on their *Lady Chatterley's Lover* list. (Can you? After all, I'm only a children's writer – whose opinions surely would not weigh with the adult public! Don't you think there is something slightly comic about E. B. solemnly declaring that *L. C. Lover* is a fit and proper book for everyone's reading?)

I'd love to help Penguins Ltd – they are doing a fine job with their publications – but I don't see how I can. For one thing I haven't read the book – and for another thing my husband said NO at once. The thought of me standing up in Court solemnly advocating a book 'like that' (his words, not mine – I feel he must have read the book!) made his hair stand on end. I'm awfully sorry – but I don't see that I can go against him. I feel impelled to read the book now of course (what MARVELLOUS publicity it is having, and how pleased Penguins must be!) though a woman author (for adults) once told me that it was dull and badly written.

Can you convey my apologies to Penguins, and let them know that while I *am* against too much censorship of books, I really cannot go against my husband's most definite wishes in this. ('To think of *my* wife standing up and advocating the reading of pornographic books – a well-loved author for *children* – you'd be condemned by every parent!') I think possibly it *would* be stupid for a children's author to join in, and I have a feeling that you would probably agree with me in that? I still feel most astonished that anyone should have thought my opinions would carry any weight with the *novel*-reading public.

Do your best for me, won't you – and *don't* let Penguins think I'm too uncooperative for words, anyway, they'll have a long string of scintillating names of critics and writers – and don't *really* need such small fry as children's writers at all!

Enid Blyton to Michael B. Rubinstein, 20 August 1960

In the same category – curious bedfellows indeed – were to be found Robert Graves, Godfrey Winn, C. P. Snow, Evelyn Waugh, Lord Boothby, Geoffrey Faber, Bernard Levin and Lawrence Durrell. The reasons for this categorization ranged from simple unwillingness to participate, to illness, other engagements, and potential problem areas which the prosecution might conceivably exploit.

Your MBR/VS of 18th. I have not read *Lady Chatterley's Lover* since it first came out. My memory of it is that it was dull, absurd in places and pretentious. I am sure that most of its readers would be attracted by its eroticism. Whether it can 'corrupt' them, I can't tell, but I am quite certain that no public or private 'good' would be served by its publication. Lawrence had very meagre literary gifts.

Evelyn Waugh to Michael B. Rubinstein, 21 August 1960

I fear I cannot offer to support your case about the publication of *Lady Chatterley's Lover* being for the public good; but this has nothing to do with its being pornographic. D. H. Lawrence, even at his purest, is the writer I like least of my contemporaries and I won't have a book of his on my shelves; can't explain it, some antipathetic element, I suppose. Of course I'm not the public.

I'm sorry because I owe a lot to Allen Lane and I think it's ridiculous that he should have to publish an incomplete series of Lawrence's works just because *Lady Chatterley* contains words like f**k which have been approved in *The Mint* (by his namesake) and a thousand other books of less merit, and descriptions of the sexual act, such as occur in most modern novels; also in my translation of Apuleius, *Golden Ass*.

Thus far you may quote me, if it's any use.

Robert Graves to Michael B. Rubinstein, 20 August 1960

Of course I will be glad to attest to the genius of D. H. Lawrence and to the importance of *Lady Chatterley*. I could also make out a convincing case about its publication being 'to the public good'. It is a fine work of art and by conscious intention a passionate artistic defence of real feelings against perverted ones. If England understood what the word 'artist' means, all this tedious and silly puritanism would be swept aside and the artists granted the same rights as doctors are granted. No one objects if a doctor wants to undress a patient; but people do not realize that a major artist is a moulder of the national psyche. He is a soul doctor – a witch doctor – the unacknowledged legislator. He should be allowed to shock when he deems it necessary; sometimes these harsh shocks wake people up and purge them, purge their psyche. We know that Lawrence's first title was 'Tenderness' and we know clearly what his notions were concerning love and marriage; there is no further doubt that his intentions were as moral as those of a great surgeon who is forced sometimes to cause pain. He should be free to speak his mind; the moral health of the public would be much benefited by reading him thoughtfully and carefully. *Lady Chatterley* is really an Epithalamium, a marriage celebration of the Blakeian kind. But I have said enough I think to show the line I would follow if I had to defend the book in open court.

Lawrence Durrell to Michael B. Rubinstein, undated (received 23 August 1960)

Thank you for your letter from which I note your very interesting views of the book . . . There is a matter which disturbs me slightly in regard to your appearance in court as a witness. I am thinking of *The Black Book*, published by the Olympia Press (who are clients of mine). It occurs to me that you might be embarrassed (I do not mean personally, but on behalf of Penguin Books Limited in relation to this action) by questions which might be put to you by a hostile Counsel in the course of cross-examination. You will appreciate my Clients' motives in deciding to publish *Lady Chatterley's Lover* at this time are not to be taken as an indication that they would have decided to publish any book which some people might regard as obscene in the same way. I cannot, of course, say whether *The Black Book* comes into the category of those which Penguin would or would not publish, but cross-examining Counsel is likely to look into the background, so far as he can, of witnesses on the other side and it would help me if I could have your views on this aspect of the matter in early reply to this letter . . .

Michael B. Rubinstein to Lawrence Durrell, 26 August 1960

Thank you for your letter which I had the opportunity to discuss with a lawyer friend. He rather echoes your view that the author of *The Black Book* might be a weak rather than a strong link in the line of defence. I leave it to you to decide. I think *The Black Book* would run into the same trouble if printed in England and that is why I have withheld my permission to publish over there. However whatever the state of affairs I would be happy to associate myself in any way with a defence of Lawrence. I don't know if the new addition of the law will help the defence. The question is rather to define 'public good'; presumably any true work of art which could be vouched for by five known artists would be very much to the public good if published. Would a jury accept that? The whole question turns upon a misunderstanding of the artist's role and his position in society – his rights, so to speak.

Lawrence Durrell to Michael B. Rubinstein, 30 August 1960

Thank you very much for your further most helpful letter of 30th August. Since we are agreed, you will not now be troubled to give evidence in this matter.

Michael B. Rubinstein to Lawrence Durrell, 6 September 1960

I should be glad to stand up for *Lady Chatterley* though I hardly think I should be regarded as a literary expert.

I do not think it a very great novel, or Lawrence's best; but I regard it as an important expression of the outlook of a major novelist, and as marking a stage in his development which cannot be overlooked.

It is, strictly, pornographic, since it portrays the sexual act, but the sexual act has its important place in human life, and cannot possibly be excluded from serious art. Lawrence in no way vulgarizes this theme, as it is vulgarized in the trashy novelettes against which any laws relating to obscene literature are, presumably, meant to apply; on the contrary, he treats it with almost excessive solemnity and reverence.

It is unthinkable that this book should be banned in a civilized country.

Tom Driberg, House of Commons, to Michael B. Rubinstein, 26 August 1960

It seems to me absurd that this book should ever have been classed as obscene and I should say that its tendency as Lawrence intended is to treat the sexual side of a love affair in an adult fashion. I can't imagine that even a minor could draw any other conclusion from the book than that sexual activity was at least enjoyable.

I am myself dubious how far Lawrence was successful in his intention. I find some parts of the book rather absurd and for that reason I would prefer not to be called as a witness in case I was forced into any admission harmful to the Penguin case.

Graham Greene to Michael B. Rubinstein, 23 August 1960

It must have been particularly heartening to Penguin that members of one group, very much in the same potential boat, should lend what support they could. Here was common cause indeed, beyond professional rivalry, or imagined antipathies.

I read *Lady Chatterley* over the weekend with, for the most part, unutterable boredom. Subject to what I am going to say in the next paragraph, it is a pretty bad novel, and a pretty badly written one too, full of Lawrence's abominable trick of repeating words and phrases for emphasis.

But there is an exception to all this: all the love scenes – all the parts, that is to say, for which the book is being prosecuted – are superb, and, in the main, superbly written. To call them either pornographic or obscene would be fantastic. In their modern terms, they don't fall very far short of the Song of Songs: I would go so far as to say that they glorify the Creator of human bodies.

In a word. As a whole, I would not describe the book as a high work of art or great literature: but it has great things in it: and anyhow the question doesn't arise, for presumably one only has to prove that a book is a work of art if there are obscenities in it that have, so to speak, to be excused. Here is no trace of obscenity.

I could not imagine a more deplorable piece of topsy-turvydom than that *Lady Chatterley* should be condemned, and the really vile *Lolita* get through. Such a contrast must stink in the nostrils of honest people who have any taste whatsoever.

I shall be delighted, if you wish, to give evidence.

Victor Gollancz to Michael B. Rubinstein, 22 August 1960

Geoffrey Faber, Rupert Hart-Davis, Desmond Flower of Cassells, Robert Lusty of Hutchinson and John Lehmann were among those also willing to uphold the publisher's right to publish. Sir Stanley Unwin was called, while Faber's colleague and co-director, T. S. Eliot, waited patiently for the call to give evidence, which was not found to be necessary. He too was in good company – with Iris Murdoch and Aldous Huxley who was prepared, in consideration of £1,000 expenses, to fly over from the States to help the cause.

As for the prosecution, of course not one expert witness was called, although several potential witnesses had been identified in advance by the defence. Edith Sitwell, who according to Rubinstein 'claimed with only partial justification, that Lawrence had based the character of Sir Clifford on her brother Osbert', was known to be hostile to the defence cause, as was John Sparrow, Warden of All Souls College. The great champion of Lawrence, F. R. Leavis, did not appear to be considered as a potential witness for either side. The reason – if not the logic – from the defence point of view became evident a year or two later on the publication of his inaugural volume in the Peregrine series:

Undoing the parcel of copies of *The Common Pursuit* I have just found the unexpected note and the label. I return the sixth copy, which I have not autographed. I do not think Sir Allen Lane did a service to literature, civilization or Lawrence in the business of *Lady Chatterley's Lover*.

F. R. Leavis to Penguin Books, 12 January 1962

Allen Lane's library copy has the signature of Leavis, cut from an earlier letter, glued to the title page.

In all, thirty-six witnesses were called for the defence in the *Lady Chatterley* trial although only thirty-five actually gave evidence. Kingsley Amis was called, but did not appear: 'I must apologize for being absent when called in Lady Chatterley. I left Swansea just in time to miss your letter and got back six hours or so after I should have been available in court.'

Thank you for your letter of 23rd November. I must say that I was puzzled to know what had happened to you since it was rumoured (evidently without foundation) that you had in fact come up to London the day when we intended to call you as a witness.

As you may have gathered from reports of the last days of the trial we were concerned to impress upon the jury the weight and number of witnesses available to the Defence but who were not in fact called since this in itself added to the very valuable impression made by those who were called, but the jury may very well have tended to be bored by the prolongation of the evidence. It was consistent with this that Mr Gerald Gardiner was able to call your name when we thought you might have been waiting outside the Court to give evidence, thereby bringing your name as a Defence witness to the attention of the jury but when you did not answer the call he called the next witness who was available. So even *in absentia* you may very well have served a useful purpose.

Michael B. Rubinstein to Kingsley Amis, 25 November 1960

The rest, as they say, is history. The following year, Penguin announced the sale of shares in the Company in a public flotation. Boosted by the boundless publicity resulting from the case, and the excellent sales of more than just this one title, the offer was oversubscribed 150 times. Sir Allen Lane, according to the newspapers, became a millionaire overnight. Rubinstein, Nash & Co., the firm that had been Penguin's solicitors from their inception in 1935, was subsequently dropped in favour of another practice, who handled the flotation.

* * *

A NEW GENERATION
1960–1970

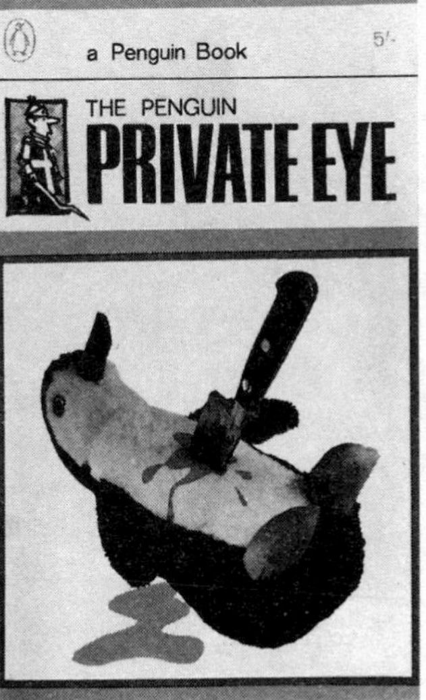

Tony Godwin

. . . It arises out of my intense admiration and enthusiasm for your book and a burning desire not only to see it published in Penguins, but also to see that it is read. It isn't so much a question of money but I have never seen the purpose in the act of merely publishing a book. I quite passionately desire that they should also find their audience. Especially yours I would like to see widely read here. It articulates marvellously what many of us are feeling.

Tony Godwin to Jane Jacobs (author of Pelican edition *The Death and Life of the Great American Cities*), 22 December 1964

The publication of *Lady Chatterley's Lover* alone would have marked 1960 as a pivotal year for Penguin. In May of that year Alan Glover retired, while Bill Williams, as ever involved in other ventures, limited his involvement more and more to an executive role, as did Eunice Frost. Eleanor Graham was similarly preparing for retirement. A new generation of editors had already begun to be assembled. First Nikolaus Pevsner's son Dieter in 1958, and Tom Maschler, Richard Newnham and David Lutyens. These were joined, or replaced, by Tony Richardson, Charles Clark, James Cochrane and Giles Gordon, and several others. All young, well educated and exceptionally able. One further editor was appointed, in May 1960, initially on a casual consultancy basis. He rose rapidly to become first fiction editor and then editor in chief with a seat on the board of Penguin Books. 'He had been a brilliant bookseller and rapidly proved himself a brilliant publisher.' (Oliver Caldecott, *The Bookseller*, 30 June 1989). This was Tony Godwin.

As E. V. Rieu soon found out, it was impossible to be indifferent about Godwin. But even his detractors would concede that he was possessed of a certain instinctive genius. He could be abrasive, irascible – never intimidated by authority or tradition. He was a born editor. More to the point Penguin was perfect for him, just as he was perfect for Penguin at this particular time. In many ways he could be uncomfortably reminiscent of the young Allen Lane. But above all he was a genuine and passionate lover of books and their authors. That passion also extended to readers, and booksellers.

Some believed that his passions extended further – in a ruthless quest for power. There was talk of his abortive 'palace revolution' to usurp Allen Lane. Godwin was undoubtedly at the forefront of a revolution – adapting and changing Penguin to a new generation of readers, and to his own vision, but to take the conspiracy theory to its logical conclusion would be to place Godwin in a position which was fundamentally against his nature. Every letter and memorandum he wrote clearly attests that he was a man interested in words, not figures, and his prime motivation was always to encourage and nurture his writers.

It was on the second reading that I began to recognize just how marvellously good *A Fortunate Man* is and became aware of the depths of the insights and appreciative of the masterly form of the book as a whole . . . I am moved and grateful the way one always feels when someone has written a good book with complete integrity and overjoyed on your behalf as I know how much this book must mean to you.

Tony Godwin to John Berger, 3 March 1966

Fundamentally, publishing is exploiting. It exploits talent: the talents of authors, rich and poor, mediocre and gifted, celebrated and obscure. It is also establishing them, securing readers for them and money and fame – and what follows? An uneasy see-saw resulting from an inevitable conflict of interests – the contrary demands of literature and commerce as well as the resounding clash of egos . . .

Are people conscious of various publishers' imprints? Do all those names at the foot of rows of spines in a bookshop convey anything? Certainly there are two imprints which do mean something to the general public: the Oxford University Press with its superb range of reference books and its reputation for scholarship, and Penguin with its unique cultural and social ubiquity. For the rest I wonder. Does it even matter? After all it is the author and the book itself that count. Yet to most publishers the mystique of the list is the Holy Grail: his imprint and all it stands for is the most important thing in a publisher's life. Most take a craftsman's pride in the quality of their list and strive to leave on it the hallmark of their taste and standards. Understand this and you've already understood much of the deepest motivations in publishing.

Tony Godwin, *The Listener*, 28 January 1971

During the time I was at Penguins Allen Lane took small interest in the editorial side. From talking to him there was never any doubt in my mind of his editorial flair, with one exception a far stronger flair than any other publisher I have known. He was also blessed with that most useful of traits to any good publisher – swift opportunism that could seize with infectious enthusiasm on an idea, plucking it at times out of the air, and converting it into a book or series. Yet by the time I arrived he seemed to have lost touch and interest. In the main he seemed content to take the editorial for granted and concentrate his time and attention on an almost interminable effort to sort out Penguin Australia, to getting Penguin Educational under way and most absorbingly of all, the financial side. What Allen very much understood to the very marrow of his bones was power and the use of power and that the key to power lay in finance and financial control. Yet I often wondered how sophisticated his understanding of finance was – not that mine was anything to boast about.

Tony Godwin, reminiscence

Never one to mince words, his letters – in his capacity as editor or friend, but more often both – are never cold and purely businesslike. Uncompromising, maybe. They are almost too open – revealing failings in almost equal measure with care and devotion and a passionate interest in every subject he encountered. Again, to John Berger:

I hope my hurried scribble about Neizvestny didn't upset you by its resolutely non-intellectual and non-metaphysical approach. It is because of the very unfamiliarity of the context in which he works that I think it calls for an approach of extreme simplicity. Were this an introduction to a Western artist, whose idiom, context, background and tradition had already made themselves familiar, and the validity of whose work is taken for granted and acknowledged, *then*, then one can loop the metaphysical loop and carry the reader with one. Not so with Neizvestny, in my opinion; there one has to build the foundation at this stage. If there is a burning necessity to explore the theoretical, then I would suggest that the book not only has an introduction, but that it has an afterword which would come at the back of the book, so that you would get a sequence in which people would read the introduction, look at the pictures, and then, at least partially prepared, read the afterword.

I am going to run a competition for *A Fortunate Man*. This will be for bookshop assistants. These are the inconspicuous of the book trade, yet it is they who arrange the books on display, who arrange the window displays, it is often they who make up the stock, it is they who recommend books to the elderly, the travelling, the gift-giving, etc etc. The intention of the competition is to try and coax as many as possible bookshop assistants to read your book, and as a natural corollary thereto, recommend it. The competition is for the best personal letter written to you and Jean Mohr. Therefore I shall be suggesting that they write direct to you in Geneva. I hope that's all right by you; and you and Jean Mohr will have to pick one of the letters as winner. I don't suppose it will result in more than 100 letters. For the first prize I should like to suggest a three-week holiday in Provence. Would it be possible to borrow your cottage for this? Then all we would have to do would be to pay the fare of the winning assistant and family and some holiday money over there. What do you feel? Don't hesitate to tell me that you would consider it a violation of the cottage if that's what you feel. I could think up some other prize in case.

I am now back in London again, but unfortunately caught flu on my arrival, so I'm back in bed again, believe it or not. I'm beginning to feel a bit bed-ridden. By the way, I should be greatly interested to see the article in *The Realist*.

Tony Godwin to John Berger, 2 March 1967

A pedestrian crib without much trace of the imagination or the power of a good historian to select and shape his material to give force, coherence, point and pace to his narrative. This, in the main, is a painstaking, pedantic, plodding, chronological account of a tedious progression of names and place-names, and a wearisome parade of the author's pedantry. This is the poor cut of the beef of history, dull and lacking in immediacy, and only really suitable for the earnest student. That endless succession of names were actual people of flesh and blood, each with individual characters, aspirations, fates; those incidents of maritime exploration, expeditions, exploitation and revolt were in fact hair-raising, sublime, exciting, tragic.

Tony Godwin to Charles Clark, 12 December 1961

The author may be illiterate. I don't give a damn. They have got talent, which to me is a damn sight more important than a great many other qualities, especially in publishing. In publishing, talent is what counts, not the ability to punctuate . . . Writers are not like business people. We may be publishers, but basically we tend to think like business people, and we must remember, if we are going to keep authors, that they are talented people with large egos and difficult to deal with.

Tony Godwin to Hans Schmoller, internal memorandum, 15 May 1962

The cover is a poster and the purpose of a poster is to catch the eye and attention. Will this do so? I daresay that the lighting and composition of the photograph have an intended symbolic depth, but a poster speaks in a fleeting shout, not in a long ruminative whisper. Incidentally, this is an orange job and not a blue one.

Tony Godwin to Tony Richardson, internal memorandum re John Berger's *Picasso*, 8 January 1965

That was a marvellous letter and I want to thank you a lot for writing to me. The only time I ever feel 'safe' about one of my books is when someone actually tells me. I mean reviews, even good ones, are meaningless in a private sense. Also, as you probably know from others I have enormous respect for your opinion and trust in you as a person so I am very happy because of your letter . . . I am off to Positano to join Anne Graham Bell for two weeks. And then I hope to begin another novel. The awful thing, or perhaps the good thing about writing is that by the time others read the book the writer is already awake at night trying to do another one and if possible a better one. That's how it is.

Edna O'Brien to Tony Godwin, 31 May 1966

Charlie, here's a beautiful one for you. As you know we publish a number of Hemingway titles and we are publishing *The Essential Hemingway* next spring. Included in that volume is *Fiesta* complete. Can you tell me whether contractually I now have the right to publish it on its own because I have the right to publish it inside *The Essential Hemingway*?

Tony Godwin to Charles Clark, internal memorandum, 8 August 1963

It is a nice idea, but I would not have thought that we could publish *Fiesta* separately. The essence of the agreement for *The Essential Hemingway* is for a number of works which together make up a volume and it is, as it were, the togetherness that we are buying.

On the other hand I don't see why you could not try to slide the point over to Tom over a cheery drink. I imagine everything will depend on the Pan edition of *Fiesta*.

Charles Clark to Tony Godwin, internal memorandum, undated

... Incidentally, the difference between our sales and Dell's is due to the fact that Dell of course do low-priced, mass marketing of paperbacks. We, as you know, do a bookshop distribution at a rather higher price in that somewhat more staid English fashion! In other words, Dell market like Pan, and we market like Penguins.

Tony Godwin to Roger Machell, Hamish Hamilton, 4 December 1962

I have now managed to stagger through *The White Deer*. It took the whole of one bath to get through it. I think it would make a very nice Penguin. Can I make a modest offer, say an advance of £150, because I am getting a slightly haunted feeling that my stocks of unpublished Thurber may well end up by engulfing me.

Tony Godwin to Roger Machell, 20 March 1963

Here is our standard form – disregard anything you think is irrelevant; remember it is mainly for our dedicated Pelican writers, plodding away on Electrolysis, or a Geography of Eastern Europe, and so on.

Tony Godwin to Mike Rumaker, New York, 24 March 1966

The proofs arrived and I'm dismayed to see that you persist in calling this book *Exit Three* when you assured me some time ago that this would be corrected to *Exit 3* – with the numeral 3. The title of the book is *Exit 3*. The title of the book is *Exit 3*. The title of the book is *Exit 3*. I will correct this on each and every page of the proofs you sent me in the hopes that this time there will be no mistake.

Exit 3 is a turnoff on the New Jersey Turnpike (where the action of the title story takes place). Numerals are used for all the exit signs and are not spelled out, as your editors insist on doing. Please don't goof on this as it is very important: Exit Three is not the same as Exit 3.

I will set to work on the proofs right away. Please send me a note re the above. Please make reassuring sounds.

Agitatedly,

Mike Rumaker to Tony Godwin, 11 June 1966

Loud reassuring noise.

Tony Godwin to Mike Rumaker, 15 June 1966

Industrial Safety: I look back at six years at Penguins, count the bruises on my shins and the abrasions on my elbows, the pouches under my eyes, and a sense of humour that has almost been eroded, and in the course of a thousand and one precepts learnt during this Armageddon, one of the most prominent, hard-learnt and carefully heeded is – unless you've got a very strong masochistic yen do not commission a book by someone who cannot write for toffee. Invariably these are the ones who think they can write, so for a start you will have a frightful time trying to convey to them the failings of their manuscript. You will also have an even more frightful time trying to edit their manuscript into readability. You have been warned.

Tony Godwin to Giles Gordon, 13 February 1967

Prior to joining Penguin in 1960, Tony Godwin had been in book-selling, having taken over Better Books in 1946, which was turned, according to the press, into an 'avant garde' bookshop. He had also been managing director of Bumpus – of which Allen Lane, too, was to be a director. He maintained his interest in Better Books – despite the occasional setback. As he wrote in a letter to *The Bookseller*: 'I love bookshops and bookselling is a way of life to me.'

We have just had the most perfect summer in England for the last fifty years, culminating in a Labour Government, which might zing things up a bit here. Summer was only marred by the absence of your splendid presence and poor old Better Books coming out in fires just like someone with boils. I don't know whether news has reached you in San Francisco but we had another fire at the end of September when one of our staff took it into his head to rob the safe and set fire to the shop, presumably to cover his traces. I can now tell you that one's office records, order system, and accounts burn more zestfully than books themselves do. Those customers the Better Books have still got are now resigned to the shabby, crestfallen, sooty shop. We certainly now have the finest kippered stock in London. You can smell all our books for about 50 yards off but we're not charging extra. What makes it all worse is that it was someone whom I liked and who was the apple of my eye. He'd been with us a couple of months and now I suppose they'll put him in prison for several years.

Today we are going to open at last the paperback-coffee-shop, which is a crazy tour de force and I think it is going to knock them all for a loop. We are starting in the coffee shop a weekly series of Writers' Nights where poets can hold readings, writers can read from work in progress and discuss it, and there can be discussions on literary themes and so on and so forth. But all to a small audience of about 40 which should add a note of intimacy and informality that might really get something going. John Calder, the publisher, is giving me a hand and I am recruiting people for dear life to help as 52 evenings in a year is a lot to arrange. So if you should show your nose in this country and they let you in, I shall certainly try to get you in there declaiming one of your plays . . .

Tony Godwin to Lawrence Ferlinghetti, 29 October 1964

. . . What kind of publishing house is MacGibbon & Kee? They have just made an offer to New Directions to publish the *Collected Ferlinghetti* (three books of poetry, a short novel and plays) and I am wondering about them. Are they obscene? Perhaps you could give me one of your famous one-line answers.

Love to you all,

Lawrence Ferlinghetti, City Lights Bookstore, San Francisco, to Tony Godwin, 23 February 1966

Contract coming post-haste: we absentmindedly filed it in a rare burst of Anglican efficiency. I guess our minds were elsewhere at the time – Vietnam for instance. Will inform Maschler of your machinations.

For the record, after six years in publishing, I think I regard all publishing houses as obscene, but I don't believe that MacGibbon & Kee have a greater access of obscenity than anyone else. They publish William Carlos Williams, Doris Lessing, Colin MacInnes. They are the lonely outpost of a TV empire. They fall between innumerable stools, such as they are neither the whizz kids like Cape, nor a great big commercial shop like Heinemann, nor hellish literary and avant garde like Calder. They are not bad, but they are not wonderful.

We are having lovely summer weather in advance over here now – why don't you come over to Europe where all the folk-singing is done?

Tony Godwin to Lawrence Ferlinghetti, 9 March 1966

Close personal contact with a number of the younger generation of writers, particularly in the United States, coupled with a belief that 'the state of English writing is somewhat quiescent at present . . . whereas in the USA there is a great deal of vitality' led him briefly to revive the title *New Writing* with a series of anthologies designed to give a flavour of literary trends and introduce new and often experimental writing from around the world. *The New Writing in the USA* initiated the series. Later volumes came out as Writing Today – with Latin American, Polish, African, Italian and several further volumes planned. This international outlook was mirrored in Penguin Plays and the poetry series, particularly with the rapidly expanding Penguin Modern Poets. The impending launch of the Penguin Press, and a near-fatal illness, necessarily turned his attention closer to home, in what were to be his final few months at Penguin.

Out of hospital at long last and now working from our country cottage. And it's glorious to be restored to oneself so to speak, and to become a private individual again instead of an object to which things are done at regular intervals. I intend to take things a little quietly for a while, and we are going off on holiday to Provence in April for three weeks. By the time I return I shall be right back on form.

Meanwhile I was delighted to hear from Tony Richardson that you had had a meeting, and that you did not appear to be too depressed, upset or disturbed by the verdict on the chapters of *Cultures*. I like your suggestion for a book on great architectural patrons of the 19th and 20th centuries. It sounds as if it might be fascinating, nor do I think that anyone has ever written about them.

Victorian Architecture has done nicely in its first two months, having sold 9,500 copies. Now I shall wait for the first six months of this year's sales with great interest to see at what level it establishes itself. Have you had much correspondence from people writing to you about it yet? Meanwhile, amongst everything else, I am tying up the final ends for the launching of our hardback firm, which is quite exciting. Yesterday the binder drove across to my cottage here to bring me the first four titles on our list. I am feeling greatly pleased with them – they have a real look, and an elegant one at that, of their own. I do think that publishers have tended to forget nowadays what lovely objects books can be as objects in their own right. I am hoping to restore this balance a bit with the Penguin Press.

Tony Godwin to Robert Furneaux Jordan, 14 February 1967

As I potter around here on what I suspect to be my last day, I thought you would be interested to know how your book (Penguin Handbook: *How to Drive Safely*) is faring now it is published. It would seem that we have sold something in the region of 4,500 since publication, which I think is very good. We seem to have about 10,500 left in the warehouse (I have just counted them), so I think that probably a reprint will be called for at the beginning of next year. I hope you thought it worth the effort and you enjoyed writing it, and that you have had the pleasure of seeing your book on sale everywhere.

By the way, if you see a decent house going cheap in Provence let me know.

Tony Godwin to John Howard, 17 May 1967

The Times and *The Bookseller* carried the following letter in May 1967:

Sir, – Tony Godwin's departure from Penguin Books has attracted extensive press comment. As yet, little has been said of his extraordinary achievements as editor in charge of the whole Penguin list: he extended the range of the list with vision, and we who were his editorial colleagues felt at every point his intense concern for quality and purpose.

Furthermore we know that these feelings are shared by Sir Allen Lane and his fellow directors.

Yours faithfully

Oliver Caldecott	Dieter Pevsner
Charles Clark	Fred Plaat
James Cochrane	Tony Richardson
Giles Gordon	John Summerscale

Robert Hutchison	Kaye Webb
Jill Norman	Peter Wright

Soon after, Tony Godwin was pointedly invited by the Society of Young Publishers in October 1967 to speak on the subject 'Is Publishing a Worthwhile Profession'. Seven years at Penguin had not dented his enthusiasm. It remained a matter of passion for him:

The reason why publishing had been regarded as an occupation for gentlemen, he suspected, had been because the upper class considered themselves – possibly they still did – as the custodians of culture. Publishing was a collaboration between the distinguished amateur and the vulgar salesman . . . However, as a result of the education acts raising the school leaving age and the steady 'democratization' of culture, the distinguished amateur in publishing was, he liked to think, being supplanted by the passionate professional.

The passionate professional was a person who believed to his very marrow in the importance of good books; that novels, besides entertaining, could convey unique truths; and the affairs of mankind in all their variety merited a high seriousness. Accordingly he was passionate in his determination to publish as well and as professionally as possible. He did not regard systematization as beneath his notice, salesmanship as vulgar, production and design problems as plebeian and analytical accountancy as beyond the pale. He regarded it as his responsibility to the author and to publishing itself to concern himself with every aspect of publishing – to see that the book was produced well, that it was efficiently promoted and vigorously sold, to be able to offer his author meticulous professional advice and publishing service, whether on subject matter, income tax or presentation.

The Bookseller, 14 October 1967

Tony Godwin took up a senior post with Weidenfeld & Nicolson. Later, against the advice of friends he went to work in the States. 'I feel compelled to move on, to learn something new, and America will be completely new. It is all an adventure.'

His health deteriorated, and he died in 1976, still relatively young, his full potential still unfulfilled.

* * *

Poison Penguin

The pheasant is an enigma, the answer to which is revealed only to the initiate; they alone can savour it in all its excellence.

The Philosopher in the Kitchen, Jean-Anthelme Brillat-Savarin, Penguin Handbook, 1970

The Specials were a seeding ground for a number of further Penguin series: wartime issues, in green, dealt primarily with matters of immediate importance to families on the home front: *Soft Fruit Growing, Tree Fruit Growing, The Vegetable Grower's Handbook, Preserves for all Occasions.* The 1941 *Keeping Poultry and Rabbits on Scraps* became by 1944 two separate Specials *Poultry Farming* and *Rabbit Farming*, though, in a somewhat early anticipation of a return to dietary normality, they were destined never to be reprinted in the Handbook series, despite having places reserved for them.

Similarly S127 *Wartime Good Housekeeping Cookery Book*, published in 1942, did not survive, and is now extremely rare. 'Cookery books must alter with the times; the recipes in this book are chosen to meet to-day's needs, when it is of primary importance to make the best use of the foods available.' So ran the brief introduction to this modest volume. Featuring dishes such as Economic Cheese Soufflé, Mock Mince Pie, 'Dig For Victory' Dish, Mystery Pie, Brains on Toast, Mock Fish, and Marmalade (Made from the skins of sweet oranges), the book was hardly likely to feature among the new Penguin Handbooks which began to flourish in the new spirit of peacetime.

By 1970, Penguin had published some forty cookery books, laying the foundation for a selection as comprehensive and international as their treatment of poets, authors and dramatists. It all started in earnest in 1948, when Penguin approached the Ministry of Food. As ever, their timing was immaculate.

They were directed to the author of *The ABC of Cookery*, compiled for the Ministry of Food Experimental Kitchens between 1943 and 1946. The author, a regular speaker on BBC cookery programmes and a journalist, was Mrs A. R. Nilson.

Bee Nilson's *The Penguin Cookery Book* was first published in 1952 and was an instant and lasting success, still remaining in print today. Before very long the book began to make an impression in the most unlikely places.

On our bookshelves there are many cookery books – all well thumbed and liberally bespattered with margarine, butter and lard. Flour rises in clouds as the pages are turned. One of these, however, shews more honourable battle scars than any of the others: namely your *Penguin Cookery Book*.

This base, like five others dotted around the Antarctic is essentially a bachelor establishment; consisting of five men spending a period of up to two years under Antarctic conditions. We perform Meteorological, Biological, and Geological observations on behalf of the Falklands Islands Government. Thereby increasing the scientific knowledge of these little known regions.

Each of us, in turn, spends a week in the kitchen, providing three meals a day for the others.

Due to the isolation, and possible monotony of routine, an interesting and varied diet is essential to high morale. In this respect the general run of cookery books have been quite useful, but, since the arrival of your book, these others have been relinquished in its favour. Indeed it has now proved itself to be an invaluable asset. The Sauces section alone has been the means of transforming a hitherto 'commonplace' dish into an exciting one.

May I therefore offer my congratulations, and thanks for such a comprehensive and 'easy-to-follow' cookery book. I shall certainly recommend its purchase to anyone in need of guidance in the kitchen. I have already decided to get a copy for my own use as soon as I return to England.

The book, from our geographical point of view, is aptly titled. Penguin meat is served at least once a week, and forms an integral part of our diet.

We were vaguely disappointed, therefore, to discover that a recipe for preparing these birds was not included in the book. We have, however, our own recipe handed down from previous Antarctic travellers.

Allow the decapitated corpse to hang for a week; after which time, make a slit down its middle. The outer feathers, skin, and layer of blubber will then peel off, rather as a rabbit skin does, revealing the deep red, almost black breast meat beneath. Only the breast is eaten, the rest is too muscular and sinewy. The meat should be cut into strips, rolled in flour, and fried in deep fat. The taste is unlike anything else I have eaten, having a distinct, but not unpleasant oily flavour.

Trusting this has added to your wealth of recipes, I conclude by thanking you once more for the pleasure your book has given to all our palates.

T. G. Owen to Bee Nilson, 17 March 1953

This letter was used as the basis for an advertisement to publicize the second edition of the book – headed: 'Cooking Your Penguin – Antarctica Provides a Supplement to the Penguin Cookery Book.'

In one of your publications – *Herbs and Spices*, by Rosemary Hemphill – there is an error in the index which I thought perhaps should be brought to your attention.

'Angelica and rhubarb leaves, stewed', is listed in alphabetical order in the index, although, of course, the recipe is really for stewed Rhubarb and Angelica Leaves.

Rhubarb leaves, as you are doubtless aware, are poisonous, and if some twit should try cooking them you might be in all sorts of trouble.

R. V. Gooch to Penguin Books, 24 February 1967

It may have been far fetched to think of anyone preparing a dish on the basis of its entry in the index rather than the printed recipe. Slavish adherence to the recipe does indicate a certain lack of adventure: as every good cook knows, the recipe should merely be regarded as the starting point – the basis from which to explore and expand and gradually develop one's own individual style. With one Penguin Handbook, however, it might prove an unknown quantity . . .

A Reader's Report (signed JGP) set the tone:

I have read the first seventy pages and glanced through the rest. I began prejudiced. The idea of a mêlée of recipes and literary reminiscences didn't appeal, and I was somewhat sickened by the seemingly false modesty of the last sentence in the book. But I was won over. One is fired with the enthusiasm to cook her dishes, and to cook them well, and is encouraged to feel that one can achieve mastery, so clearly are the methods explained. I should like to see Penguin publish the book . . . Should there be an explanatory note actually on the front cover, discreetly reminding people who Alice B. Toklas is and outlining the form of the book. The latter is particularly important – it is by no means a handbook but should be read first and cooked from afterwards. People are going to be disappointed if they think it is recipes in handy form, and they won't get the proper enjoyment from it.

In the event, it was not felt necessary to remind readers of the salient facts in the career of its author.

There was a kind of veiled warning from Alice B. Toklas in her introduction.

As cook to cook I must confide that this book with its mingling of recipe and reminiscence was put together during the first three months of an attack of pernicious jaundice. Partly, I suppose, it was written as an escape from the narrow diet and monotony of illness, and I daresay nostalgia for old days and old ways and for remembered health and enjoyment lent special lustre to dishes and menus barred from an invalid table, but hovering dream-like in invalid memory.

This evocative last phrase was to provide an all too apt description of one unfortunate reader's exact state.

Last Thursday I gave a dinner party, and made as a sweet the Orange and Lemon Dessert, the recipe for which is given on page 307 of the Penguin *Alice B. Toklas Cook Book*. The next day all the guests complained of suffering from a terrible doped feeling, headaches and a very dry mouth. Three of the guests were confined to bed all day, and only finally recovered on Saturday afternoon. The effects were most unpleasant, particularly the complete inability to salivate, and perpetual dizziness.

The doctor is of the opinion that the cause of the illness was the large quantity of nutmeg (¼ cup) called for in the recipe. Apparently in this quantity nutmeg is narcotic, and has prolonged after-effects of the sort I describe above.

I do not know whether this has been brought to your notice before. In view of the rather drastic consequences I thought it worth pointing out to you.

Lisa Bronowski, Newnham College, Cambridge, 5 June 1966

Thank you for your letter. I am very grateful indeed that you have pointed out the mistake in the Orange and Lemon Dessert recipe in the *Alice B. Toklas Cook Book*. This really is a serious error and it should, of course, read ¼ of a teaspoon. This will be corrected in the new edition.

I am terribly sorry that this mistake should have been brought to our notice in such an unfortunate way and I do hope that this experience will not have put you off Penguin cookery books for ever.

Jill Norman to Lisa Bronowski, 5 July 1966

The book having been published in 1961, readers had, presumably, been doped and dry-mouthed for some five years before this particular error was pointed out. For those who eschewed the Orange and Lemon dessert, there were further potential sources of discomfort:

I have just bought a copy of the above work and am surprised to find that it falls into the all-too-frequent error among cookery books of translating *laurier* by laurel. *Laurier cerise* is the common English garden laurel, while the *laurier-sauce* is the English bay. This would be a minor point, were it not for the fact that laurel contains cyanide. As one medical book says: 'an infusion of three or four laurel leaves in milk will produce headaches, vertigo, loss of consciousness, convulsions and paralysis'.

I hate to think of the effect of laurel-leaf soup, page 274, for which one has to 'boil a branch of laurel with its leaves for 20 minutes in a saucepan'!

A single laurel leaf is also apparently required for quite a number of recipes throughout the book.

Perhaps this point has already been brought to your attention by those lucky enough to have noticed it before trying the recipes. To my mind, it is serious enough to warrant correction in subsequent reprints.

P. H. Collin to Penguin Books, 16 November 1962

I am not sure to whom this letter should go, perhaps you could pass it on to the right person.

Enclosed is a copy of a letter we have had from a reader. Do you know if anyone has mentioned this before? How can we find out if this is true, and what shall we do about it if it is? I will hold up my reply to Mr Collin until I hear from you.

Incidentally, a few months ago Scotland Yard were on to us about the Haschich Fudge recipe on page 306 of the Penguin, as this apparently also contains a recipe in the last paragraph for some dangerous drug, I have forgotten which one. We put them on to you. Was anything specific decided about that, I mean should any cuts or alterations be made if this is reprinted?

Patricia Siddall to Raleigh Trevelyan, 21 November 1962

Thank you for your letter of November 21st about the *Alice B. Toklas Cook Book*. Scotland Yard didn't seem inclined to pursue the matter of the Haschich Fudge. Now that cyanide has crept in, the matter is getting more and more serious. I have written to Miss Toklas's agent and will let you know what transpires. Obviously, if you decide to reprint the book, it will mean, I am afraid, either cuts or alterations.

Raleigh Trevelyan (one-time Penguin staff member and author, then at Michael Joseph) to Patricia Siddall, 3 December 1962

A copy of a letter from Joe Barry to Madame W. A. Bradley in December 1962 read:

Miss Toklas wants me to tell you that she is vastly amused by the letters on the English edition of the cook book, but, of course, is doing nothing about them. She sends you devoted remembrance and thanks for sending her the correspondence. And I join her in best wishes for the New Year.

Sincerely, Joe Barry

By March 1963, however, there was a change of mind.

On receipt of your letter of the 15th I got in contact with Miss Toklas about the little affair of the mis-translation in her cook book.

She quite agrees that Penguin should make the necessary alterations in their future reprints, changing 'laurel' into 'bay' throughout the book, and also removing the last paragraph giving the recipe for preparing one's own Haschich.

W. A. Bradley, Paris, to Raleigh Trevelyan, 26 March 1963

The last sentence in the book?

And now it amuses me to remember that the only confidence I ever gave was given twice, in the upper garden, to two friends. The first one gaily responded, How very amusing. The other asked with no little alarm, But, Alice, have you ever tried to write?

As if a cook book had anything to do with writing.

* * *

The Lucky Country

You may be interested to know that, in the first six months of the year our turnover was as big as our first complete year here. I am tickled pink. It is now showing the fruit of the first couple of years hard grinding and I think is some indication of what the US market can be worked up to. It has struck me that you might like to come here for a year. The sunshine and change of scene plus two long sea voyages would do much to put you completely back to full health, youth, vitality and what have you.

Bob Maynard to Eunice Frost, 11 July 1949

Bob Maynard had been one of the pioneers: he had worked in the Crypt, and made the move down the A4 to Harmondsworth. Returning from the war, in which he had distinguished himself, he felt, like many others, restless at the thought of an office routine. The solution had been a compromise: he had rather liked the idea of going to South Africa. Instead Allen Lane decided he should go out to Australia, a pioneer once more, and set up an office and distribution network there.

In July 1946, when he landed there, Australia was still very much a Colony. It soon became obvious that there was a great opportunity to exploit the statistic that Australia and New Zealand shared the largest reading public in the world per head of population. Maynard's reconnoitring visit became a permanent posting. Penguin's Australian headquarters were found in half a tin shed in south Melbourne, where stocks soon arrived, to be packed and dispatched personally by Maynard and his wife.

The operation grew over several years, to provide steady, if unspectacular

Marginally preferable to an inverted penguin – the Australian Penguin device.

income to Harmondsworth. All went well, until Allen Lane decided that it would be expedient to remove his brother from the immediate sphere of influence. As Richard Lane had married an Australian, sending him out to take over the Melbourne operation made sense to Allen and suited Richard perfectly too. But it meant first removing Bob Maynard. This was accomplished by a process of undermining Maynard's authority and a series of humiliations that amounted to constructive dismissal. The settlement was handled by their mutual solicitors. Years later, Lane was to concede it had been a mistake: though not to the extent of resuming a working relationship with Maynard. Richard Lane remained in charge, as a Penguin director, until he resigned just prior to Penguin's public share issue.

Tremendous growth in population, coupled with an increasing appetite for reading and an undeniable sense of national identity, all pointed to the necessity of developing the Australian business into more than just a distribution centre for books published in Britain.

Attached is a memorandum on Australian publishing by Geoffrey Dutton who is a Professor of English Literature at Adelaide University and is very highly regarded in literary circles in that country: a letter from Dr Coombs with whom I had conversations about the possibility of setting up an Australian Universities Press and a letter from Brian Stonier dated 26th September.

I have a feeling that the time is ripe for a modest beginning in Australia and I think that the three schemes might be tied in together. I would be glad to have your comments.

Allen Lane to editorial colleagues, internal memorandum, 20 October 1961

Geoffrey Dutton reported that:

The situation looks to be extremely optimistic. Sir Allen Lane's recent visit has created high expectations in the retail trade, and great enthusiasm in academic, educational, and literary groups. This keen expectation has not faded after Sir Allen's departure, but if anything has increased. There seems to be no likelihood in the immediate future of Australian publishers entering the field in competition with the kind of programme we have prepared.

There were drawbacks – the most pressing being the lack of suitable best-sellers in hardback. Consequently most of the quick turnover mass market titles would have to be commissioned. For that reason it was proposed that the initial list be split between world market and Australian titles – gradually integrating titles published from Harmondsworth with truly locally produced books.

Brian Stonier pressed the point that a real rebirth in Australia would depend on publishing locally; and commissioning books on Australian Literature, Art, Folk Songs and Children's Stories. Dr Coombs's letter suggested something quite different: setting up Penguin Books Australia as a reprint arm of the Australian National University. Bill Williams, in typical forthright style, pulled no punches.

I have read the Australian memoranda which you have sent me, and offer the following comments.

I see no prospective benefits at all in teaming up with the Australian National University. We have never formed a partnership of this kind with any British University, and I agree with Geoffrey Dutton's opinion that it might hamstring us to be attached to the ANU. It is very unlikely indeed that any exciting book would come to us via ANU. On the other hand, what we should probably be offered would be dreary academic theses which would have very poor sales indeed. I think we should maintain the detachment we have always practised in this country and express ourselves as willing to receive books from any source. I know Coombs very well and, indeed, had lunch with him the other day. We were not discussing Penguin affairs, but I did gather, from his incidental remarks, that he was astutely trying to shed various commitments, including publishing commitments, on any innocent partner he might find. Let us face it: from the academic point of view Australia has precious little to offer, certainly nothing equivalent to books we have had from academic people in this country. Coombs's proposals seem to me entirely the kind which would result in us carrying the can, in that good old Australian phrase, for University academic publishing.

The ideas put forward by Dutton and Stonier seem to me eminently sensible. Stonier, particularly, seems to have both feet on the ground. I have no first hand knowledge of conditions in Australia, but it does seem to me that the proposals put forward by Dutton might really put Penguins on the Australian map . . .

W. E. Williams to Allen Lane, 23 October 1961

I think your letter of 23 October is an extremely good summing up of the Australian situation and I will paraphrase it for consumption in Melbourne. My own feeling is that Australia is about to emerge, speaking from a publishing point of view, into a creative phase in place of an absorbent one . . .

Allen Lane to W. E. Williams, 25 October 1961

The establishment of Australian Penguins is a short study in Anglo-Australian relations . . . The beginning of the 1960s was exactly the right time to start a Penguin Australia series, to tap a wide readership that would buy paperbacks of quality, to give the prestige of the world's greatest paperback publishing house to works by Australian writers . . . In the best Lane tradition we were to do all the work ourselves and be paid very little, but the enthusiasm still surged and such practicalities seemed not to matter.

Geoffrey Dutton, *Snow on the Saltbush*, Viking Melbourne, 1984

Tony Godwin was defensive, and expressed his grave reservations in a memorandum to Allen Lane:

Where is the money to come from? Will it come out of my present budget, and how many titles a year? . . . Are we undertaking production or work on manuscript preparation, proofreading etc., or are they going to do the whole thing over there?

His strongest reaction was to the modest proposals for Australian Specials:

I would be completely against these being published as Penguin Specials unless it is made quite clear that they were Australian Penguin Specials as opposed to our own. We have a very clear conception of Penguin Specials and by the sound of the Australian set up we would not have any editorial control.

Finally I feel the timing of the programme seems unrealistic.

An initial bungling would cause loss of their own confidence, while a launch of this project below our standards would slow up the whole project getting under way. I would therefore press most strongly that the earliest they could launch their first titles would be during 1963 at the beginning of the academic year, whenever it happens to be.

The Australian Editorial Board was set up and met in December 1961, agreeing to aim for November 1962 as the date for the first publications.

Sir Allen has asked me to add a rider to his letter of 7/8 March in reply to yours of 28 February and 1 March.

We discussed the question of your printing in Australia, and were all in agreement with the force of your argument. We are looking forward with enthusiastic interest to the day when you will launch your own publications. However, it does raise one or two problems.

I have just received a letter dated 1 March from Geoffrey Dutton, to which I shall be replying today. In it he instances the four titles which you are to launch in November 1962, and one of those titles is Randolph Stow's *To the Islands*. You will probably have seen my previous letter in which I said we would be able to use 15,000 copies here were we to publish it in collaboration with you. This, of course, was under the condition that we should publish it over here and send you a bulk consignment of your own copies. If you are going to print and publish in Australia, I think the picture changes, because the higher Australian printing prices plus the consignment charges would greatly add to our costs.

It also raises at this early stage the problem of the cover. For instance, would we send you artwork for our 15,000 copies, or use your cover adapted to look like our normal fiction cover?

It seems to me, on reflection, that there will be sufficient problems involved in the launching of Australia's own publishing programme without involving ourselves in unnecessary problems. I would suggest, as a principle, that during your first year's programme any titles which you publish in Australia should be published without any expectation of any aid from England. We shall, of course, try to sell as many copies as we can; but I think, personally, that they should be regarded as a bonus rather than essential to your planning on printing figures . . .

Tony Godwin to Brian Stonier, 13 March 1962

I was completely stunned and taken aback by your letter of the 13th March.

I agree we must resolve at once this principle of whether we can count on any UK and/or USA sales, as I have not the slightest doubt that we cannot economically support a publishing programme in this country, without your sales support.

Probably we shall always have to rely on overseas sales, but most particularly for the first year, so there is not much point in indicating that you may support us after the first year, for there wouldn't be any publishing!

I assumed that the whole point of Penguins publishing in Australia, was to give an experienced world-wide marketing to Australian titles which had not had such a chance before – and to take advantage of overseas interest in one or two aspects of Australia . . .

But if all that is intended is that we shall become a parochial Australian publisher (maybe selling a few overseas by accident), then we shall be a very second-rate version of Angus & Robertson, Rigbys and Horwitz. These are the only three paperback distributors in this country, and none of them approaches Penguins (Ltd) as to product, standing, or experience . . .

As far as I can see, if we do not have active support in obtaining overseas sales for the proposed titles, there is no point in wasting time by publishing here. What is the point of our doing *Australian Art* under these circumstances, we might as well wait for a few years till you can do it, at Harmondsworth . . .

Brian Stonier to Tony Godwin, 21 March 1962

Thank you very much for your letter of 21 March from which I was distressed to learn that you were stunned and taken aback by my letter of 13 March.

The crux of the matter is, of course, that the amount of support which we can give you by placing a firm order for a title for us to sell both at home and in the other export markets is subject to exactly the same considerations as operate from here. I absolutely sympathize with everything you say, but, nevertheless, one does have to be practical about these things. . .

I think that you are jumping to conclusions when you say that this principle can be resolved whether or not you can count on UK and/or USA sales. What I said was that I thought it would be wisest to try and cost up your projected titles without counting unduly on UK sales, but tending to regard them as jam on the bread and butter. Of course you can count on UK sales and when you can manage to give us sufficient concrete details on which to work we will probably give you a provisional order.

Tony Godwin to Brian Stonier, 3 April 1962

From this point, Hans Schmoller took over, ostensibly as Tony Godwin had now given the Australian team the benefit of his practical editorial experience. Schmoller could add to this matters of production and pricing. That advice, based on locally produced copies of *Breakfast at Tiffany's*, was comprehensive, typical of the care and knowledge he applied to all his work – and delivered with rather more tact than recent exchanges had led the Australian team to expect.

Thank you for your letter of 3 April and the two advance copies of *Breakfast at Tiffany's*. The speed with which these have been produced leaves us breathless and you deserve to be congratulated on having managed it so quickly.

The printing quality, you will forgive me for saying, is indifferent. Admittedly a printed paperback is not ideal photo copy, and I can well believe that the printer had some difficulty under that heading. But much of the unevenness must be due to poor plate-making and machining . . .

The paper is good – in fact too good for the purpose – but I note that it was only used because you were unable to get hold of Burnie Directory in time. Judging by the specimen, Burnie Directory at £100 sterling per ton compares quite favourably with the paper we often use for offset litho printed text at £98 sterling, but even this is a lot more expensive than our standard paper at under £70 sterling per ton. Admittedly it is somewhat better quality.

One thing that is wrong with your paper is the direction of the grain: it runs across the page instead of down. It is this which prevents the book from lying flat when opened, and if you ever order a whole making, you should try to insist that the paper is supplied with the grain running parallel with the spine on the finished book. There are various ways of testing this. The simplest perhaps is to fold the sheet both ways: it will fold more readily and smoothly if the fold runs with the grain than across it.

There is perhaps an excessive contrast between the almost blue-white of the cover and the cream of the text paper.

Lastly, the imprint page: its only, and major, blemish is the excessively wide word-spacing throughout. Close word-spacing is one of the basic rules of good composition and your printer evidently does not know it.

Hans Schmoller to Brian Stonier, 10 April 1962

In March 1963 the first Australian titles were published, with their own national identity: the Penguin, Pelican or Puffin colophon flanked by crossed boomerangs.

Allen Lane's visit to Australia to open the new Penguin headquarters at Ringwood, and Tony Godwin's trip to sample Australian culture first hand (or, some said, as a subtle hint of possible exile), were not enough to mend a relationship that had been soured. Godwin's initial refusal to distribute copies of *The Lucky Country* and *The Australian Ugliness* in Britain was crowned by his casual dismissal of Dutton's collection for *New Australian Writing*. His action was due to a ludicrously ill-informed report. The report itself was leaked to the press:

This writing combines the vices of parochialism and an attempted superiority about parochial society; it is like a school magazine in which the school's few intellectuals parade their dislike of the school, but betray their inability to think beyond it.

The Australian, 10 October 1964

It was the final confirmation to the Australian editors that:

The local Penguin organization does not enjoy the full confidence of Harmondsworth and is therefore frequently bypassed. People suggest to one that Australian Penguins must be a pretty crumby bunch if they need another publisher to run their business. The result is that one is made to feel a bit of a galah in the local scene.

Geoffrey Dutton to Allen Lane, 21 August 1964

Like their earlier American counterparts, Brian Stonier, Geoffrey Dutton, Max Harris and George Smith all resigned in order to start their own publishing firm, Sun Books. Worse was to follow. In February 1966 the major publication *The Art of Australia* was withdrawn shortly before publication, for failing to meet production standards. It was announced to the press that

Robert Hughes's book would be brought up to date and reprinted – in the United Kingdom – in a year's time.

Nevertheless, *The Lucky Country* did sell out its first edition, with significant help from British sales, and, like the American branch, Penguin Australia settled down to grow steadily and prosper, despite occasional minor setbacks and changes of staff. As Morpurgo observed: 'There were other overseas adventures and Allen's urge to travel was never stilled, but with Baltimore and Melbourne firmly established his imperial pretensions were satisfied.'

* * *

Britain in the Sixties

What's happened to the Common Sense About Smoking*? Do you realize that the longer you delay, the more people are going to die of cancer? I want it for January. Please.*

Tony Godwin to Dieter Pevsner, July 1962

After the spectacular successes of the years leading up to the war, Penguin Specials adapted to the new circumstances by turning their attention to more practical matters and generally broadening the horizons of the series. So, alongside the continuing political volumes, were a good many handbooks dealing primarily with food, books of Low cartoons, *The Case for Family Allowances*, *Ley Farming*, *Venereal Disease in Britain*, *God and Human Progress*; as well as a number of books detailing the progress of the war: *Signalling and Map Reading for the Home Guard*, *The British Way in Warfare*, *An ABC of the Pacific*, *How the Jap Army Fights*, *Our Settlement With Germany*. And, most popular of all, two volumes of R. A. Saville-Sneath's *Aircraft Recognition*.

In the immediate post-war period the series dried up, as books on the big issues of the day – *Hiroshima*, *The Nuremberg Trials*, and Emery Reves's *The Anatomy of Peace* – were issued in the main series. As Allen Lane pointed out to the MP Tom Horabin: 'At the present time there is, unfortunately, a very definite trade recession going on in publishing and bookselling, and in no other class of book is it more noticeable than those dealing with current affairs either at home or abroad.'

With the purely practical consideration that in the immediate post-war period, the average time for getting a book through the press was around eighteen months, and with no single editor managing the Specials series, they searched mostly in vain for causes that would remain current for long enough. Barbara Ward's *Policy for the West* and a collaborative effort *Attitude to Africa* came out in 1951. 1952 saw Bob Darke's *The Communist Technique in Britain*. Then there was *The Kingship of Christ*, *Communism and Christianity* and *Spotlight on Asia*. There were few other Penguin Specials during the early 1950s.

The latter half of the decade began to see a revival of interest, and the burning issues of the day – the Middle and Far East, the atomic revolution and the bomb – were all treated, along with a slightly incongruous look at *Sixty Seasons of League Football*.

But it was British politics that was to prove the salvation of the series. Shortly after the war, J. E. D. Hall was commissioned to write a summary of the sweeping changes introduced in *Labour's First Year*, 'a session of Parliament in which legislation has been passed providing for the nationalization of the coal mines and of the Bank of England, and for the implementation of a nationwide scheme of State provision for safeguarding the health of the whole people . . . a landmark in British history'. Some months after publication, however, Allen Lane wrote to Hall: 'As you know, our intention was to continue with this series reflecting year by year the progress of this country into Socialism, but from the present reaction of the public – I don't honestly feel that this is merely a temporary outlook – it does not appear as if the venture is going to be economic. For this reason I feel that perhaps it might be wise to face up to this now, rather than let it drift on for a second and third volume.'

It was followed up, all the same, some ten months later with a more balanced approach – a Labour and Conservative politician had both been approached to put their particular points of view. This was to cause Penguin no little embarrassment: John Parker's *Labour Marches On* was delivered on time, and to the specified length of 70,000 words. The manuscript of Quintin Hogg's *The Case for Conservatism* ran to 160,000 words, and even after substantial editing still topped 120,000.

So Penguin were obliged to sell the Labour offering at one shilling, and the Conservative version as a double volume at twice the price. Richard Lane was at some pains to point out: 'I do feel very strongly – and my Sales Department agrees with me – that to publish the two books together with so marked a difference in the price would inspire purchasers and reviewers to feel that we were giving your party a very unfair deal and, indeed, would expose us to accusations of political partisanship, which, as I feel sure you will agree, the very fact that we arranged for these two books to be written at the same time indicates, are unjustified.' Which would seem to suggest that another item of Penguin mythology, that 'the road to Number Ten Downing Street was paved with Penguin Specials' was not yet common currency. Indeed a Publisher's Note in both volumes stated, 'The difference in price between the two books, therefore, does not mean that the publishers wish either to penalize the advocacy of Conservatism by charging the reader more than a fair price for it, or to suggest that Labour policy is worth only half as much as Conservative policy! As publishers we have no politics. We hope that both the political friends and political opponents of each of the authors will spend three shillings on both books; and we are sure they will feel that in both cases they have had good value for their money.'

Penguin's avowed pragmatism in the quest for readers' three shillings led William Gallacher to test Penguin by offering a further volume, *The Case for Communism*, which Lane naturally accepted. The embarrassment caused by the price differences of the previous two were eclipsed by this prospect. Bill Williams agonized:

There still does linger in my mind the repercussions on the firm's prestige which publication might create. The public is a rather foolish animal, and might well jump to the wrong conclusion. We can, of course, make it abundantly plain in the blurb that we are only doing for Communism what we have already done for Conservatism and Socialism. But I think we ought to consider some further announcement on the front cover itself, i.e. saying that this is one of a series on, political beliefs. Such a course would, I know, make the cover look ugly and distress Tschichold, but I think this case deserves special treatment.

Conflicting opinion within Penguin's ranks was mollified by an odd compromise. Gallacher's book was published, not in the main series with the other two, but as the first of a new series of Penguin Specials, with the prominent cover statement. As if to emphasize their neutrality, it was priced at 1/6d.

It did prove finally possible to shorten Quintin Hogg's book, which reappeared in 1959 as *The Conservative Case* by Viscount Hailsham, along with two newly commissioned volumes of almost identical length, Roy Jenkins's *The Labour Case*, and Roger Fulford's *The Liberal Case*.

All this was only a brief prelude to a complete revival of the Specials on the lines of social and political criticism which had so caught the public mood before the war. It was initially Allen Lane's idea, who invited Richard Hoggart, the author of *The Uses of Literacy*, and Dieter Pevsner to discuss the issues of the day: a meeting once more of missionary and mercenary ideals, and the beginnings of a new interpretation of the phrase 'paperback revolution'. Once again – and all the more so when Tony Godwin took a close personal interest and overall control of the series – it was to be Penguin's aim to set a new agenda and, with a series of polemical works, define Britain in the sixties.

At whom is this book aimed? I would like to see much more, in the opening chapters, on the sociological aspect of insufficient housing and on the connexion of housing and literacy – can you produce a nation of scientists and technicians where families still live in two rooms, with or without Granny? What is a socially reasonable standard of housing? Social justice or equity and housing are burning questions. I would really like, at the beginning of the book, to see the whole of this side put into perspective . . .

Tony Godwin to Dieter Pevsner, 22 August 1962

Britain in the Sixties: Housing was published in September 1962, and attracted the following comments from 'Economos' in *Estates Gazette*: 'Today Penguins have grown into a tremendous weapon of the Left. True, they published Quintin Hogg's book, but then one swallow doesn't make a summer; find a pop socialist work, and the odds are considerable that Penguins have put out an edition of it at some time or another . . .'

Further Specials asked *What's Wrong With the Church, Hospitals, Unions, Parliament* and *British Industry*. *Housing* was joined by *The Family and Marriage, The Crown and the Establishment, The Other England, Education for Tomorrow*, *Communications* and *Vagrancy* in the Britain in the Sixties series.

Anthony Samson believes that Macmillan will make a convulsive effort to drag Britain into the Common Market by this early Autumn, that the governmental position will continue to deteriorate, and that Macmillan will hold a snap election in November.

I suppose there is a possibility of this. The general view I have obtained from the *Guardian* and the weeklies seems to be that we would be damned lucky to be in the Common Market a year next Autumn, and that a general election is unlikely before next Spring.

However, under these circumstances, we ought to discuss those three little Specials – do you remember them? *Why I Believe in Labour*, *in Liberal* and (hollow laugh) *in Conservative Governments*.

Tony Godwin to Dieter Pevsner and Charles Clark, internal memorandum, 17 July 1962

S201, published in July 1963, was Nora Beloff's *The General Says No: Britain's Exclusion From Europe*. Preparations eventually went ahead with a further trio of Specials detailing the relative merits of the parties. Jim Northcott's *Why Labour?* and Timothy Raison's *Why Conservative?* were published together.

I hope you will be pleased to receive the enclosed after all this time. And this seems a good moment to thank you for all the work you have put in. I hope you make thousands of converts.

We are publishing it, together with *Why Labour?* (of which I thought you might like to see a copy), on 2 April. Unfortunately the Liberals rather let us down. We still hope to be able to publish one before the Election, but it is not certain.

There are thirteen copies of your book and I would be awfully grateful if you could sign one of them and return it to Sir Allen Lane who keeps a collection of autographed Penguins.

Once again, congratulations and many thanks.

Dieter Pevsner to Timothy Raison, House of Commons, 23 March 1964

Harry Cowie's Liberal manifesto finally appeared in July, at the same time as another political offering.

Here is a proof of the cover of your book. I hope that you approve. *The New Britain* quoted in the title will be printed in white, not in red as here. I would like to take the opportunity of thanking you for all your help in preparing your book for press. We are very pleased with the result and hope you will be as pleased as we are when you see a finished copy.

PS My imagination was particularly caught by your Edinburgh speech in March, 'A First-class Nation'.

Tony Godwin to Harold Wilson, Prime Minister, 30 June 1964

Many thanks for your letter of 30th June, enclosing the proof of the book. I think it is excellent and am very pleased with it, as are all who have seen it with only one exception.

I appreciate what you said about the preparation side. My regret is that I could not have been quicker than I was, but know you understand the difficulties.

I am looking forward to seeing the finished article but in the meantime would like to express my thanks to you and your colleagues for all the help you have given, and your great patience and courtesy.

Thank you again – and particularly for your postscript.

Harold Wilson to Tony Godwin, 3 July 1964

Tony Godwin was not able to resist a further letter concerning the marketing of Harold Wilson's *Selected Speeches*:

I should welcome any personal suggestions or requests you might wish to make. I also wonder whether you might happen to be making a policy speech on or about the eve of publication, Thursday 30 July. A policy speech that referred to the book or one of the speeches in the book would give an enormous fillip towards the necessary impact to make the country aware of its presence in the bookshops and on the bookstalls.

The international front was not ignored during this period – just like the Specials of the 1930s, the titles act as a chronicle of the times: *Berlin: Hostage for the West*; *Torture, Cancer of Democracy* (*France and Algeria 1954–62*); *The New Cold War: Moscow v. Pekin*; Bertrand Russell's *Unarmed Victory*; *Cuba: an American Tragedy*; *Legacy of Strife: Cyprus from Rebellion to Civil War*; *South East Asia in Turmoil*; and, inevitably – *Vietnam*.

Another cause that Penguin supported with considerable vigour, and not only through Penguin Specials, was the Anti-Apartheid movement. This was due predominantly to Tony Godwin's association with the exiled South African Ronald Segal, who was to become a prolific freelance editor for Penguin, producing a number of political Specials, commissioning and editing for the Pelican series on Political Leaders, as well as founding and editing for many years the Penguin African Library, which took as its standard the editor's own first contribution to the series, *African Profiles*.

There were clear echoes of Penguin's early, fervent years in his first meeting with Godwin as Ronald Segal recalled: 'The founding of the Penguin African Library is part of South African political as well as British publishing history. During the Sharpeville emergency of 1960, I took Oliver Tambo, the ANC leader, across the border into exile, and subsequently *Africa South*, the international quarterly I had been publishing and editing in Cape Town, to Britain. Sometime in 1961, I was informed by the authorities in South Africa that all my inherited money, with which I had long been subsidizing the quarterly, was frozen there, and I had little choice but to announce an end to the publication of *Africa South in Exile*. I got a telephone call from Tony Godwin inviting me to meet him and Dieter

Pevsner at a pub in St Martin's Lane. There he suggested to me that Penguin might consider financing and publishing the quarterly. It was a tempting offer, but the quarterly, radical and militant, owed much of its character to its independence and I believed that it was better dead than sustained in any other form. When I rejected the offer and gave my reasons, Tony proposed that I should start a Penguin African Library and be given, as an assurance of its autonomy, complete editorial control over it.'

There were similar resonances in the preparation to publish Segal's first Special.

An international conference on Sanctions Against South Africa will be opening in approximately a fortnight in London. This is a large scale international affair under the patronage of about seven Prime Ministers. A number of eminent people have been asked to contribute papers examining specific aspects of this problem such as the effect of sanctions against South Africa on gold and the effect on the British economy, the position vis à vis international law, etc.

We shall be publishing a Penguin Special on this in July and as you can see this is a rush job. I want you to prepare three covers, one of which we shall finally choose. Cover number one will feature a photograph showing the South African delegation missing from the UN's session. Cover number two will feature a quote or quotes from the conference. Cover number three would be a design/typographical cover featuring some or all of the contents and some or all of the authors.

I realize that this somewhat opportunistic approach to the cover causes a lot of extra work but I think the signal importance of the book merits it. Could you please act on this at once.

Tony Godwin to Germano Facetti, internal memorandum, 26 March 1964

Sanctions Against South Africa was published with just those words in black and white text on a plain red cover. Ronald Segal was already working on a second Special, published early in 1965 as *The Crisis of India*.

This is a brilliant, beautiful, maddening, mad, filthy and pitiful place. I am almost out of my mind myself with interviewing politicians, economists and religious fanatics. But I'm glad I came, and I will certainly write a provocative book for you, though it may take me a year to do it in, and it will never be allowed into India, what a political scandal! But the Indians are sensitive and so am I.

The Penguin African Library has sold out in Bombay, though there are still a few copies on the pavement in a mosaic of pornography. I am much less impressed with Penguin coverage anywhere else. I cannot say whether the fault lies in your agents or your inhibitions, but you're much less in evidence than Four Square or Pan or the interminable Americans.

I see that *Into Exile* has got some good pre-publicity in the *Guardian*. Advance copies should be ready quite soon, and if you and Dieter want any – I should like you to read the final version – do please phone up Tom on my behalf and ask him for a couple, from me to you.

I am travelling everywhere by car, which is a laboured, expensive but valuable business, and I should be in Calcutta, staying at the Great Eastern from the 25th of January to about the 6th of February, if you want to write to me.

Ronald Segal, in India, to Tony Godwin, 12 January 1963

* * *

Has Man a Future?

I should like to interest you in writing for us a brief Penguin Special, the starting point of which would, of course, be your present campaign for non-violent resistance in the cause of nuclear disarmament but would also, I hope, deal with some other matters.

In the welter of controversy over defence, we seem to have forgotten to ask not only whether there is anything to fight against but also what are we defending ourselves for. For Democracy? For the Western Way of Life? For Christian values? (And what do these phrases mean in 1961?) If for mere survival, then survival of what sort of people in what sort of society.

A short book by you on, in effect, ends and means in the 1960s, would as a Penguin Special reach a very large audience which is, privately at least, becoming increasingly uneasy about the answers to the sort of question which I have suggested.

I very much hope that this idea appeals to you. Perhaps we could meet to explore it further. I look forward to hearing from you.

Tony Godwin to Bertrand Russell, 7 March 1961

I wanted to write straight away to say how very pleased I was to meet you, to thank you and your wife for your hospitality and to tell you again how delighted we all are that you are willing to write *Has Man a Future?* for us.

I will, as I said, let you have a suggested rough outline based on the discussion we had on the various points you feel should make the book. I shall let you have this next week when I have had a little time to put our thoughts in order.

Thank you very much again for your kindness.

Dieter Pevsner to Bertrand Russell, 29 March 1961

Bertrand Russell is writing us a Penguin Special which we hope to have in the house ready for press at the beginning of September. The book will be linked to his support of nuclear disarmament, but will not basically be an argument in favour of nuclear disarmament campaigns. Rather it will be concerned mainly with the far more fascinating question of why this great and universally esteemed man of nearly 90, with no belief in God or a life to come, should feel that it is so important for mankind to survive and is prepared to devote a considerable effort to backing such a campaign . . . I don't think I need to point out to you what a privilege it is for Penguin to be given the chance to do the first publication of a new book by Russell.

Dieter Pevsner to Peter Janson-Smith, 3 July 1961

As you probably know, we publish practically all Bertrand Russell's work, and he wrote to us expressing the hope that we should not feel aggrieved that he had fallen for a proposal you had made him for a short book on *Has Man a Future?* Our reply was to the effect that we should never want to prevent him from doing anything he wanted but that we felt, in view of our unique connection with his writings, a cloth bound edition should be simultaneously published by us. He tells us that you are agreeable and that the contract should be with you. We accordingly enclose a formal agreement which we hope will meet with your approval.

Stanley Unwin, George Allen & Unwin Ltd, to Dieter Pevsner, 22 June 1961

The typescript of *Has Man a Future?* is enclosed herewith. I hope that you will not think it too different from your suggested synopsis. I also hope that the population of Britain will survive long enough for you to get it published . . .

Bertrand Russell to Dieter Pevsner, 20 July 1961

I am writing to explain that, if I am given a considerable prison sentence next Tuesday, as seems likely, I shall not be able to correct the proofs of *Has Man a Future?* I am very sorry and hope this will not cause you trouble . . .

Bertrand Russell to Dieter Pevsner, 8 September 1961

Of course I understand that should you be sent to prison tomorrow you will have difficulty in correcting the proofs, but I sincerely hope that it may not come to that. I have noted your two corrections and passed them on to Stanley Unwin.

Dieter Pevsner to Bertrand Russell, 11 September 1961

Bertrand Russell, a prominent member of the Committee of 100, had earlier been arrested during a CND demonstration in Downing Street.

I have great pleasure in enclosing six personal copies of your book *Has Man a Future?*

I would like to take this opportunity to thank you once again for having agreed to write this book for us and then for working so hard to produce it quickly. As things have turned out, it could hardly have been more timely, and we feel both fortunate and proud to be able to bring it out at this moment. For your part, I hope you will feel that our presentation of the book is exciting.

Publication is, as you know, on 25 November, and the *Sunday Times* is to publish its first extract next week.

Dieter Pevsner to Bertrand Russell, 30 October 1961

* * *

Tony Richardson and the Liberal Arts

. . . Will be in touch when nostalgia for trad, old socks and the hard floors of segregated schools or the Aldermaston march becomes too great – if not before. Senility at twenty-five is a curious experience. It must be the angst and schmerz and schmaltz of the post-Nagasaki, post-Sinatra generation. Looking forward to more of your viscera.

Tony Richardson to Jeff Nuttall, 2 December 1966

Herewith the Black. When are you going to do a Penguin Concrete Poetry – and drive all your typographers into nervous breakdowns?

Edward Lucie-Smith to Tony Richardson, undated

Very many thanks for the copyright holders on *Satirical Verse* and for D. M. Black. Everyone now wants us to do Concrete Poetry – which is why we are not. Or, to put it less succinctly, it would be a real commercial disaster with our print runs. However, Horovitz has delivered a part of his anthology proposals and I hope that we would have a fair section of Concrete Poetry here. Never let it be said that we languish in the race to be fashionable.

Tony Richardson to Edward Lucie-Smith, 4 November 1966

My reasons for wanting to omit the poems I did were, generally speaking, just a matter of personal preferences. I am not at all worried about the British reader – you are neither a British reader's poet nor an American reader's poet, just a poet. And to be fair I do think you rather over-estimate the Englishman's susceptibility in certain matters. For example, I didn't omit 'Matins' because of the toilet seat. Even we, primitive and insular as we may be, have long ago accepted the flush toilet and the processes connected with it as legitimate material for the artist. Let me reinforce this with a digest of the theme of one of the poems by George MacBeth which we published in the latest volume of the Penguin Modern Poets Series:

'The Crucifix'. A Neo-Nazi in England keeps a photograph above his bed of Sigrid von Lappus, one of Hitler's mistresses. She wears a chain around her ankle with a swastika attached to it. He treats this as a crucifix, and regards the photograph as an image of the Virgin Mary. Each night before going to bed, in a ritual sperm-letting, he abuses himself before the picture.

As this may demonstrate I have no real qualms about our audience, unless it be about their capacity to know good poetry when they see it.

Extracts from a letter from Tony Richardson explaining to Denise Levertov his initial selection of her poems for Penguin Modern Poets 9, 16 November 1964. 'Matins' was ultimately included in the selection of her work.

It was very nice meeting you and talking about the Penguin Modern Poets project. I hope you can persuade Longmans – if in fact they need persuading – that your appearance in the series would be a good thing. Meanwhile I am looking around to see if I can find a suitable male playmate. Can't think of anybody offhand but there must be enough poets to make a fully equipped brigade – I will start with the NCOs and work downwards. I enclose copies of the five volumes in the Penguin Modern Poets Series to date. They should give you some idea of the way the thing works, and it may elucidate what I myself told you.

I hope you found your glasses without too much difficulty and that the Arts Council will find me some promising poets . . .

Look forward to seeing you again some time when we know better how we stand.

Tony Richardson to Stevie Smith, 6 March 1964

I am sorry being so long over this job, somehow I always mean to get on with it and then everything crops up in the way of various domestic crises, going away, and so on. But I expect the real reason is that as soon as I start thumbing over the wretched old ones I begin to want to write new ones, and so do, and that means further delay. But this letter is just to let you know that the ghastly bundle really is getting sorted out and I hope to let you have it soon. By the way, have you got a copy of the Longmans book – the *Selected Poems*? If so, and there are any you particularly like, do send me the titles and I will include them.

Stevie Smith to Tony Richardson, 10 September 1964

I've got so many letters that I haven't answered by this time that yours . . . dated Oct. 15th . . . seems like only yesterday.

As you have guessed, I certainly have no objections to your list, in fact I think it's v. good and marvellous of you to have sorted it out at all.

I now seem to do nothing but sing my poems around the poetry groups . . . so that will be an added complication, getting the music score in too, as well as the drawings.

Do hope you are well and not having too trying a time of it.

Stevie Smith to Tony Richardson, 9 November 1964

Glad you liked the selection. I will now go ahead and get a contract with Longmans drawn up. Sorry your correspondence is piling up. I swear I will not add to it – for the moment at least.

Tell me one thing – do you sit at the piano, play the guitar, or are you backed by a jazz group? At this rate you will make next year's Royal Command Performance, if not Covent Garden. You might, incidentally, let me know where and when the next poetry sing-song is taking place. It sounds so much more fun than a dry old reading.

Tony Richardson to Stevie Smith, 11 November 1964

In addition to his Poetry duties, the gifted Tony Richardson also looked after Penguin's burgeoning Art list – and the dedicated and epicurean external editors of the Pelican Style and Civilization series, Hugh Honour and John Fleming, whom Allen Lane had met by chance when staying next door to their permanent home in Italy.

Your letter of the 10th May – my fault, I'm afraid, the £200 was paid to Fleming–Honour in March. Apologies. It is difficult to keep track of payments sometimes – not because they come in so fast, I hasten to add, but because the bloody banks are too bloody lazy nowadays to say on their accounts who made the payments.

Don't bother about the lark pâté for the moment: Tory has just discovered a patch of truffles in our woods so we shall be all right for another week or two . . .

John Fleming to Tony Richardson, 20 May 1965

I enclose first proofs of the illustrations for Pre-Classical. The reason I am sending them to you will, I am sure, be immediately obvious – as you can see, the designer has used a large number of cut-outs.

I believe I have discussed the idea of the cut-out with you and Hugh before, but I indicated then that I was against it. I have also, in the past, indicated this feeling to the designer. On the one hand, his argument in relation to this book is the following – the illustrations are themselves dull. No amount of sizing or extravagance of page-layout will mitigate this. In cut-out form, however, they can present shapes which look very exciting on the page. He is using cut-outs precisely for this reason.

I can personally see a lot of justice in this and feel that in many cases the touching out has been sensitively done. I also feel that the vases especially gain greatly from this treatment. Their contours are brought into play as an essential factor and to my mind this somewhat alleviates the monotony of so heavy a reliance on vase painting. Paradoxically, they have a far stronger physical presence in cut-out form than they ever had in the original photographs.

I am less sure about the sculpture, since I have always believed that cut-out, by abstracting a work in the round from its natural space, produces a dreary, flat, and artificial result which invalidates all the sculptural qualities of the object.

On the other hand, I feel the results are not in every case so monstrous as I would have expected . . . I would therefore appreciate your comments upon the individual quality of each of the proofs . . .

Tony Richardson to John Fleming, 6 May 1966

Your letter of the 6th has just arrived with the proofs of Boardman's plates. Hugh and I are pretty horrified by some of them though we understand and to some extent sympathize with what Gerry was trying to do. I don't think cutting out matters very much with the pots and I suppose in some cases they will undoubtedly look a bit better. But it is a different matter altogether when we come to sculpture. I really cannot see how this possibly can be defended. Cutting out not only tampers with the silhouette but distorts in other ways as well, especially when there are any holes, i.e. between the thighs. When cut out one gets a bright white patch between the thighs, with distorting effect and the whole looks quite unlike what it ever looks like in reality . . .

So what it comes to is this. Hugh and I would think it absolutely essential to have new blocks made (with no cut outs) of the following:

Plate 58. I can't remember what the original background was in the photograph. But it couldn't be worse than it is now. Just *look* at those arm-pits! It's too vulgar . . .

John Fleming to Tony Richardson, 11 May 1966

I can tell you now about the job I am going to since everything is signed and my fate sealed. Briefly, Granada, who as you know already own Panther, Hart-Davis, MacGibbon & Kee and a substantial chunk of Cape, want to add another paperback imprint. I will be going there in September as Chief (and only) Editor, with lashings of money at my disposal and the invitation to build a strong competitive list. As you can imagine, I am delighted with the whole thing – since if one is committed to publishing this is precisely the kind of situation one dreams of waking up in. But it also scares the pants off me, and I only pray that it will work.

Tony Richardson to John Fleming, 18 July 1967

Tony Richardson left shortly afterwards, to set up the Paladin imprint for Granada. This immensely gifted editor died in 1969 before his thirtieth birthday, a victim of Hodgkin's disease.

* * *

Kaye Webb and Puffin Books

Tell Allen from me that Austria is a much better bet than Tring. I wish I had been able to see him soon after my return to prove my point (seven pounds lighter and a suntan).

Kaye Webb to Eunice Frost, 9 April 1954 – her earliest appearance in the Penguin archive.

The transition from one generation to the next that took place in most corners of the Penguin empire during the early 1960s affected the Puffin list no less profoundly, with the retirement of Eleanor Graham and the arrival of her replacement, Kaye Webb. In this instance, at least, the passage was smoothed by the able interregnum of Margaret Clark. And just as the 1960s took a little time to get going, so too did the rejuvenated Puffin list. But like the decade itself, once it really got moving, there was no stopping it.

Kaye Webb was able to see the opportunity that existed for Puffin and create a phenomenon. For under Kaye, editorial decisions and marketing decisions were inextricably bound.

The Story of Puffin Books, Sally Gritten, 1991

What had happened was simply another of Lane's hunches paying off. Kaye Webb was not the obvious choice for the job: she had plenty of experience, but none specifically in book publishing. This was more than compensated for by her attitude and sheer enthusiasm. There is no doubt that Eleanor Graham loved books and was passionately concerned with producing the very best for children. Kaye simply loved children, and used Puffin to engage their hearts and minds in equal measure.

A remote stance and occasional formal meetings were unthinkable for her. She mucked in. At one level this involved increasing dramatically the output of new books: forestalling competition by persuading a series of hardback publishers into deferring their plans to launch their own children's paperback list. She raised the profile of Puffin with her natural instinct for publicity. But more than anything else she set out to get to know her readers, and get her readers to know Puffin. Huge parties were laid on at Harmondsworth where readers met both the staff and authors; exhibitions were mounted, competitions organized and on one memorable occasion a trip arranged for a party of children to meet real puffins on Lundy Island, finishing up with a barbecue on Allen Lane's farm. Books had to be as exciting as television. Through her constant personal involvement and stream of ideas, allied with an astutely chosen list, Kaye Webb made books come alive.

Do you feel yourself settling in to the Chair comfortably now? I am sure you must, the new books have such a nice positive look.

Eleanor Graham to Kaye Webb, 21 September 1961

I have just heard that I am going to be allowed to have a reprint of *Black Beauty*, and I wonder whether you would feel like redesigning the cover for us . . . If you feel like doing it for us we should like something rather less gentle and more arresting since I find that it's the immediate attraction of the cover itself that does half the selling of a Puffin. I am sending you one or two covers which I think have been particularly successful.

Charlotte Hough's first thoughts on illustrating *Black Beauty*, casually interposed halfway through her letter on the subject.

If you would do the roughest sort of rough I could perhaps pop over and discuss it with you. We can offer a fee of 20gns for a new design.

One of the books I am sending you, *Snow Cloud Stallion*, isn't really a very good book, but it has sold entirely on its cover. Apparently dramatic horsey covers are in. Perhaps you could do Black Beauty in a close-up. If you don't want to wrap the design round the jacket you needn't, but we should like some design on the back as well if it is a separate one.

Kaye Webb to Charlotte Hough, undated

Older readers were courted first with the introduction of Peacocks – designed primarily for teenagers, and more specifically teenage girls. The Penguin backlist was raided for suitable titles – the series was launched with *National Velvet*, and was soon followed by John Buchan, C. S. Forester and Georgette Heyer titles. But the majority of books were new to Penguin, as were a good many of the authors.

Only one original book was issued, *The Peacock Cookery Book*, written by Betty Falk with an educational market in mind. Kaye Webb's hands-on approach to the children's series was much in evidence when it came to producing a cover for the book.

I'm going to make your Stuffed Eggs and Doreen has very nicely said she'll make a Lemon Meringue Pie, but if you could make just one of your recipes which would look attractive on a photograph it will obviously ease the strain. If this is inconvenient I'm sorry, and if you really can't manage it we shall just have to go and buy something.

Kaye Webb to Betty Falk, 24 May 1963

Kaye Webb's assistant Doreen Scott had her kitchen requisitioned for the cover photograph.

For Kaye Webb, whose primary aim, supported for many years by Allen Lane, was to make readers rather than profits, any practical scheme towards this end was worth pursuing. None was pursued with such vigour and energy as the Puffin Club, her inspired creation which took the involvement of the readership in the processes of writing and publishing to new levels altogether.

The Club was almost launched on an unfortunate note, or at least with an unfortunate choice of words: 'CENSORED: Sir Allen Lane orders the Puffin club to drop "psychedelic"' ran the headline of Charles Greville's article in the *Daily Mail* of 27 February 1967.

Even 64-year-old Sir Allen didn't know at first when I asked him about it last night. So he asked his wife, Lettice. She knows all about the psychedelic bit. She's a psychiatrist. And after she had explained to him that the word comes from the hipster world of drugs like LSD, Sir Allen said: 'I don't know how we came to use it. It's a very silly word to have chosen. It must be dropped at once.' It will mean changing thousands of pounds' worth of bookshop display material designed to make children join the Puffin Club, which starts next month.

Trying to 'think of exciting words beginning with a P', they had come up with the slogan 'It's P'Super – It's Psychedelic'.

Four years ago today we were writing you the Very First Editor's Letter, and it felt quite different; because we didn't really know what our Club Members, if we got any, would be like. It was like going into a new country with only text-book knowledge of the language. But it was a very exciting time, as well; opening the first membership applications and reading your letters. In those early days there were only three of us, and Rosemary, Doreen and your Editor spent one entire weekend sealing up Club badges in pieces of cardboard. And while we worked we used to wonder what we'd do when we had the 20,000 members we dreamed of.

Kaye Webb, *Puffin Post* Editorial

The 20,000 figure was almost reached by the time the second quarterly edition of *Puffin Post* was sent out to members in the summer of 1967. Before too long, membership topped 100,000: 'Sniffup Spotera' indeed.

The visual style of *Puffin Post* and all Club publicity was largely the work of the young and distinctive artist, Jill McDonald.

The magazine really has to have the McDonald flavour. I really feel our own club notepaper ought to be redesigned. Could you do this for us? . . . We ought to have cards acknowledging good manuscripts which we do not think we can use, but would like to encourage the children. I am enclosing the brief text. Could you make something nice out of it?

Kaye Webb to Jill McDonald, 4 June 1969

One of the children's manuscripts that was used had been written by Janet Aichison, five and a half – a one-page story, *The Pirate's Tale,* which was published in *Puffin Post*. Jill McDonald turned this story into one of the early volumes of the new illustrated series for younger children, Picture Puffins. Janet Aichison thus became Puffin's youngest author, and quite possibly the only one to have bought herself a climbing frame with the advance.

* * *

Penguin English Library

You probably know the Brodie series which I gather have a very wide following. I would be interested to know what has happened about the editions of the English Classics we were proposing to have edited on, I imagine, similar lines to these.

Allen Lane to Tony Godwin, 25 November 1963

The Penguin English Library is a new series of English Classics which are designed to take their place alongside the Penguin Classics which are, of course, all translations. The format, appearance, and price will be similar. Each volume in the Library will have a separate editor whose task is to present for publication an introduction of between 4,000 and 7,500 words, an authoritative text and explanatory notes.

The audience to aim at is the intelligent general reader who has always meant to read the English Classics, but has either never got round to all of these or at least not looked at them since his school days.

Notes for volume editors, Penguin English Library, 1963

In this way the Penguin English Library was set up, initially under the editorship of David Daiches of Sussex University, with eight titles selected to launch the series. Tony Godwin suggested Daiches edit the first volume, as a guide for further contributors: 'Much of Dr Rieu's authority as editor of the Penguin Classics came from the fact that he translated the first volume which has been both a prestige and commercial success.'

Before the first batch could be published David Daiches decided to resign the editorship on a matter of policy. It was subsequently decided to keep in-house control of the series, but at the end of 1963 Godwin's initial choice Charles Clark was already fully occupied:

As you have a very full programme at the moment with Studies in Social Illness, which looks like being one of the most successful ever sub-series, and the Law books especially needing to be concentrated on; the changeover of advisory editors on Psychology to accomplish this year and I am particularly keen, after the success of your Edinburgh trip, that you should spend as much time as possible at the

Universities, I suggest that on the commissioning of new titles and the titles which require recommissioning etc. I take over personally with Jim Cochrane. In due course he can take over the whole series when it is safely launched on the right lines.

Which indeed was the case.

How very kind of you to write about this project of yours – one that seems very interesting and needful. I should be very happy to contribute an introduction and notes to one of the classics on your list. Let us indeed meet to discuss the matter. As I am fairly free from next week on, would you like to suggest a time, day, place?

Anthony Burgess to James Cochrane, 29 September 1964

Many thanks for your letter of September 29th. How about meeting for a drink in the Café Royal at 6 o'clock next Thursday or Friday. Let me know which if either of these days would suit and perhaps you'd better let me know what colour tie you'll be wearing. I think I shall probably recognize you but there's no point in taking unnecessary risks.

James Cochrane to Anthony Burgess, 7 October 1964

An excellent idea. The downstairs bar on the left? – the one with the Oppen picture? Good. Election night – 15th at 6.0 – would suit very well. I can't describe my ties, so I'll wear dark glasses. I am jowling and morose.

Anthony Burgess to James Cochrane, 8 October 1964

The meeting was a success: Burgess chose Defoe's *A Journal of the Plague Year* from the list on offer, and all subsequent correspondence is conducted between Jim and John.

23 October 1964: Dear Jim, Many thanks for your letter and offer and all. It was nice having you. We will junket again when I return, like Marvell-hymned Cromwell, from Ireland . . . As ever, John

5 November 1964: Dear John, Sorry I didn't have a chance to speak to you last night. You had disappeared by the time I escaped from the coffee machine. You spoke persuasively for Burroughs but I am not as yet convinced . . . Jim

6 November 1964: Dear Jim, Forgive my nodding technique at the

automat the other night. Speech had become painful. I'm not convinced yet either . . . John

As usual in cases of this kind, I've sent out your introduction to *A Journal of the Plague Year* for an independent report on matters of scholarship, etc.; and I now have this before me. My reader likes the piece in general as much as I do but goes on to say 'any comments on it would be qualifications of definite statements which would blur the general lines of Burgess's argument' and makes a number of detailed points which I attach with this letter.

I think the comments he makes on noblemen at Oxford, Oxbridge education and Elizabethan prose style are just, but that the others are mainly scholarly tentativeness and reluctance about generalization. On the matter of Defoe in the pillory I simply don't know. But I am quite sure that all his points can be accommodated with very minor modifications.

Jim to John, 4 June 1965

Sorry about the delay in doing what had to be done, but Lynne and I have been in Wales for a fortnight and had no mail forwarded to us. I've gone carefully through the material you sent, for which thanks, and concede what has to be conceded, correcting the text accordingly. But I'm scared of making the whole thing too scholarly and have not added anything to what I've written. If you yourself would like to incorporate anything I shan't complain, my deathless prose not being all that deathless here, but I do feel that one should keep the average reader in mind and eschew nice qualifications. I hope you agree.

We'll be down at our COUNTRY ESTATE from Wednesday next – so do get in touch with us there, socially or professionally. I have a couple of books to write. And in the Autumn we'll meet for another General Election or just for pure boozing.

John to Jim, 11 June 1965

Burgess was a shrewd choice: the success of the series hinged on the editor for each title. Malcolm Bradbury, at the time in America, and also involved in editing *The Penguin Companion to American Literature*, not unnaturally took on Mark Twain. Michael Foot tackled *Gulliver's Travels*; Richard Hoggart,

The Way of All Flesh; and Angus Wilson, *Oliver Twist*. Particularly imaginative was the choice of J. I. M. Stewart of Christ Church to tackle what had previously appeared in the fiction list as a crime novel, Wilkie Collins's *The Moonstone*. Stewart, too, was a regular in that guise – as the author Michael Innes.

The Penguin English Library, along with the changing and developing sister series Penguin Classics, and the establishment of Peregrines all demonstrated an increasing flirtation with formal education: a trend which, in truth, had started in 1937 with the establishment of Pelican. For the time being, however, the solution remained a compromise.

The problem is this: we have to print 20,000 copies and upwards of any book that we publish and this cuts out immediately a large number of books, however good they are, that we would dearly like to do. One solution is to create a forum for a particular area and we then find that we can do books in that area that we were not able to get away with on the general list. Thus we have created the Penguin African Library and have been able to do one or two books there that we certainly could not have done on the general list. Similarly with Shakespeare, the creation of a New Shakespeare Library will give us the chance to do some books which in our terms will have a minor sale. But the first thing to do is to establish the Library in the minds of booksellers and the public with absolutely central volumes. Then, if the series gets under way properly, we can start doing books like your own which we would dearly love to do and which are good but which we cannot do either on the general list or on the first run or so of titles in the Shakespeare Library.

Charles Clark to Terence Hawkes, 4 March 1964

* * *

Betty Radice and Penguin Classics

E. V. Rieu's lasting contribution was to make the Classics accessible to the general reader. The very act of publishing them in Penguin editions made them considerably less forbidding to the uninitiated, and while there was no lack of scholarship in the translation or accompanying introduction, the emphasis was nevertheless on providing the general public with a translation that was primarily readable. When Rieu's successors Betty Radice and Robert Baldick inherited the series, this relaxed policy was under some scrutiny. To meet the burgeoning demand for accurate and academically impeccable texts from colleges, particularly in the United States, a change of emphasis and direction was called for. Steady progress towards this objective was hampered by the untimely deaths of both Robert Baldick and his successor as co-editor. Several years earlier, Betty Radice's first contribution to the series was her translation of the *Letters of the Younger Pliny*, which she dedicated to her mentor, E. V. Rieu.

Thank you so much for piloting Pliny's *Letters* through the publishing. It looks very nice and I am most grateful for all you did. I hope I was not an unduly Anxious Parent. I learned such a lot from our conversation and resolved that in future (if I have a future) I will be less fussy and more trustful. I also realize that I have a great deal to learn, when any of you have the time to educate me.

Betty Radice to David Duguid, internal memorandum, 6 May 1963

As both contributor and editor of the series once called 'the greatest educative force of the twentieth century', she soon realized that trust and fussiness needed to be tempered with the founder editor's example: 'his rejections were always reasoned and courteous and I learned how difficult that can be'.

Your opening sentence is feeble. There are two silly slips of the pen and some over-long sentences, but what worries me is that you have not got inside the piece; though of course it is too short to show much sequence of thought . . . I should like to see at least three chapters – consecutive ones. I'm sure you will understand that I must satisfy myself that you can make a scholarly and readable job of this. My typed letters sound fiercer than I intend them to be, so don't cast yourself into the Bournemouth seas clasping Frazer and Leake to help you to sink. I hope we shall have a chance of meeting sometime.

Overseeing a major change in policy could not be undertaken without hurting feelings, as long-standing translations were abandoned. Rieu had held strong feelings about the translation of verse: 'Verse into verse conveyed as much, or more, of the writer as his subject'. With very few exceptions – such as Dorothy L. Sayers's Dante – poetry ought to be rendered into prose. It was on this basis that David Wright's translation of *Beowulf* had been commissioned in 1951. In 1967 it had become out of place, despite its continuing steady sales, and a new verse translation was commissioned from Michael Alexander. There were other similar casualties.

In setting out to please both academics and the general reader, one likely consequence was that representatives of both camps would fail to be satisfied, and be vocal in their dissatisfaction.

There were outside criticisms, notably that of the American journal *Arion*; there were internal battles to be fought as the Penguin Classics were threatened with dilution through the introduction of Pelican Classics. And there was the related constant, and generally unwelcome, presence of Dr Moses Finley.

The dilemma was complete and insuperable. To make a relatively dull work relatively interesting necessitated taking liberties with the act of translation. Added to this was the simple fact that to continue expanding the series indefinitely would ultimately require a new definition of the word 'classic'; and the more obscure the text, the more specialized the audience, and the more demanding that audience would be.

The introduction of the Pelican Classics series did not help clear the atmosphere. An internal memo, summarizing an August 1968 meeting to discuss the two series, attempted a definition:

> It was agreed that in most cases the definition of Penguin Classics as classics of literature and Pelican Classics as classics of non-literature would make a clear demarcation between the two series, provided that a proper liaison is maintained between the editors, both inside and outside, when new books are commissioned.

But to make things more complicated, Moses Finley, who edited the Pelican Classics series, had, in addition, a brief to study and report on existing volumes in the Penguin Classics. He found little to his satisfaction: 'I find this a shocker, I'm afraid.' 'This is not for me. The second sentence stopped me.' 'This performance is flawed throughout, in addition to being careless. I therefore have not bothered to read beyond the general introduction.' 'The introduction seems to me to fall between all possible stools, and I am unable to understand whom it is aimed at, or who would get much out of it.' 'I can't cope with this. It would require too many pages, and then it wouldn't be worth the effort.' 'This defeats me completely.' 'As always, you catch the tone and level just right, I think.' This last was in relation to Betty Radice's Pliny translation.

Before very long Betty Radice found it necessary to take something of a stand.

I have given a lot of thought to the discussion we had with Dieter Pevsner. I don't suppose it will surprise you to hear that this was the first time I had been told anything about Pelican Classics.

Of course I welcome the revision and fresh introducing of the historical works; I urged this four years ago and at intervals since, but Tony Godwin was never willing to spend extra money on the Classics. Least of all on what were judged academic or non-'popular' works. These were mostly brought out years ago by Dr Rieu: I think *The Byzantines*, Wellesley's Tacitus' *Histories* and Jane Mitchell's *Civil War* (which *CJ** in March '68 reviewed as a model of what a Penguin Classic should be), are the only ones for which I have been wholly responsible.

I shall be glad to hear your opinion of the introduction to *The War with Hannibal*, which was my attempt (after long experience of VIth form teaching and tutoring for the Oxbridge awards in classics and English) to present Livy in a wider context and as more enjoyable reading than a limited set text generally suggests. You may not like it, but I rather hope it doesn't come under the axe. On reprinting I should like to add a full index.

Pelican Classics will fill many gaps and sounds a most promising venture. I will pass any would-be translator of such works to you, and I am sure if we keep each other informed there will be no problems. Polybius presumably comes under me with the other historians, and if Dieter finds there is US support I have two academics on the files who want to try a translation if we can settle on the selection.

I agree that the Digest should come into the Pelicans, and I have written to Colin Kolbert. But the more I think of it, the more strongly I feel that no other published or commissioned Classic should be moved out of the Penguin series. It would have a damaging effect on the series as a whole if it is whittled down when it has aimed at being comprehensive, and if, by definition, your new series is to take in important non-literary books, then to take works like More's *Utopia* and St Augustine's *Confessions* out of the Penguins is to deny

* *Classics Journal*

them literary status. This is surely quite wrong in principle: such books can be read for many reasons and in many contexts, but they are undeniably great works of literature. And as regards the *Laws of Plato*, I follow Dieter in thinking that all the works of Plato should be together.

You have such a wide field with untapped resources and a sympathetic chief editor, and I am sure you can quickly build up a valuable series of your own. So this time it is I who am asking you to retire gracefully from something you had in mind, and I do so in the interests of the longest-established whole series in Penguin Books which I do not wish to see broken up. Change in presentation there must be, in line with changing trends in education, and translations must be redone to match development in current speech, but the achievements of this series have in general been remarkable as you yourself said, and it will long outlast the work you or I do for Penguin Books.

Betty Radice to Moses Finley, 17 August 1968

Finley's reports continued to arrive, and, with the prospect of the new series, carried occasional hints of a new agenda:

As a Pelican Classic, this is a non-starter. S. has deliberately aimed at a low, if not the lowest, level of political and intellectual literacy. If one checks his introduction and notes against the general memo for Pelican Classics, he fails on every point, except the bibliography, which is tendentious by the way, but which is very excessive and pointless for a Penguin Classic. Even as a Penguin Classic, it rouses few cheers in me.

It all culminated in a letter of September 1970, quoted in full in William Radice's introduction to *The Translator's Art, Essays in Honour of Betty Radice*, edited by William Radice and Barbara Reynolds (Penguin 1985):

How nasty your letters can be to receive; I often dread the sight of the Cambridge postmark, though I know better than to take them personally. And I do appreciate how it is a great saver of your time not to have to choose your words, and how the building up of what the *TLS* calls your famous bite is a very useful ploy in the gamesmanship of the academic rat-race. It must be an agreeable feeling to use it . . .

Betty Radice to Moses Finley, September 1970

On the other hand, however, the job did have its compensations – and none more so than the sheer pleasure to be gained tackling a particularly recondite translation, helping out a colleague: in this case, Jill Norman, who had some odd snippets of Latin to translate for the Handbook, *The Philosopher in the Kitchen*.

Certainly I will do your small chore; it is an agreeable weekend relaxation, and you could have had it immediately if I weren't held up by the recipe for dormice, which must, I think, come from Apicius. I will look this up next week when I am in the Institute of Classical Studies.

This should be a delightful book, and the odd pages are most tantalizing. I shall not take to quinine as a slimming aid.

Have you ever thought of taking over Apicius's *Roman Cookery Book* which was translated very well by B. Flower and E. Rosenbaum about 1950? They actually cooked and ate the recipes (but not dormice). Or would it be better with me? It certainly is a Classic of its kind.

I am well, fearfully busy with Erasmus, translating *Praise of Folly* for which Anthony Levi of Campion Hall has written a brilliant Introduction and is preparing notes. I think the result should be rewarding, and the combination of Jesuit authority and the renaissance and down to earth agnostic has taught me a great deal, and has at any rate taught him that he can't take for granted that everyone knows what terms like grace, justification and Pauline folly mean.

This is such fearfully difficult allusive Latin that the back has fallen off my Lewis & Short big dictionary (so your 8 guineas will be welcome) and I think that I shall stick to high renaissance Latin in future – so few people are prepared to cope with it, and I have already done some Bembo and Petrarch for the Officina Bodoni at Verona. I should also like to do some Erasmus with Anthony as I find him such a very interesting person: Erasmus, I mean though. (Anthony is also interesting as is his brother Peter, also an S. J. and poet, whom you may know. Don't know why two such handsome brothers are wasted in the Jesuits.)

I hope you flourish and are not too overworked. Some day we must have our promised lunch together.

Betty Radice to Jill Norman, 29 November 1969

Stuffed Dormice: Stuff the dormice with pork forcemeat and the minced flesh taken from all parts of the dormice, along with pepper, nut kernels, asafoetida and fish sauce, stitch them up and put them in a clay dish in the oven, or bake them when stuffed in a pot oven.

* * *

Penguin Education

Publishing is a vocation as well as a trade – or so it seems to me – and it is that distinction which enables us to claim that we are public educators. Even an astute man like Allen so intuitively understood that it was only by a combination of commerce and conscience that he could make a fresh mark on British publishing.

W. E. Williams to Victor Weybright, 6 March 1946

When Lord Reith, nearly forty years ago, formulated the precepts which were to govern the BBC, he declared that it must educate as well as entertain. It is true, I think, to say that Penguin Books have done the same. It remains our purpose to maintain a balance of that nature.

Allen Lane, Chairman's Statement, 18 April 1962

Drawing comparisons between Penguin and the BBC was hardly accidental – and long before 1962 was entirely justifiable. Penguin Books were an institution, and a major cultural force, and it was largely the 'educational' arm of their publishing that made this so.

Despite the fact that books were not specifically published for the educational market, the distinction between informing and teaching had been gradually breaking down for years. Penguins were used as text books, and in America most of all, the adoption of a Pelican or Classic as a set text guaranteed excellent sales. The question was not a new one, and it is hardly surprising that in the immediate aftermath of the war the matter should be seriously discussed.

Finally, have you ever considered the possibility of entering the schools market? Teachers and education authorities are burdened with relatively expensive text books and reference books, which in consequence of their price have to last a long time, and are often not discarded until they are falling to pieces. Many teachers would welcome cheap books, which could be discarded after a year or two. Particularly valuable would be the kind of reading and reference books so much needed for class use and so rarely available. For example, in geography, a book of illustrations, of physical geography, landscape in various countries, etc. would be of the greatest value. In history, a book containing extracts from original material, or one with extracts from historical novels would be useful, as would a book containing descriptions of towns and countryside from descriptive works by good authors, dealing with Britain and foreign countries, including descriptions from novels and other literary works.

James Gregory to Hans Oberndorfer, 10 July 1945

In response to a similar request from W. T. Williams, the author of various Penguin Problems books, who also served on the Kent Education Committee, Alan Glover wrote in January 1946:

I do not think there is a great deal of prospect of our being ready to undertake a series of educational readers at the present time. We have such a lot of commitments left over from the war years, and are travelling up so many streets at the moment, that we have as much as we can do for the next two or three years, and we are not terribly keen on going into the directly educational field. None the less we would like to give your idea full consideration.

Williams replied immediately, elaborating his ideas further:

What I had in mind was the vast new population in the so-called Secondary 'Modern' School. No one has any notion what to do with these lads and lasses (who will be about 75% of the whole Secondary School population). Certainly, in English work, the type of reader must be rather less literary and academic than those which serve in the Grammar School type. I should like to edit a series of Prose Readers with a punch. Such books as *Tschiffely's Ride*, *The Cruise of the Cachalot*, *The Man-Eaters of Tsavo* occur to me as having a good standard of writing and a strong appeal to adolescents. The books would perhaps serve better if they were (very slightly) abridged. I realize, of course, your difficulty, and that your commitments are very considerable. But I also feel that there is a big market here, and that even if you feel disinclined to start a new series (I suggested 'Peacock' Books in my letter), it might be useful to stake a claim by publishing a few books in your regular series.

As with Peacock Books, a name adopted for the 'adolescent' market, the idea of a separate educational list was not to bear fruit until the 1960s. Immediately after the war Penguin were restricted still by paper rationing, delays and difficulties in printing and distribution, and a readership still coming to terms with peacetime. Nevertheless, Penguin were travelling up a number of streets, some of which had no apparent end. Quite apart from the new Penguin Classics and rejuvenated periodicals, Noel Carrington and Allen Lane had gone a long way towards commissioning and producing what would have been a 'definitive' natural history of Britain in several bound and paperback volumes. Distinguished artists, who had already produced successful Puffins, were hard at work on their particular subjects: Richard Chopping on *Wild Flowers*, R. Talbot Kelly on *Birds*, Bernard Venables on *Fish*, S. R. Badmin on *Trees* and Paxton Chadwick on *Animals*.

Even larger in conception was a scheme to publish worldwide an international Atlas, to be masterminded by George Kimble, at McGill University, Montreal, and commenced in 1944. This progressed to the extent that the *Montreal Gazette* of 15 May 1945 announced:

Convinced that geography has been shot by the war into a place of prime educational importance, Mr Lane has earmarked $1,000,000 for the business of putting out a world atlas of the type hitherto only found in large reference libraries and of a type never before put out by an English-speaking firm. This new atlas, which will be 'a sort of photographic representation of the contemporary world' will be at a price which the ordinary man can afford.

The million-dollar investment was apparently news to Richard Lane, who was despatched to Canada to sort it all out. The overall cost, printing difficulties at home and the real prospect of Harmondsworth being taken over to extend Heathrow Airport, all conspired towards its eventual abandonment.

In 1963 the question of educational books was raised once more by an acquaintance of Tony Godwin, Ian Rodger.

There is probably a deep-seated hostility in schools and Local Education Authorities to the paperback book. But it could surely be pointed out quite successfully that the cost of supplying a fresh paperback text book each year could not be very much more than the cost of supplying hard covers once every five years. A paperback text book service could also incorporate a system of slip pages for revisions and second thoughts and new revelations. This particular system could also be applied to the university field where for example science text books are out of date at a phenomenal rate. A paperback text book system could overcome this. I am sure the initial outlay in this field would be enormous. But once it was established, the returns would multiply yearly.

He concluded with a specific suggestion for prose anthologies designed for foreign students, and opined that such an educational series might be known as Plovers.

I entirely agree with the burden of your letter. As a matter of fact we have been discussing this at Penguin for the last two years and J. E. Morpurgo, the director of the National Book League, is taking charge of an effort on our part to do precisely this. I am therefore passing on your letter to him except for the last paragraph which I am passing to Richard Newnham, who deals with our language books.

Tony Godwin to Ian Rodger, 20 March 1963

Richard Newnham was already involved in the production of the *Penguin English Course*, due for publication the following year, which already set out to achieve largely what was being suggested 'with contemporary texts and passages that are really interesting in themselves, taken from such diverse sources as the *Times* Leader columns, *Woman's Hour* talks, *Time* magazine, and George Mikes'.

Changes in educational philosophy were seen to be causing a shift towards a market where Penguin might thrive alongside the more traditional educational publishers such as Longmans and OUP. Particularly important was the market in developing countries. J. E. Morpurgo, in his National Book League role, had pointed this out in his 1960 pamphlet *Paperbacks Across Frontiers*:

All over the world, but especially in Africa and Asia, millions are stumbling out of illiteracy into literacy. Nations, new to the excitements and to the responsibilities of independence, and eager to establish economic and social health, are attempting to compress into one generation the processes which Western Europe has achieved only after four hundred years of gradual development.

The equally well-travelled Chris Dolley, originally appointed in the early 1960s to work in the export market before taking over the management of the Education series, developed the theme:

I would like to tell you that one of the reasons we are going into textbook publishing is because we hope to use our knowledge of cheap book production to reduce the cost of textbooks, particularly in those countries where education is being seriously prejudiced by the high price of many books. I am thinking of places like India, South East Asia and Africa.

Of course the Third World was not the only potential market.

You may wonder why Penguins are bothering to do a series of readings at all, as I know the American market is flooded with them. The fact is that nobody has bothered to produce a series of readings in this country and in any case our advice is that many of those prepared in the States are of a rather low standard. As you will see from our list of editors, we have a number of American psychologists collaborating in the project so we are hoping to get a share of the American market ourselves.

Chris Dolley to Professor Robert Franz, 12 July 1965

Chris Dolley was soon on the move once more, this time taking the place of Harry Paroissien in Baltimore in order to give the American company fresh impetus. The new education list became the responsibility of Charles Clark, another of the able and versatile young editors appointed in the early 1960s.

Charles Clark had grown in stature with responsibility and he was now making something viable out of the unpromising, and to Penguin eccentric, Penguin Education list. He had launched some brave pioneering ventures. Although Allen was not then, nor ever would be, competent to judge the pedagogic venturesomeness of such series as *Success with English*, the Nuffield A-level books or the Education Specials, his ear was to the ground. He heard the approving voices of the leaders of the teaching profession and his eye, as ever on the sales sheets, was quick to recognize better than satisfactory turnover.

J. E. Morpurgo, *Allen Lane: King Penguin*

All the same, the Education list was on surer ground when dealing with the Arts, to which many of the established editorial staff naturally gravitated.

Students on the whole don't thank you for solemnly informing them that 'The Miller's Tale' is a bit bawdy: it sounds too much like those old-style Oxford men who were always piping 'Ah, but *Macbeth* is a story' to everyone's constant irritation. If you were to do anything with Webster's wit you would have to go into (on the one hand) styles of Jacobean satire and character writing, and (on the other hand) large-scale comparative gestures involving ... well, I think involving Pope, Rostand and possibly Skelton. (I.e. anger for most of us is a helpless, hot, stomach-crimping, inarticulate thing. How can Pope and Webster manage anger of that credibility while still being articulate. Articulacy of that kind, in most people's experience, is like Cyrano's – cool, distanced, untouched by other people entirely. But then is it really anger we are talking about . . . and so on.)

Martin Lightfoot to Charles Clark, 26 February 1969

They were less certain in dealing with a new offshoot of the Education list, the Library of Technology.

Library of Technology

The more I think about this series, the more I am convinced that it is going to need a special effort from us over the next few years. It is not only a new market for us, but also a highly complex one.

The list of problems is formidable and we have not helped ourselves by getting the books off to an indifferent start. There is a grave danger that the rather mediocre initial impact could set off a downward spiral.

It is now clear that the size of the market is dictated almost entirely by the number of candidates for the C&G examinations. This means, as I explained at the last price meeting that the market for the Stage II of the Fundamentals book is 6,140 people, and when we come to price the second Telecommunications book it will be 3,535. Any prospect of our selling to the Industrial Training Board market is fast disappearing as the boards themselves establish their own training programmes which rely heavily on teaching machines, programmed learning and similar units of instruction. In conclusion, I feel that although we may have begun the Library of Technology not knowing a great deal, we are now both older and sadder, and I believe wiser, and that we are faced with the fact that we incorrectly assessed the prospective market for technological books from the very beginning.

John Hitchin to Charles Clark, 22 August 1969

Penguin Education was, all told, considerably more than a brief experiment. It was a substantial gamble, but one backed by a powerful logic, which appealed particularly to Bill Williams, Penguin's educational mentor.

Charles Clark ensured that Penguin Educational would revolutionize the rapidly expanding market for text-books at all levels, from the primary school to the university, and this thriving and lively enterprise has become a field of major growth and another brilliant manifestation of the educational motive which Pelicans first demonstrated nearly forty years ago.

W. E. Williams, *Allen Lane: A Personal Portrait*

The following year the Education list was dismantled, an inevitable consequence of the merger with Pearson, which also included Longman, an established publisher in the educational field, with whom Penguin had previously competed and cooperated.

Nevertheless, as some eighty-seven contributors and supporters understandably pointed out in a letter published in the *Times Educational Supplement* in March 1974:

In its short life it has produced a list that has made school books into a different species. Not only have they set an altogether different standard of design and illustration – so powerful that other firms have had to follow Penguin's lead – but the content and direction of books like *Voices*, *Connexions* and the *Penguin English Project* have in themselves made a major professional contribution to the practice of education in schools . . . We regret that a team which has shown itself capable of these kinds of innovations should be destroyed.

* * *

The Paperback Commodity

. . . There is something very gingerly about the manner in which Mr Warburg handles the word 'commodity'. You can almost picture his wry distaste. He states that paperback publishing is commodity-selling, and that by this he means 'that the size of the edition is comparatively large and that what is sold is already a more or less known article . . .' But all publishing is commodity-selling of one sort or another. If the commodity (books) is not produced with the intention of selling it, what is publishing supposed to be about? What most frequently confronts a publisher is not the question 'Is this a good book of its kind?' but the problem of just how he is going to secure the widest audience for it. Anybody can sell a best-seller, although some are much better at boosting them than others. But the art of publishing lies in the ability to secure for each book its potential readers. This, as much as anything, is what publishing is all about. In other words, commodity-selling.

Mr Warburg then says, 'Furthermore the "commodity" books are, by and large, books with some considerable popular appeal,' and I seem to detect a note of disparagement in his tone. That there is something derogatory about books with considerable popular appeal is a fallacious and snobbish cliché on a level with the hoary old favourite that if you give the working class baths they will use them to put coal in. The implication is that a book must have been vulgarized in some way to enjoy considerable public appeal. And the corollary is that the only books of true merit are the ones with only a minority appeal. What rubbish!

Letters to the Editor, *Times Literary Supplement*, 17 June 1965

Thus in no uncertain terms Tony Godwin chastized Fred Warburg. Perhaps in his uncompromising attitude towards the publishing establishment there was just the slightest touch of the young Allen Lane. By this time Lane himself was of course very much part of that establishment.

Godwin's theories about the paperback as commodity were soon to be put to the test by a 'half-Irish Londoner' with similar disdain for the establishment.

Having studied the James Bond phenomenon, Deighton had devised his own formula on which to base efficiently successful thrillers, and was determined to write five of them to prove it. He gave the first of them to Fleming's publisher, but found himself at loggerheads with Daniel George who, while he liked the laconic style, tried to persuade Len to simplify its convoluted plot. Deighton walked out and gave *The Ipcress File* to Hodder & Stoughton; but they under-estimated its potential and ran out of stock soon after publication, leaving the author far from satisfied with their performance . . . Len Deighton is as versatile as he is dynamic. While writing thrillers he was devising the illustrative strips which appeared each week in the *Observer*, from which he then compiled his *Action Cook Book*; and was also assembling a serendipitous miscellany of information for his *London Dossier*.

Michael S. Howard, *Jonathan Cape, Publisher*, 1971

By 1964 Len Deighton was one of the hottest properties in publishing, and while Pan were selling the James Bond books in their millions, Penguin were having to work extremely hard to convince Deighton that they were the best publishers to handle this particular commodity.

The most immediate and arresting thing about Len Deighton's Penguins is their outward appearance. They did not look like Penguin Books – they looked like Len Deighton books. But Deighton himself was not ignorant of the art of cover design. As he recalled:

After I left the Royal College of Art Penguin covers were among the jobs I did. In those days the Penguins were still colour-coded with vertical bands of orange, green and so on categorizing the books. The illustrators had to produce simple black and white drawings that would fit between the bands.

Since childhood I had always read a great many books but working for publishers extended my reading. I suppose that reading some of the less good ones persuaded me to try writing.

Horse Under Water: Len Deighton

May I suggest that we commission Ray Hawkey, art editor of the *Daily Express*, to do our cover. Hawkey has done the Deighton covers for Capes and also, with conspicuous success, the Fleming covers for Pan Books, for which I am told he was paid £200 a throw. As he is fond of Deighton I believe he would do our Deighton cover for £75. He will probably suggest at first that we use the Cape cover. You know that I hate and disapprove of using the same cover as the hardback so don't be persuaded.

Tony Godwin to Germano Facetti, internal memorandum, 8 April 1964

Having secured the rights and published the book, Tony Godwin was soon being pressed by the author to fulfil his claim that 'Anybody can sell a best-seller, although some are much better at boosting them than others.'

Further to my letter about your complaint about the distribution of *Horse Under Water*, the Marketing Director has now agreed that we will re-promote with great vigour to the wholesalers and other specialist outlets from May onwards, as well, of course, as trying to get our normal sales force into a renewed frenzy of action.

There is one comment I think I should make, and that is that our experience has shown that where *Horse Under Water* and *The Ipcress File* have been shown side by side, *Ipcress* considerably outsells the other, which has been making it difficult for us. It may be due to the fact that it has the same title as the film; or of course to the fact that it has enjoyed a much greater success review-wise, etc. as a hardback than *Horse*.

Tony Godwin to Len Deighton, 29 March 1966

A similar vigour had been contemplated for the promotion campaign for a quite different Deighton book, this time a Penguin original.

We have had an enquiry from a customer who is considering producing a cookery book which he would like to contain an aroma of garlic! I know we have done a lot of research on the removal of odours from print but I would be grateful for any information and suggestions you can make for introducing them.

I believe in America a certain amount of printing is done with an introduced odour, but normally of a less noxious type, and one of the points which we will have to consider carefully is to avoid the contamination of other work during the manufacturing process. I wondered whether the insertion of a small impregnated card into the bound books might be possible and would avoid repercussions from the factory floor.

Any information you are able to give will be of the greatest value.

Richard Clay, of Clays printers, to V. G. W. Harrison, of Printing, Packaging & Allied Trades Research Association, 8 December 1964

In reply to your letter of 8 December, we are fairly used to getting some pretty extraordinary requests but this one beats most. My first reaction was to suggest that you printed the books and left them for three weeks in a basement in Soho, but this might give rise to difficulties.

We find on more serious investigation that Proprietary Perfumes Ltd of Ashford, Kent has worked and is working with a number of large paper organizations on the 'odorizing' of paper and board. We have not given them your name but we understand that they would welcome a general discussion of the problem and would probably be able to offer you technical advice.

Should this lead nowhere, please let us know so we can think again.

V. G. W. Harrison to Richard Clay, 11 December 1964

We have been going into this matter since it was raised in December last and have been advised by the printers that it is impossible to introduce any pungent odours into the printing ink, sprays or paper making. The only alternative seemed to be to insert an impregnated card into the book and we have obtained bottles of various odours from Proprietary Perfumes. We tested these by using stacks of eight books, the inner four of which had cards, and separated these from the next stack by an intermediate stack which contained no cards, with the object of seeing whether the odour travelled within the stack or to adjoining books. After we had left the cards for two days we found that no odour remained except where we used the full strength garlic, and this only resembled the aftermath of garlic consumption and not the true smell of garlic. It is impossible to hold for any length of time a mild concentration and it is obvious that by the time the books reached the bookseller all trace of smell would have disappeared, and I believe that this is true even of the concentrates.

Jimmy Holmes to Tony Godwin, internal memorandum, 24 March 1965

As I told Ray, it has proved quite impossible to get a printer to impregnate ink, paper or anything else with garlic. They say the smell won't come off the machines for months. Tony [Richardson] sent you the sample not as proof of success but as an indication of how the thing might have worked out. Sorry about this. In any case the view here is that its value as a promotion gimmick would have been more than outweighed by possibly disastrous effects in the bookshops – contaminated stock, unbreathable atmosphere etc.

What we can do, however, is charge all the review copies with garlic – or, rather, give them a discreet odour.

Tony Godwin to Len Deighton, 4 June 1965

The Penguin edition of *Où Est Le Garlic?* was not a strong seller, although it is highly prized today as a Deighton first edition.

It did eventually sell out its first edition, and was later reprinted with a new cover, the original one having been largely held to blame for the slow sales. There was, in truth, little wrong with the look of either cover; both versions are models of good taste and restraint compared with the later *Len Deighton's Action Cook Book*. For this it was originally planned to have Michael Caine indulging in culinary arts on the cover: a none too subtle reference to the recent Deighton films. In the event two models, one with shoulder holster, the other with false eyelashes were to be found paying somewhat scant attention to a pot of spaghetti on both the front and rear covers. *Garlic*'s main problem was its landscape format, which made it difficult to display in bookshops. *The Action Cook Book*, and the reprint of *Garlic* got over this by having one cover in landscape format and the other in the customary portrait mode.

As more of Deighton's books appeared in Penguin, the commercial realities of commodity selling began to tell on Tony Godwin. In the wake of Corgi's promotion of James Munro's thriller *The Man Who Sold Death*, Godwin wrote to the author: 'I have had a look at the announcements for the Corgi Munro promotional plan. I took it from what you said on the phone that this is the level of promotion which you now feel your books should get. I therefore asked our Sales and Promotion Departments to get out a full-blooded promotional plan for *Funeral in Berlin*, and perhaps when I have it (I hope shortly after the New Year), we could meet and see if it is at the right level, and the sort of thing you want.'

On the same day, something more of his true feelings were revealed:

I have been attacked extremely harshly by Len Deighton, who feels that our marketing and promotion for both *Horse Under Water* and

Où Est Le Garlic? have been extremely inadequate. As a result of his dissatisfaction, it is very likely that we shall lose Deighton as an author. However, I am trying to do what I can. I am sending him the details of the promotion and marketing plans we have for each of the two books, and I shall try and manoeuvre him into agreeing to suspending any decision about paperback rights to *Billion Dollar Brain* until we have demonstrated what we can do with *Funeral in Berlin* this Spring.

If, as I am assured, it is in Penguins' interest to have a number of top-selling authors on the fiction list, to lend sparkle, etc., in the shop, then it is a mistake in policy to lose Deighton, because he is undoubtedly one of the top popular authors, and likely to become even more so during the next two or three years. On authors of this popularity we undoubtedly are going to have to compete with the marketing and promotion that they would receive from Corgi, Pan, etc. If we are not prepared to promote top popular authors to somewhat the same extent as our competitors, then, I really do think it is a waste of my time – and it does take really an awful lot of time and patience and luck to go out and try to obtain authors such as these for our list.

I should be grateful if you would take your time to give me a report, and your personal opinions on these two campaigns, and whether you think the author has a justifiable grievance.

I would also be grateful if you could give me an outline promotion programme of the sort the author seeks for *Funeral in Berlin* so that we might see what is involved, and whether it is possible, and what the Company's policy should be.

Tony Godwin to John Hitchin, internal memorandum, 21 December, 1965

Funeral in Berlin

This is to place on paper and confirm in writing the substance of our discussion about this title yesterday.

Penguins will plan a £5,000 promotional campaign to launch and sell this title, which is scheduled for publication in June 1966. I have given Len our undertaking that the initial printing shall be 250,000 copies; you and Len have given me an assurance that if *Funeral in Berlin*'s sales and promotional campaign are satisfactory, we will be offered *Billion Dollar Brain* at an advance of £15,000, and that in the meantime it is not on offer elsewhere.

Tony Godwin to Tom Maschler at Cape, 12 January 1966

There is no mention anywhere in the Penguin archive of the near-legendary party held in Berlin to celebrate the publication of *Funeral in Berlin*. One or two photographs exist, which suggest a rather staid affair. It was, according to many, a supremely extravagant and wasteful gesture. Len Deighton remembers it differently: 'Afterwards he was criticized by people who didn't understand what he was doing. Even some of the trade press tried to prove that he wouldn't get his money back from the sales of the book. But Tony was clever; he knew that the uninformed controversy added to the publicity for Penguin Books. In some ways it was a turning point in Penguin's history marking a change to competitive publishing in a market that was becoming ever more cut-throat.' In Tony Godwin's case it was, unfortunately, his own throat that was about to be cut.

* * *

Massacre

Cartoonists, as I discovered when I was editor of Punch, *are desperately serious men, who seldom laugh themselves, and deeply resent laughter in others.*

Malcolm Muggeridge, Introduction to *Siné Massacre*

A copy of the book *Massacre* by the French Cartoonist Siné had been circulated to each Director. Having expressed his concern that he had not been informed about the book at an earlier stage, in the light of its possible controversial impact, the Chairman [AL] said that he had called the Meeting primarily to ensure that all the Directors were acquainted with the full facts about the book, thus affording them the opportunity to express their individual views on the subject matter, also their opinions as to the advisability or not of proceeding to publication.

Siné Massacre: there were few survivors from the first edition.

The Chairman felt the board would be interested to learn that Mr Arthur Crook, Editor of *The Times Literary Supplement*, thought the book 'rather good'. Mr Crook had offered to circulate a copy of the book to a cross section of his office staff and the Chairman had agreed to this. Mr Crook was able to report that of the members of his staff ranging from 16 to 54 years of age to whom the book had been circulated, not one had found the book offensive. Opinion had varied from 'Terrific' to 'Funny but Macabre' and 'Gallows humour, Ealing style'. . . .

The decision to publish Siné was not the outcome of any sudden or rash impulse, but as part of the result of four years of calculated Editorial Policy aimed at representative comprehensiveness across the whole range of Penguin titles.

Siné was considered to be an important cartoonist working in the long tradition of Graphic satire whose language and attitudes to convention have always shocked. Penguin's cartoon series by tradition embraces a wide range of cartoonists, satirists and humorists stretching from Steinberg and André François to Charles Addams and Brockbank. In the cartoon series, Siné at the one end of the list and Thelwell at the other, seems therefore a natural corollary of any objective towards a representative list.

A. Godwin then went on to say that Penguins has always been contemporary, publishing to the younger generation of eighteen to forty. Personal taste does not unduly influence Penguin's choice of Authors; more influential are the aims of an Editorial policy to produce a comprehensive list phased to meet all legitimate reading needs.

If our aim is to publish books representative of the age we live in, then it is impossible to ignore the whole movement of art and literature towards explicitness and the exposition of controversial subjects such as sex, sadism and religion. There always has been and always will be, a gap in literary and artistic tastes between the thirty and under age group, and the forty and over age group, yet if because of this we turn our back on this movement, then we are turning our back on any pretensions to being the most exciting, contemporary and adventurous Publisher, and on the tradition implied by the publication of *Lady Chatterley*.

A. Godwin conceded that the question of controversial books is a problem, but stressed that it is disastrous if they are to be raised as late as Siné where copies are in the Warehouse and Representatives already subscribing. A decision not to publish at this late stage would obviously have repercussions, and the direct loss from pulping copies could exceed £2,000 . . .

H. F. Paroissien considered the book as being blasphemous and not compatible with the image and publishing policy of the Company . . .

A. M. Walker personally took exception to the book . . .

R. Blass found the book tolerably humorous . . .

J. A. Holmes found the book distasteful . . .

C. Clark considered his personal views on the book to be irrelevant to a decision whether to publish or not . . . Jointly with A. Godwin was extremely disturbed by the situation which had arisen where the question of a controversial book could be raised at such a late stage, such circumstances in his estimation tantamount to abrogation of

Editorial responsibility especially if the Group Board were against publication of the book.

D. Pevsner was for publication of the book. Agreed with C. Clark concerning the danger of abrogating the editorial responsibility of the Chief Editor.

R. G. Holme informed the Board that W. H. Smith's Central Buying Department had seen the cover and blurb and had authorized subscription to branches . . .

H. P. Schmoller felt . . . that six or seven of the drawings were not only incompatible with the company's image, but might cause shock and pain to some people as to do lasting harm to them . . .

Following some discussion it was agreed that a poll should not be held and the Chairman informed the board that the consensus of opinion which was in favour of publication would be reported to the Group Board.

Minutes of a meeting of the Directors of Penguin Books Ltd, 5 October 1966

Siné Massacre has been given very careful consideration by the Penguin Board. We are publishing this book for the following reasons: Siné is a cartoonist and graphic artist of international reputation and importance, occupying a position in the satirical tradition of Hogarth, Goya, Daumier and Grosz – a tradition where conscience has often led to extreme forms of statement. Much of Siné's own work is a passionate reflection of a contemporary crisis in moral and religious values. For the French this was crystallized by the Algerian War and its psychological consequences.

Penguin has frequently published books without a consensus of agreement on the Board for it has always been a major part of Penguin's policy to publish books across the widest range of taste. This is a guarantee of the alertness of the firm to the mood of society as a whole.

Draft press statement, 1 November 1966

Siné Massacre; reserve press release

I showed the draft release to Ben Huberman, who as you know advised on the legal side, and his reaction was very much the same as mine. The first paragraph is excellent, but the second paragraph rather points the door to what could be damaging speculation. Whatever the differences of opinion within the firm, I feel we should present a common front as far as the outside world is concerned. A very simple amendment would meet this point if you would accept it, and I attach a copy duly amended.

[The amended second paragraph reads: 'It has always been Penguin's policy to publish books across the widest range of taste and to be alert to the mood of society as a whole.']

Charles Clark to Tony Godwin, internal memorandum, 26 October 1966

A strange story follows:

Well, what I remember is this: one night roughly about 12 o'clock in the evening, I was in bed of course, the phone rang, and it was Bosley. He said I'm with Sir Allen here now, at the office, and he wants you to come up straight away. From then I got up, dressed, out, and back to the firm, and who should I see up here but Sir Allen, Bosley, Derek Singleton, and another person who shall be nameless.

He said George, open up the building will you. Those bloody Sinés – those were the exact words he said to me. So we opened up the building, we walked up to the warehouse. He said, I've got Singleton round the back with the farm wagon. He said I'm going to pinch all those Sinés. Crikey, I said. He said, George, that bloody Board outvoted me today but I'll have my own back on them. So we thereupon unloaded the whole and entire stock of Siné in the bulk warehouse, in flat form, loaded them on to the truck and after a period of time we finished off the bulk, and we suddenly remembered there was the open stock in the distribution area. Well, of course we got down there, got the cartons together, loaded them aboard, and did the same thing with them: loaded them on to the truck. And that was the whole edition of Siné gone, literally gone.

He said to me, now we'll keep this a secret, we won't tell anybody, will we. I said, as far as I'm concerned, it never happened. You're the governor – who am I?

Of course, one must remember that was a short time after the publication of Siné, which we had had some rather adverse comment from, particularly religious leaders, quite rightly, and he felt the same.

The next day I naturally kept my eyes open to see whether anything was noticed, but strange to relate, nobody did; and for a long while I never heard not a word about the Siné books, and I just can't believe it myself, being ex-warehouse. But nobody apparently noticed it, I don't think it was until a long while afterwards, when a stock check was taken. There were no orders of course, because it had been stopped, if only temporarily, so people would not have noticed the temporary stock position. But even so no one did notice it until the stock was taken, and then of course questions would be asked.

Sir Allen and perhaps a couple of us were then doing a little giggling to ourselves.

George Nicholls, reminiscence, 9 October 1970

From this point on, the story becomes speculation. In the best tradition of Penguin myth-making, there is more than one version of the story concerning the eventual fate of the books. What is reasonably certain is that they were taken to Lane's farm near Reading. There, the books were, according to the various versions of the story, burnt, buried, or composted. The book was reported as out of stock, and no further orders taken. Allen Lane then, as was his wont, took himself off to Spain.

This book had been commissioned in 1963 by Tony Godwin, who had chosen Malcolm Muggeridge to make the selection and write a short Introduction, for a fee of £50. Muggeridge, a 'great admirer of Siné', had immediately agreed. This was duly delivered in March 1964. Godwin found this first selection

. . . a most disappointing representation of his work. Very little of the savagery and unique quality of his humour is represented . . . I am certainly not at all happy about introducing the non-whimsical Siné to the English public with this selection. I don't think it stands much chance of success, nor do I think they will readily grasp how good he is. So I hope you will temper a very natural impatience with a little charity towards me.

I rather share your feelings about the Siné selection and was a bit doubtful when I sent it off, though reassured by your first letter. It was the best I could get out of the material I had, though not, as you say, savage enough for him. There's the additional difficulty that a lot of the political drawings (e.g. on Algeria) are now out of date and liable to be incomprehensible to English readers. I'll send the remaining bits and pieces back to you. If you could manage to collect some more examples of his work, and you'd like me to, I'll gladly come along sometime to your office, and we could look at it together.

Malcolm Muggeridge to Tony Godwin, 15 April 1964

Publication was delayed, while new material that was more representative was sought from Siné's publishers Pauvert.

The incorporation of this material only added to the book's problems, as two firms of printers refused to handle what was now a most controversial publication. With the benefit of past experience, Penguin were already actively gathering witnesses for the defence.

'Siné is such a good draughtsman. His drawings are splendidly funny. He provides valuable social comment on our times and I cannot see why anyone should object to this volume. It is quite harmless.' A. J. P. Taylor

'Siné's cartoons are bitter, vicious and funny. They are nonetheless valid observations of the behaviour of his fellow men. I fully approve of publication.' John Mortimer

'Re Siné. I think he's a remarkable cartoonist with a very engaged and honourable record in French politics. I used to follow his work in both *L'Express* and *Nouvel Observateur*. I would have thought he was one of the most significant graphic commentators of the last ten years, reflecting very well the grisly underside of this time. Certainly in France he is highly respected. I think the idea of doing a book of selected drawings by him is a very good one – I would certainly vote for it. (You might follow it with one on Gerald Scarfe.)' John Berger

Quite apart from my admiration of Siné's draughtsmanship, I feel that the book deserves publication – not despite its subject matter but because of it. And however shocking some of the ideas presented by his drawings, they still remain ideas which cannot damage anyone whose own ideas are truly held; to be 'upset' by such work can happen only to people with a poor sense of balance. To prevent its circulation is to reveal how afraid one is of the aptness of his comment.

The fact that Siné goes so far is in itself a testimony to how seriously he feels. And there is a long tradition in art and literature – as I need hardly remind you – for witty presentation of serious and even moral convictions. His work is making a point, whether about General de Gaulle or Roman Catholicism, which has as much right to be made as any other expression of human reaction to authority. Indeed, you might say that there is a duty for all human beings constantly to question all forms of authority, to ensure that tolerance is preserved.

Gillray and Goya were allowed to make their 'shocking' comments. No harm came of it, but people were allowed the freedom to be amused by them, or made to think by them. And I hope that such tolerance will now be extended to Siné.

Michael Levey, Deputy Keeper, The National Gallery, to Tony Richardson, 3 October 1966

Thank you so much for the letter on Siné, which was quite the best of the endorsements we received. In the event the day was won without reference to them, but it was very reassuring to have your support and certainly it enabled us to make the best possible case.

Tony Richardson to Michael Levey, 7 October 1966

I was sorry but not really surprised that trouble should have arisen over the Siné book. The point is that Siné, like Swift (and Scarfe for that matter – his nearest equivalent in this country), is a moralist, which is commonly regarded as an intolerable position today. As a hater of pornography and aspiring Christian I find his furious indignation over the present moral confusion in State and Church very much to my taste, which was why I undertook writing the Introduction. There is, I confess, something very funny to me in the thought that a publishing house which made enormous profits out of the perverse sexual ravings of D. H. Lawrence should fear to sully its reputation with Siné. However, that is how things are.

Malcolm Muggeridge to Jill Norman, 28 September 1966

The book was duly published, and the complaints duly rolled in. 'This book constitutes a mixture of vulgarity and blasphemy which is unique in our experience and we are surprised to find it published by a firm of such repute.'

'This book is a disgrace.' A number of Lane's oldest friends, apparently, also made their objections known to him.

Long after he had left Penguin, Tony Godwin contributed his own reminiscences of this and other events in his eventful time at Penguin. About the Siné affair, he recalled:

It is revealing of the sort of conflict Allen experienced in consciously and conscientiously trying to provide a successor to carry out the tradition of Penguin when he retired. It shows the conflict he was involved in with his uneasiness and intuitions about the younger generation – the twenties to the thirties, and his instinct for the necessity of Penguin publishing for them – and at the same time his inability now to understand them and their attitudes and their tastes. The generation gap had become too wide for him to bridge. Really his own personal tastes had been formed during the thirties and forties as far as I could see. I don't believe he ever really latched on to Salinger, Amis and all those fifties writers and it was interesting that the only time I saw him thrilled and excited over a prospective publishing venture in fiction was when we negotiated another ten Somerset Maughams. Then he took a sudden personal interest in all the details of cover design, blurb, promotion, etc. And I think this is the only time while I was there that he did so.

This episode also shows the fits of diffidence he would have as a result, every now and then, over a particular controversy. It shows his instinctive deference to the establishment by seeking an opinion from the *TLS* and its editor.

There is no doubt he was against publishing Siné from the start, yet he would not come out and say so. If he had, then that would have ended the matter then and there. But he preferred to leave it to the democracy of the Board and even, himself, voted in favour. It also demonstrates how difficult he found it to accept consensus Board decisions that he disagreed with.

* * *

Allen Lane The Penguin Press

'In that same chapter we might pin our colours to the mast and declare our intention of sticking to our own particular field instead of wandering after false gods in hard covers,' wrote Bill Williams to Allen Lane with his first ideas for the 1956 celebration, *The Penguin Story*. That book detailed the existing relationship with hardback publishers: having originated in suspicion, it had since given way 'to a general spirit of co-operation'. This spirit was ratified in a 1948 agreement with a group of publishers – Heinemann, Hamish Hamilton, Faber, Chatto & Windus, and Michael Joseph – which 'gave Penguin first call on paper-bound editions from their lists'. This in turn led to a series of 'tens', based on the model of the Shaw and Wells millions, celebrating Agatha Christie, Evelyn Waugh, D. H. Lawrence and countless more.

This relationship was further cemented by the reciprocal arrangement, whereby original Penguins – Classics translations, Pelicans and even Puffins, found a subsequent hard cover edition with a 'conventional' publisher.

Penguin had themselves wandered after the false god: quite apart from the King Penguins, odd hard cover editions had turned up occasionally long before the Pelican History of Art in 1953. And in 1951 Bound Penguins and Pelicans were introduced, sold in parallel with their paperback versions. As soon as Penguin started issuing original works, there was a further problem to contend with – that of illicit rebinding of paperbacks to make library editions. 'By the end of the 1950s binding up was a widespread practice and indeed some library binders circulated to their customers lists of bound-up paperbacks that they had available in stock.' (Charles Clark, *The Bookseller*, 15 January 1966)

By the 1960s, the special relationship with other publishers could no longer operate. Penguin were in serious competition with other paperback imprints for every fiction title, of course; but there was a further consideration. Many of the hardback publishers were at last waking up to the viability of publishing their own paperback series. There was a real prospect of Penguin losing a good many of its authors.

Directly in the wake of the share issue, Allen Lane saw one particular means of adapting to this changing relationship. He began the process of entering into a series of negotiations with publishers on both sides of the Atlantic. Countering press speculation that Penguin itself was the target for an American takeover, September 1961 saw the purchase by Allen Lane of almost 40 per cent of the shares of Associated Book Publishers, a firm which included Methuen, Eyre & Spottiswoode and Chapman & Hall. The following May he sold the entire holding. By this time he had already entered into negotiations for the reconstruction of Cape as a sort of co-operative venture, ostensibly (and prophetically) to help prevent the takeover by Americans of a 'one-man publishing house set up between the wars' whose founder had recently died. Widely reported in the press as a takeover, it ultimately came to nothing. An agreement had been concluded with Houghton Mifflin to form a partnership with the Baltimore arm of Penguin; but, as W. E. Williams observed: 'he began to regret it and did not rest until he bought back his independence from them . . . Allen's basic allergy to all alliances was bound to prevail.'

Such was the general background when the Penguin Press was first discussed. There are those convinced that setting up this imprint, in the very same Vigo Street office where he first started at the Bodley Head, was an act of pure nostalgia and vanity and a prelude to rounding off a fifty-year career for Allen Lane. Others see it as further evidence of Tony Godwin's ambition, and equally an undertaking that Penguin could not afford, which was bound to lose money, and alienate the very publishers on whom Penguin still depended for a good proportion of their income.

Whether or not ulterior motives existed, Tony Godwin saw sound practical reasons for the new imprint:

> The argument for establishing a hardback subsidiary was roughly based on the fact that we found increasingly that more and more authors who we desired to commission to write for us insisted that their projected book should appear first in hardback – a cumbersome and expensive procedure for us. The hardback publisher always wanted a cut of the paperback royalty, often there were difficulties over the time lag between publication of the hardback and the paperback, and it was rare for the hardback to contribute to the higher and higher advances demanded of us. Our own hardback imprint would solve these difficulties and bring other benefits such as increased turnover, provide an added inducement to attract authors, etc.
>
> Tony Godwin, reminiscence

In a 1968 interview Allen Lane confirmed this: 'It was always intended that it would feed books into Penguins and in return Penguins could give all the authors who wanted it the full treatment . . . providing something that very few other people can.'

It certainly started with 'the full treatment' – an updated version of Lane's 'aphorism that books could only sell for sixpence or six guineas' (Morpurgo). Having published the best designed and produced paperbacks, it was time to renew his acquaintance with fine books in the tradition of the Bodley Head.

The first book, lumbering rather than rolling off the press, was the sumptuous and magnificent *Bibliopola – Pictures and Texts about the Book Trade* by Sigfred Taubert, Director of the Frankfurt Book Fair. It was priced in advance at £16, or after publication at £21.10s., for an edition of 750 sets of the two volume work. It was a labour of love for its compiler Taubert – the result of ten years' research and collecting. For Hans Schmoller, a close friend of the author and the inspiration behind its choice at Penguin, it was a minor masterpiece:

You may be interested in what is perhaps the most elusive production refinement in *Bibliopola*: the reverse of the colour plates has been printed with a pale cream tint so that it closely matches the shade of the text paper. Without this there would have been some 40 or 50 glaring white rectangles, even though they appear on that side of the mounted plates which is not meant to be looked at. This is just one example of the loving care that has gone into the making of this book. The credit belongs entirely to the designer, printer and binder in Germany.

As it developed, 'consuming money rather than providing any', ALPP showed scant heed of the avowed intent of the two founders, and the sacking of Godwin made little difference to the direction on which it was already embarked. A good many of the books in the series could never possibly enjoy a mass sale in a later Penguin or Pelican edition. The list assumed an unpredictable and often esoteric character, with titles such as *The Labyrinth of Solitude: Life and Thought in Mexico*; *German Rococo*: *The Zimmerman Brothers*; *Coup D'Etat: A Practical Handbook*; *The Levittowners: Anatomy of Suburbia*; *Revolutionary Silhouettes*; alongside the Nikolaus Pevsner Festschrift, the acclaimed *Complete Pelican Shakespeare* and the works of authors such as Marcuse, McLuhan, Isaac Asimov, Erich Fromm, A. Alvarez, Edward de Bono and John Berger. As a series it was not a disaster, and certainly not lacking in interest: but never a commercial success.

The Chairman's Statement for the 1967 year end results reads:

The hardback subsidiary's programme was launched in April 1967, and twenty-eight books had been published by the end of the year. Most of the books were widely and seriously reviewed, and the excellence of production was noted. The establishment of a new imprint demands judgement, patience, and capital, and I do not expect any profit contribution before 1970. However, the list now taking shape is making an impact, particularly in the social sciences. In 1968 we expect to publish a further fifty titles, and I discern the nucleus of an effective back-list. Although immediate profits cannot be expected, the group benefits from our being able to offer authors the complete range of hardback and paperback publishing techniques.

In a 1969 interview with Alex Hamilton, on the verge of retirement, Allen Lane was more resigned to its likely fate:

Your recent venture into hardbacks, with Allen Lane The Penguin Press, looks like a return full circle for you which hasn't quite connected.

It hasn't made a profit.

Is it doing as well as it ought to?

No, it's not.

Will it go on?

I don't think we should keep it going for more than three or four years if it doesn't break even.

Would you give it any popularizing shots in the arm?

No, I don't think so. If we are wrong on it, we are wrong basically and fundamentally. I started it from sentiment. In London one day I saw the old premises in Vigo Street where the Bodley Head was in the 1890s, where I started publishing, was empty. I thought it would be a fitting end to my career to go out through the same door I came in. I'm told the trade thinks it an old man's folly. Maybe, but I thought there was a purpose in it, linking the books to Pelican. But if it's not viable, it perhaps will stop. I should be sorry.

Allen Lane was being uncharacteristically pessimistic. He had already invited Charles Clark to take on, in addition to his role as head of Penguin Education, the revival of the ailing hardback series, and by the time Clark left the firm in 1972 the imprint had been stabilized and had earned its reprieve. Its real importance, an early move by the most senior paperback publisher into vertical publishing, was viewed with deep suspicion by many in the hardback trade. Today this is publishing orthodoxy.

* * *

The Village Book

The Village Series began not as a series but as one book, Jan Myrdal's *Report From a Chinese Village*, a study of a Chinese community which translated for Western readers both Chinese feelings for the old China and Chinese experience of the new order. It was an analysis of the process of change, of how people as individuals and as groups of individuals became adapted (or failed to adapt) to a new organization of society. It made use of interview and direct speech. It happened to be about the aftermath of a Communist revolution. It related the small society of the village to the large society of the State. It had theoretical insights of value to sociologists and political theorists and, at the same time, it had the immediacy, and the concentration upon the individual and his situation, of good journalism.

From the introductory blurb to the Village Series

Myrdal's work found its way into Penguin as a Pelican reprint, but the subsequent volumes were to become joint ventures between André Schiffrin of Pantheon Books in the States and Tony Godwin in Britain, in the new hardback imprint Allen Lane The Penguin Press. Several further 'village' books were planned, to be published simultaneously in Britain and the States. Along with Studs Terkel's study of an American 'village' in Chicago and further volumes featuring North African, Cuban, French villages, it was natural that a British contribution too should be considered. Ronald Blythe's book was to be in many ways autobiographical – unlike the writers of all the other Village Series books, he was born into the community that he was to describe more as a poet and storyteller than rural sociologist.

I thought about the village book all the way home – and a good bit of the night – and I honestly don't remember when I have felt so interested in a project. I have often thought of just writing a 'country book' out of sheer self-indulgence but how exciting it is to conceive one in, so far as this country is concerned, entirely revolutionary terms.

Your amalgamated village idea is excellent. It enables me to have total freedom in which to work. I look forward to reading the Chinese book – which I have read so much about – and by the time we next meet I hope I can talk about the whole thing in detail . . .

Patricia Highsmith comes to supper tonight – and it's snowing. Perhaps a long walk this afternoon, as you suggest, is imperative. Grotty time ahead.

Ronald Blythe to Tony Godwin, 12 February 1966

I have just written to Pantheon Books about you, and to ask whether they will be prepared to jointly commission the 'Village' book.

What we expect each author to do is to take the community, and draw together an integrated picture out of all the different threads that go to make up the village. The final work will answer such questions as: in what sense is it a community, and what sort of community is it? What roles do people play, and what do they actually do? What is their economic level and pattern, and what are the physical conditions in which they live – land, etc.? And of course the evolution of all these things gradually over the lifetime of the oldest inhabitant. What sort of social organization has the village got? Hierarchy? Kinship? Power? What about movement and immigration, and the relationship and view of the larger world of the surrounding country, county, city and nation as a whole?

If I were to sum up the intention of the books in one sentence, I would say that it is an attempt at making one understand in social and historical terms what a village is, and how it became so. I will let you know as soon as I hear from America.

Tony Godwin to Ronald Blythe, 17 February 1966

I had not forgotten you, and although things have been hellish busy since I got back, and I have also been battling both with bouts of asthma, and trying to get the Penguin Press under way, I have been doing something about your English Village: I think I have the right author, and at present he is writing a synopsis so that I can send it, plus examples of his work, for your approval . . . I am sorry that you should think that 'out of sight, out of mind' and I assure you this is not so.

Tony Godwin to André Schiffrin, Pantheon Books, 1 March 1966

Will this do, do you think? I have not gone into great detail but have emphasized my own position and have also tried to show the Suffolk village by means of a mixture of facts and emotive impressionism. The point I wish to make is that I am out to explore a familiar territory in order to discover its unfamiliarity.

I could have given a great number of thumbnail sketches of all kinds of locals, but I felt this would prove very little. What Pantheon Books really want to know, I imagine, is the depth of my involvement in village life and my ability to understand it from the sociological and historic – and political – point of view. I do indeed understand these things and the synopsis has been made to show what kind of man it is who is going to make his neighbours talk! I also suspect that no one who didn't know them would get a word out of them.

The value of the book will come from the actual 'voices' and the way they are edited and arranged – as in the Myrdal book, the great thing will be to escape from the question and answer technique, so that people will talk freely. It could be surprisingly interesting as a book – and this without trying to do a rustic Nell Dunn.

I hope it comes off. It is perfect timing for such a book.

Ronald Blythe to Tony Godwin, 16 March 1966

I am immensely impressed by your synopsis etc. to Anglia. I suddenly felt full of confidence that this is going to be a very good book indeed, and that you are absolutely one of the very few people who could write such a book. I will show it to one of my editors just to make sure I have not overlooked any pages and then will send it off to André Schiffrin of Pantheon, asking him for a reply as soon as possible, as I am sure you would like to get under way.

Tony Godwin to Ronald Blythe, 28 March 1966

Thank you very much for your letter. I am very relieved and pleased that you like the Anglia synopsis because the more I think about this book, the more I want to write it. Like most writers who live in the country I have always had it in mind to write a country book but I have always, too, had great reservations about the 'country book' per se. This book really could be something. I don't feel cocksure about it, neither do I feel – as one does about some books – that by a certain professional use of the right techniques it will simply 'come off'. I now simply hear and see the book all the time. In a personal sense it will be a 'steadying' thing for me to do, and I am eager to do it. Thank you again for your generous reception of the Anglia synopsis: it is just the kind of reassurance I need.

Ronald Blythe to Tony Godwin, 30 March 1966

I think the American reader will be more interested in discovering a microcosm of contemporary England than in immersing himself in the kind of close study of the qualities of village life, which have been described so very well by British writers of the past. I'm sure that Blythe realizes this, and I hope you will remind him. The other aspect which concerned us was the very serious tone of Blythe's prospectus, which again I hope will be mitigated by the realities of the villages . . .

André Schiffrin to Tony Godwin, 12 May 1966

I bicycled 22 miles yesterday for the Village book, staring about me as though I was in Africa. You are quite right, it could be a tremendous book. A ditcher: 'All them stones, piled one on one, so that you can get to the top and see the boats on Aldeburgh water . . .' He was looking at the church tower at Cretingham.

Ronald Blythe to Tony Godwin, undated (March 1967)

I am back in bed again, blast it! 'Flu this time. I enjoyed seeing you and your 'area'. I haven't forgotten your book; Production are costing it at the moment and you should have it as soon as they've finished with it. I think I shall come down and see you again in three months, if you're agreeable. I have great ambitions for your book.

Tony Godwin to Ronald Blythe, 2 March 1967 (tape-recorded, signed in his absence)

Thank you very much for your letter telling me about the changes at ALPP. I had not, as a matter of fact, seen any announcement that you were taking Tony Godwin's place. I would like to wish you every happiness and success in this new venture, and also hope that we may meet on one of my somewhat rare visits to London. I owe, as I believe does any writer who had any contact with him, a very great deal to Mr Godwin and I am particularly pleased that someone like yourself should be following him.

Ronald Blythe to Sir Edward Boyle, 1 July 1967

I had lunch with Ronald Blythe and can thus report on progress on the English volume in the 'Village' series. After an initial period of difficulty, Blythe feels he has found a way into his subject and that is to concentrate on what he calls the 'field men' of East Anglia. This is the peasantry of one of the most totally agricultural areas of England, who have been underpaid to the point of starvation for something like 200 years and still receive only about £11 a week. While I think there is a special toughness about these people in East Anglia, they are representative of the agricultural worker throughout England, and in that sense I think our book will be as much about the whole country as Terkel's work on Chicago has revealed all of America.

I have seen finished versions of two interviews of the many he has so far carried out, and feel very excited indeed at the prospect of the complete book. Blythe is a very sensitive person and a very skilful writer, and he has managed to coax fairly inarticulate people into exactly the sort of eloquence that this series needs. He works at such a level of concentration that he finds it difficult to predict when he will be finished, but I think it is reasonable to hope for a manuscript by Easter 1968, and I believe you will be as pleased by it as we have been by Terkel.

David Thomson to André Schiffrin, 8 November 1967

How very kind of you to write so soon and with such appreciation. I cannot tell you how relieved and happy your letter made me. I felt at heart that the book had really 'happened', as it were, but I have been so immersed in it, particularly this last year, that I was beginning to lose all sense of its impact – or indeed have any idea of whether it possessed impact. So you can imagine what real pleasure your words gave me.

Ronald Blythe to David Thomson, 4 April 1968

I genuinely had not the faintest idea that you and the Americans, and the other people who bought it, would like it as much as you do. I suppose this is because I am so on top of the whole thing and take it all for granted . . .

It is very strange sometimes how little a writer knows about his work. It is a completely different thing to him to what it is to those who read it. I do hope that *Akenfield* repays you for all the confidence you have put into it. I tried bits of it on the dog – i.e. one or two nice conventional friends in the neighbourhood, and they listened in amazement. They were very moved.

Ronald Blythe to Charles Clark, 22 January 1969

ALPP100: *Akenfield*

We all thought that we should send you a copy of the hundredth title from your imprint with an inscription from all the staff at Vigo Street. We are all delighted that the book we chose to be the hundredth title has had such a marvellous reception.

Unidentified writer to Allen Lane, 16 May 1969

* * *

Life After Godwin

The first week's sales of *A Fortunate Man* were 231 copies which is thought to be good. A tentative enquiry from the Readers' Union, which we are following up vigorously. We will let you know the result.

The Godwin sacking farce continues its dreary course. Allen Lane has made an unspeakable buffoon of himself. We sent out a joint statement and then agreed neither of us would talk. He then talked rapidly to everyone in sight. The main burden seems to be that I was sacked because I thought that Penguins should be popped into petrol stations and pubs, and published Penguins with naughty, racy covers. This has caused a certain degree of hilarity among the more intelligent British public.

Meanwhile, I have had several grotesque offers, including the offer of a boost of extra capital into a small 'tedious firm' by someone or other who owns five motor-racing courses, three chemical companies, seven property companies and other oddments. I am taking on all comers placidly, and will probably sort through the cards at the end of next week. It's more a problem of deciding what's worth doing and whether one can do it well and with people one respects than anything else. The trouble is, it's so easy to be wise after the event and unbelievably hard to be wise before the event.

As soon as it has been confirmed who will take over the Penguin Press, I will discuss the Neizvestny. The Césaire contract is now pretty well complete, so I will have it wrapped up for you.

Tony Godwin to John Berger, 10 May 1967

The sacking of Tony Godwin was either the disastrous mistake of a man out of touch, the saving of Penguin, 'the saddest event in publishing in the last twenty years', or simply anticipation of creative burnout:

When I was in a ferment about what was happening editorially and with Tony Godwin, I was involved in one of the new groups of television which were going for the Yorkshire station actually, and I used to go up occasionally to meetings in Leeds. One of the people I used to travel with sometimes, on the plane, was in television and he said one of the worst problems he had to face was wastage of human material in television – and that the pace is so terrific they burn themselves out. It's a very ruthless game and they go up very quickly but they also come down very quickly. I was wondering whether perhaps that wasn't happening.

Allen Lane interviewed by Heather Mansell, 1968

The disagreements between Allen Lane and Tony Godwin were widely reported, and blown out of all proportion. As ever, Penguin was news. In the main the press stories were concerned with the general appearance, and photographic covers in particular, and the marketing of Penguin books: 'Board Clash on Penguin Image', read *The Times* of 5 May 1967. Three days later, the *Daily Express* quoted Lane in an article by Anne Batt: 'So much dignity was going out of my books. Some of the frightful young marketing whizz-kids just wouldn't realize a book is not a tin of beans.'

The prospect of selling Penguins in garages, chemists' shops and supermarkets, and even vending machines was nothing new; Allen Lane, in his 1935 manifesto 'All About the Penguin Books', stated that they were:

designed primarily to reach these people, where they congregate on railway stations and in chain stores with the hope that when they see these books are available in the regular bookshops, they will overcome their temerity and come in. I know that I am not alone in thinking that when once this public has been induced to cross our threshold, it will be but a short step to turning them into regular book-buyers.

Vending machines too: the pre-war version was called the Penguincubator. It was largely a rerun of the critical differences which had broken up Penguin's original American partnership. By 1967 paperback books were largely – some said as much as 90 per cent – sold on impulse in Britain. This demanded the use of arresting cover art. It also necessitated a short shelf life, which in turn meant large scale returns – in the States, as much as half of an entire print run. Any step in this direction would be anathema to Lane, and ultimately suicidal from a business point of view.

All these headlines and articles gradually gave way to new and more insidious stories: the steadily growing rumours of successors and takeovers. In all this speculation the continuing achievements of Penguin during the 1960s tended to be ignored.

There is another quite different way of looking at these years, as Allen Lane's last, and not least achievement. After the decline of the fifties, he succeeded yet again in brewing up a cauldron of people who gave Penguin another renaissance at least as fruitful as its earlier peaks. Of course there was politicking, of course Godwin went around saying 'Allen is past it. It's all quite *hopeless*. Something's got to be done.' But there had *always* been politicking. The truly remarkable fact is that Allen Lane, at sixty odd, was able to find and set alongside his unbeatable production and marketing organization yet another set of doers (of whom I had the great good luck to be one). All of them, including Godwin, looked beyond their older colleagues directly to Lane for inspiration, leadership, and above all for understanding of their aspirations.

Dieter Pevsner, *The Author*, Winter 1979

In the centre of all this was Allen Lane, as contradictory as ever. The dynamic version, passionate about his creation – desperately seeking a worthy successor, but unable to let go of the 'reins', or the 'tiller', or similar agricultural or nautical metaphors. The cynical version – lunching for ever with potential suitors: 'Let them sort it out when I'm dead.' The practical version, undertaking significant collaborations with Longman over a number of years – with the Nuffield Science Teaching Project, and sales arrangements in certain remote markets – gradually acquainting themselves and preparing for the inevitable. Yet another Lane – the Olympian version, believing himself immortal, or at least trusting in the fact that his parents had both survived well into their eighties, and with the impressive example of Bill Williams, emerging unbeaten from a stroke, heart attack and throat cancer. A final version – heroic, struggling placidly through a long debilitating illness, never losing his interest or his grip, clinging tenaciously to life and Penguin.

For the last few years of his life after considerable haemorrhaging of editorial staff, Penguin gradually began to achieve the stability which allowed Lane the satisfaction of stepping back, easing himself into a retirement which he would never enjoy. He was satisfied with the three senior editors, Oliver Caldecott, Dieter Pevsner and Charles Clark. There were Chris Dolley and Harry Paroissien – a blend of dynamism and maturity allied with a commitment to the export market, backed up by the impressive and urbane figure of Sir Edward Boyle. The ever-dependable Ron Blass – and Hans Schmoller, Penguin's conscience and passionate advocate of the highest design and production standards. Most of all in his final years there was a concerted move to regain financial stability – a severe cutting back on expenditure, particularly on the advances paid, to the general relief of the paperback market, and an end to the overproduction associated with courting the best-seller market.

It was the backlist: the growing number of classics, original translations and commissioned books that provided the foundation. The only cloud on this otherwise untroubled financial horizon was one common to virtually every company seduced by the first generation of computers, which promised everything but tended to deliver little more than administrative nightmares. Mundane tasks like speeding distribution and checking credit-worthiness were one thing; 'the real impact of the machine lies in its devilish capacity for spotting winners. In effect it will supply data to advise editors on books worthy of publication. An ominous prospect.' (*Daily Mirror*, 15 December 1967)

The Directors of the Penguin Publishing Company Limited announce that consequent upon teething troubles following the introduction of a computer, the final results for 1967 will not be available for a further four weeks. It will be recalled that in his interim statement last October, the Chairman anticipated that in the second six months of the year some part of the set-back in the first six months would be recovered. The indications are that this has been the case and that profits will be sufficient adequately to cover the maintained dividend.

Draft press release, 23 April 1968

As for Allen Lane:

My plan is, as far as the firm is concerned, to mould it into what I think it should be as of now, because obviously you can't plan how it's going to be in ten or twenty years time, and then stick around as long as they can put up with me. My relationships are pretty good with the majority of people and I like to be kept informed about what's going on. The rest of my time I can spend farming which I'm enjoying more and more and increasing productivity on the farm which I find is very visually and physically satisfying.

Allen Lane interviewed by Heather Mansell, 1968

* * *

Lanesday – The Penguin *Ulysses*

Ulysses

It struck me that it might be interesting to know how far *Ulysses* had got into public libraries, as obviously if it has to any great extent it would make it more difficult to make a case against its general sale. This is Stevenson's reply to my enquiry (he, as you know, is our 'tec' reader – Librarian of Hornsey and an official of the Library Association).

A. S. B. Glover to Allen Lane, internal memorandum, 23 June 1953

I wonder if you happen to know to what extent *Ulysses* is now available in public libraries. Have you, for example, got it at Hornsey? We have been considering the possibility of a Penguin *Ulysses*, but don't all feel quite sure that it might not cause trouble if we launched this once controversial work on an unguarded world at a price which would enable the so easily corrupted masses to get it. If, on the other hand, *Ulysses* is already easily and widely obtainable through the public library service it would seem to suggest that it is worth nobody's while to attempt its suppression any longer. Please don't mention this possibility which is still a secret locked in our own hearts.

A. S. B. Glover to W. B. Stevenson, 19 June 1953

Your letter about *Ulysses* interested me very much. The policy of public libraries regarding the book has become in the last few years much more liberal. I put *Ulysses* before my committee some five years ago as a special item, and had little difficulty in inducing them to purchase it. After it had got in the catalogue, the demand grew, and I now have five copies, though none of them ever go on the open shelves. We even had a University Extension class reading it a year ago. The general policy depends much on the librarian. The book knocked me down when Harold Edwards got me a copy in 1930 and I've been lending my own copy out ever since. Thus if the librarian has read it, and believes in it as I do, he will have bought it. I know there are a good many copies in public libraries – the Lane edition and its reprint did that. But I am practically certain that none of them are openly on the shelves. You want facts however: I will write to the South Eastern Regional Bureau and find out how many copies there are in the South of England, and let you know.

W. B. Stevenson to A. S. B. Glover, 22 June 1953

I am grateful for your observations on *Ulysses* and will be glad to hear the result of your enquiries from the South Eastern Regional Bureau. I can't myself feel that a court would expose itself to ridicule by deciding at this stage in history that we weren't old enough to read *Ulysses*, but with English courts you never know and some of my colleagues are not quite so happy. If it were *Lady Chatterley* unexpurgated I should feel more doubts.

A. S. B. Glover to W. B. Stevenson, 24 June 1953

I believe that you act as trustees of the estate of the late James Joyce.

We have been contemplating the possibility of a Penguin edition of *Ulysses*, but are not sure what the present position of the copyright of the book is, and how far the market is restricted by agreements with other publishers. If this matter is in your hands and you would be prepared to consider whether an arrangement for the publication of a Penguin edition would be feasible, perhaps you would kindly let me know so that we can go further into the matter.

A. S. B. Glover to Munro Saw & Co., Solicitors, 21 July 1953

We have your letter of 21st instant and confirm that we act for the Administrators of James Joyce.

We had some negotiations with you between 1946 and 1947 over a proposed publication of a cheap edition of *Ulysses*. We think that Messrs Richard Steele & Son were negotiating the matter but in the meanwhile, we suggest that you should clear up the position with John Lane The Bodley Head and then communicate with us again. We would mention in passing that John Lane The Bodley Head have, under the terms of an Agreement with them, the right to publish a cheap edition.

Munro Saw & Co., Solicitors, to Penguin Books, 22 July 1953

In slightly different circumstances, James Joyce's *Ulysses* might have become the first publication in hard covers of Penguin Books Limited. Allen Lane had succeeded to the Chairmanship of the Bodley Head, whose situation was already being described as 'desperate' in 1932. An agreement was reached with the co-directors whereby the Lanes would raise their own money to fund personal ventures. It was in this way that Penguin Books was launched in July 1935, the first eighty books carrying the Bodley Head imprint on the cover along with that of Penguin. It was not until early in 1936 that Allen Lane put the Bodley Head into voluntary liquidation, severed his connections with the firm and formed Penguin Books Ltd.

Ulysses was published in America in early 1934 after the test case invited by the publishers was won by Morris L. Ernst, who would later become not only Lane's friend and adviser, but also a Penguin author in his own right. Lane was in America at the time and was, ultimately, the only British publisher to make an offer for it. The Bodley Head co-directors would only sanction its publication on the basis of the loose agreement which placed all the costs and the real risk of prosecution on the Lanes. Even so, by the time it was published, under the imprint of the Bodley Head, the Lanes were no longer involved in the company. *Ulysses* was to become one of the foundations on which the fortunes of the Bodley Head slowly revived.

Between 1936 and the time of the Penguin edition, the Bodley Head had sold just over a quarter of a million copies of the book – averaging at 10,000 copies a year, until, in 1961, the film of *Ulysses*, and the Countess of Dartmouth's denunciation of both the book and the film (which she had neither read nor seen), raised the sales for that year, according to *The Bookseller*, to almost 40,000 copies. From then on sales declined to little over 2,000 a year. Such figures might easily be interpreted as denoting a book that has had its day.

By the late 1960s Sir Allen Lane was in poor health, and no longer played an intimate role in the daily affairs and editorial decisions of Penguin. But he wanted *Ulysses* for Penguin.

Ulysses by James Joyce

We have not hitherto solicited offers for the British paperback rights to this book, as we were not in a position to conclude the negotiations. The time has now come, however, for us to arrange for a paperback edition, and we are asking the four or five interested paperback houses to make us an offer.

Subject to suitable terms being agreed on, we hope to sign a paperback contract this year.

Guido A. Waldman, the Bodley Head, to Oliver Caldecott, Joint Chief Editor, Penguin Books, 14 September 1967

Ulysses

I am glad we came so close to agreement last night, and both Sir Allen and I welcomed your assurance that Penguin would have the book for release in April 1969, subject of course to our making you a reasonable offer.

I understood you to express a desire that the offer should represent a series of recurring payments rather than an enormous lump sum and perhaps you would consider an advance for the first year of £10,000, followed by guaranteed minimum of £3,000 per annum for ten years, as meeting your requirements. Sir Allen would very much like this to be against 10% rather than the crippling 12½% royalty.

Finally, although I have talked above about a guaranteed minimum sum for ten years, I am assuming that in the event of this being a successful operation the paperback rights would be renewable at the end of ten years.

Perhaps you would let me know after Frankfurt whether this offer seems reasonable to you.

Oliver Caldecott, Joint Chief Editor, to Max Reinhardt, 12 October 1967

Ulysses

Thank you for your letter of October 12th. I do not think your offer is reasonable, for we have had much more substantial ones. We are not putting the book up for auction, but I think it is important that the Penguin offer should be as good as some of the others we have had. If it is, then I will be glad to put it forward to the Joyce Estate for their acceptance.

I should have thought that the advance should be £15,000 the first year and £6,000 per annum for the next ten years. I also feel that the royalty should be 12½% for this is considered by many authors, and certainly by literary agents, as a matter of prestige.

It seems to me that you could easily sell 200,000 copies the first year of publication and certainly 75,000 copies a year in subsequent years. These sales would earn more than the advance that we are asking.

Let me know what you think of this.

Max Reinhardt to Oliver Caldecott, 16 October 1967

Ulysses

I've discussed your letter with Sir Allen. He is less concerned about the advance than about the royalty. We are prepared to agree to £15,000 down and to an annual figure in the region you suggest (though we should prefer £5,000 per annum), but the extra 2½% does represent approximately an extra 1s on the selling price and since our sale is likely to be largely to students, a low price is essential.

Would you be prepared in any way to modify your insistence on 12½%? I have in mind that we go to 12½% after we've cleared our origination costs, i.e. after the initial 250,000.

If you do agree this, I shall be at Harmondsworth tomorrow and if you were to let me know on SKY 1984 (between 2.30 and 4.30 p.m.), if this is acceptable, Sir Allen and I would go off to our editorial conference with lighter hearts.

Oliver Caldecott to Max Reinhardt, 17 October 1967

I haven't replied before to your letter of October 17th as I wanted to get the approval of the Joyce Estate before doing so. I have now had their answer, and we are quite prepared to accept your offer for a paperback edition of *Ulysses* on the following agreed terms:

An advance of £15,000 on signature, plus a further advance of £6,000 a year for ten years, against a royalty of 10% on the first 250,000 copies sold and 12½% above.

The book will be published under the joint imprints of Penguins and the Bodley Head, and I understand that Sir Allen would like to publish it in April 1969. With a bit of planning I really think we could make this a great occasion, both for Penguins and for the Bodley Head, and we should be happy to contribute to this effort.

Would you now let us have a contract for this, with, perhaps, two extra copies that we can send to the Joyce Estate?

I am very pleased that we have come to an agreement about this.

Max Reinhardt to Oliver Caldecott, 1 November 1967

The April 1969 publication was designed to be the final scene in the last act of Sir Allen Lane's long career, played out appropriately at the Vigo Street premises where Lane had first started out as little more than an apprentice to his 'uncle' John Lane, fifty years earlier.

Some thirty-three years after the Bodley Head name was removed from the covers of Penguin Books, *Ulysses*, the book that Allen Lane had acquired for the Bodley Head at his own risk, was finally to be published by Penguin, under the joint imprint, and on the fiftieth anniversary of Lane's introduction to publishing.

It was a highly charged event for Lane, and at £75,000, the highest price ever paid for paperback rights, an event not insignificant for Penguin.

Daily Mirror, 16 January 1969

Max Reinhardt, managing director of the Bodley Head, explained: 'We have, of course, had many offers for the paperback rights, but there was really no reason to sell when *Ulysses* was doing so well in hardback. I suppose it is really a kind of anniversary present to Sir Allen.' One point he did make though was that friendship has some limits in business. For Reinhardt added: 'To get the rights, Penguin paid more than anyone in Britain has ever paid for the paperback rights to a book.'

Penguin 3000 was indeed published on 23 April 1969, as Sir Allen Lane's swan song, prior to his 'retirement' from publishing. *Ulysses* appeared in the guise of a Penguin Modern Classic, embellished on the rear cover with Augustus John's drawing of Joyce. The front cover was perhaps the starkest and simplest typographical design ever produced by Penguin – the Penguin colophon in one corner and James Joyce *Ulysses* set in type on a black background, suggesting, perhaps, serenity and a calm progress through the thirty-five years of Penguin's Progress.

* * *

Allen Lane – The Final Years

23 April is Shakespeare's Birthday, St George's Day, and this year, exactly fifty years to the day since I first entered publishing with my uncle John Lane at the Bodley Head. This is the day I have chosen to retire as Managing Director of the firm and when Harry Paroissien and Chris Dolley will take over jointly in that capacity. Both of them have had experience in all aspects of publishing, and it is with the utmost confidence that I place the Directorial Management in their hands.

It is almost thirty-five years since the first ten Penguins appeared at sixpence. Since then 6,000 titles have been published in the various series, and there is no doubt that ours is a list to be proud of. Perhaps you feel that I should now sit back and enjoy a satisfied retirement, but with so many exciting projects in hand this is impossible! Penguin will remain very much my company – I will stay on as Chairman and intend to visit the office once or twice a week, so my involvement with the firm will be as great as ever.

Letter to the Staff from Allen Lane, 1969

And that is as close as it was possible for Allen Lane to come to retiring. Chris Dolley recalled:

As he was an insomniac, he would get up at 3 a.m. and write countless little notes to himself with which to harry his staff and others on the following morning. I have one such, written only a few days before he died and given to me when I visited him for the last time in Mount Vernon. It is a collection of trivial, inconsequential jottings written on a flimsy sheet torn from a notebook, but oh, how typical right to the end.

Stories circulate from time to time that Lane is contemplating selling Penguin Books Ltd, and he admitted to me at lunch the other day that death duties would make him an 'expensive corpse'. Offers have undoubtedly been made to him, but my guess is that he would find it beyond endurance to sever himself from this national institution.

Leonard Russell, *Sunday Times*, 7 February 1960

Business is incredibly good. In October we sold over a million books for more than £100,000. I haven't a clue what I'm going to do next. I've got the firm, the farm, the Zoo, Bumpus and such sidelines as the insurance company, a host of acquaintances, a few friends, an enormous capacity for enjoyment but a rather empty personal life.

Allen Lane to his cousin, Joan Collihole, undated (October 1958). Written on the 8.45 to Bristol

One must appreciate how much change there has been in publishing during the last ten years. When we started Penguins we had virtually no competition, we did not take our work terribly seriously – our editorial decisions were made over lunch at the Barcelona – and although we had our travellers there was no real sales policy: in fact we were all amateurs. The situation today is that we are, whether we like it or not, in a tough, highly competitive industry, and we have to fight every inch of the way, from the facing of colossal advances if we are to keep books away from Pan, Corgi, Ace, Panther, etc., to the real struggle to retain space at the retail outlets. As you know, this has led to our having to drop some of the people who were with us from the start in order to replace them by highly trained executives. The result of this can be seen in our balance sheets, and were it not for the fact that we have reorganized ourselves, there is no question but that we should have slipped swiftly back in the race. I had dinner with Bob Lusty last night, and we both bemoaned the fact that life in publishing today is entirely different from what it was when we came into it, and that the change as far as we are concerned personally has not been for the better. I can contemplate my retirement when the time comes without any regrets in advance.

Allen Lane to Richard Lane, 22 July 1959

The AGM is to be held at Harmondsworth in the new room we have had fitted out at the far end of the canteen. Our canteen caterers have turned out to be a success and for the occasion I have ordered melon, double lamb chops with haricots verts and mushrooms, asparagus served as a separate dish, followed by strawberries and cream.

Allen Lane to Richard Lane, 18 May 1960

The matter which is engaging a good deal of our attention at the moment is, of course, the *Lady Chatterley* case . . . I am afraid I will have to give evidence and WEW will also speak as representing the literary side of the firm. We are now working on our list of witnesses, which is an impressive one, and from now on we shall have to spend a good deal of time with counsel planning the main lines of our defence. We are studiously avoiding letting out the names of the witnesses we are proposing to call and the prosecution is being equally reticent as to the people whose support it is counting on.

Allen Lane to Richard Lane, 26 September 1960

As you know one of the main reasons why I was negotiating with the *Economist* was that I felt that this was as sure a way as could be devised of ensuring the continuity of the business, but from the events of the last few days it seems we might have been doing exactly the opposite. I am now contemplating the possible flotation of a public company which I imagine would suit you quite well as you could then dispose of your shares on the stock exchange in the ordinary way.

Allen Lane to Richard Lane, 25 October 1960

Tony Godwin is now settling in well although there have been and still are tensions . . . HFP was over for a couple of weeks just before I left and I think he sees the size of the problem he has to face in fifteen months time. I've made it clear to him that I propose to adopt a three day week or a six month year as soon as he is in the saddle. With my interests out here, the bit of land in Ireland which the new airport at Cork is going to make a difference to, and the farm I think I can give myself enough to do to keep me out of more mischief than I'm in already.

Allen Lane, Los Antillas, Carvajal, to Richard Lane, Christmas Day 1960

I won't be coming to Australia this spring for a number of reasons, the principal one being that I have been strongly advised by Machell of Martins, by Whatmore, and by Dickson among others that it would be very foolhardy if I let the present financial structure of the firm stand as it does at present. At the same time I don't feel that the best interests of all concerned lie in the direction of a take-over bid and the only practicable alternative available is some form of public issue.

Allen Lane to Richard Lane, 25 January 1961

In anticipation of the thing going through I have postponed my visit to Spain. I am building this house on the beach at Carvajal and not on the piece of land I bought at Marbella, as Marbella is now developing as a sort of Cannes, Monte Carlo, and Nice rolled into one and this is not the sort of life which I enjoy, so I will probably sell the land sometime. I might even consider planting it out to citrus fruit.

Allen Lane to Richard Lane, 3 February 1961

In addition to America there is Australia where I'm afraid we've lost a lot of ground which if we are to pick it up will require a major effort. There's the Africa project and India to follow. Plus Peregrines, the Loeb Classics' successors, a new Puffin drive and the educational approach. In all of this I don't see myself as more than a paternal figure as I am convinced that it's a bad thing to have a near sixty-year-old as active chief. I've seen too many people reach that age and carry on as if they were in their prime with very bad effects down the line.

Allen Lane, en route for Isfahan, to Hans Schmoller, 17 May 1961

I'm very glad that we were able to see each other last night although it was only for so short a time. Although we said that we hadn't changed much and certainly you looked exactly the same to me I think that in fact the years have made their mark. We are two more serious people with a different and more responsible attitude to life and I look forward to seeing you again after a shorter gap than the last one. This has been a tough trip and I'm ready to go home but I think the results will justify the efforts.

Allen Lane, in flight between Adelaide and Melbourne, to Bob Maynard, 7 July 1961

I thought that you were looking well, far better than you had led me to expect. After all we are not in the first flush of youth. As you know I enter my sixtieth year next month and as I told you, I enjoy my life very much, irregular as it may appear to some. Both of our parents went on to their mid-eighties and I don't see why we shouldn't too. Father told me when he was well over eighty that he thought that the right age to retire was somewhere between fifty-five and sixty, the only 'must' being the ability to take up something to fill the gap one's work had filled until that time. I'm hoping the farm will do that for me. How about you?

Allen Lane, en route to Quebec, to Richard Lane, 12 August 1961

The greatest excitement at the moment is still on the secret list but I thought you might like to know something about it. For a long time we have been allowing a certain number of our original titles to be published by other firms. The number of books available has now increased and we have decided to set up a wholly owned subsidiary to handle these. In going down Savile Row I noticed that the windows of the Bodley Head looked very scruffy and that there was a notice posted in the window. From this I learnt that Bertram Rota had moved to larger premises. Before lunch I rang up Julie Belcher and asked her if she would start making enquiries as to the possibility of taking over the lease. This resulted in our doing this and we will be opening in the spring a new firm to be known as Allen Lane The Penguin Press. I felt it was very fitting to go a full circle and end up where I began nearly fifty years ago.

Allen Lane to Richard Lane, 28 September 1965

Until we were turned into a public company I took full responsibility for every aspect of the business but now that we are as we are I feel that the board or boards should, or rather in fact must, assume corporate responsibility for the editorial, financial, art, sales, production and promotion policy. My own taste editorially is towards Maugham, Wells, Hemingway, Graham Greene and Evelyn Waugh, and in the theatre to Shaw and Wilde and Noel Coward; typographically to Oliver Simon and Tschichold; and in art to Turner and Ivon Hitchens and I find myself out of sympathy with much of contemporary literature, theatre, typography and art which is why I have adopted the attitude I have of recent years when such matters have been discussed.

I have just over a year to go in active business life and during that time I intend to effect a staged retirement which I consider to be in the best interests of all concerned. In this way the final break will be easier for me to face and those who remain will have been able to work out a modus vivendi.

Allen Lane, El Fenix, Carvajal, to Hans Schmoller, 15 August 1966

Sir Edward Boyle who was the Minister of Education in our last Conservative government and who has been a director for over a year is willing to become vice-chairman any time now and to step into my place when I vacate the chair which will either be in September 67, Feb. 68 when my present seven-year agreement ends or April 69 when I will have completed fifty years in publishing. HFP's agreement runs out in July 68 when he will be sixty two and I'm in two minds as to whether to let it run on for a further three years or not. Neither HPS nor Tony Godwin want to be managing director so I'll probably have to look outside. Chris Dolley or Charles Clark are the best bets but the former is doing a very good job in Baltimore while the latter has his hands full as OC Education which is becoming an increasingly important side of the business.

Allen Lane, El Fenix, Carvajal, to Richard Lane, 16 December 1966

During the talk I had with Tony he said that he wanted to give up fiction and hand it over to Caldecott. I said that I would see him and that I would make myself responsible for fiction covers working with Caldecott, Tony Richardson and anyone else I thought fitting . . . Tony said that he thought that Alan Aldridge would leave if I insisted on the art department moving to Harmondsworth . . . Tony wrote to me about *New Writing USA*. I dislike the biographical note on Ed Saunders on page 328 and find I am developing a phobia about the four-letter word we defended at so great a cost – and profit. I'm quite content to abide by your and Harry's decision.

Allen Lane, El Fenix, Carvajal, to Hans Schmoller, 28 December 1966

So many of my friends and contemporaries are either retired or dead that my social/business contacts don't give me as much pleasure as they used to and as I have as much as I need to get by on for the rest of my life there's really not much point in doing anything which gives me little satisfaction . . . The new warehouse is now in use and the automated distribution section should be in use on Jan. 1. At the same time we switch over to the computer from the punched card system which has been in use for twenty years.

Allen Lane, El Fenix, Carvajal, to Joan Collihole, 28 December 1967

To return to the firm, my feeling is that we should go for a period of consolidation in 1968 with a real drive to curb all unnecessary expenditure and as we are fundamentally sound I think we may well turn in outstanding results, which I would like to do for my last full year in the saddle.

Allen Lane, El Fenix, Carvajal, to Hans Schmoller, 31 December 1967

Fiction is a difficult section just now and as I've said before I am of the opinion that we should be more selective even if it means reducing the number of titles quite considerably. At the present time there are too many unimportant books which clog up the list. I've just finished my chore of going through the stock sales for the year and I think it would be well worth your while to take the Penguin section home sometime and give it the once over. One can pick up a lot from it which could be useful as a guide.

Allen Lane, El Fenix, Carvajal, to Oliver Caldecott, 30 December 1967

I won't return to the office again. It's in good shape and the major battles have been fought and won but I just haven't the energy to get down again in the scrum especially as there's no need for it as far as I'm concerned personally. What I would like to do is to spend more time with my family and friends in the peace which I find in the country.

Allen Lane, Middlesex Hospital, to Joan Collihole, 8 August 1968

Memorandum

Proposed Acquisition of Penguin Books by Universities, Colleges and Similar Institutions . . . The matter was discussed in greater detail at a dinner on the 23rd April at Lord Goodman's home, attended by distinguished University representatives: Professor Alan Bullock, St Catherine's College Oxford – The new Vice Chancellor: Sir Roger Stevens – Vice Chancellor, Leeds: Lord James – Vice Chancellor, York: Professor Briggs – Vice Chancellor, Sussex: Professor Hoggart; and Others.

At this meeting there was a cordial endorsement of the project. Lord Butler could not attend because of commitments in the North but asked to be kept in touch. At the meeting it was agreed to proceed with the scheme which should be sufficiently attractive to the Universities and provide Sir Allen Lane with continuity of control and a guarantee that no quick profit would be made by anyone . . .

Lord Goodman, 25 October 1968

I was very glad to get your letter from Melbourne and to learn that everything is going well there. Chris told me that we weren't able to get the strip of land next door. I'd be interested to know how you've solved the problem of the new buildings . . . I've made a recent discovery and that is that white wine is not good for me but that whisky is. It's a bit more expensive but the result is OK.

Allen Lane, El Fenix, Carvajal, to Ron Blass, 31 March 1969

Harry Paroissien retires at the end of the year. I am afraid he is a bit unhappy about it but on the other hand the firm is so different these days that I do not think he would have enjoyed going on much longer. The staff is now around 500 and I do not know more than about 10 per cent myself. I have been into the office twice since I left hospital but I am not going to make any attempt to become involved in day-to-day administration. Ron Blass is going to become Deputy Managing Director in the new year and he is my closest contact.

Allen Lane to Richard Lane, 31 December 1969

* * *

It is obvious if the elder members of a firm attempt to keep youth from taking an active part in the management of a concern, they are, at the same time, keeping out new ideas, one might almost say, progress. After a certain age it seems as if one is forced into a rut which often seems to be little more than a fad. There is a tendency to take shelter behind the slogan, 'What was good enough for me or my ancestors is surely good enough for you' – meaning youth. On the other hand, youth, by itself, in command without the steadying hand, is by no means a good thing. Experience, though discounted by youth, is quite as valuable, if not more so, as originality.

Allen Lane, unidentified newspaper, 22 August 1927

Sir Allen Lane, CH, founder and chairman of Penguin books and creator of the Paperback Revolution, died on Tuesday of this week, 7th July, in Mount Vernon Hospital, Northwood, Middlesex, after a long illness. He was sixty-seven.

The Bookseller, 11 July 1970

PENGUIN NOW A SITTING DUCK
Evening News, 8 July 1970
PENGUIN TO MERGE WITH PEARSON GROUP
Daily Telegraph, 9 July 1970
AMERICAN BID FOR PENGUIN THWARTED
Sheffield Telegraph, 10 July 1970
LONGUINS
The Economist, 11 July 1970
LORD COWDRAY BAGS A PENGUIN
Observer, 12 July 1970
PENGUIN BATTLE LOOMS LARGER
Evening Standard, 16 July 1970
McGRAW HILL'S WAITING GAME
Investors Chronicle, 24 July 1970

Book publishing is a pretty personal business. Very few publishing firms survive the death of their founder in recognizable form.

Allen Lane, 1969

I hope Penguin business will straighten out, even though so many fine people have left that I know it can't ever be the same again. I don't know why I feel so very personally about it – perhaps because a few very fine people are still there. Well, enough said. Keep in touch, and if I can help in any way, just let me know.

Peter Mayer, Avon Books New York, editor of the 1966 Pelican *The Pacifist Conscience*, to Jill Norman, Penguin Editorial, 16 May 1967

Bibliography

Allen Lane: A Personal Portrait, W. E. Williams; Bodley Head, 1973

Allen Lane: King Penguin, J. E. Morpurgo; Hutchinson, 1979

The Ample Proposition, John Lehmann; Eyre & Spottiswoode, 1966

The Bantam Story, Clarence Petersen; Bantam, New York, 1970

The Bodley Head 1887–1987, J. W. Lambert and Michael Ratcliffe; Bodley Head, 1987

The Book of Paperbacks, Piet Schreuders; Virgin, 1981

Dorothy L. Sayers: Her Life and Soul, Barbara Reynolds; Hodder, 1993

Essays in the History of Publishing, ed. Asa Briggs; Longman, 1974

Fellows in Foolscap, Desmond Flower; Robert Hale, 1991

Fifty Penguin Years, Linda Lloyd Jones, Jeremy Aynsley; Penguin, 1985

A Guide to Paperback Progress, Nicholas Joicey; *Twentieth Century British History*, vol. 4, no. 1, 1993

How the Law was Changed, Roy Jenkins; Encounter, 1960

I Am My Brother, John Lehmann; Longmans, 1960

An Imagined Life, Richard Hoggart; OUP, 1993

Jan Tschichold: Typographer, Ruari McLean; Lund Humphries, 1990

John Lehmann's New Writing, Ella Whitehead and John Whitehead; Edwin Mellen Press, 1990

Jonathan Cape, Publisher, Michael S. Howard; Cape, 1971

The Making of a Publisher, Victor Weybright; Weidenfeld & Nicolson, 1968

Master of None, J. E. Morpurgo; Carcanet Press, 1990

The Monotype Recorder – Hans Schmoller, ed. Gerald Cinamon; Monotype Corporation, April 1987

The Mushroom Jungle, Steve Holland; Zeon Books, 1994

Orwell, The War Broadcasts, ed. W. J. West; Duckworth/BBC, 1985

The Paperback; Its Past, Present and Future, Desmond Flower; Arborfield, 1959

Paperbacks Across Frontiers, J. E. Morpurgo; Bowater Paper Corporation, 1960

The Passionate Intellect; Dorothy L. Sayers' Encounter with Dante, Barbara Reynolds; Kent State University Press, 1989

The Penguin New Writing 1940–1950, ed. John Lehmann and Roy Fuller; Penguin, 1985

The Penguin Story, W. E. Williams; Penguin, 1956

Penguins Progress 1935–1960, Compton Mackenzie, Michael Grant, Richard Hoggart, Elliott Viney, Reuben Heffer; Penguin, 1960

Picture Post 1938–50, ed. Tom Hopkinson, Penguin, 1970

Publishing and Bookselling, Harold Raymond; J. M. Dent & Sons, 1938

Snow on the Salt Bush, Geoffrey Dutton; Viking Melbourne, 1984

Suffolk Lives, Josephine Walpole; Richard Castell Publishing, 1993

The Translator's Art, ed. William Radice and Barbara Reynolds; Penguin, 1987

The Trial of Lady Chatterley, ed. C. H. Rolph; privately printed and Penguin, 1961

Tributes to Allen Lane, Harry Paroissien, Richard Hoggart, Robert Lusty; privately printed, 1970

Mass-Observation Reports

PCS Newsletter, *The Penguin Collector*, *Miscellany*; The Penguin Collectors' Society, 1974–1994

The Times, *The Times Literary Supplement*, *Sunday Times*, *Observer*, *Guardian*, *The Bookseller*, *The Author*, *The Book Collector*, *Antiquarian Book Monthly Review*, *Signal*, *Book and Magazine Collector*

The books, pamphlets, publicity material published by Penguin, 1935–1995

Acknowledgements and Sources

Between 1935 and 1970 Penguin Books Ltd touched the lives of everyone who cared about good writing, the arts, sciences and social sciences, education, politics – and more. The great majority of these were readers; the rest were Penguin authors, editors and the many backroom staff, as dedicated as any at Penguin, but whose contributions are rarely, if ever, recorded. So these acknowledgements should start here, with all those many people involved in the Penguin story whose names and achievements have been, once more, ignored.

In the time and space available, I have merely scratched at the surface of Penguin history, and barely hinted at the range and depth of the list. But I have managed to meet and contact a great many people, and have received their limitless help and enthusiastic cooperation. I have plundered the files and correspondence of many, many others. Whatever credit is due belongs to them.

The book would not have existed without the Penguin archive, and more particularly without the unceasing help of Nick Lee and Michael Richardson at the University of Bristol Special Collections, who, in addition to everything else they did, trusted me.

Sir Allen Lane's family – his sister Nora Bird in Australia, his widow Lady Lettice Lane, his daughters Clare Morpurgo and Christine Teale, his cousins Joan and Eveline Collihole, and Richard Lane's daughter Elizabeth Paton – provided invaluable help and, in addition, made large contributions to the archive in the form of copies of personal letters between Allen, Richard and John Lane, papers relating to the Bodley Head, and the surviving diaries Sir Allen Lane kept on his business trips abroad.

Eunice Frost OBE has acted throughout as my conscience and mentor, her energy, care and unceasing commitment an example it would be foolish to ignore. Margaret Clark similarly never failed to provide detailed answers to my constant questioning. Chris Dolley travelled halfway round the world to meet and help me.

Michael Rubinstein came to my rescue, at the same time making a significant addition to the Penguin archive.

To these must be added the many more who answered questions, contributed material, corrected errors and generally helped and encouraged me: Miriam Allott, H. A. W. Arnold, Ian Ballantine, Stanley Baron, John Berger, Ian Cameron Black, Helen Blass, Ronald Blythe, Cliff Bosley, Sylvia Bradford, Jane Carrington, Lee Chadwick, Charles Clark, James Cochrane, Peter Cochrane, Mark Cohen, Elizabeth Creak, John Curtis, Len Deighton, John Dreyfus, Peter du Sautoy, David Duguid, Geoff Dutton, Russell Edwards, Jean Faulks, John Fleming, Dr Desmond Flower, the Rt Hon. Michael Foot MP, Emeritus Professor Boris Ford, Norman Franklin, Eric Gadd, Abram Games, James Gardner, Fay Godwin, William Gompertz, Tom Hanley, Susie Harries, Robin Harrison, Beryl Hedges, David and Brenda Herbert, John Hitchin, Uta and Ian Hodgson, Grace Hogarth, Professor Richard Hoggart, Baron Holme of Cheltenham, Lord Horder, Charlotte Hough, Professor Lisa Jardine, the Rt Hon. Lord Jenkins of Hillhead OM, Nicholas Joicey, Peter Kite, Sir Michael Levey, Marjorie Lloyd, Linda Lloyd Jones, William McGuire, Ruari McLean, Bob Maynard, John Miles, Professor J. E. Morpurgo, Jill Norman, Bella Olney, Joe Pearson, Dieter Pevsner, June Pipe, His Honour Judge David

Pitman, Alexander Potter, Fred Price, Isabel Quigly, Dr William Radice, Max Reinhardt, Dr Barbara Reynolds, C. H. Rieu, Richard Rieu, Professor Ian Rogerson, Doug Rust, Tanya Schmoller, Doreen Scott, Ronald Segal, Tishy Sharma, Barbara Smoker, His Honour Judge Owen Stable QC, Joan Steele, Richard Stoneman, Brian Stonier, Jack and Dorothy Summers, J. R. Tanner, Martin Taylor, Neil Thomson, Raleigh Trevelyan, Ralph Tubbs, Shirley Tucker, Bernard Venables MBE, Elliott Viney, Kaye Webb, John Whitehead, Brian Wildsmith, Tatiana Wolff, Edward Young. Sadly Ian Ballantine, James Gardner and Peter Kite died before I had the opportunity to meet them.

I must, too, thank Penguin for indulging me initially, and then encouraging and guiding me: Peter Carson, Miranda McAllister, Andrew Cameron, Betty Hartell, Donald Muir, Carol Jones, Bridget Sleddon, John Rolfe, of Penguin Books Ltd, and Bob Sessions of Penguin Australia. And finally my thanks go to the Penguin Collectors' Society whose officers, members and publications have provided a constant source of help, information and friendship.

The editor and publishers would like to express their thanks to the following authors and their representatives who have kindly given permission to include their correspondence or quotations from their work: the Peters, Fraser & Dunlop Group Ltd, for the statements and letter of Kingsley Amis; the letters and text of W. H. Auden included in this book are copyright © the Estate of W. H. Auden; Darrell Waters Ltd, for the letter of Enid Blyton; Leslie Gardner, for the letters of Anthony Burgess; the Estate of Jonathan Cape and Jonathan Cape Ltd, for the letters of Jonathan Cape; extracts from the late Lord Clark are published here by permission of Margaret Hanbury, 27 Walcot Square, London SE11 4UB, representative of the Estate of Lord Clark. All rights are reserved and no reproduction of copyright material may be made without permission of the proprietor or his representative; the Peters, Fraser & Dunlop Group Ltd, for the introductory text to *Penguin Russian Review* 4, and letter of Edward Crankshaw; Reed Consumer Books, for a letter by Grace Cranston; Len Deighton's letter is copyright © 1994 Pluriform Publishing Company B.V.; the Estate of Lovat Dickson, for the letter of Lovat Dickson; Bruce Hunter, Literary Executor, for the letter of Tom Driberg; the letters of Lawrence Durrell are reproduced with permission of Curtis Brown Ltd, London, on behalf of the Estate of Lawrence Durrell, copyright © the Estate of Lawrence Durrell; Hilary Barrow, for permission to use the letter of B. Ifor Evans; Lawrence Ferlinghetti, for permission to reproduce his letter; the extracts and letters of John Fleming are reproduced with his permission; the Provost and Scholars of King's College, Cambridge, for the letter of E. M. Forster; letter from Victor Gollancz reproduced by permission of Livia Gollancz; A. P. Watt Ltd, for the letters of Robert Graves; Francis Greene, Executor, for the letters of Graham Greene; the extracts and letters of Kathleen Hale are reproduced with her permission; Chambers Harrap Publishers Ltd, for the letter of Walter G. Harrap; the Estate of G. B. Harrison, for the letters of G. B. Harrison; Mrs H. M. Higham, for the letter of David Higham; HarperCollins Publishers, for the letter of C. Walter Hodges; quotations from *Jonathan Cape, Publisher* are reproduced with the permission of the Estate of Michael Howard and Jonathan Cape Ltd; Random House UK Ltd, for the letter of F. R. Leavis; Messrs Miles Huddleston and Charles Osborne, Executors, for quotations from the works of John Lehmann; the Peters, Fraser & Dunlop Group Ltd, for permission to use the letters of D. B. Wyndham Lewis; Edward Lucie-Smith and Rogers, Coleridge & White Ltd, for the letter of Edward Lucie-Smith, copyright © Edward Lucie-Smith; The Mass-Observation extract (M-O Archive: FR2545C, December 1947, 'A Report on Penguin World', pp. 287–90) is copyright the Trustees of the Mass-Observation archive at the University of Sussex, reproduced by permission of Curtis Brown Group Ltd, London; Agence Hoffman, for the letter of Henry Miller; quotations from *Allen Lane: King Penguin*, *Paperbacks Across Frontiers* and a *New Statesman* review, with permission of Professor J. E. Morpurgo, and from *Master of None*, also with permission of Professor J. E. Morpurgo, and Carcanet Press; the Peters, Fraser & Dunlop Group Ltd, for the letter of John Mortimer; the Estate of Malcolm Muggeridge, for the letters of Malcolm Muggeridge; John Murray (Publishers) Ltd, for the letter of John Grey Murray; Nigel Nicolson, for the letter of Sir Harold Nicolson; Edna O'Brien's letter is included with her permission; sections from *Orwell, The War Broadcasts* are copyright © the Estate of the late Sonia Brownell Orwell and Martin Secker and Warburg Ltd; the Peters, Fraser & Dunlop Group Ltd, for the letter of J. B. Priestley; Dr Barbara Reynolds, for the letters and quotations from the work of Barbara Reynolds; Bertrand Russell's letters are copyright © The Bertrand Russell Archives, McMaster University, Hamilton, Ontario, Canada; Nigel Nicolson, for the letter of Vita Sackville-West; the Trustees of Anthony Fleming, deceased, for the letters of Dorothy L. Sayers; unpublished Bernard Shaw letters copyright © 1955 the Trustees of the British Museum, the Governors and Guardians of the National Gallery of Ireland and Royal Academy of Dramatic Art; James MacGibbon, for the letters of Stevie Smith; the letter of A. J. A. Symons is reproduced by permission of Curtis Brown Ltd, London, copyright © A. J. A. Symons, 1941; Mrs Eva Haraszti-Taylor, for the letter of A. J. P. Taylor; the Peters, Fraser & Dunlop Group Ltd, for the quotation from Ben Travers; the Estate of Charles F. Tunnicliffe, OBE, RA, for the letters of C. F. Tunnicliffe; HarperCollins Publishers Ltd, for the letter of Stanley Unwin; A. P. Watt Ltd, for the letter of A. S. Watt; the Peters, Fraser & Dunlop Group Ltd, for the letters of Evelyn Waugh; extracts from *Allen Lane: A Personal Portrait*, by W. E. Williams, are reproduced with the permission of the Bodley Head; the letter of Harold Wilson is reproduced with the permission of the late Lord Wilson; the letter of Leonard Woolf of the Hogarth Press is reproduced with the permission of Random House UK Ltd; correspondence and original illustrations by John Wyndham reproduced with permission of Wyndham Case Pty Ltd.

All correspondence remains copyright to the original author, except where otherwise stated. While every effort has been made to contact all copyright holders and correspondents, this has not been possible in every case. The editor and publishers will be pleased to hear from anyone represented in the book whose contribution is not acknowledged, and to rectify this for future editions.

Index